Simon Glen lives in Townsville on the north-east coast of Australia. He has five children (Ruth, Ellen, Adrian, Aisha and Jacob) and three grand-children. When not lucky enough to travel overseas, his outdoor leisure interests have been sailing, photography and camping in the Australian bush. He also takes an amateur interest in motor vehicle maintenance and repairs. Trained as a teacher, he has taught at schools and teachers colleges in Australia, Zambia and Nigeria. He has a masters degree in Education and is currently working on a PhD in Australian Aboriginal history. He is also committed to the redress of social inequalities and the abuse of women.

Simon has driven overland extensively in Canada, New Zealand, Europe, Asia and Africa, as well as Australia. He has lived and worked in various parts of Africa for more than twenty years and first became fascinated by the Sahara while teaching at Sokoto in the north of Nigeria. He has also travelled in the Kalahari, Namib, Iranian, and Baluchistan deserts as well as those of central Australia. They are all magnificent but he has found none that can compare with the Sahara in terms of size, aridity, isolation, challenge and quite awesome beauty.

Publisher's Note

The gradual opening of the Sahara to tourism has been a welcome development following the independence of Algeria in 1962.

The road from the Mediterranean south to Tamạnrasset in the Hoggar Mountains is now tar sealed, and the Algerian Government reportedly has further sealing in mind. Air services have joined with bus services and expedition organisers in opening up this superb region, and increasingly requests are coming in for up-to-date information on this area where much of the body of literature is either quite old, or, in the case of post-war books, acceptable when first printed, but rendered obsolescent by the passage of time.

This book, carefully compiled over a period of years and not always in the easiest of circumstances, will, we believe, go a long way towards helping all those with an interest in the Sahara.

Certainly it is the most detailed of the English language guides to that part of the Sahara which lies in southern Algeria and Niger, and will be received with open arms by Sahara aficionados everywhere.

Sahara Handbook

Simon Glen

Roger Lascelles, Cartographic and Travel Publisher
47 York Road, Brentford, Middlesex TW8 OQP. Tel: 081-847 0935

Publication Data

Title	Sahara Handbook
Typeface	Phototypeset in Compugraphic Palacio
Printing	Kelso Graphics, Kelso, Scotland.
ISBN	1 872815 20 0
Edition	1st Edition April 1980, 2nd Edition March 1987, 3rd Edition September 1990
Publisher	Roger Lascelles 47 York Road, Brentford, Middlesex, TW8 0QP.
Copyright	Simon Glen

Distribution

Africa:	Enquiries invited	
Americas:	Canada —	International Travel Maps & Books, P.O. Box 2290, Vancouver B.C.
	U.S.A. —	Hunter Publishing Inc., 155 Riverside Drive, New York, NY 100 24
Asia:	Hong Kong —	The Book Society, G.P.O. Box 7804, Hong Kong Tel: 5-241901
	India —	English Book Store, New Delhi
Australasia	Australia —	Rex Publications, 413 Pacific Highway, Artarmon NSW 2064
Europe:	Belgium —	Brussels, Peuples et Continents
	GB/Ireland —	Available through all booksellers with a good foreign travel section.
	Italy —	Libreria dell'Automobile, Milano
	Netherlands —	Nilsson & Lamm BV, Weesp
	Denmark —	Copenhagen — Arnold Busck, G.E.C. Gad, Boghallen
	Norway —	Oslo - Arne Gimnes/J.G. Tanum
	Sweden —	Stockholm - Esselte/Akademi Bokhandel Fritzes/Hedengrens Gothenburg - Gumperts/Esselte Lund - Gleerupska
	Switzerland —	Basel/Bider: Berne/Atlas; Geneve/Artou; Lausanne/Artou: Zurich/Travel Bookshop

Contents

Appendices

Preface

In colonial times, before the 1960s, the French organised restricted tourist access to the Sahara. Travel was confined to the winter months. Even then, permission was granted only after rigorous vehicle inspection and often on condition that travel was with a military escorted convoy. Today such controls and restrictions do not exist. Consequently, travel within the Sahara is much freer but at the same time more dangerous.

The aim of this book is to give actual information: addresses; facts; opinions of products; and straight advice. It is also intended to show where one can go in the Sahara, in sufficient detail to enable tourists to plan realistically, and not fall into the traps that could either cause them to lose their lives, or cause them not to go somewhere that they **could** have gone, had they had sufficient information.

However, the cover highlights a point worth stressing about the Sahara. The desert is like the sea. You must respect it; and it will reward with pleasures unimagined and unsurpassed. If you don't, it will eventually kill you. Do not accept tall stories about how impossible or how easy it is. Find out about it with the aim of understanding and enjoying it, and go prepared on that basis.

In compiling this book, actual personal experience has been used as much as possible. But, where it was not possible, we are particularly indebted to the following authorities on travel in the Sahara for their practical advice and assessments of some Saharan routes:

Ida and Pieter Kersten of Amsterdam, Holland.
Duncan Gough of Devizes, Wiltshire, U.K.
I am also grateful for the opinions and information given by:
Alhaji Abdul Rahman of Ain Salah, Algeria.
Les Petites Soeurs de Jesus of Beni Abbes, Algeria.
Russell Ebeling of the Gold Coast, Australia.
Dennis Laird of Townsville, Australia.
Ian and Kerrie Norrie of Sydney, Australia.
Freddie and Marie Hicks of London, U.K.
Arne Glud of Copenhagen, Denmark.
Alain Cottereau and Yolande Sigwalt of Muttersholtz, France.
Ahmed Mohammed Ahmed of Wau, Sudan.
Rita and Reinhardt Hammerli of Geneva, Switzerland.

Reinhold Wepf of Berne, Switzerland.

Special thanks must also go to Mike and Pathma Beckwith of Maldon, Essex, U.K., for the extensive and invaluable use of their Range Rover (RAY 333M).

Unless otherwise indicated, all photographs were taken by the authors. All maps and diagrams were drawn by Simon Glen. Virtually all the town and oasis maps in the Itineraries section were drawn initially on location and in sketch form as the authors drove around these settlements. They are therefore totally original and, of course, copyright.

Distances, weights and measures are given in the S.I. Metric system because most countries use it now. Probably only Britain and U.S.A. are still in the process of changing over. Tyre pressures are an exception and have not been quoted in 'Kilopascals' but in the more commonly used but older metric values of 'kg/cm²'. Vehicle wheel rim sizes have been given in radii of inches.

Finally, a quote from the Koran:

> *"If thou findest faults, then better them. Only one*
> *is infallible, and that is Allah!"*

Therefore, I would be pleased to receive corrections, opinions, criticism and further information on Saharan travel, vehicles, products discussed and any other ideas useful to other Sahara travellers.

Simon Glen

The Sahara is forever changing. In the middle foreground a section of track has become impassable because a sand dune has drifted across it and motorists have had to find another route several kilometres away. It is impossible for a book of this nature to keep up with changes of this sort but the traveller in the Sahara should be constantly prepared for the unexpected

1
The Sahara

The word Sahara is a derivation of the Arabic word 'Sahra' which means desert, or empty area. Today this name is applied to a vast region that extends from the Atlantic Ocean in the west, to the Red Sea in the east, and from the Mediterranean in the north to a large semi-desert zone or 'Sahel' to the south. It is a monster of a desert, more than 5,000 km across. It is so big that the whole Australian continent could fit into it and still have large areas of desert left over.

There is no other desert in the world that even approaches its area. There are tiny areas of the Atacama or Namib deserts which are totally arid, but by comparison the Sahara's totally arid areas are each many times their size. There is nowhere in the deserts of central Australia where one could stand and not see vegetation. In the Sahara it is possible to drive for three days at 175 km a day and see absolutely no vegetation at all! There are vast areas of rolling sand dunes, totally devoid of vegetation, and yet each area is bigger than England, or the American state of Oregon, or the Australian state of Victoria.

Because of the Sahara's immense size and its extreme aridity some of the scenery is quite spectacular. It offers the tourist as much scenic grandeur as the Himalayas, Alps or Rocky Mountains. The beautiful mountains of the Hoggar, Air and Tibesti as well as the gigantic ergs and sand seas are quite awe-inspiring in terms of their tremendous size and pristine condition unblemished by modern man. Sunrise at Assekrem in the Hoggar Mountains is a sight not to be missed even if it means deviating thousands of kilometres out of one's way. It is on a par with other magnificent places such as the Victoria Falls in southern Africa, India's Taj Mahal, America's Grand Canyon and New Zealand's Fjords.

On the other hand, when you are camped out in the desert — in the Ténéré for example — the stars are wonderfully bright and clear and the sky so very black. It is so quiet that the silence is almost deafening. It is also quite humbling to know that within a radius of 200 or so kilometres there are no other human beings, let alone any vegetation. When one thinks of the size of this desert and of the 4,800 million years it took for the Sahara to reach its present state, it makes one realize just how puny and insignificant mankind is. The overwhelming sense of peace and timelessness experienced in these desert nights is wonderful.

The World's Deserts (Based on Koppen's classification.)

Desert	Countries	Km²	Sq.miles
Sahara	Morocco, Algeria, Tunisia Libya, Egypt, Mauritania, Mali, Niger, Chad, Sudan, Senegal.	5,600,000	3,500,000
Australian	Australia	2,080,000	1,300,000
Arabian	Jordan, Israel, Oman U.A. Emirates, Kuwait, Saudi Arabia, South Yemen, Yemen, Qatar, Iraq.	1,600,000	1,000,000
Turkestan	U.S.S.R., Afghanistan	1,200,000	750,000
North American	Mexico, U.S.A.	800,000	500,000
Patagonia	Argentina, Chile	420,000	260,000
Iranian	Iran, Pakistan, Afghanistan	390,000	230,000
Kalahari-Namib	South Africa, Namibia, Botswana	350,000	220,000
Takla Mahan	China	320,000	200,000
Gobi	Mongolia, China	320,000	200,000
Thar	India, Pakistan	240,000	150,000
Atacama	Chile, Peru	220,000	140,000

N.B.
Some of these deserts include many others within the general region. For example, the Australian desert also includes the Gibson, Simpson, Victoria, Tanami, Sturt's, etc. The same applies to the North American (Mojave, Sonoran, Gt. Basin, Chihuahuan, and Baja Californian) and to the Sahara (Tanezrouft, Ténéré, Bilma Erg, Western Hoggar, Tibesti, Rebiana, Empty Quarter, Fezzan, Tademait, etc.)

These figures cannot be 100% accurate. They are estimates.

Source: TIME-LIFE, The Desert, Amsterdam, 1963.

The Sahara is ideal for those who enjoy solitude. Indeed, the monastery at Assekrem in the Hoggar Mountains is a perfect place for meditation and quiet thought especially with a view so inspiring.

The Sahara can offer a challenge. Not everyone is able to conquer Mount Everest or take part in an expedition across the Antarctic. Yet in the Sahara, for only moderate cost, it is possible for the private individual to cross some of the harshest terrain on earth and have first-hand experience of difficulties and privations unthinkable in most of the western world. It is a considerable feat to drive from Algiers on the Mediterranean to Kano on the edge of the Savanna in West Africa even on the easiest and most commonly used route: the one via the Hoggar. Distances are very great, the heat and dryness can be intense and exhausting, the roads vehicle-destroying, the dust choking and the sand sometimes seemingly endless and bottomless. The novice must quickly learn how to cope with corrugations, broken-up and washed-out roads, and getting a bogged vehicle out of the sand. Similarly, there are logistical problems to be overcome like obtaining fuel, food, water, spare parts and mechanical repairs, as well as coping with the bureaucratic complications of African border crossings. One also has to come to terms with relating to people of totally different cultures and economic backgrounds. To intensify the difficulties and challenge involved, one needs even more preparation to take alternative routes or visit more remote places in the Sahara.

Apart from its magnificence, soul-healing properties and challenge, the Sahara offers special things for a wide variety of travellers. It is a photographer's paradise and is steeped in pre-history. It offers surprises for the naturalist and gem stone fossicker. It provides inspiration for those with an artistic bent or literary potential. Yet, no matter what the background or interest may be, it is rarely possible to lose all the sand from one's shoes. On every acquaintance the Sahara has a tendency to leave its indelible mark.

2
Flora and Fauna

In the Sahara all wildlife is activated by the never ending struggle to obtain and retain water. All plants and animals have evolved various, often ingenious, methods of maintaining adequate supplies of moisture. Plants have extensive underground root systems for extracting as much water as possible from the ground. They have fleshy leaves with hard shiny sclerophyl surfaces to reduce water loss. Among the animals, the addax (*Addax nasomaculatus*) and the gazelle (*Gazella dorcas*) are able to obtain all the moisture they require from the scattered vegetation they feed on — they never drink. The jerboa (*Jaculus jaculus*) conserves water by having specially adapted kidneys which concentrate urine thus minimising the amount of water excreted in urination. Even man, the Touareg, wears cloth over his mouth and nostrils in order to maintain a layer of moist air through which he breathes.

The list of adaptations that plants and animals have developed to minimise water loss is almost endless. Yet the desert environment has also brought about other adaptations and specialised behaviour patterns which because of their interest value and the lessons to be learned are worth mentioning. Some plants such as the hadh (*Cornulaca monacantha*) establish micro-climates by living together in clusters thus encouraging wind-blown sand to accumulate around them. Inside the resulting mounds of vegetation and sand temperatures are marginally but crucially lower and humidity slightly higher. Cold blooded reptiles spend the heat of the day well below the desert floor where temperatures are lower.

Some further adaptations are evident. The fennec (*Fennecus zerda*) has very large ears which not only aid hearing and the search for its prey of reptiles and insects during the night but also act as radiators, dispersing body heat through a myriad of fine specially adapted blood vessels close to the surface of the ears. Touaregs and other people often wear black cloth, as opposed to heat-reflecting white, because black minimises the penetration of harmful ultraviolet 'B' rays from the sun. Some plants (halophytes) are especially adapted to survive very saline conditions. Some animals like ostriches (*Struthio camelus*) can survive on saline water. Ostriches are also able to allow their body temperatures to rise several degrees above normal before they pant. In this way water is not used for evaporative cooling until it becomes absolutely necessary.

In a desert climate it may not rain for many years (e.g. Farafra in Egypt receiv-

The addax (Addax nasomaculatus) is rarely seen in the Sahara, its native habitat. It is able to obtain all the moisture it requires from the very scattered vegetation it feeds on and never needs to drink (Photo by courtesy of The Zoological Society of London)

The sand fish, a skink which literally swims through the sand to escape from predators and to keep cool during the hottest part of the day

The fennec has very large ears which give it acutely sensitive hearing and help this nocturnal desert fox find its prey of small reptiles and insects. These ears also act as radiators, dispersing body heat through hundreds of fine specially adapted vessels just beneath the skin

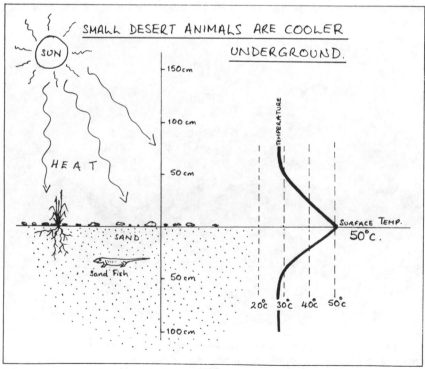

ed rain in 1945 and then again in 1973). For plants and animals with short life spans existing in these conditions there are special problems to overcome or the species would die out. Seeds are able to lie dormant for many years encased in a hard outer cuticle which prevents moisture loss. When rain finally does come, the desert bursts into life. Plants go through their complete life cycle from seedling to flower and seed dispersal within weeks, even days. Often the flowers are very bright and beautiful in order to attract equally short-lived pollinating insects. Rapid growth becomes a matter vital to the survival of the fittest.

Similarly, insect eggs hatch having lain dormant for many years. In oueds, gueltas and other places where water collects temporarily, thousands of tad-pole frogs and toads emerge as well as numerous tiny fish like the ubiquitous tilapia (*Tilapia* and *Astatotilapia*). The catfish (*Clarias senegalensis*) which can lie dormant in a cocoon of dried mucus in the dried up mud is stimulated out of its long sleep by the presence of water.

Tilapia — a fresh water fish caught with pride in the Oued Saoura at Kerzaz in Algeria

15

Rain will also stimulate mammals like the jerboa (*Jaculusjaculus*) and the fennec (*Fennecus zerda*) into breeding for it heralds a brief period of plentiful food supplies when the young are most likely to survive. Similarly, the

Camels have dozens of remarkable adaptations to desert conditions. Saharan camels with one hump are 'dromedary camels'; those with two humps, 'bactrian camels', are found in cold mountainous parts of Asia

sudden increase in the humidity stimulates reptile embryos to hatch from eggs that their long since dead mothers may have laid many years previously.

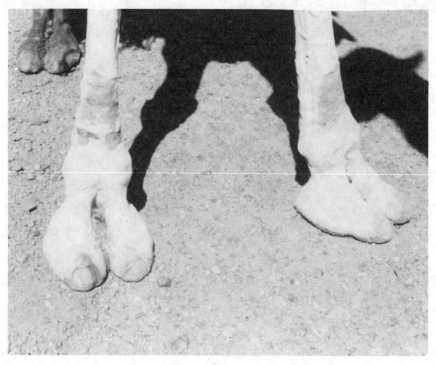

The camel's feet are specially adapted to provide flotation as it walks across sand

The camel (*Camelus dromedarius*) and the addax have feet and hooves specially adapted to walking on sand by providing flotation through spreading the weight of the animal over a relatively large area. Camels have an amazing variety of other desert adaptations. They have a special arrangement of blood vessels at the base of the brain that allow it to be kept at a tolerable temperature even while the rest of the body rises to about 46°C. Moreover, as a camel loses water it adjusts the volume of the vascular system so that the heart's functioning is not impaired (see T.J. Dawson in **Scientific American,** Aug. 1977). They are also able to reduce their kidney filtration by 20 per cent of normal during dehydration. Thus a camel without water will lose only 1000th of its body weight daily through urination. It hardly sweats at all. By contrast, a man can sweat up to 3 litres an hour walking in the desert which can amount to over 10 per cent of body weight in a day : leading rapidly to circulatory collapse and death. A camel's stored body fat can keep it fed for up to six months (provided it doesn't have to work). A camel can also withstand up to 1.8 per cent salt in water. This volume would kill a man and even other hardy arid land mammals such as Merino sheep and kangaroos. Perhaps the ultimate desert adaptation a camel has is its limited ability to combine hydrogen (H) with the oxygen (O) it breathes to produce water (H_2O)!

Among reptiles, the sand fish (*Scincus scincus*) and the sand swimmer (*Phrynocephalus nejdensis*) are skinks and agamid lizards which literally swim in the sand to escape predators and to descend to cooler temperatures deeper down in the sand.

SH 2

The darkling beetles (of the family *Tenebrionides*) do not have wings like most beetles and their outer wing cases are fused together leaving an air pocket beneath. This not only provides insulation from the heat of the sun beating down on them and maintain warmth during the cool night, but is of even more importance by reducing the amount of water loss through evaporation, for the breathing holes open out into this cavity.

Darkling beetles have no wings but a pocket of air beneath the hard casing that covers their backs provides insulation from desert heat

Most animals and insects in the desert are nocturnal, living in burrows during the day to remain relatively cool and coming out at night when the accumulated heat of the day radiates up into the night sky. This applies to fennecs, camel spiders (solifuges), scorpions, jerboas, lizards, insects, etc. It is quite amazing to get up in the morning and to discover by the tracks and disturbed sand that the apparently lifeless desert you stopped to camp in became a hive of activity during the night.

Scorpions not only have hard outer skeletons but are also covered with a thin layer of hard and impervious wax which gives them a shiny appearance. This makes them extremely resistant to water loss. There are many species of scorpions in the Sahara. Among them are *Androctonus amoreuxi, Buthotus franzwerneri, Buthus quinquestriatus, Buthus occitanus, Prionurus australis* and *Androctonus australis*. Most have a sting which though only localised is worse than that of a bee, very painful and can last for several days. The poison injected by the sting of *Androctonus australis* (found around Ain Sefra, Biskra, Ouargla, as well as throughout the southern Sahel) is neuro-toxic. Its toxicity is equal to that of a cobra (*Naja haje*) and can kill a man in four hours, (see chapter on Survival for antivenine). The stings of *Buthus occitanus* (in the southern Sahel) and of *Buthus quinquestriatus* (in the Tibesti) are similarly neuro-toxic. For the non-expert it is worth treating all scorpions as if they were neuro-toxic ones. Being nocturnal, scorpions usually lie in wait for their prey of insects. However, they will emerge to catch insects that are attracted by the lights or fire of a campsite. At dawn they will curl up for the day in any potentially dark and cool place, like inside shoes or sleeping bags.

Conservation

Modern man has made a big mess of parts of North America, Europe, Japan, and Australia. There is evidence to suggest that his mess is spreading to the Sahara. Oil exploration parties, expeditions and tourists continue to leave piles of rubbish scattered everywhere: empty cans, beer bottles, motor vehicle parts, etc. All this sort of rubbish is easily buried for little extra cost and effort. The earth is pretty good at dispersing man's garbage, but in the Sahara it takes a long time; nothing rusts and plants don't grow over the rubbish. Indeed it has been said that if Queen Nefertiti had thrown her empty Coke can in the desert, it would still be there today!

Also, please don't take advertising material to the desert. In recent years, several truck manufacturers have, with much publicity, taken to organizing grandiose expeditions across parts of the Sahara. They erected balises (beacons) as they went, apparently to mark out new routes across the inhospitable desert, to promote their vehicles, and so that a route will become known as 'Berliet Piste' or 'Piste Saviem'. Often those balises are so far apart that they serve little real purpose, other than littering the desert with more rubbish. They may even confuse. Indeed one expedition is known to have found nowhere useful to place its balises. Instead, they indiscriminately erected two, with much flourish and photography and then buried the rest!

Many sites of ancient relics have been pillaged by tourists seeking souvenirs in the form of fossilized wood, paleolithic adzes and arrowheads, and even ancient bones. Some tourists have scrawled obscenities over ancient rock paintings and engravings. It is up to governments to protect their nation's heritage but more often than not they are too pre-occupied with other concerns like poverty, development and stability to have the will to do anything about these sites.

It is often sad to see what man is doing to this desert, especially as it has

It is amazing to get up in the morning and to discover that the apparently lifeless desert you stopped to camp in was a hive of activity during the night

19

taken so long for the Sahara to become what it is today.

There are many creatures which are now so rare and shy, partly due to man's encroachment into their habits, that it would be very unusual if a tourist were lucky enough to see them. Unfortunately, some of these will be extinct very soon if they are not already.

Fennecs, especially pups like this one, are adorable. However, they are protected by law. So please do not buy them from scruffy little boys. This would only serve to perpetuate a market which could put them on the endangered species list. Moreover, they can be carriers of rabies

Some rare species

The desert cat (*Felis libyca*) is sand coloured, has large ears and is about the size of a domestic cat. Extremely rare, it is nocturnal and eats small rodents and birds, probably reptiles as well.

Two rarely seen species of antelope, no doubt remnants of bygone centuries when the Sahara was a considerably more fertile place, are quite large, have long horns, and are swift of foot. They are the addax (*Addax nasomaculatus*) and the oryx (*Oryx algazel*). Both these herbivores live in sandy areas such as the Ténéré and in the Sahel to the south of the Sahara.

Small mountain goats, like the antelopes, were once more plentiful than they are now. They inhabit the rocky mountainous regions. This mountain goat or 'moufflon' (*Ammotragus lervia*) is limited to the rocky Saharan massifs (Tassili, Hoggar, Tibesti, Air, Ennedi, and parts of the Moroccan High Atlas).

The desert fox (*Vulpes vulpes*) is similar to its European counterpart but is much lighter in colour and more the size of the still common fennec. Its diet is similar to that of the European fox (birds, reptiles, insects) but its metabolism is slower. It is strictly nocturnal like the fennec.

The hedgehog is still fairly common in the Atlas ranges and is not unlike its European counterpart but has long ears like the fennec. It is strange to find it (*Hemiechinus auritu aegyptiacus*) again in Nigeria when it is almost totally unknown in the drier regions in between.

Gazelles (*Gazella dorcas*) can frequently be seen in the main Saharan massifs (Hoggar, Tassili, Air, Tibesti, Ennedi). Some people think it sporting to chase these exquisite creatures in cars. There are no controls on this sort of activity by governments. In fact, idle soldiers have been known to enjoy this pastime especially as it has given them shooting practice. One day gazelles will join the ranks of the endangered species and will not be there for the foolish to hunt or for the wise to observe.

The fennec is still quite common in Tunisia and northern Algeria but is unfortunately frequently trapped and sold to tourists. This is quite illegal but because there is a ready market for these cute animals there are always people willing to sell them.

The jackal is also the victim of such poachers and is found in sandy and 'reg' regions where it eats similar food to the fennec, i.e. small rodents, beetles, birds, lizards; and if it can find them it scavenges on dead herd animals.

The desert hare (*Lepus capensis*) is sand coloured with large 'radiator' ears, and has nocturnal habits. It is common in rocky oueds and is incredibly fast but should not be chased and it is not a pest as its cousin the rabbit has become in Australia.

The little desert rodents can often be seen by quiet watchful tourists during the evenings. In fact, they are quite partial to western food if any happens to be lying about in the cool of the evening when they become active. They include the little, large-eyed sand rat (*Psammomys obesus*), the gerbil (*Meriones crassus*) and the jerboa (*Jaculus jaculus*). Sadly, some are caught and smuggled back to Europe where they spend their lives in cages, not on the cool sands, and are played with by little European children. It seems a great shame that pet shop owners should benefit from the relative tameness and sweetness of these little creatures. Hopefully, one day, controls will be stricter and put a halt to the exportation of such animals.

Some of the mouse-sized creatures which scurry about in the sand eat beetles and other insects and some eat grass seeds but they are in turn eaten by the horned viper (*Cerastes cerastes*) which is very poisonous and is a good reason for not going about totally bare footed. It lies just below the surface of the sand with its horns just protruding as it waits for its prey but is most unappreciative of tourists walking on it. On the move it has a distinctive

21

sideways movement which is similar to that of the North American sidewinder.
Solifuges (known variously as camel-spiders, wind-scorpions and taran-tulas) are commonly seen at night in the southern Sahara. Noticeable because of their hairy bodies and legs as well as the speed with which they run around with outstretched forelimbs, they are relatively harmless, although they can give a small sore but venomless bite. Some of the species to be found are *Othoes saliaraes, Galeodes granti, Galeodes arabs,* and *Galeodes olivieri*. Looking like large hairy spiders, they prey upon insects.

Birds

The variety of birds to be seen in the Sahara is so wide and complex that a list of all the species is impractical. Moreover, often birds seen in the desert are only temporary visitors, stopping only to rest or to die of exhaustion during their annual migrations from Europe and Siberia to the forests of equatorial

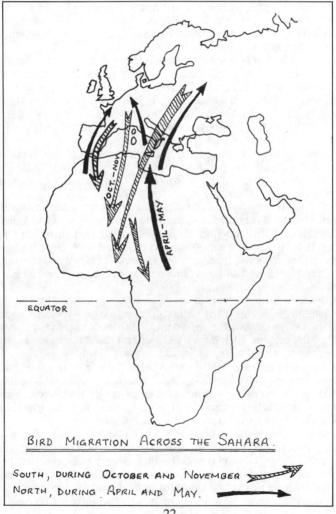

BIRD MIGRATION ACROSS THE SAHARA.

SOUTH, DURING OCTOBER AND NOVEMBER

NORTH, DURING APRIL AND MAY.

Africa. Ultimately, the best guide to bird species seen in the Sahara is a detailed book like Serle, W., Morel, G.J., and Hartwig, W., **A. Field Guide to the Birds of West Africa** Collins, London 1977. It should also be stressed that the distribution of several species in the Sahara region is not only debatable but in some cases unknown. There is scope for considerable research.

Many species of bird may be seen dead or dying in the Ténéré, during May or June, when they return to Europe for the summer, after winter in the tropics. These birds which didn't make it are a pitiful sight as the crouch in the transient shade of Ténéré balises, or burrow under a petrol drum, or lie exhausted in the shade of a tourist's vehicle. (They even come into cars sometimes and settle down amongst the luggage where it is marginally cooler than outside.) These migratory birds die from sheer exhaustion and heat fatigue after flying from Cameroon, Ghana, Ivory Coast, and other West African countries. They include thrushes, larks, nightingales, shrikes, doves, pigeons, buntings, flycatchers, pipits, swallows, some water birds and even birds of prey.

In the southern regions, in Sahel and Savanna country, and even some of the southern oases, live a wide variety of vividly coloured birds such as the weaver birds, sunbirds, scrub-robins, starlings, shrikes, barbets and bee eaters.

Among some of the more noticeable birds in the Sahara are:

White Rumped Black Chat (*Denanthe leucopyga leucopyga*): a small (12cm long) black and white bird which tends to live in rocky areas and is noted for its inquisitive nature which often brings it very close to stationary vehicles.

The White Rumped Black Chat, an inquisitive little bird seen all over the northern Sahara

23

Chestnut Bellied Sand Grouse (*Pterocles exustus*) and Spotted Sand Grouse (*Pterocles senegallus*): well camouflaged medium size birds which tend to give the approaching human more of a fright when disturbed and in flight. Eggs are laid in a slight hollow on the bare ground hardly visible among the other stones of the hammada. After eggs have hatched the parents take turns to fly great distances to find water which is soaked up in the breast feathers and brought back to the young nestling on the scorching earth.

Vultures: around oases like Bilma, Agadez and Gao four types of vulture can be found:

— Ruppell's Griffon Vulture (*Gyps rupelli*): a large bird standing about a metre high. Known to nest at Kotorkoshi in Sokoto State, in Nigeria.

— Hooded Vulture (*Neophron monachus*): the more commonly seen vulture especially in the southern Sahel, it is only half the size of the griffon, of slender build and a long bill. Gregarious. The authors used to have one as a pet.

— Egyptian Vulture (*Neophron percnopterus*): the smallest of all three, it has a bare yellowish face, short neck and slender bill. It is known to be able to pick up rocks in its beak and drop them on eggs in order to smash them.

— Nubian Vulture (*Torgos tracheliotus*): a large brown bird standing about a metre high. It has a bare pink head and neck and conspicuous white down underbelly. Can be seen throughout the southern Sahel from Senegal to Chad and has even been seen as far north as Beni Abbes in Algeria.

In the southern fringes of the Sahara some of the more obvious birds are:

— Ground Hornbill (*Bucorvus abyssinicus*): a massive bird standing about 1.5 metres high, it usually feeds in pairs on the ground walking very sedately. Large very prominent beak.

— Grey Hornbill (*Tockus nasutus*): seen in swooping flight from tree to tree.

— Hoopoe (*Upupa sengalensis*): a lovely cinnamon red bird with a long slightly curved beak and a magnificent red and black crest which it raises

A Hooded Vulture: this particular bird was raised by the author as a family pet from the time it fell out of its parents' nest prematurely

every time it lands.
— Ostrich (*Struthio camelus*): seen frequently in the thorn Sahel country in southern Mali and Niger but also in the Air. The male is larger than the female and has black body feathers. The females and the immature are grey-brown.
— White Pelican (*Pelecanus onocrotalus*): large fish eating bird which nests colonially not too far from rivers and lakes. Confined to the southern Sahel.

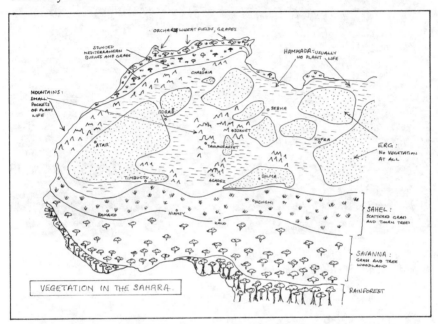

VEGETATION IN THE SAHARA.

Vegetation

To detail all the variety of Saharan vegetation would involve a major academic study. Nevertheless, one is continually surprised at how small plants manage to survive in such arid and apparently soil-absent conditions.

Some of the more noticeable plants are listed, generally in order of size.
— Chou Fleur or Champignon de Bou Hammama (*Fredolia aretioides*): at first sight it looks like a large rock standing on its own in a large flat, dry and hot, stony reg. On closer examination, it is seen to be a plant with tightly packed branches and small fleshy leaves. Usually it is found in the north-west of the Sahara.
— Desert Melon (*Colocynthis vulgaris*): inedible because it is an emetic (will induce vomiting). When dry, the melons blow great distances in the wind considerably aiding seed dispersal.
— Cram-cram (*Cenchrus biflorus* and *Cenchrus echinatus*): a low tussock grass which generally marks the end of the hyper-arid desert and the beginning of the southern Sahel. Usually it grows in association with the *Acacia seyal* thorn trees.
— Had (*Cornulaca monacantha*): like the cram-cram, it is a grass which grows at the outer limit of the Sahara. It grows in the 100 to 150mm rainfall band.
— Calotrope or Sodom Apple (*Calotropis procera*): a bush with large fleshy leaves and delicate pink flowers. A native of the Sahara, it has spread to

25

the deserts of Iran and Australia. It has a white sap which industrialists may one day refine as an oil substitute.

At first sight the Chou-Fleur looks like a large rock (in right foreground). On closer investigation it is clearly a plant

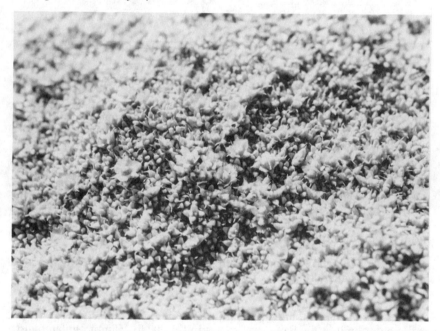

A close-up lens photo of the Chou-Fleur reveals that this deceptive plant is really a mass of tiny fleshy leaves

26

The Desert Melon is inedible. In fact, if eaten it will induce vomiting

This photo taken just north of Agadez shows the 'cram-cram', a low tussock grass which is generally taken to indicate the southern edge of the Sahara. The scattered acacia thorn trees are also typical of this area

27

An Oleander flower. Native to the central and northern Sahara, these flowering shrubs are now grown in gardens in many Mediterranean and tropical parts of the world

A Sodom Apple or Calotrope bush is native to the central Sahara

Acacia thorn trees seen in the Hoggar area (Acacia radiana)

— Oleander or Laurier Rose (*Nerium oleander*): pink flowers, white sap (poisonous) and grows close to water at oases. Now grown as a garden shrub in many Mediterranean and tropical parts of the world, it is a native of the Sahara.

— Cypress (*Cupressus duprziana*): these large trees are remnants from a much cooler and humid climatic era. Largely found in the Tamrit area of the Tassili N'Ajjer near Djanet, some of them are many centuries old and there are no young ones.

— Laperrine Olive (*Olea laperrini*): a low olive bush to be found in the Hoggar, Mouydir, Tassili and Tefedest mountains in southern Algeria and at Mt. Greboun in northern Niger. Like the Cypress, it is a remnant from a time when the Sahara was a much wetter place. As a species it is dying out.

— Tamarisk: there are many species of these trees with fine needle-like leaves. They are salt resistant and often grow in almost vegetationless oueds that are too salty for other plants (e.g. in the Oued Saoura just south of Tarhit near the rock engravings). The large trees which line the streets of Tamanrasset are Tamarisks. The two most common species are *Tamarix articulata* and *Tamarix gallica*.

— Acacia: there are many varieties of acacia thorn trees throughout the Sahara. In the centre and north (Hoggar, Tassili and north) the most common is *Acacia radiana*. In the south on the edge of the Sahel the *Acacia seyal* predominates. Being legumes, acacias are hosts to bacteria which live in nodules in the roots and are able to fix nitrogen in the soil. The trees have small yellow puff-ball flowers and large thorns which drop to the ground, cause punctures and discourage camping near them. Camels are able to eat the leaves by nibbling between the thorns and even eating the young green thorns.

— Date Palms (*Phoenix dactylifera*): dates have been cultivated by man for thousands of years. They are monocotyledons (like grass, orchids, tulips, bananas, etc.) and need lots of clear sunlight and access to underground water for the best fruit. The 'Deglet Nour' variety grown in the Souf area around El Oued and Touggourt are renowned for their large size and sweetness.

— Neame or Nim Trees (*Azadirachta Indica*): native to northern India, these medium to large exotic trees were introduced by British and French colonial authorities in the countries of the southern Sahel (Mali, Niger and Nigeria). They can be seen lining the main streets of hundreds of little villages and towns. With foliage all year round, their long pendant leaves on drooping stems provide excellent shade for small roadside stalls and to park under. Widely known in India for their medicinal qualities, the leaves can be eaten to relieve constipation and when dried and put in drawers and cupboards they will keep away cockroaches and earwigs.

— Eucalyptus trees of many varieties can be seen in the streets of many northern Saharan towns like Tozeur, Laghouat and Ain Sefra, especially the tall Blue Gum (*Eucalyptus globulus*) a native of the eastern part of Australia.

— Golden Wattle Trees (*Acacia cyanophylla*) are used extensively throughout the Atlas ranges in re-afforestation programmes. Natives of western Australia, they are fast growing and virile soil-enriching (nitrogen fixing) legumes. Between Bou Saada, Ksar el Boukhari, Tiaret and Tlemcen there is now a massive 20 kilometre band of these Golden Wattles which were planted during the 1960s by the Bou Saada Trust (established by New Zealander Wendy Campbell-Purdie).

The Sahara Desert is still largely untouched by modern man. As such it is worth trying to keep it that way as far as possible. Therefore, please never kill or molest desert creatures. Don't buy animals from horrible little boys.

Date palms in the Souf area of Algeria. The owner of these trees has the daily task of removing sand from the area where his trees are growing. If he does not, the trees will be drowned by the encroaching sand. Note the grass fences built to slow sand encroachment

The Baobab tree (Adonsonia digitata) with its characteristic fat and fleshy trunk is a native of the Sahel area to the south of the Sahara

30

This creates a market, causing more to be caught, and more to be bought. Jackals and fennecs can carry rabies which would usually be fatal in the Sahara. Moreover, they are protected by law, and in Algeria one could face problems with the police.

"Take nothing but photographs, and leave nothing but your footprints!" Though the saying is trite, it is really worth remembering, especially in such a beautiful and fascinating region, which has been left in relative peace, by comparison with Europe and North America and the other so called 'civilised' countries of the western world.

Animals to be found in the Sahara region, from the Atlas ranges to 13° North:

1. Mammals

Camel	*Camelus dromedarius*
Donkey	*Equus asinus*
Addax	*Addax nasomaculatus*
Gazelle	*Gazella dorcas*
	Gazella dama
	Gazella leptoceras loderi
Mountain sheep (Moufflon)	*Ammotragus lervia*
Hyena	*Hyaena striata*
	Hyaena crocuta
Desert cat	*Felix libyca*
Jackal	*Canis aureus*
Fennec	*Fennecus zerda*
Desert fox	*Vulpes vulpes*
Gerbil	*Meriones crassus*
	Meriones libycus
	Gerbillus gerbillus
Sand rat	*Psammomys obesus*
Jerboa	*Jaculus jaculus*
Hare	*Lepus chadiensis*
Desert hare	*Lepus capensis*
Hedgehog	*Hemiechinus auritu aegyptiacus*

2. Reptiles

Spiney tailed iguana	*Uromastyx acanthinurus*
Sand fish	*Scincus scincus*
Sand gecko	*Hemitheconyx caudinctus*
House lizard	*Agama agama*
Naja viper	*Naja nigricollis*
Horned viper	*Cerastes cerastes*
Desert monitor	*Varanus griseus*
Crocodile (miniature)	*Crocodilus niloticus*
Sand racer	genus *Psammodromus*
Chamelon	*Chamaeleo chamaeleon*

3. Others

Giant millipede	genus *Spirostreptus*
Black millipede	*Tachypodoiulus niger*
Velvet mite	*Dinothrombium tinctorium*
Green centipede	*Scolopendra cingulata*
Centipede (large)	*Orya babarica*
Centipede (small)	*Orya almoliadensis*
Tibesti scorpion	*Buthus quinquestriatus*

Small yellow scorpion	*Buthus occitanus*
Brown scorpion	*Prionurus australis*
Fat tailed scorpion	*Audroctonus australis*
Hunting-spider, Tarantula,	*Othoes saliaraes*
Solifuge, Wind-scorpion,	*Galeodes granti*
or Camel-spider	*Galeodes arabs*
Darkling beatle	*Prionotheca coronata*
Flightless mantis	*Eremiaphila reticulata*

Perhaps the most useful non-academic but still authoritative book on plant and animal life in the Sahara is by the French couple Yves and Mauricette Vial, **Sahara Milieu Vivant,** 1974, Hatier, Paris. It is an ideal book to take in the glove-box of a car. For birds, however, it is best to take Serle, W., Moral, G.J., and Hartwig, W., **A Field Guide to the Birds of West Africa,** 1977, Collins, London.

3
Climate and Desertification

Although ecologists are not in full agreement about what exactly constitutes a desert, generally deserts have hot temperatures for at least part of the year and receive less than 250 mm of rain per year. Using these criteria the Sahara is by far the largest desert in the world. Covering up to ten million square kilometres, it occupies an area equal to that of the USA, nearly double the area of Europe and 25 per cent larger than the total area of Australia.

There is no denying the Sahara's heat either. During the summer months the Sahara becomes very hot indeed. In July the average daily maximums for Ain Salah and Agadez are 45°C and 44°C respectively and it is nothing unusual for these shade temperatures to go into the fifties!

In the winter months the Sahara is not quite so hot. Agadez has an average daily maximum in January of 29°C and a minimum of 10°C. The same January figures for Tamanrasset (high up in the Hoggar massif) are 19°C and 4°C. The Sahara in winter is actually very pleasant. Temperatures do drop during the nights but it is only in high exposed places that it becomes very cold at night (e.g. Assekrem in the Hoggar : -2°C).

The Sahara is probably the driest place on earth, 80 per cent of it receiving less than 100 mm of rain per annum. Oases such as Adrar, Bilma, Djanet, Ain Salah and Farafra may not receive any rain in 20 years. Indeed, at Farafra in the Egyptian desert it rained in 1945 and then next in 1973!

Rainfall

The following is a list of annual median (50 percentile) rainfall figures for a variety of places in the Sahara region. It is followed by a list of rainfall figures for other desert places in the world for comparison purposes.

Adrar	16mm	Khartoum	157mm
Agadez	164mm	Kidal	130mm
Ain Salah	16mm	Maiduguri	658mm
Aswan	1mm	Nguigmi	225mm
Beni Abbes	32mm	Niamey	625mm
Bilma	19mm	Nouadhibou	39mm
Cairo	28mm	Ouagadougou	899mm

33

Dakar	554mm	Sokoto	707mm
Djanet	20mm	Tahoua	390mm
Farafra	6mm	Tamanrasset	41mm
Gao	235mm	Timbuktu	244mm
Luxor	1mm	Tripoli	389mm
Kano	890mm	Zinder	575mm

(Note: some of these places are not in the Sahara desert but are not far from it. Towns like Kano, Sokoto, Niamey and Tahoua may look exceptionally arid for much of the year but with their "Sahel" rather than "Sahara" climate they receive heavy rain for two to three months in summer to make up for the other dry nine months. Nevertheless, for the dry months desert conditions prevail.)

Rainfall figures in other deserts:

Australia		**Middle East**	
Alice Springs	251mm	Amman	279mm
Birdsville	115mm	Baghdad	140mm
Kalgoorlie	226mm	Bahrein	74mm
Oodnadatta	103mm	Tehran	246mm
North America		**South America**	
Albuquerqu	206mm	Arequipa	109mm
El Paso	200mm	Lima	31mm
Las Vegas	112mm	**Asia**	
Phoenix	183mm	Astrakhan	78mm
Reno	182mm	Kandahar	178mm
Tucson	279mm	Kashgar	78mm
Southern Africa		Ulan Bator	229mm
Gaberone	280mm		
Luderitz	48mm		
Keetmanshoop	127mm		
Swakopmund	15mm		
Windhoek	235mm		

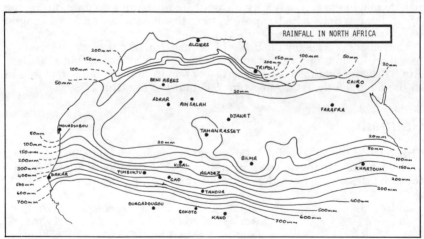

It should be noted that rainfall in deserts is extremely erratic. Thus while the average rainfall for Beni Abbes is 32 mm per year, the annual rainfall has varied between as little as 10 mm and as much as 100 mm. Although the

34

annual average for Tamanrasset is only 41 mm for the whole year, one day in September 1950 the town received 44 mm of rain in only three hours! These sudden and even unseasonal downpours cannot be ruled out anywhere in the Sahara. Indeed, during 1981 just such a cloudburst was responsible for the death of one of the Petits Frères du Jèsus in Tamanrasset when one of the mud walls which characterise much of this town collapsed on top of him.

Similarly, temperatures can be just as erratic. The Hermitage at Assekrem in the Hoggar once received a light fall of snow early in 1977.

Droughts

Generally the Sahara is in an area of descending air or a high pressure zone. Winds tend to blow from the Sahara outwards and, although the direction varies seasonally, very rarely do rain carrying winds penetrate the centre of this massive desert.

Droughts or abnormally long periods without rain are endemic to most desert areas and their margins. Three to six 'good' years may be followed by two to five years of drought, causing considerable distress for agriculturalists and pastoralists alike unless their cultivation or grazing is managed to cater for these entirely natural droughts. However, for the past 8,000 years the Sahara has not only become increasingly dry and arid but has been expanding. Indeed, one researcher in the Sudan has estimated the Sahara's southward expansion at 100 kilometres in the seventeen year period from 1958 to 1975.

Sand Storms

Normally between early July and late August the southern fringes of the Sahara, namely the southern Sahel, do receive some rain. Agadez, for example, has a short rainy season in these months during which it receives all of its average annual rainfall of 164 mm. It is not much but it can be heavy and occurs when cells of marginally cooler but moist equatorial air occasionally extend northwards into the very hot Sahara from the low pressure zone over West Africa. These isolated sorties into the oven-like north are quite spectacular. Preceded by still, sultry and very hot days, the front between the two masses of different air can be quite clearly seen as a turbulent wall of dust extending thousands of metres into the sky. As this wall of dust approaches people, livestock and birds race for shelter. Within minutes it hits one. All vision is blotted out as one frantically battens down loose objects and winds up windows. The sand stings one's face and legs. Inside the house, tent or car it becomes unbearably hot as the wind howls outside. Soon it begins to pour with rain. Gutters, streets and oueds become raging torrents of muddy water. The wind dies down and the rain eases right off. Emerging from shelter or winding down windows, there is a wonderful sense of relief as the cool, moist and sweet smelling air hits one.

These sand storms invariably come at the beginning of the rainy season which in the southern Sahel occurs during June, July and August. In the northern Sahel (north of the Sahara in a band just south of the Atlas ranges extending across northern Libya and Egypt) these sand storms occur in November and December at the start of the northern winter rainfall period and are just as spectacular. During November and December cold moist air extends from southern Europe, across the Mediterranean, to the Atlas ranges. This is when occasionally even the southern Saharan Atlas range can experience light falls of snow (e.g. near El Bayadh and Aflou).

35

July: summer
An area of high pressure descending air over the Mediterranean blowing dry rainless
wind south is pushed northwards by an area of low pressure ascending air bringing
rainfall to West Africa and the southern limits of the Sahara. Where the two air
masses converge, the air rises rapidly, cooling, condensing and raining heavily along
along a front that extends right across Africa.

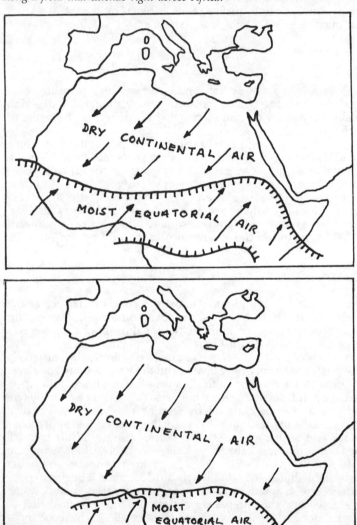

December: winter
The moist equatorial air mass is pushed southwards away from the southern Sahara
by the cooler continental air from southern Europe. As it travels across the Sahara it
dehydrates even further and also picks up a lot of dust. This is the cold and dry
Harmattan wind

In the Sahara itself, when there is no wind, the days are usually beautifully clear and the sky a lovely blue. When the wind blows, all is hazy, as the air is filled with a suspension of fine dust particles that even prevent the sun from creating shadows. Following a windy period it may take days for the dust to settle. During windy periods the front of one's car can have all the paint sand-blasted off. Similarly the abrasive action of the sand will make headlight lenses go opaque.

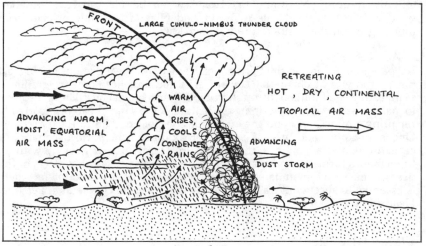

A sand storm

Harmattan

In the southern Sahara and the southern Sahel between November and February a cold north-easterly wind known as the Harmattan may blow for several weeks or months. To the local people it is bitterly cold. There are no shadows and for much of the time there is no trace of the sun in the sky because the dust is so dense. When the Harmattan is blowing, eye diseases, colds and 'flu become very common. It is also a dangerous time for head-on collisions between vehicles on some of the pistes in Niger and Mali. During these dust storms (as opposed to the sand storms which occur at the onset of the rainy season) the strong wind can pick up so much sand and dust that forward vision can be completely blocked off for days on end. Terrible accidents have occurred in these conditions.

Temperatures in the Sahara are generally hot. The highest ambient temperature ever recorded on earth was 58°C at Azizia in Libya (about 50 km south of Tripoli). Nevertheless, temperatures do vary from season to season, the highest in July/August with the lowest in December/January. However, the difference between the middle of the day and the middle of the night temperatures (the diurnal range) can be quite considerable. Agadez, for example, has a diurnal range of 20°C in January (the cold season — winter). This contrast between day and night temperatures can make nights seem freezing cold especially during this drier time of the year. In the Hoggar overnight temperatures in December to February regularly go below freezing and, coupled with very low humidity of even less than 10 per cent, this makes for bitterly cold nights and early mornings. (Camped at Assekrem in January it is a very bracing run up to the Hermitage to catch the sunrise.) In winter it pays to take warm clothing to the Sahara.

On the other hand, to people who have lived most of their lives in the Sahara, high temperatures seem quite normal. At Seguedine in the Ténéré Desert in May one year with the shade temperature at 46°C, the local Guard Nomadique or policeman calmly told the authors that "When the hot season comes in July, one cannot walk in the palm grove during the afternoon." To him 46°C was not hot.

Similarly, during November to February when the cold and dry Harmattan wind is blowing, the locals in Niger and Nigeria feel bitterly cold each morning when the temperature is a low 10°C.

A Warning

For people travelling in the Sahara, its dryness and heat present the biggest threat to survival. Dehydration can be a slow and unnoticed process, gradually manifesting itself initially through irritability and headaches. These lead one to make mistakes like misjudging the texture of the sand ahead or incorrectly repairing a puncture. Soon the errors are compounded and disaster strikes. One is off-course and there is a major break down : the perfect scenario for catastrophe and a slow but horrible death. Hardly a year goes by without the Sahara's furnace-like heat claiming lives. Awareness of the effects of the desert climate on the human body and the steps necessary to counteract them is essential to successful travel in the Sahara. (See the chapters on Personal Health and on Survival.)

Desertification

During the Sahara's current trend towards increasing aridity there have been good and very bad periods. It has been a fluctuating but nevertheless con-tinuous change. The severe drought of 1968-1974 was a 'bad' fluctuation. The high rainfall of 1974-1976 was a 'good' one. Drought returned for 1980-1984. However, the Sahara is not only becoming drier but is also expanding. Its southward advance into the West African savanna has been known since the 1930s. But, some have blamed man for his cutting of the savanna and sahel bush for firewood, his shifting cultivation and his uncontrolled grazing (especially by his voracious goats). Today this is seen not as human error but rather as the attempts of poor, disadvantaged, and simple people trying to cope with a long term climatic change, totally beyond their control (to some, determined by the unquestionable designs of Allah).

It may also be argued that some aid programmes have actually made things worse for some of the nomads of the southern Sahara. French and FAO policy of sinking more wells in the Sahel region may have made the 68-74 drought worse. These extra wells encouraged more nomads to keep larger herds of livestock. These extra herds had to be grazed more intensively and therefore allowed less chance for the vegetation to recover after grazing. Consequent-ly, when a normal bad fluctuation occurred, and the drought came, the nomads were ill-prepared for it. Their newfound affluence in terms of live-stock died off rapidly without adequate grazing, and mass starvation resulted. To drive through the Sahel and southern Sahara in 1973 was quite shocking for a westerner. Death was everywhere.

Recent archaeological and geological evidence has shown the land mass of what is now the Sahara to have alternated between wet and dry climates during the past million or so years. Radar images from US Shuttle spacecraft of parts of the Sahara have revealed ancient watercourses and drainage patterns underneath some of the giant ergs or sand seas. These have confirmed the findings on the ground of archaeologists working in the Kalanshio sand sea and the Selima sand sheet in the Egyptian Western Desert. In vast areas of what are now sand seas, human beings, probably simple hunter-gatherers, lived some 100,000 years ago during what archaeologists call the Late Acheulean pluvial period. This was followed by a long hyperarid period during which the Sahara became much drier than it is today. The water table dropped and humans and animals disappeared. This is when most of the large ergs or sand seas were formed. In later pluvial or wet stages when life returned to the desert the dunes were often stabilised and compacted by vegetation.

Human occupation of the Sahara then oscillated between 60,000 years ago and the beginning of relatively 'recent' times some 25,000 years ago. During pluvial periods life returned to the desert while the alternating dry climates brought about the desertion of all life forms. Then, for about 15,000 years a relatively long dry period endured. It was not until about 10,000 years ago during the last 'Ice Age' that plants, animals and man returned to the area now covered by the Sahara. Paleolithic and then Neolithic people brought domesticated animals from surrounding areas to the south. They practised limited agriculture and established fishing economies around the shores of former lakes which have long since dried up such as Lake Arouane in Mali and the Aouker Basin in Mauritania. The final drought did not begin to set in until about 5,000 years ago. Indeed, 2,000 years ago it was still possible for horse drawn chariots to cross the Sahara. Man soon found it necessary to import the camel from Asia and today it is the only animal capable of crossing this increasingly hyperarid desert.

The extreme aridity of the Sahara today is not a permanent condition. Man's excessive pressure on the fragile surrounding semi-desert environment may temporarily exacerbate the aridity but in the long run it would seem another pluvial period will return to the Sahara. However, this will certainly not be in our, or even our grand-children's, lifetimes. Desertification in the Sahara should be seen not as man-created but in terms of different cycles superimposed on one another: cycles operating over thousands of years and those which operate only over decades. Thus, the terrible Sahelian drought of 1968-1974 which was followed by a period of good rainfall was merely a minor oscillation within a much greater cycle which seems to be currently leading towards increased aridity.

4
Sand, Stones and Rocks: Geomorphology

The rocks underneath much of the Sahara are pre-Cambrian and being more than 3,000 million years old are some of the oldest on earth. However, as recently as 225 million years ago (recent in geological time), there was only one giant continent on earth. Known by geologists as 'Pangaea', it began to split up along the lines of enormous rift valleys which in turn widened out into vast oceans as breakaway land masses (today's continents) drifted away. The present African continent is all that is left of the original 'Pangaea' on or near its original site. Other chunks of it or 'cratons' like Western Australia and NE Brazil have drifted away from Africa.

However, Africa too is not stationary and is actually moving incredibly slowly northwards, crashing into Europe on the way. As it collides so the impact areas of the two continents are wrinkling or folding, thus forming the Atlas Mountains, the Pyrenees and the Alps.

This oversimplifies what is actually happening for as the two continents or 'plates' collide they are also moving very slowly sideways in opposite directions. As the two massive plates scrape alongside each other, huge chunks

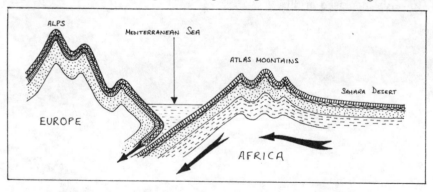

As the African plate moves north and collides with the Eurasian plate it causes mountains to be formed. Along this impact zone there will be frequent earthquakes as the plates scrape alongside each other. There will also be volcanic activity (e.g. Vesuvius and Etna) as fractures in the folding rock allow molten magma from deep inside the earth's crust to come to the surface

40

of continent break off and, as well, giant mountain blocks are pushed up. Sometimes the sideways movement of the plates is impeded slightly, maybe for a few hundred years only. The pressure from behind each plate builds up until quite suddenly there is a violent movement, usually in the form of an earthquake. Just such an earthquake killed thousands at El Asnam in northern Algeria early in 1980. Other recent major 'quakes have occurred at Agadir in Morocco, Naples in Italy and Skopje in Yugoslavia and will undoubtedly occur again and again on both sides of the Mediterranean.

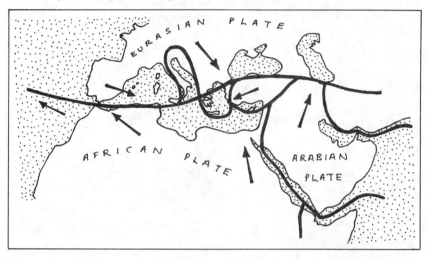

Approximate position today of the major plates of the Mediterranean area. While the African and Eurasian plates move slowly in opposite directions, the north-westerly movement of the African plate tends to force the Eurasian plate below the surface (Map was adapted from N. Calder, The Restless Earth 1972 BBC, London)

Granite hills to the south of Arak in southern Algeria. These rocks are some of the oldest on earth, being part of the original continent: Pangea

41

The Atlas Mountains to the north of the Sahara lie along the rim of this continental collision area. They are largely very old sedimentary rock which was once flat as it was being laid down many millions of years ago, forming layer upon layer of compressed sediment. With continental drift or plate movement, these sediments have been very slowly bent and contorted and folded into the several mountain ridges of the Atlas ranges.

To the south, the centre of the Sahara is relatively flat, consisting mainly of ancient pre-Cambrian rock overlain with more recent sedimentary material. In some places, such as the Hoggar, the pre-Cambrian rock or craton is exposed on the surface and is clearly seen as massive, bare, dome-shaped, granite mountains sticking up out of the sedimentary plains.

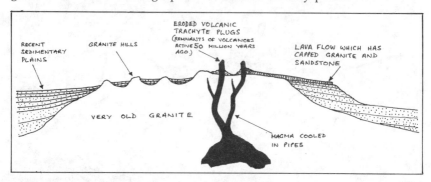

Granite and volcanic magma intrusion in the Hoggar. To the left of this photo are ancient granite rocks (lighter colour). Volcanic lava has forced its way to the surface and can be seen as the darker rocks in the right background; the large dome being a plug of trachyte lava which has cooled in the pipe which brought the lava to the surface

Trachyte volcanic plugs in the Hoggar Mountains. These are made of trachyte rock (an alkaline form of igneous or volcanic rock) which was once lava that cooled inside the exit pipes of now extinct volcanoes some 50 million years ago. The outer surface of the volcanoes has been eroded away. In the foreground are rocks which are the remains of a lava flow and of molten debris blasted out of the volcanoes

Actually, the highest peaks in the Hoggar Massif such as Illamane (2918m), Akar Akar (2132m), Tahat (3003m), Assekrem (2918m) and Tellerteba (2455m) are made of volcanic magma which has pushed itself up through the granite and cooled on the surface before gradually becoming eroded during the succeeding few millions of years.

These spectacular peaks in the Hoggar Massif are cooled trachyte lava plugs blocking the exit pipes of what are now extinct volcanoes.

In the Tibesti Mountains of northern Chad the situation is slightly different. Volcanic material or magma had protruded through the sedimentary sand-stone plateau forming volcanoes which are still semi-active (Eli Mousgou, Trou au Natron, Sobourom and Emi Koussi). In some places hard basalt rock (a remnant of past lava flows) has formed a cap over sand-stone slowing down the rate at which the sedimentary base rock has been eroded; such is the case with the Fadnoun Plateau south of Illizi in Algeria. Roads built over these ancient lava flows are invariably incredibly rough and vehicle destroying because the rock is so hard, as any journey from Illizi to Ft. Gardel and from Tamanrasset to Assekrem will show.

However, the largest proportion of the Sahara's surface is sedimentary, or made up of sand, soil and debris laid down over millions of years through wind deposition, sediment deposited by ancient rivers and even by glaciers during various ice ages. The material deposited by water has usually been eroded and washed down from higher mountains like the Hoggar and Tibesti and deposited on lower ground gradually building up layer by layer even-tually forming vast plains like the Tanezrouft and the Hammada du Guir In some places the Sahara was clearly covered by ocean hundreds of millions of years ago. There, limestone plains consist largely of fine seafloor silt and

43

Iharen or Pic Laperrine just north of Tamanrasset in the Hoggar Mountains is a typical volcanic plug and the diagram below illustrates its formation

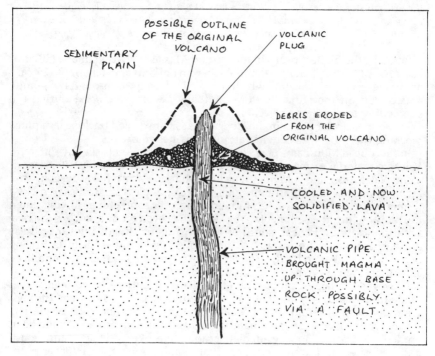

The Tanezrouft: vast featureless plain of sedimentary gravel and sand up to 900 kilometres across. A typical 'Reg', the name Tanezrouft means 'Land of Terror' because its great size and total absence of water and vegetation made crossing it a daunting task to be avoided at all costs

A close-up of fossilised coral polyps embedded in rock that forms part of the escarpment overlooking the Oued Zousfana at Tarhit in Algeria. Clearly parts of today's Sahara Desert were once below sea level and covered by a warm ocean

45

the fossilised skeletons of millions and millions of sea creatures. Most of these were almost microscopic but it is very easy to find larger fossilised shells of molluscs, snails and brachiopods as well as the remains of large coral reefs. Just two of the places where one can find such fossils are in the cliffs overlooking the Oued Zousfana at Tarhit and in the Plateau de Tinrhert between Bordj Omar Idriss and Ohanet in the eastern Algerian Sahara.

Similarly, one can find the fossilised remains of primordial swamps (in the Dunes of Guadoufawa) and even of temperate rain forests (near Ain Salah). Time has compressed these remnants and preserved them.

Fossilised molluscs seen in rocks about 100 kilometres north of Adrar in southern Algeria: further remnants of ancient sea bed life in what is now desert (The car keys in the centre lower part of the picture indicate the scale)

Time has brought about radical changes in the climate of the Sahara area. For example, 12,000 years ago while the climate of southern Europe and the Mediterranean was glacial, the central Sahara was experiencing a bitterly cold arid steppe climate rather like that of Mongolia and the Canadian prairies today. At the lower levels of the Atlas ranges alpine glaciers flowed south into what is now desert. Gradually, as the continental shield glaciers which covered Europe receded northwards, the Sahara's climate became warmer and changed through several climatic types to the present one of hot desert.

With these and much earlier climatic changes there has been a constant process of erosion varying in its intensity and means from climate to climate. Also during this time the results of 'Plate Tectonics' (the movement of continents and its accompanying mountain building processes) have been worn down by climatic factors to create the sedimentary plains which account for perhaps half the area of the present Sahara.

These sedimentary plains have been classified by geomorphologists into several types:

Hammada : Flat or undulating plateaus or uplands of rocks and stones such as the Tademait Plateau and the Hammada du Guir. Sometimes these stones

Fossilised tree trunks a few kilometres west of Ain Salah in the Tidikelt region of Algeria. These fossils are the remains of a once prolific forest of Araucarian trees, a type now found only in SE Australia, New Zealand and southern Chile. Similar fossils have been found in the Antarctic

Date	Vegetation	Climate type and classification*
-10,000	Grassland steppe	Arid steppe Bsk
-8,000	Mixed forest	Temperate humid Dwb
-5,000	Grass, olives and cedar trees	Warm Mediterranean CSa
12,500	Thorn trees and graminated trees	Sahelian BShw
-500 0 + 2,000	Varying from almost nothing to nothing	Desert BWh

* the Köppen system

Climatic Change in the Sahara Region
(adapted from Hugot, H.J. (Ed.) Missions Berliet: Ténéré et Tchad, 1962 Paris.)

are blackened by heat forming a pavement of desert armour or 'patina' (known as 'gibber plain' in Australia). Sometimes these stones are the result of a gradual breakdown from larger rocks caused through the chemical action of capillary water either during a more humid previous era or through overnight dews. A close examination of such stones under a microscope has revealed bacteria and microscopic lichens living on the surface. These, together with capillary water, will cause a gradual breakdown.

47

Left: A stone taken from the floor of Hammada desert with the characteristic striated erosion pattern on it. This has resulted from a gradual chemical breakdown and dissolution of its surface which has been brought about through a combination of microscopic bacteria and lichens working together with capillary water derived from frequent overnight dew. These microscopic organisms extract nutrient from such rocks and are able to survive in the tremendous extremes of temperature that occur on a Hammada desert floor: from 85°C in the middle of the day to below zero during the night

Reg : Endlessly flat plains of sand and pebbles. Much of the northern Ténéré and the Tanezrouft are like this. Regs are perhaps a more eroded or more advanced form of Hammada.

Serir : Plains of fine sand. Some are totally flat like parts of the Ténéré.

Erg : Large areas of sand dunes or sand seas. The distinction between Serir and Erg is not necessarily very clear as they often blend into each other.

There are several types of sand dunes some of which are shown in the diagrams.

There are many theories on exactly how different dune formations develop but none is really definitive and none accounts conclusively for why large dune areas are where they are. The detailed physics of blown sand have been much studied but the pioneer and still recognised authority on this is R.A. Bagnold, who studied dune movement in Libya and Egypt during the 1930s and in Saudi Arabia in the 1950s. He also led daring British attacks behind enemy lines in the eastern Sahara during World War II. His best known works are : **Physics of Blown Sand** (1941) Methuen, London and 'The Transport of Sand by Wind' **Geographical Journal** No 89, 1937.

Sand saltation, or the way in which blown sand particles jump or bounce when they hit the ground has been determined in terms of detailed mathematical formulas. This saltation can be seen in the way footprints and tyre tracks may be obliterated within minutes. Generally, coarser sand particles do not bounce more than a metre above the ground and sometimes it is possible to walk in flat sandy areas without eye protection while the lower parts of one's legs are constantly stung by sand grains. For this reason it also pays to work under cars or engines during the night when the wind may have died down.

Very fine dust particles are picked up by the wind and may even remain in suspension in the air for many days. Sometimes this air/dust mixture will obliterate the sun for weeks, even long after the wind has dropped. If the air/dust mixture reaches a very high altitude, upper atmosphere winds can take it great distances, which accounts for the fall-out of Saharan dust that occurred in Britain in 1968 (see article by A.F. Pitty in **Nature** No 220, 1969).

An excellent reference book on the geology of the Sahara is Jean Fabre **Introduction à la Géologie du Sahara Algérien et des Régions Voisines** (1976) S.N.E.D., Algiers. In French, it is primarily concerned with structure below the surface. Full of diagrams and using many different examples throughout Algeria, it is particularly good on the volcanic structures of the Hoggar. A good general book on surface features of deserts is R.V. Cooke and A. Warren **Geomorphology in Deserts** (1973) Batsford, London.

SH 4

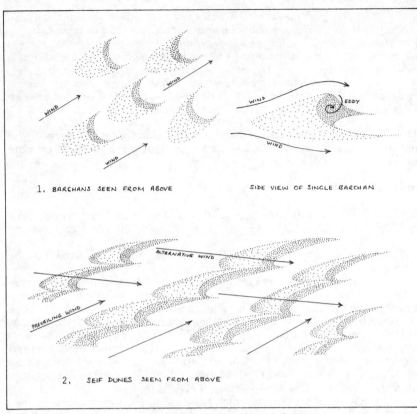

1. BARCHANS SEEN FROM ABOVE   SIDE VIEW OF SINGLE BARCHAN

2. SEIF DUNES SEEN FROM ABOVE

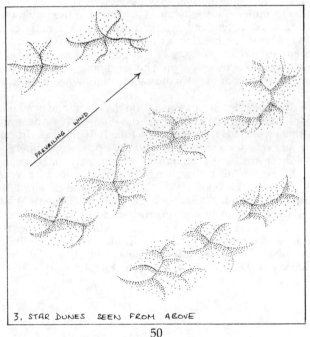

3. STAR DUNES SEEN FROM ABOVE

Longitudinal or 'Sief' dunes in the Ténére seen from a Boeing 707 airliner at an altitude of 10,000 metres and viewed from the south. These dunes are about 2 to 3 kilometres apart and up to 30 metres high. Although the prevailing wind is from the NE (top right hand corner), when this photo was taken an alternative wind from the NNW had been blowing. Unlike similar but stable dunes in the Kalahari Desert and in central Australia, these longitudinal dunes are moving all the time and there is absolutely no vegetation on the ground below

51

Sand near Kerzaz in Algeria — part of the vast Grand Erg Occidental which is up to 400 kilometres across. Typical of sand seas, this erg appears as a mass of chaotic dunes of soft, constantly moving sand. Some dune peaks, like the one in the right background, rise to over 300 metres above the surrounding landscape

Sedimentary sandstone outcrops at Gara Eckar about 50 km north of Ain Guezzam in southern Algeria. These rocks have been eroded by the abrasive action of wind-blown sand

Longitudinal sand ridges in the Ténére Desert between Bilma and Fashi. These dunes are constantly shifting and for this reason hazardous without a guide. This photo was taken looking towards the NE from where the prevailing wind comes but an alternative wind from the SE has been blowing as indicated by the ripples in the right lower corner

Star dunes — looking from one dune towards a neighbouring dune on the left. On the horizon, three kilometres across a bare gravel plain, is another parallel range of star dunes. These dunes in the Grand Erg Oriental near Hassi Messaoud rise to about 150 metres above the plain

A boy offering a Sand Rose for sale at Nefta in the South of Tunisia. These roses of crystallised gypsum are relatively easy to find just below the surface of the sand in the dunes of the Souf area of eastern Algeria and SW Tunisia as well as other areas. This crystallisation takes place very gradually as dew or rain (rarely) dissolves gypsum in the sand and is dehydrated repeatedly over many years. The gypsum crystals cling together to form these beautiful roses

5
Pre-History

In the mountainous massifs of the Sahara one can find a wealth of information about the early history of man. The rock engravings and paintings of
the Hoggar, Fezzan, Tassili N'Ajjer, Tibesti, Uweinat and Saharan Atlas areas
in particular show that more than two thousand years ago the Sahara was
a much greener and wetter place. These ancient drawings depict hunting,
herding and domestic scenes which indicate that much of the Sahara was
a type of savanna grassland over which giraffe, rhinocerous, buffalo, antelope
and other game roamed freely. They also show how man hunted them and
later how he grazed his own domesticated livestock.

The Sahara really started becoming a desert in geologically recent times at
the end of the last ice age or about 8000 BC. That is not to say that it had
not been a desert before. However, at this time it was largely a rolling
savanna grass and woodland with volumes of wild animals not too dissimilar
to the game reserves of East Africa today. Rainfall was higher and there were
also large lakes and swamps such as the Lake Chad basin and the ancient
Lake Araouane, once an inland sea into which the Niger River flowed near
the present day Timbuktu and Mopti. Areas now desert were mostly only
semi-arid. Hunters roamed the plains and eventually domesticated wild
animals, while fishermen camped on the shores of the lakes.

At this stage most of the Sahara was peopled by Caucasoid peoples as
distinct from the negroids of West Africa and the Khoisan of central and
southern Africa (the latter being now largely confined to the Kalahari Desert).
Later, in neolithic times, there were considerable migrations within and across
North and West Africa leading to the present mixed population. Essentially
the people of 8000 years BC were hunter-gatherers, catching and trapping
game, collecting fruits and seeds, and digging for roots and tubers. Classified
as Paleolithic, they used only extremely simple stone tools. As the climate
became more arid and temperatures increased, early man had to adapt.

This resulted in the so-called Neolithic Revolution. There appeared much
more sophisticated and specialised stone tools, ground and polished rather
than simply chipped and flaked. There was also the invention of baskets and
pottery to enable men to store and transport food and water. Semi-permanent
dwellings or huts began to develop. But the real breakthrough was the
discovery that animals could be tamed, kept, bred and not just hunted, and
that seeds and roots could be cultivated and not just collected.

Typical of stone tools found in the Sahara. Remnants from a time when what is now desert was once a vast savanna plain like those of East Africa today: teeming with wild life. Up to 8,000 years ago early man hunted antelope, giraffe and other game with some of these tools. The largest one on the right and the small top centre ones are probably Paleolithic, being very simple. While the others, being more complex, are likely to be Neolithic. They were all found in the Djado Plateau area in the north-east of Niger

Domestication and cultivation led to increasingly larger and more permanent settlements situated close to the best sources of water, grazing lands and crop land. Storage of food enabled man to exist independently of the seasons and gave him time for more specialised pursuits like pottery, basket weaving and improving weapons and tools. Ultimately, this increasing sophistication led to the evolution of metallurgy and tools of copper, bronze and then iron — the so-called Bronze Age and Iron Age.

All of this occurred in the Sahara while it was becoming increasingly arid over the last 10,000 years and is reflected in the pre-historic art to be found scattered all over today's desert. There are probably thousands of paintings and rock engravings out in the desert, some as yet unseen by modern man. The authors, for example, have uncovered engravings of wild animals south of Djanet and were probably the first humans to set eyes upon them for four to six thousand years. On another occasion near Bechar, a stone picked up to use as a wheel chock prior to jacking up the car was discovered to be an ancient grindstone used possibly by neolothic man to grind the seeds he had collected. In the Massif de Termit, between the Ténéré and Lake Chad, travellers have stopped and found that they had been driving over thousands of ancient stone tools scattered across the desert floor.

Increasing desertification has slowed the decay and breakdown of these remnants of early man's existence. At the same time it has driven man from the area thus ensuring that they are left undisturbed. Sadly, however, this preservation has been rudely interrupted by modern man. Rock engravings near Tfout and Targhit in Algeria have been desecrated by graffiti. The danger of

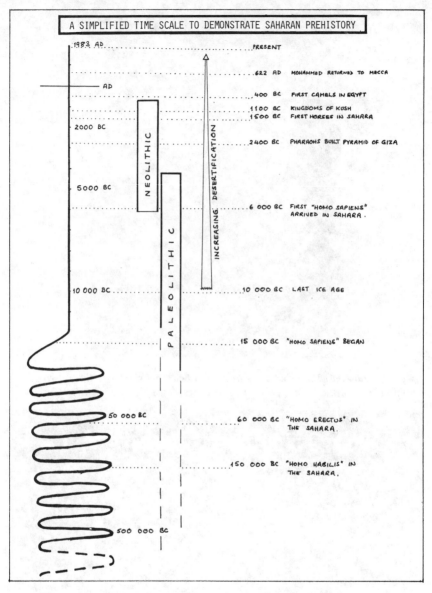

A SIMPLIFIED TIME SCALE TO DEMONSTRATE SAHARAN PREHISTORY

1983 AD .... PRESENT

.... 622 AD MOHAMMED RETURNED TO MECCA

— AD

.... 400 BC FIRST CAMELS IN EGYPT

.... 1100 BC KINGDOMS OF KUSH
.... 1500 BC FIRST HORSES IN SAHARA

2000 BC

NEOLITHIC

.... 2400 BC PHARAOHS BUILT PYRAMID OF GIZA

INCREASING DESERTIFICATION

5000 BC

.... 6 000 BC FIRST "HOMO SAPIENS" ARRIVED IN SAHARA.

PALEOLITHIC

10 000 BC .... 10 000 BC LAST ICE AGE

.... 15 000 BC "HOMO SAPIENS" BEGAN

50 000 BC

.... 60 000 BC "HOMO ERECTUS" IN THE SAHARA.

.... 150 000 BC "HOMO HABILIS" IN THE SAHARA.

500 000 BC

1. The terms 'neolithic' and 'paleolithic' are used to describe cultural periods in the past which can be separated by the methods of making stone tools
2. For a brief and succinct account of this time scale, see: S.L. Washburn, 'Tools and Human Evolution' Scientific American, September 1960 and D. Pilbeam, 'The Descent of Hominoids and Hominids' Scientific American, March 1984
3. This chart is a generalisation based on the pre-history of the Sahara area and should not necessarily be applied to other areas. Moreover, pre-historic evolution is not susceptible to a rigid classification. New discoveries continually render rigid classifications obsolete

A pair of stones used to grind grass seeds into flour and similar to those used by neolithic man in the Sahara (The box of matches shows the size of these stones)

Rock engravings thousands of years old at Tfout in Algeria which have been desecrated by modern vandals

the puerile actions of a few vandals despoiling art that is milleniums old accounts for the sensitivity of governments to the impact of tourists in certain areas. Thus, tourists are not allowed into the Tassilli National Park near Djanet unaccompanied by a guide. For the same reasons, the Niger Government has forbidden unauthorised people to go to the area of the Dunes of Guadoufaoua where intact fossilised dinosaur skeletons have been found under the shifting sand.

The rock art of the Sahara has been classified by experts into eras or periods which are summarised in the following chart:

Bubalus period 10,000-7000 BC
when large wild buffalo type animals roamed
the plains hunted by early man.

Roundhead period 8000-5000 BC
when early man painted strange people
with large round heads.

Cattle period 5000-2500 BC
when man became a herder of
domesticated cattle.

Horse and chariot period 1500 BC - 800 AD
when the horse was the main means of
transport in this increasingly arid land.

Camel period 400 BC - present day
when the horse, being incapable of coping
with the aridity, was replaced by the camel,
imported from Asia.

Some of the foremost experts on pre-historic rock art and cultures are:

L. Frobenius   — Libyan Fezzan
Henri J. Hugot   — Hoggar and Tassili
Henri Lhote   — Hoggar, Air and Tassili
Theodore Monod   — Mauritania
R. Capot-Rey   — Tibesti and Ennedi
Yolande Tschudi   — Tassili

Some of the best museum collections can be seen at:
— Musée de l'Homme, Paris
— Collection Sahariennes de la Fondation Berliet at Abbaye de Senanque, near Avignon, France.
— Musée du Bardo, 3 Ave. Franklin Roosevelt, Algiers.
— Musée du Sahara, Ouargla, Algeria.
— Musée de la Centre Nationale de Recherches sur les Zones Arides at Beni Abbes.
— Musée National, Niamey (Pre-history & present)
— Horniman Museum, Forrest Hill, London, (Touareg collection, contact 153 Club first)
— Museum of Institut Français d'Afrique Noire at Place Tascher, Dakar, Senegal.
— Musée National Njamena, Chad (Tibesti engravings).

The following are just some of the many, many sites of interest involving rock engravings, rock paintings, and other archeological interest. There are hundreds of others, some as yet awaiting discovery.

Ain Sefra Numerous rock engravings to be found at village of Tfout along the main road to El Bayadh. One kilometre east of village after crossing the oued seen on north side of road and also 11 km east of village along a track (guide needed).

Ain Guezzam About 60 km north of Ain Guezzam are the picturesque wind eroded sandstone rocks of Gara Ekar. At the foot of some rocks are camel period etchings and some Touareg 'tifinar' script (sometimes covered by sand).

Bardai in the Tibesti. Rock engravings of wild animals of the savanna near Azoua, at the Enneri Dirinao, at Gonoa, near the Soboroum hot springs, and just north of Zouar. 15 km east of Bardai are some pre-Islamic tumuli.

Bir Moghrein in northern Mauritania. Paintings of wild savanna animals at Oumet el Ham.

Adrar Bous north of the Air Plateau, Niger. Berliet Expedition in 1959-60 made important discoveries of paleolithic (Aterian and Acheulian) and neolithic stone tools.

Adrar Madet east of the Air Plateau and on the edge of the Ténéré. Neolithic stone tools.

Djanet Massive quantities of rock engravings and paintings within the Tassili National Park and in surrounding areas like the Oued Indebirenne and Erg d'Admer. (See itinerary section on Djanet for details.)

Chirfa There have been important finds (by Berliet Expeditions) of paleolithic and neolithic stone tools in the Enneri Blaka area of the Djado Plateau NE of Chirfa. Also, many engravings of wild savanna animals.

Rock engravings near Targhit in Algeria which are probably of the Bubalus period

A Roundhead period painting. The 'Gorille' at Sefar in the Tassili area (Photo: courtesy of Dr Rheinhold Wepf)

Horse and chariot period. 'Le grand mouflon' at Ti-n-Zoumaitak in the Tassili near Djanet (Photo: courtesy of Dr Rheinhold Wepf)

A Cattle period engraving in the Oued Indebirene near Djanet

Camel period paintings in the Fadnoun Plateau south of Illizi in Algeria

An example of fairly recent engravings and some Touareg 'tifinar' script seen at Ain Guezzam in the very far south of Algeria

El Bayadh 75 km along a piste directly to the south of El Bayadh is the village of Brezina. Take a guide to be shown dozens of early neolithic engravings. Main sites are at Ain Marshal, Fouaij Tamara, Hadjera Driess, Keradka and Merdoufa. 92 km NE of El Bayadh along the road to Aflou are many more engravings at the oasis of El Gicha.

El Beyed About 200 km NE of Atar on the edge of the Mauritanian 'Empty Quarter', paleolithic stone tools litter the desert floor.

Fada North of Fada in the Ennedi Mountains of northern Chad are rock paintings in purple of wild animals and hunting scenes. Also, there are pre-Islamic tumuli.

Faya Largeau In northern Chad to the north of Faya are paintings in caves and some tumuli.

Ft. Gardel (Zaouatenlaz). At Tinterhert in the foothills of the Tassili — rock engravings. (Ask at 'Hotel-Café' for Ibrahim Ben Balous as guide.)

Guadoufaoua Among the crescent dunes of the western edge of the Ténéré are the fossilised skeletal remains of dinosaurs (*Ouransaurus nigeriensis)* and giant crocodiles (*Sarcosuchus imperator*). It is forbidden to visit this area without specific approval.

Ghat In the Tadrart Acacous sandstone rocks to the east of Ghat are caves with paintings of hunting scenes, family life and festivities as well as explicit engravings of sexual activities, unfortunately despoiled by more recent graffiti.

Gilf Kebir Neolithic stone tools and pottery remains.

Hassi El Mounir and Bou Akba in the Hammada du Draa area north of Tindouf in Algeria there are rock engravings of wild animals of the savanna.

Iforas Adrar near Tademeka in the north east of Mali. Petroglyphs or rock engravings of chariots.

Iherir At this tiny Touareg oasis hidden in a massive canyon are rock paintings and engravings some 5 km by foot from the village (ask for a guide).

Illizi It was here that a French Lieutenant Brenans in 1934 made the first modern description of pre-historic rock art in the Tassili. The Oued Djerad is a canyon some 40 kilometres long and it is only possible to travel up it by foot with camels but there are more than a thousand engravings and paintings to be seen! Ask at the Police for a guide.

Ideles Engravings in the south of the Tefedest range between Hirafok and ✔ Ideles at Oued Zarzoua, Immaara and Oued Isharrar.

Kidal Rock engravings.

Jebel Uweinat Paintings and engravings among the mountain massif which straddles the confluence of the Libyan, Egyptian and Sudanese borders.

Mertoutek Engravings north of the village but well to the south of the Garet El Djenoum mountain. Travel by donkey and with guide is essential.

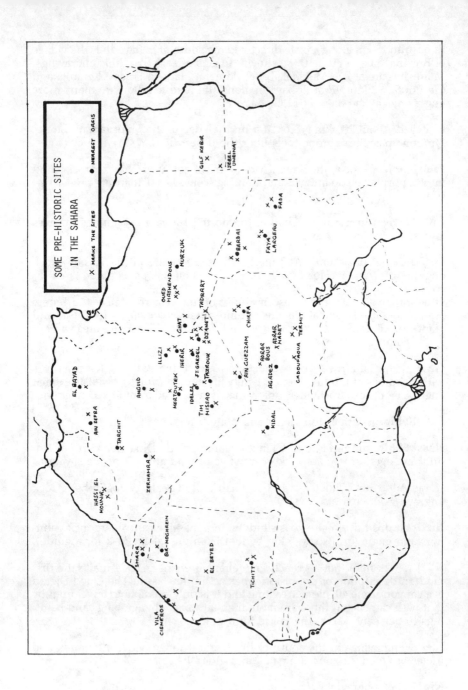

SOME PRE-HISTORIC SITES
IN THE SAHARA

X MARKS THE SITES   ● NEKABET OASIS

Oued Mathendous Large number of rock engravings.

Smara Throughout the Saguiet el Hamra valley there are engravings and stone hand tools (even as far back in time as 'Chellean') which can be found at many points.

Targhit Rock engravings (and a few paintings) south of the oasis in a rocky escarpment overlooking the Oued Zousfana. Easy to find. (Let tyres down and just follow tracks.)

Tazrouk Rock engravings, fairly recent with 'tifinar' script.

Termit Neolithic stone tools.

Tim Missao Rock engravings of savanna animals and of chariots.

Tichitt Top of the Dahar Tichitt, an escarpment which runs all the way to Oualata in the east, at the edge of what was once lake Aouker, there are remnants of fortified neolithic 'villages'. Some of the fortification walls still exist as do some tumuli. Discovered by Teodore Monod in 1954.

Villa Cisneros Up and down the coast are middens of discarded shells left by neolithic men. Some of these mounds also contain remnants of pottery, stone tools and decorated ostrich eggs.
  Engravings: 200 km SE of Villa Cisneros near the peak of Gleibat Mosdat and a further 100 km SE in the hills of Leyauf are many engravings of wild animals and chariots.

A pre-Islamic stone circle in southern Algeria. Possibly a tumulus or ancient grave, there are literally hundreds of similar stone structures all over the Sahara and in most cases their origin is still unknown (Photo: by courtesy of Jim Taylor)

65

Yei Lulu Yoga A pass along the Berliet piste very close to the Chad frontier. Camel period engravings, late neolithic stone axes and hippopotamus skeletons.

Zerhamra 55 km SW of Beni Abbes beyond the tiny oasis of Zerhamra at the Oued Merlouk are rock engravings and neolithic artifacts. (Enquire at Museum in Beni Abbes first.)

Today, big changes are taking place in the Sahara. In Libya, massive agricultural programmes at Sebha and Kufra oases are having spectacular success. Wheat and citrus fruits are now growing on a scale seen previously only in California, Israel, and the Murray Valley in Australia. Uranium mining in the Air region of Niger is bringing about big social changes for the Touaregs. The Algerians have ambitious plans for a sealed, trans-Saharan highway to open up trade with West Africa.

But how long will these man-made changes last? Man used to hunt and graze livestock a long time ago, where now there are gigantic seas of rolling sand dunes. In the solitude, silence and enormous emptiness of the central Sahara, one thinks about the four thousand eight hundred million years of the earth's history, the relatively short existence of the Sahara as a desert, and the complete insignificance of man. Will the Sahara, the ultimate of all deserts, be changed? Or will man's current efforts end up like the ancient rock engravings and tools found among the rocks of the empty plateaux?

6
History

At the end of the last century an Oxford historian described African history before the colonial period as 'blank, uninteresting brutal barbarism' a view now thoroughly discredited for its ethnocentric approach. At the outset of the Iron Age 2,000 years ago, the people on both sides of the Sahara were developing societies with social systems, economies, religions, art and cultures as advanced as any in Europe. The complex societies of the Egypt of the Pharaohs, Nubia, Axum and Kush were fully fledged states which considerably predated the ancient Greek, Phoenician and Roman states.

During Roman and Phoenician times, when Carthage and Tripoli were at their height, considerable trade across the Sahara was conducted by Berber traders. Some of these Berbers were referred to as 'Garamantes' by the ancient geographers Herodotus and Strabo and the Alexandrian Ptolemy. All three classical geographers reported that the Garamantes used to carry out raids across the Sahara to attack the 'Ethiopians' and to the Niger River via the Hoggar mountains. Moreover, they used four-horse chariots! (Quite a feat!) Evidence of these can be found among the rock paintings of the Tassili at Tin Abou Teka, Ala-n-Edoument and Adjefou. Henri Lhote, the foremost authority on prehistoric rock paintings in the Sahara, is also convinced that Romans were involved in these raids. However, at that time the Sahara was not quite as arid as it is now; such a journey by horse would be virtually impossible today.

Under the Romans, Christianity replaced Judaism and spread throughout the Maghreb but with the demise of the Roman Empire, in 429 AD Germanic Vandals overran Roman North Africa. Over a hundred years later in 534 AD they in turn were overcome by the Byzantine Empire which soon became oppressive and inefficient. It lost the loyalty of the Berbers and ultimately collapsed in the face of the Arab conquest in the seventh century which effectively replaced Christianity with Islam.

However, during the 11th century there was a large scale migration into the Maghreb and what is now northern Libya of nomadic Bedouin Arab tribes known as the Beni Hillal and Beni Sulaym. Ibn Khaldun, the most respected of the Arab historians (born in Tunis 1332, died in Cairo 1406), likened this Bedouin migration to that of a swarm of locusts, destroying all in their path. Until this point the Arabs had been, like their predecessors the Romans and Phoenicians, a numerically small urban elite. Now the invading Arab

67

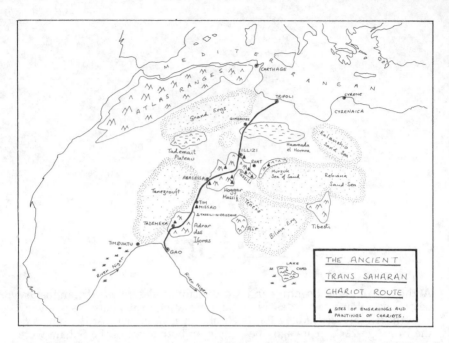

At several places strung out across the Sahara ancient rock art has been discovered that depicts horse drawn chariots. With one or two exceptions, the sites of these paintings and engravings are to be found along a route that some authorities like Henry Lhote believe was an ancient path across the desert to the Niger River used by these charioteers to avoid the more treacherous sandy areas. The pictures of chariots were probably drawn between 1000 BC and about 500 AD when the Sahara was not as arid as it is today. But who actually rode those chariots has been an open question for some time. Some have suggested the Romans or perhaps the descendants of Mycenaean invaders from Crete. The Greek historian Herodotus wrote of the Garamantes of Libya driving chariots all the way to Ethiopia. A major breakthrough in this controversy may have occurred early in 1985 when a U.S. National Geographic Society expedition discovered wheels from two chariots and other Roman remains at Tassili-N-Eridjane in the far south of Algeria

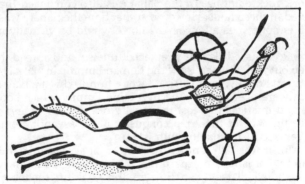

A horse drawn chariot at flying gallop. Drawn from a photo of an engraving at Tin Smad, Oued Djerad near Illizi (Courtesy of P.J. Morgan)

settlers displaced the Berber population which retreated into the more inaccessible confines of the mountains (such as the Kabilye region) and into the desert. Thus, although Islamicised since the seventh and eighth centuries, Berbers have tended to remain separate from the Arab populations in Algeria and Morocco, retaining their own language and jealously guarding their own traditions. Some modern academics now see Touareg origins as stemming from the Berber retreat into the desert at this time.

Meanwhile, by the ninth century, on the other side of the Sahara powerful states like ancient Ghana, Mali and Kanem-Bornu in West Africa were engaging in thriving trade throughout the region, to the Middle East and across the Sahara to the Mediterranean. This was a trade in commodities ranging from gold, copper, slaves, cloth, salt, beads, and even books; all of which were regulated and taxed by the empires concerned. During this same period, northern Europe was in the grip of the so-called Dark Ages.

By the ninth century Islam had reached the West African empires through these trade routes. It gave a new sense of unity in some states and encouraged trading alliances throughout the Moslem world. The Sahel and northern Savanna belt of West Africa was especially favourable for the development of complex societies. The well-watered fertility of the upper Niger and the area north of the Niger and Benue Rivers encouraged the growth of a relatively dense agricultural population. These areas were also well placed to trade local products for those of the forest areas to the south and those from across the Sahara, lying at the ends of the great caravan routes. Alluvial gold deposits in what are now modern Ghana and Ivory Coast provided an especially potent stimulus to trade.

The powerful ancient Ghana Empire, essentially a trading state, with its capital Kumbi (200 km north of the present Bamako) on the fringe of the Sahara flourished from the eighth century. When in 1076 the Moslem Berber armies of the Almoravids (or 'Al Murabethin' in Arabic) from southern Morocco con-

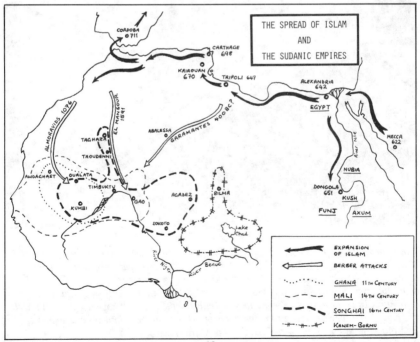

quered the region (as well as most of the Maghreb and Spain) trans-Saharan trade continued but the Almoravids were unable to master it themselves and to hold onto the region. During the thirteenth century a Moslem convert from the Mandinka people in the Cassamance area of what today is Senegal, Sundaita Keita, established the new Mali Empire with his capital at Niani. The empire reached its peak with the reign of Mansa Musa (1312-1337), a period of stability and immense wealth. In 1324 on a pilgrimage to Mecca, he created a sensation in Cairo with his wealth and lavish gifts of gold; the gifts actually ruined the value of the Egyptian gold-based Dinar for several years afterwards. Under the Mali Empire cities like Timbuktu and Djenné became important centres of Islamic learning and scholarship, with books becoming a major item of trade.

However, in the fifteenth century internal disputes gradually weakened the Mali Empire and it was eclipsed from within by the Songhai people of Gao, a trans-Saharan trading city. Sunni Ali and his successor, Askia Mohammed Turé, took over Mali and established the new Songhai Empire which grew into the largest of the Sudanic African kingdoms with control over the Hausa city states in the east, Agadez in the north-east, Taghaza in the north, Oualata in the west and Djenné in the south-west. Nevertheless, this potent and sophisticated empire with its organised systems of administration, justice and revenue collection, collapsed virtually overnight with the sudden arrival of raiders from the north.

El Mansour, King of Morocco, sent his forces aided by Spanish mercenaries all the way across the desert in a daring raid to capture the centre of the West

The mud-walled Djingareber Mosque at Timbuktu was built in the 14th century and is the oldest surviving Mosque in West Africa. It has been partially rebuilt many times since that date and most of the present structure dates from 1571. One of its doors has been closed since the Mosque was first built in 1325. It is guarded continuously because it is believed locally that should it ever be opened it would spell the end of the world. Nobody knows what is behind the door and no one wants to find out (Photo by courtesy of Freddie and Marie Hicks)

African gold trade. In 1591 Timbuktu and Gao fell and the Empire collapsed. El Mansour could not control it from across the Sahara and had to withdraw. Smaller states arose in the vacuum and Islam went into decline throughout West Africa.

Eventually, out of the ruins of Songhai arose smaller kingdoms like the Bambara estates of Segou and Kaarta (in present day Mali), the eighteenth century Berber kingdom of Kunta based on Timbuktu, the Hausa Bokwai city states and at the start of the nineteenth century the Sokoto Caliphate established through an Islamic revivalist war or Jihad by the Fulani Shehu Usman dan Fodio.

To the east of the Sahel belt, the Kingdom of Kanem-Bornu had evolved from about 700 AD in the area to the east of Lake Chad. In the fourteenth century its rulers had become Moslem but because it was not ideally situated in relation to fertile agricultural lands and supplies of gold, it never prospered as much as the empires further west. However, its influence was widespread and it was owed allegiance by states as far away as the Funj Sultanate in the Nile Valley and parts of the Fezzan to the north where it controlled the trans-Saharan slave trade. Moreover, this empire can be regarded as being still in existence today with the Sehu of Bornu as its current leader based in the Kanure town of Maiduguri in the north-east of Nigeria.

To the north, across the Sahara Desert, the Almoravids, who had taken over the Maghreb and Spain, in the eleventh century gradually lost control. They retreated from Spain and Christians invaded the north African coast. This united Moslems into 'Brotherhoods' to carry on the fight and the Turks came to the aid of their fellow Moslems in the sixteenth century. In Morocco a new and vital dynasty, the Sa'dids, came to power and decisively defeated the Portuguese at the Battle of Three Kings in 1578. Although the victorious Moroccan ruler was killed in the course of the battle, his brother succeeded to the throne and the glory of the title of El Mansour (the victorious).He restored the power of the state in Morocco and acquired much wealth through his capture of the Songhai Empire in 1591.

It wasn't until the seventeenth century that another Sa'did, Mulay Ismail, who based his power on negro slaves from the Niger area, won back from the Spanish and Portuguese all the Christian holdings except for Ceuta and Melilla which remain Spanish to this day.

By the beginning of the nineteenth century both the Sa'did dynasty and Ottoman Turkish rule in Algeria and Tunisia were in a weak position, having lost control of Berber populations and being unable to keep pace with the technological progress of European countries. They soon collapsed under pressure from the French who were embarking on empire-building expansion plans.

Algeria became a French colony in 1830, Tunisia in 1881, but Morocco was not divided between Spain and France until 1911. However, French rule was relatively short-lived. Morocco became independent under descendents of the Sa'did dynasty in 1956 and the present King, Hassan II, remains to all intents and purposes a ruler with all the prerogatives of absolute monarchy in spite of a constitution.

Algeria, occupied by the French in 1830, became independent in 1962 after eight years of exceedingly bitter guerrilla warfare in which literally millions of Algerians died and a million French settlers or 'Pieds Noirs' were repatriated to France. Since independence Algeria has followed a socialist policy, redistributing land to form collectives and nationalising vital sectors of the economy. Since 1977 Algeria has devoted much energy to supporting the Polisario cause in Western Sahara, severely straining relations with Morocco.

In Tunisia's case independence was achieved after a relatively short two-

71

The Fort at Zinder in Niger Republic. Built towards the end of the last century by the French, it served as the base for the French colonial military forces, the 'Narine' (composed of French officers and local soldiers) who were used to subdue most of the eastern half of Niger

year guerrilla war in 1956. Tunisia has since had good relations with European countries, becoming an associate member of the EEC as well as a major tourist destination for the people of affluent Europe.

Libya's history is somewhat different from that of the Maghreb. In the sixteenth century it became part of the Ottoman Turkish Empire and remained that way until 1911 when the Italians, in a last minute bid for colonial possessions,' took it over. With only a small population and apparently little of value at the time, it was placed under United Nations trusteeship in 1946 and became independent under King Idris in 1951. Following a coup in 1969 Colonel Gaddafi established a fundamentalist Islamic socialist regime which now enjoys tremendous oil wealth as well as considerable distrust on the part of some of the less radical countries on both sides of the Sahara.

However, the greatest disruption to society economics and trade along the southern fringe of the Sahara came with the European conquest in the last two decades of the nineteenth century. The French took over almost the entire southern Sahelian perimeter of the Sahara from Senegal to the Sudan. The states of Segou, Sikasso, Borgu (1894), Mossi (1896), and the Samori of Tucolor (1898) provided stubborn and intelligent resistence. No kingdom or state gave in without a fight as the French advanced from the west and south. The wars were bloody, long and bitter despite the technological advantages held by the French (for example, the Maxim machine gun). The repression was conducted with a harsh and often indiscriminate brutality. Few rulers were prepared to act as agents for the French who therefore tended to destroy traditional authority wherever they met it, concentrating all power in the hands of their own commanders or administrators.

In the centre of the Sahara, the French were able to defeat the Kel Ahagger Touaregs in 1902 at the Battle of Tit but out of necessity and through clever

In 1903 the British captured Sokoto, the seat of Hausa-Fulani power, but they had to rule through the Sultan and his Emirs. Thus, today the Sultan of Sokoto, Abubakar II, a direct descendant of the Shehu Usman dan Fodio, is venerated by and commands more loyalty among the people of northern Nigeria and southern Niger than do the modern rulers of those countries. He is seen here addressing his people during the festivities (Id el Fitri) at the end of the Moslem period of fasting, Ramadan

politics were able to rule indirectly through the Amenokal or Touareg chief. However, Touareg society has not recovered from the French conquest and current socialist Algerian policies could ensure that it never does.

Yet, when, in 1903, the British captured Sokoto, the seat of Fulani-Hausa power, they had to use traditional rulers like the Sultan and the Emirs to maintain some semblance of occupation. British numbers were thin on the ground. Thus, while the French tended to destroy traditional authority, the British probably even bolstered some of it up. Today, long after independence, traditional rulers are still a major force in Nigerian politics while in Niger, Mali, Chad and Burkina Faso (Upper Volta) they are insignificant.

In 1960 all the French colonies of the Sahel received independence under republican regimes. Some of these territories have totally incongruous borders which could have proved disastrous. For example, the Niger Republic includes large segments of the former Songhai Empire, the Sokoto Caliphate, and the Kanem-Bornu Empire. The other segments of these former states are within the borders of neighbouring Mali, Upper Volta, Nigeria and Chad. Yet, probably because traditional rule had been stamped out by the French, there have been no significant secessionist movements and for more than twenty years now this country with its polyglot mixture of peoples has survived intact.

Nevertheless, the outcome of European colonial rule was not only a complete breakdown of empires but also the collapse and disappearance of the centuries old trans-Saharan trade and contact between Arab and Black Africa. It has only been in the late 1970s and the 1980s that this trade and contact is being re-established as present day Algeria and Libya compete for markets and influence in the Sahel. Every day, dozens of large Algerian and Libyan trucks can be seen arriving and departing from the Niger oasis of Agadez at the terminus of two major and ancient caravan routes.

Summary Information on Saharan Countries

Algeria
Population : 23 million (1987)
Algiers 1,720,000; Oran 663,000; Constantine 448,000; Annaba 348,000; Tizi Ouzou 101,000; Blida 191,000.

1954	FLN (Front de Liberation Nationale) started open warfare against the French administration.
1958	French settlers form OAS (Organisation de l'Armée Secrète) as anti-FLN guerrilla movement.
1962	Independence following talks at Evian. Ferhat Abbas, President. Ahmed Ben Bella, Prime Minister.
1963	Ben Bella elected President. Internal unrest concerning the compatibility of socialism with Islam.
1965	Military coup : Colonel Houari Boumédienne, President.
1973	Asphalt road reached Ain Salah.
1978	Asphalt road reached Tamanrasset.
1979	Death of Boumédienne.
1980	Colonel Bendjedid Chadli, President.
1980	Earthquake at El Asnam

Burkina Faso (formerly Upper Volta)
Population : 8.5 million (1988)
Ouagadougou 442,000; Bobo-Dioulasso 231,000; Koudougou 52,000.

1960	Independence, Maurice Yameogo President.
1966	Coup : Lieut-Col. Sangoule Lamizana President.
1969-74	Drought.
1980	Coup : Colonel Saye Zerbo President and Prime Minister.
1982	Coup : Major Ouedraogao Head of State.
1983	Coup : Capitaine Thomas Sankara Head of State.
1983-84	Drought
1987 and 1989	Further coups. Current leader Capt. Blaise Compaoré

Chad
Population : 5.4 million (1988)
Njamena 512,000; Moundou 87,000; Sarh 124,000; Abéché 71,000.

1960	Independence : President Ngarta Tombalbaye
1973	Libya occupied Azaoua region north of Tibesti.
1974	FROLINAT movement engaged in civil war against government. Largely Toubou based and supported by Libya.
1975	Coup : General Felix Malloum, President (Tombalbaye assassinated.) Fragile peace.
1979	President Goukouni Oueddi following coup. Resumption of civil war.
1981	Hissene Habré with Libyan support took control of Njamena. Bitter fighting.
1982	Habré President.
1987	Cease fire. Libyan forces confined to Aozou Strip.

Libya
Population : 4 million (1986)
Tripoli 858,000; Benghazi 368,000.

1911	Italian occupation, expulsion of Turks.
1943	British and French military administration.
1946	United Nations trusteeship.

1951	Independence : King Mohammed Idris Al Senussi.
1969	Military coup : Colonel Muamma Gaddafi, leader.
1973	Intervention in Chad.
1977	'Jamahiriya' or State of the Masses proclaimed. Gaddafi retains position as leader of the revolution but has no formal post.

Mali
Population : 7.8 million (1988)
Bamako 404,000; Mopti 54,000; Segou 65,000; Sikasso 47,000; Kayes 45,000; Gao 16,000; Timbuktu 15,000.

1959	Independence from France, but as a Federation with Senegal. After only a few months Senegal broke away. Modibo Keita, President of Mali.
1961	Major break with France. Increasing alliance with eastern bloc countries.
1968	Coup lead by Leiut. Moussa Traoré (now General). Keita believed sent to salt mines at Taoudenni.
	Improved relations with France.
1969-74	Drought.
1985	Moussa Traoré elected President.

Mauritania
Population : 1.9 million (1988)
Nouakchott 500,000; Nouadhibou 22,000; Kaedi 21,000; Atar 16,000.

1960	Independence, President Moktar Ould Daddah.
1976	Spanish cession of southern part of Western Sahara to Mauritania but war against POLISARIO a big economic drain.
1978	Military coup : Colonel Mustafa Ould Salek became President.
1979	Lieut-Col. Mohammed Mahmoud Ould Ahmed Louly chosen President by military council. Mauritania ceded its share of Western Sahara to Morocco.
1980	Lieut-Col. Mohammed Khouna Ould Kaydalla chosen as President.

Morocco
Population : 23.6 million (1987)
Casablanca 2,140,000; Rabat 596,000; Marrakesh 436,000; Fez 426,000 Meknes 403,000.

1956	Independence and end of international status for Tangier. Sultan Sidi Mohammed ben Youssef became king as Mohammed V.
1960	Agadir earthquake — 4500 killed.
1961	Succession of Hassan II upon his father's death.
1962	Constitutional monarchy established.
1969	Spanish enclave of Ifni ceded to Morocco.
1976	Spanish Sahara ceded to Morocco and Mauritania.
1979	Mauritania ceded its Wad Ed-Dahab province to Morocco.

Niger
Population : 7.2 million (1988)
Niamey 400,000; Maradi 65,000; Zinder 82,000; Tahoua 42,000; Agadez 27,000; Arlit 28,000.

1960	Independence, Hamani Diori, President.
1969-74	Drought.
1974	Military coup, Lieut-Col. Seyni Kountche President. Hamani Diori imprisoned at N'guigmi.

Nigeria
Population : 119 million (1988). (Population figures are controversial.)
Lagos 1,477,000; Kano 450,000; Zaria 228,000; Kaduna 210,000; Sokoto 120,000.

1954	Federation of Nigeria formed.
1960	Independence : Sir Abubakar Tafawa Balewa as Prime Minister and Nnamdi Azikwe as Governor-General.
1963	Republic, Azikwe as President.
1966	1st Coup : General Ironsi, Head of State. Tafawa Balewa assassinated together with Saudana of Sokoto (Sir Ahmadu Bello). 2nd Coup : Ironsi assassinated and General Yakubu Gowan Head of State.
1966-70	Civil War : 'Biafra' seceded as a separate Ibo state under Ojukwu. With collapse of 'Biafra' Ojukwu fled to Abidjan.
1972	Beginning of massive oil wealth.
1975	Coup : Murtala Mohammed Head of State, but was assassinated soon afterwards. General Obasanjo, Head of State.
1979	Military government stepped down. Shehu Shagari elected as President by Parliament under a new constitution.
1984	Military Coup : General Muhammad Buhari Head of State.
1985	Military Coup: Major General Babangida Head of State.

Senegal
Population : 7 million (1988)
Dakar 1,400,000; Thies 156,000; St. Louis 92,000; Kaolack 132,000.

1960	Independence from France, but as a Federation with Mali. After only a few months Senegal broke away. President Leopold Senghor. (Much revered throughout Africa for his literary works.)
1980	Senghor resigned. Succeeded by Abdou Diof.
1982	Senegal and Gambia formed "Confederation of Senegambia".

Sudan
Population : 23.6 million (1987)
Khartoum 1,160,000; Port Sudan 205,000; Wadi Medani 153,000; Kassala 149,000; El Obeid 118,000; Juba 116,000.

1820	Sudan conquered by Egyptian-Turkish regime.
1881	Mohammed Ahmad Al Mahdi revolted and set up an Islamic state based at Khartoum.
1898	British General Kitchener captured Khartoum and established an Anglo-Egyptian Condominium.
1956	Independence with parliamentary government. Civil war : Moslem-Arab north against the Christian south.
1958	Military coup and military regime led by Ibrahim Aboud.
1964	Military coup.
1966	Coup. Sadiq al Mahdi, great grandson of the Mahdi, came to power.
1968	Military coup. General Gaafar Mohammed El Nimeri head of state.
1971	Nimeri elected President.
1972	Addis Ababa agreement ended 17 years of civil war. Regional autonomy for the south.
1977	Period of bad relations with Libya began.
1983	Civil war in the south resumes.
1985	Military coup led by General Abdul Rahaman Swar Al Dahab.
1989	Military coup led by Brig-Gen. Omar Hassan Ahmad al-Bashir.

Tunisia

Population : 7.8 million (1988)

Tunis 596,000; Sfax 232,000: Sousse 84,000; Bizerte 95,000; Kairouan 72,000.

1955   Independence.

1957   Habib Bourguiba elected President following deposition of the Bey.

1969   Associate membership of EEC.

1974   Merger of Tunisia and Libya, but nothing came of it.

1987   President Ziue Ben Ali.

Western Sahara

The total population of Western Sahara was only 75,000 in 1974

El Aioun 28,000; S'mara 7,300; Dakhla 5,400.

1900   Franco-Spanish partition of Morocco and the western part of the Sahara.

         Spain established three provinces : Tarfaya (given to Morocco in 1958), Seguiet El Hamra and Rio de Oro, collectively known as Spanish Sahara.

1957   Revolt by Reguibat people against the Spanish.

1973   POLISARIO formed (Popular Front for the Liberation of Seguiet El Hamra and Rio de Oro).

1975   International Court at The Hague affirmed the right of the Saharaoui people to self-determination.

1975   Spanish Sahara ceded by Spain to Morocco and Mauritania. Insurrection continued.

1979   Guerrilla war proved too expensive for Mauritania which ceded its portion to Morocco.

         Note: Algeria has consistently supported the POLISARIO movement which set up a government in exile entitled République arabe sahraouie democratique (RASD) or Saharawi Arab Democratic Republic (SADR).

1981   Morocco constructed a giant 450 km long fortified wall of sand and rocks to isolate the economically important towns of El Aioun, S'mara and Bou Craa (phosphate mines) from Polisario guerrillas who usually attacked from the south and east. Tindouf in Algeria has for long been a supply base for the Polisario.

1983   Talks on Western Sahara between King Hassan II of Morocco and President Chadli of Algeria. However, the war continued even though Libya toned down its support of the Polisario during 1983-84 and became aligned with Morocco in an extraordinary *volte-face* by Colonel Gaddafi. Algeria has maintained its support of the Polisario.

1984   Morocco and Libya were 'united'.

1991   UN sponsored referendum on whether to join Morocco or become an independent state.

Economic Factors

Sources: United Nations, (1988) *UN Statistical Yearbook*, New York.
UNESCO, (1990) *UNESCO Statistical Yearbook*, Paris.
Paxton, J. (Ed), (1990) *Statesman's Yearbook 1990-91*, London.

	GNP* per capita	Life expectancy male female		Literacy % **
Algeria	$2,570	58	61	58
Burkina Faso	$150	43	47	19
Chad	$88	41	46	30
Egypt	$760	57	60	48
Libya	$7,180	57	60	64
Mali	$170	47	50	32
Mauritania	$440	42	47	34
Morocco	$590	57	60	49
Niger	$260	47	50	28
Nigeria	$730	47	50	51
Senegal	$420	42	45	38
Sudan	$330	47	49	27
Tunisia	$1,300	60	61	51
Australia	$11,910	72	79	100
Britain	$8,920	71	77	100
Netherlands	$9,749	73	80	100
USA	$16,710	71	78	100
W. Germany	$12,080	71	78	100

(1988 figures)   (1988 figures)   (1990 estimates)

*in US dollars per annum.
**as a percentage of population over 15 years.

The chart shows that practically all the countries of the Sahara area are desperately poor. Life for their people is harsh and in many cases a desperate struggle. Consequently, when droughts occur like that of 1969-1974 they are absolutely disastrous. In Australia and North America similar droughts do lead to some livestock losses but government financial aid is substantial and in extreme cases some people face bankruptcy. In the Sahara and Sahel, not only are vast herds of cattle and other livestock wiped out but hundreds of thousands of people die of starvation, malnutrition and related diseases. Even in good years one frequently encounters the dehydrated carcasses of cattle, camels, donkeys, etc. but in 1973 the author came across similar human carcasses: people who had died of starvation. At villages in the Air Mountains people lined the track and begged for water, not money or food. Starvation and death were everywhere. Yet, just outside one village a group of lavishly equipped tourists from Europe was encountered camped and openly enjoying their own gourmet meals with beer and wine. They were quite callously oblivious to the devastation all around them. The author of the graffiti on the old distance marker seen in this photograph taken in the Hoggar Mountains must have come across a similar indifference by the affluent to other peoples' suffering. Please be discreet about your comparative western wealth when visiting the poor third world countries of the Sahara and Sahel.

7
Peoples

Religion

Most cultures in North Africa are less secular than Western societies. Religion, and in particular, Islam, is an all-pervading influence on the social fabric of life in the Sahara. Islam is the dominant religion of the whole Sahara region. The prophet Mohammed was born at Mecca (in what is now Saudi Arabia) in about AD 570. He preached a universal submission, or 'Islam', of all men to the will of God (Allah). He claimed to have received revelations directly from God. These were written down by his disciples to form the **Koran.** Although Moslems accept the Jewish **Torah** or the Christian **Old Testament,** including the Ten Commandments, fundamental to their faith is the conviction that "There is no God but God : Mohammed is the messenger of God" (*La ilaha illa Allahu : Muhammadun rasulu Allahi*). Thus, for a Moslem, Islam is God's revelation made to Adam and Noah, the religion revealed to David and the Prophets of Israel as well as to Jesus and his Twelve Apostles. For the final time, in its pure form, the true religion was revealed to the Prophet Mohammed and related in the **Koran.**

The essence of Mohammed's teaching is that a true believer, a Moslem (one who has submitted himself to and is at peace with God) is a man who professes faith that there is only one God and that it is through Mohammed that his will has been revealed. A Moslem must carry out four major ritual obligations :

1. He should pray to God five times a day no matter where he is. Before prayer, he should wash his hands, feet and face symbolically with water. (Touaregs sometimes use sand instead.) Prayers should be well spaced throughout the day but it is permissible to say some prayer sessions in close succession one after the other if it was not possible to say them earlier. This is private prayer. Congregational prayer is recommended on Fridays at noon. There is no organised priesthood intervening between man and God, though 'Mezzuens' call people to prayer (usually from the minaret of a mosque) and 'Imams' lead the prayers at congregational prayer sessions in mosques.

2. He should give alms to the needy. Sometimes communities levy a 'Zakat' or tax to replace alms-giving.

3. He should fast between sunrise and sunset without anything to eat or drink for the 30 days of Ramadan.

81

4.   If possible, he should make the pilgrimage or 'Hadj' to Mecca at least once in his lifetime. (One who has completed the 'Hadj' is generally addressed as 'Alhaji' or 'El Hadji' and traditionally is entitled to grow a beard as a symbol of this.)

The schism which divided Islam into Sunni and Shii sects came about early in the history of the religion. Sunnis, the majority today, believe that the 'community of the faithful' is the only vessel for the law (sharia) and its traditions. Shiites, mainly in Iran and Iraq, believe that the 'divine light' which guided Mohammed has been passed down through his direct descendants. Most of the Moslems of the Sahara and Sahel are Sunnis but there have been and are several smaller sects such as the Mozabites of Ghardaia today and the Kharidjites of Gao in the ninth century.

Islamic Holidays

Algeria, Egypt, Gambia, Libya, Mali, Mauritania, Morocco, Niger, Nigeria, Senegal, Sudan, Tunisia and Burkina Faso all have very large Moslem populations. They therefore have the following public holidays:

Id el Fitri
(End of Ramadan)
01 April 1992; 20 March 1993; 08 March 1994; 25 February 1995; 14 February 1996.

Id el Adha
(The peak Hadj time at the end of the season of pilgrimage to Mecca — the occasion when rams are killed)
08 June 1992; 27 May 1993; 15 May 1994; 03 May 1995; 27 April 1996.

Id el Moled el Nabowi
(Birthdate of the Prophet)
29 June 1992; 18 June 1993; 07 June 1994; 27 May 1995; 16 May 1996.

The Moslem calendar is lunar-based and has a year of 354 days. Years are counted from the date in AD 622 (of the solar-based Gregorian calendar) when the archangel Gabriel revealed the Word of God to Mohammed and he returned from exile in triumph to his native city of Mecca in order to cleanse it of idol worship.

The Tourist and Moslem Customs

The non-Moslem should always be respectful of Islamic customs and institutions, and constantly vigilant in order not to offend.

Don't just walk into a mosque. Ask first if it would be all right to do so, and if so, take off your shoes before entering. Make sure that it is all right for a woman to go in, too. Fridays are special prayer days, especially after midday. In some countries like Algeria and Libya, Friday is a public holiday, equivalent to the western Sunday, and Thursday is a half day. Saturdays and Sundays are normal working days.

Sometimes it is preferable to let a man in your group, rather than a woman, do the negotiations with officialdom at frontiers, police posts, airline offices, and hotels. Women are advised to show restraint in all social exchanges in Saharan countries, where social status is considered to be lower than in western countries. Local people will often make allowances for western women, but sometimes the official you want particular co-operation from might take offence.

Similarly, a western woman should not assume that local men will make allowances for her when engaging in normal conversation. A normal open, frank western woman can, in local eyes, be regarded as promiscuous or easy game for men so used to cloistered women, and they may try to take advantage of her. For the same reasons, a woman should not wear shorts, or at times even jeans. Long skirts are the surest and most respected. In some ways this applies to men as well. Shorts on men can be regarded as obscene. Certainly, before reaching a frontier post men should change into long pants. This applies especially to Australians, New Zealanders and southern Africans, who are used to wearing shorts as a normal business man's dress (and even get queer looks in Britain when wearing them!)

Be careful when photographing local women, especially those covered up. Many Moslems feel that westerners are scornful of the custom of keeping women in 'purdah', and consequently are sensitive. You could have your camera taken away from you, or be stoned.

Be careful not to deliberately look over the walls that surround a house courtyard. This may offend as there could be women in seclusion doing household chores in the courtyard. This custom of purdah is still taken seriously in many parts of the Sahara and Sahel, even in socialist Algeria. In some Sahelian towns the law still permits a man to be stoned to death if he rides into town on the back of his camel (which would allow him to see over compound walls).

Do not offer pork or bacon or anything cooked in pork fat to a Moslem and

A small wayside prayer ground in Niger. The area set aside for prayers is marked by the old logs. Often it is marked by a ring of stones. Under no circumstances should you walk across such hallowed ground. Note the clay calabash of water provided for the ritual pre-prayer ablutions. Moslems must wash their faces, hands and feet three times before praying

do not eat pork in front of him.

Devout Moslems are not supposed to drink alcohol. Thus Libya has a total prohibition on all beers, wines and spirits. Generally, Algeria is also a 'dry' country with alcoholic drinks being limited to hotels most likely to be used by tourists. However, many Algerian officials assume that westerners have loads of whisky and crates of beer in their cars. Sometimes, handing out a beer or two to an official will work wonders, but let him ask for it first.

During the 30 days of fasting of Ramadan, do not eat or drink openly in front of a lot of people. They are fasting during the day and might get unduly sensitive about it.

Giving alms to beggars (Saddaqua) is a Moslem custom that generates respect, even in socialist Algeria. Consequently, be discreet when sending beggars away, especially if you don't give them anything.

Education In relatively wealthy Saharan countries such as Algeria and Libya modern primary school education is almost universal. With large proportions of students completing the bulk of a secondary education, there is now sometimes a large population of educated but unemployed and idle youths. In extreme circumstances in larger towns they could cause problems for tourists. Avoid crowds of idle youths. This is a problem common to many developing countries where, although there is a shortage of skilled technical labour, most secondary school graduates have had a liberal arts education and are therefore ineligible for tertiary technical education and cannot find jobs.

By contrast, in most poorer Saharan countries like Chad, Mali and Niger,

Inside the classroom of a simple one-teacher primary school at Seguidine, an oasis in the Ténéré Desert. Note the sandy floor and bare mud walls. These students were eager and disciplined. At the time they were having an algebra lesson. Yet, they had never seen electricity apart from the headlights of an occasional Land Rover. One wonders what use a sophisticated education is when it will not help them look after their camels and tend their date palms better

84

even primary schools are rare and very rudimentary. The teacher is a highly respected member of the village community and a useful source of local information as well as a means of communication with the village or oasis population.

In some countries traditional Koranic schools offer a supplementary form of education. A man learned in Islamic precepts and able to read and write Arabic is the village 'Mallam' or Islamic teacher. Outside normal or modern school hours children attend traditional Koranic classes where they learn by rote essential passages from the **Koran** and **Hadith.** In some ways, these Koranic schools are more relevant to the simple and very harsh lives of people in the very poor countries. It is a form of education which imparts a spiritual acceptance of the inclemency of life on earth and can provide comfort in the face of high infant mortality, low life expectancy, drought, famine, disease and war. The phrase "It is the will of Allah" provides an explanation for suffering and disaster.

Gifts In many places dozens of little children will pester you for 'cadeaux', or shout "Donnez-moi stylo". If a child has been helpful in giving directions, for instance, then a gift is quite in order. But if you just stop and hand out gifts this will create a commotion and even cause a stampede. Furthermore, it will spoil things for other tourists who may not have dozens of cheap gifts to hand out, and therefore may receive a hostile reception. Here is a list of suitable 'cadeaux' for 'patrons' to give:
Matches or 'allumettes': small villages in the Ténéré.
Shirts or 'chemise': everywhere.

A traditional Koranic school at the oasis of Seguidine in the Ténéré Desert. In the afternoons children learn by rote major passages from the Moslem Koran and Hadith. Note the wooden writing board used by the teacher or 'Mallam' to demonstrate the Arabic, the pen made from a porcupine quill and, in the small gourd, ink made from indigo plants found in the Sahel region. This education imparts a spiritual acceptance of the harshness of life on earth

85

Every oasis one goes to in the Sahara, one is invariably faced with a problem of how to cope with dozens of urchins that race out to greet the foreign tourists. Some are quite charming like this group of little girls at a village near Tahoua in Niger. Some are a nuisance and hang around like flies

These proud Algerian boys near Ain Sefra are clearly much influenced by their country's military regime

Jeans: especially for young Arab boys and men.
Cigarettes or 'Taba': everywhere.
'Bic' lighters: especially in Algeria.
Digital watches: especially in Algeria.
Bright scarves: small villages in Niger and Mali.
Plastic beads: small villages in the Ténéré.
Metal chains: to Touaregs.
Aspirins and vitamin pills: everywhere, especially truck drivers.
Shoes: everywhere.
Old clothes: everywhere.
Ball point pens or 'stylos': small boys everywhere.
Old 'thongs' or 'flip flops': to Touaregs and Fulanis.
Sweets: everywhere to small children.
Balloons, or 'balon': to small children.
Bottles with screw tops, or jars with lids: to Touaregs.
Empty cans: to Touaregs.
Dark glasses: everywhere.
Sugar cubes: to Touaregs and Fulanis.
Magazines and newspapers: to teachers and officials in isolated oases.
Porno magazines: to truck drivers and soldiers.
Nail polish: to women in Niger.
Note pads: to school children.

Some of these items can be used to negotiate permission to take a photograph. Of course, money is often an appreciated gift.

Hospitality Many truck drivers in Algeria come from big cities in the north and are contemptuous (or envious?) of tourists. However, if you help them when bogged, or offer water, or cigarettes to one when broken down and awaiting a mechanic, they open up and are usually friendly and personable people. Do not refuse any tea, coffee or other sign of friendliness that they offer, as this may offend.

With Touaregs and many of the Mauritanian traders seen in Niger, the tea ceremony is crucial. If, for example, you arrive at a Touareg village or encampment, take your time about introductions and greetings. They have all the time in the world. Soon very small glasses will be laid out. You will notice blocks of sugar and salt, and a pot of tea brewing on a small wire-supported charcoal fire. Do not go away. Stay, and you will be offered these small glasses of very sweet mint tea. Still do not go away. Each glass of tea must be drunk fairly quickly and with much relish and lots of slurping noises. If after the third round of tea, no more is offered, this means that you are welcome, and welcome to stay for a while. If a fourth round of tea is forthcoming it means that you are welcome but not asked to stay, as it is not convenient. Drink this fourth glass, and slowly and politely farewell your host and go.

If asked in this way to stay you should, for at least an hour or so. This may well be a magnificent opportunity to learn about Touareg life and even (after some time) take photographs, not otherwise possible. Remember, you must not rush things, as in the western manner.

If you stay with some expatriates living and working in places like Kano, or Niamey, be careful not to overstay your welcome. All too often, kind expatriates living under fairly difficult circumstances (they can seem luxurious at first sight), get lumbered with over-landers 'sponging' off them. Don't let this happen, and when you leave you should leave a meaningful gift, or at least send a brief thank you letter or card. This is most appreciated and remembered.

If a frontier official asks you to his quarters for a drink or a meal, don't refuse.

Touareg tea ceremony

Not only does he control your movements but because he is an official in an outlying place, he will more than likely be longing for some educated company. He can also be a mine of useful and interesting information. He may even ask you to visit his home later, in Algiers or Niamey. A magazine or newspaper would be a much appreciated parting gift. On the other hand, he may be after your whisky, your wife, or whatever else he can get.

In the same way, hospitality offered by a shopkeeper may be genuine, or he may just be anxious to convince you to buy something. This is often difficult to judge.

Buying In Algeria most prices are fixed. This applies to all commodities from petrol, gas and tyres, to newspapers, condensed milk, bread, carrots and films. It also applies to services like puncture repairs, tooth extractions, cinemas and bus tickets. Sometimes prices are negotiable especially in outlying areas where tomatoes or leather-work can be haggled over.

But in the rest of the Sahara practically everything, except petrol, has a negotiable price. The first price given for a can of sardines or a bunch of carrots is not the price the shopkeeper expects to get. If you reduce it by half and then work upwards, very gradually, you might reach a mutually satisfactory mean. Sometimes it pays to ask around as to what other people have paid for things. In this way you might find that half the price suggested by the trader is still too much. Usually the tourist can expect to pay more than the going price. Yet not to bargain is often regarded as a sign of weakness. So, even if the goods are offered for less than you would pay at home, you must at least engage in some token bargaining.

Brief summary of some Saharan Peoples

Arabs They speak Arabic and are the dominant group in the northern Saharan areas. Their women are traditionally cloistered. They occupy all walks of life: truck drivers, soldiers, civil servants, oasis farmers, shopkeepers, etc. Many men and women wear western dress. Also, they sometimes wear big baggy trousers and the more cloistered women wear long garments that cover most, if not all of their bodies and faces.

Arabs first came to the northern coast of Africa during the seventh century AD with the spread of Islam: Tripoli in 647, Kairouan in 670, Tunis or Carthage in 698 and across the straits of Gibraltar and into Spain in 711. During this expansion of Islam, Arabs from the Middle East either conquered the local people, achieved their acquiescence and conversion, or the local people gradually withdrew into the inaccessible mountain or desert areas.

Berbers Perhaps the original inhabitants of the Atlas Mountains. Often they do not consider themselves as Arabs. Many feel they are oppressed by the Algerian Government. They live mainly in the Atlas Ranges, as farmers, but are also in all walks of life. They generally wear western dress. In Algeria there is a large concentration of Berbers in the beautiful mountain area around Tizi Ouzou some 100 km east of Algiers, the Kabylie region.

There are also nomadic Berbers whose low tents can be seen all over the Chott areas between the Atlas Ranges and as far south as Ain Sefra, El Bayadh, Laghouat, Biskra and Gafsa. They keep camels and goats. They are proud of their pre-Arab origins and jealously guard their own traditions and nomadic independence.

Bli Bli or Beri Beri A small mixed group of oasis cultivators who live in the villages of the Kouar escarpment in the Ténéré (Aney, Dirkou and Bilma) and at Fashi.

Chaamba A confederation of semi-nomads stretching throughout the following areas : the Souf, Ouargla, Metlili (Mzab), and El Golea. Warlike by tradition and skilful camel handlers, they were used by the French in their early campaigns in the Algerian Sahara. Captain Laperrine incorporated Chaamba men in his special desert patrols or 'Mehari' which were used in the decisive Battle of Tit in 1902 which crushed the power of the Kel Ahagger

A nomadic Berber encampment in the Chott area of the Atlas Ranges north of El Bayadh in Algeria

Touaregs. Over the centuries there has been constant rivalry between the Chaamba and Touaregs. The magnificent fort overlooking El Golea was built as a defence against marauding Touaregs.

Dogon The ancestors of the present Dogon people were part of the pre-Islamic Mandé Empire in what is now southern Mali, but with the spread of Islam during the thirteenth century in West Africa they fled north-east to the rocky and precipitous Bandiagara Escarpment. Here they were able to defend themselves from marauders and to use the meagre soil at the foot of the cliffs to sustain themselves. In this refuge they were able to resist Islam as well as maintain their culture, social structure and religion based on mythology.

The Dogon people have not been Islamicised and have escaped Christianity. Their art, still practised today on the rocks of the Bandiagara Escarpment, represents aspects of the stories in their religious mythology (Photo by courtesy of Dr Freddie Hicks)

A small tribe, their existence is confined to a 100 km section of the Bandiagara Falaise from Bankass in the south almost to Douentza in the north. Their houses and grain storage silos are built in troglodite fashion among the rocks and rubble of the cliff face. Anthropologists have found them fascinating because their successful existence in the escarpment has preserved pre-Islamic West African religion, art, culture and society like a time capsule. Life for the Dogon is hard with the rhythm between wet and dry seasons of the arid Sahel being far from even or regular and the need to provide for or reduce uncertainty is a dominating theme in their art, culture and religion.

Nommo, one of the offspring of the god Amma, represents good and the rainy season, whereas his brother a fox called Yurugu brings about disorder and drought. Both the god Amma and Nommo are on the side of the Dogon provided that they do their bit to help in this perpetual struggle. This has produced an optimistic culture with a work ethic that has led to a self-reliant and diligent people united in a fairly rigidly ordered class society. There are cultivators, administrators, cobblers, smiths, etc. and mobility between them is limited.

Much of Dogon art represents aspects of their religious mythology. As such carved masks, wooden sculptures, terracotta ancestor figures, and grass weaving work are much sought after. However, because Dogon culture is unique, the Mali government has since the 1960s taken steps to protect it. Hence the restrictions on photography and the exportation of genuine artifacts.

An excellent study of Dogon society can be found in : M.Griaule and G.Dieterlen, 'The Dogon of the French Sudan' to be seen in Daryll Forde(Ed), **African Worlds** (1954), Oxford University Press, London.

Doui Menia Nomads and semi-nomads who live in the Touat, the region through which the Saoura valley extends from Tarhit in the north through Beni Abbes, Kerzaz and Adrar to Reggane in the south. These people are Arabs who cultivate dates and wheat in the Saoura: a dried up river bed which has water flowing on the surface only once every decade or so. The Doui Menia are the people who over the centuries laboriously constructed the 'foggaras' or subterranean irrigation canals to be seen in vast numbers between Adrar and Reggane. Some of these people are very dark with negroid features. This region was once part of a major slave route between West Africa and Morocco and the Mediterranean coast.

Douz and Kebili The semi-nomads of the Nefzaoua region of southern Tunisia, an area around the vast salt lake or Chott Djerid. They grow dates and keep sheep, goats and camels.

Djerma Sedentary cultivators who live in the Tillabery, Niamey, Say and Dosso areas of Niger. They hold strong positions in government; both present and past leaders of Niger have been Djermas.

Fulani (Puels) The Fulani people are widely dispersed throughout Sahelian Africa south of the Sahara from Senegal in the west to Sudan and Ethiopia in the east. They are known by various names by the peoples among whom they live: Foulah in Senegal; Puel in Mali, Burkina Faso and Niger; Fulbe in Niger and Chad; Fellata in Sudan; and Fulani in Niger, Nigeria and Cameroun. Their language is Fulfulde.

Originally, before the nineteenth century, they were generally all nomadic cattle keepers. As such they migrated with their livestock among the more sedentary peoples of the Sahel, coexisting with them: exchanging meat and dairy products for grain and other items. But this was never a totally peaceful coexistence. Often clashes occurred between the nomads and sedentary cultivators particularly over trampled crops. Today with the population explosion in West Africa, more pressure on the land and the southward extension of the Sahara Desert, these clashes are fairly frequent. In 1973, for example, there was a major battle between Hausa cultivators and Fulani nomads near Shinkafe in the north of Nigeria. More than a dozen Hausa farmers were killed by Fulani spears.

In the late eighteenth century Islam was in decline over most of West Africa. A militant revivalist movement began in the region to the north of Sokoto. Lead by a young Fulani convert to Islam, Usman dan Fodio, a 'Jihad' or Holy War was waged between 1802 and 1809 reconverting much of the Hausa population. This Jihad established the Fulani Empire of northern Nigeria.

However, the Jihad brought about major changes in the life of the Fulani who quickly became split into four distinct groups:

1 'Fulani Toroobe'. These are now the traditional ruling families of many

91

Sometimes there is no privacy. Here Fulanis cannot contain their curiosity. In some of the poorer and more remote areas there is total amazement at western technology and the gadgets that a westerner carries with him but accepts as normal

Fulani women at Agadez. A happy people with few inhibitions. Women are noted for their elaborate hair styles and large ear rings

Hausa towns and although of Fulani origin these people no longer speak Fulfulde and have intermarried with the Hausa populations conquered in the Jihad.

2 'Fulani Siire' or 'Town Fulani'. Like the aristocratic Toroobe, they have deserted nomadic ways and settled in towns and surrounding agricultural land, intermarrying with the sedentary population.

3 'Fulani Ladde' (or 'Fulani Na'i'). These bush Fulani practise a form of trans-humance pastoralism combined with semi-sedentary agriculture. Women cultivate land while men and boys migrate with the cattle. They move south into the savanna woodlands in the dry season in order to keep their cattle grazing. However, in the rainy season when the grass is luxuriant but the tsetse fly prevalent, they have to move north into the semi-arid Sahel to prevent their cattle dying from sleeping sickness (*Trypanosomiasis*). The cultiva-tion of crops by women is usually only temporary for whole families move on the major migrations. The Nigerian Government currently has a project under way to settle the bush Fulani permanently on cattle ranches, because as the West African population continues to explode, they are in danger of ending up with nowhere to graze their cattle. (It is also hoped that this will end the Fulanis' apparent disregard for international boundaries.)

4 'Fulani Bororo'. More akin to the pre-Jihad Fulanis, the Bororo are entirely nomadic and confined to the Sahel band spreading from Senegal to Ethiopia. Perpetually on the move with their cattle (and a few donkeys and camels) the Bororo are very noticeable with their fine features, lighter skin tone and their passion for beauty in both women and men. Women are noted for their elaborate hairstyle, large earrings and sometimes for their brass anklets. For young men, to be attractive is to be heavily made-up with ochre and kohl and to emphasise their fine facial features. In towns like Agadez young Fulani Bororo are uninhibited and men and women, as well as just men or just women, can be seen in the streets holding hands and being openly very close to one another.

Every year among the Fulani Ladde and the Fulani Bororo, each clan will hold at least one of the following dances, which should not be missed if the opportunity arises:

● "Yake" — Young men and girls dance in separate lines facing each other climaxing in the modest selection of a boy by each of the girls.

● "Jerol" — A war dance at which young men perform with spears as they dance in front of the admiring girls.

● "Sharo" — an initiation dance for young men at puberty. Really quite a horrendous beating ceremony. Watched by all the young unmarried girls, they must dance and show no signs of agony as they dance and are beaten over and over again by older men wielding big long sticks.

A fascinating ethnography on the Fulani has been written by Paul Riesman, **Freedom in Fulani Social Life** (1977) University of Chicago Press, Chicago. F.W. Taylor has written **A Fulani-English Dictionary** (1932) Oxford Univers-ity Press, London.

Hausa A very large population of sedentary cultivators and traders with a partly urbanised society. They are the dominant group in the north of Nigeria and largest tribal group in Niger. Moslem by religion for many centuries, the seven Hausa trading cities ('Hausa Bokwai') were conquered during the early nineteenth century by the reforming Fulani Moslem, Usman dan Fodio, whose direct descendant, the Sultan of Sokoto, is traditionally the spiritual leader of all Hausas on both sides of the frontier.

Usually very dark negroid people, Hausa men wear long flowing white robes or 'riga', and intricately embroidered caps, though traditional leaders, like

This Hausa farmer is from the Sokoto region of northern Nigeria as indicated by the scars on his cheeks

Emirs, wear elaborate turbans. Women have a definitely subservient role in Hausa society, though it is only a rich man who can afford to keep his wives totally in purdah.

Although most Hausas are farmers, there are large cities of urban populations (Kano, Sokoto, Zaria, Katsina, etc.) whose livelihood is based on trade and commerce: a tradition developed as these cities were on the end of the

Hausa boxing: each opponent only uses one fist (tightly wrapped in cloths and clasping a lucky charm such as a rabbit's foot). They swing their fists at each other in a series of swift over arm actions. Here drummers are working their boxer up into a trance prior to a fight

A typical highly decorated Hausa house. These buildings are made of clay/mud as is the method throughout the southern Sahara and Sahel region

trans-Saharan camel caravan routes from the north, and at the end of the bush routes south to Yorubaland and the coast. Hausas can be seen as traders all over the Sahel, in places like Niamey, Gao, Tahoua, Agadez, Maradi, Zinder, and N'guigmi. They have a very long and involved greeting procedure of questions and responses. If a man shows his clenched fists at you, accompanied by the words 'Rankadidi' this is a salute of greetings reserved for people of high status and importance. (You should reply 'Sanu' to one man, 'Sanunku' to a group.)

Kanure Sedentary cultivators who live in the north east of Nigeria, at N'guigmi, and around Lake Chad. They are Moslems, and for a long time rivals to the Hausas. Their traditional leader is the Shehu of Bornu whose palace is at Maiduguri.

Maures The Maures form about 75% of the population of Mauritania. Many of them are, like the Touaregs, probably of Berber origin. Similarly, they tend to be lighter skinned and have in the past dominated the black minorities of the region. They also have a system of six castes:
- Hassan: the nobility or warrior caste. Largely of Arab origin they are the descendants of the Beni Hassan tribes from Morocco.
- Tolba: the religious caste of marabouts or holy men and their families.
- Zenaga: largely of Berber or Almoravid origin, they were conquered by the Arab Hassans during the fifteenth century.
- Mallemin: craftsmen, leatherworkers, carpenters, silver, bronze and iron artisans.
- Griots: the musicians, poets and entertainers.
- Haratin: composed largely of former slaves, these people are not only darker skinned but also for the most part sedentary cultivators or fishermen.

The French outlawed slavery and this, combined with the drought of 1968-1974 and the need to work in the modern money economy (e.g. the iron ore mines at Zouerate) effectively broke up the caste system.

Most Maures speak Hassaniyah, a Mauritanian version of Arabic. They have a tea ceremony similar to that of the Touaregs. A few Maures can also be seen in the south of Niger Republic where they are often small shopkeepers.

Mozabites The M'zab is a picturesque valley in the desert some 150 km south of Laghouat in which there are five towns: El Atteuf, Ghardaia, Beni Isguen, Bou Noura and Milika. A few kilometres to the north are Berriane and Guerara which broke away from the rest of the M'zab. Founded in the eleventh century by a group of conservatively orthodox Moslems from the Middle East known as Ibadites, these towns grew up from heavily fortified villages. Persecuted and motivated by a puritanlike work ethic, the inhabitants of the M'zab or Mozabites are a closed society zealous in their traditions. They are renowned for having created a viable urban life in the middle of the desert, their tapestry work and their business acumen.

Rebaia The semi-nomads of the Souf region of Algeria (El Oued and Tougourt). Renowned for their date cultivation, as the sand encroaches upon their date groves they must constantly and laboriously dig out the engulfing sand. Thus their date palms can be seen growing in manmade hollows among the dunes. The dates, known as 'Deglet Nour', are regarded as the ultimate in dates.

Reguibat Supposedly founded by a pious Ahmed Reguibi in 1503 they are probably a mixture of Berber and Arab origin. The Reguibat began as settled

Carpets are just one example of the artistic talents of the Mozabite people. They are also renowned for their huge decorated brass plates and earthenware pots

agriculturalists in the Asmara region of Western Sahara but gradually became more mobile with sheep rearing and then on to full desert nomadism as camel herdsmen. There are two main tribal groups: the Reguibat Legoucem in the north and in the Tindouf area, the Reguibat Sahel in the south and in parts of Mauritania and Mali.

The war against the Spanish from 1957 onwards and then against the Moroccans has resulted in the Algerian town of Tindouf becoming the largest Reguibat centre.

Saharaoui This is the emerging generic term for the diverse peoples of what was Spanish Sahara, people now largely united under the 'Polisario' in a struggle against Moroccan rule and for the establishment of an independent Saharan Arab Democratic Republic (SADR). Just some of the tribal groups which make up the population in the Western Sahara are the Reguibat, Tekna, Sba, Arosien, Filala, Delim, Fuicat, and Imraguen. For a detailed but readable account of these diverse peoples, their cultures and societies, see J. Mercer, **Spanish Sahara** (1976) Allen and Unwin, London.

Senussi Not really people or tribe, 'Senussi' is a word that has been used in Libya to describe Sunni Moslem zealots. During the latter half of the nineteenth century some of them formed armed bands and carried out a series of minor Jihads or Holy Wars. They resisted Turkish rule in Libya and a raid of 'Senussi' influenced Kel Ajjer Touaregs was responsible for the murder of Father de Foucauld at Assekrem in 1916. King Idris, who was deposed by Gaddafi in 1969, was the last of a line of 'Senussi' monarchs to rule in Libya.

Touareg Sometimes spelled Tuareg or Twareg and known as Bouzous in Hausa. Generally regarded as a type of Berber people, there has been specula-

97

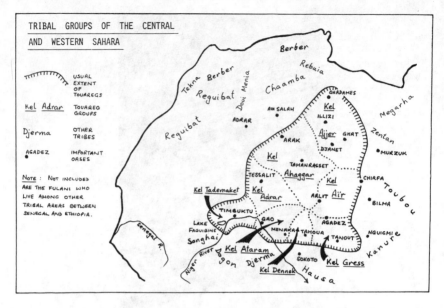

TRIBAL GROUPS OF THE CENTRAL AND WESTERN SAHARA

USUAL EXTENT OF TOUAREGS

Kel Adrar — TOUAREG GROUPS

Djerma — OTHER TRIBES

AGADEZ — IMPORTANT OASES

NOTE : NOT INCLUDED ARE THE FULANI WHO LIVE AMONG OTHER TRIBAL AREAS BETWEEN SENEGAL AND ETHIOPIA.

tion that they were originally pushed into the desert from the Atlas area by the Arab advance from the east. Today Touaregs occupy a southern area of the Sahara extending from the south of Algeria into Libya, Niger and Mali. In some areas, especially in the south, Touregs are not the majority of the population and existence is shared with other nomads like the Fulanis as well as sedentary people such as Hausas, Djermas and Songhai. Touaregs have, especially since the disastrous drought of the early 1970s, moved even further afield and can now be seen as far away as Ouagadougou, Kaduna and Maiduguri in the savanna lands of West Africa.

There are eight main groups of Touaregs:

Group:	Region:
Kel Ahaggar	Hoggar Massif
Kel Ajjer	Djanet-Illizi
Kel Air	Air Massif
Kel Gress	Lowlands south of Air
Kel Adrar	Iforas Massif
Ioulimmiden Kel Dennek	Tahoua-In Gall
Ioulimmiden Kel Ataram	Menako-Gao
Kel Tademaket	Timbuktu-Lake Faguibine

Within each group there are small regional sub-groups. Thus within the Kel Ahagger there are also the Kel Amguid, Kel Teffedest, Kel Ahnet and Kel Ohet, etc. However language, custom and dress tend to vary considerably between groups. In the Tamahaq language there are many words used for example at Mertoutek (in the north of the Hoggar) that would not be understood by Touaregs at Tazolé (south-east of Agadez). Dress, particularly the wearing of the head-dress/veil combination, varies from group to group. Similarly, details of the traditionally stratified Touareg class society will vary from group to group. For example, social structure among the Kel Ahaggar is:

- Ihaggaren — Nobles, men of the sword, camel owners.
- Imrad or Kel Ulli — Vassal goat herders.
- Isekkemaren — Vassals of mixed Touareg-Arab origin
- Inaden — Blacksmiths, artisans
- Iklan — Slaves, usually dark-skinned, now freed.

98

- Izeggaren — ('Harratin' in Arabic) First cultivators who first came to the Hoggar in 19th century and became dependent clients of the Ihaggaren.
- Imrad — Marabouts or religious men.

Among the Kel Ahaggar, there used to be three major Ihaggaren (Noble) descent 'drum groups': Kel Rela, Taitok and Tegehe Mellet. In recent times the Kel Rela, now numbering about 275 individuals, have become the most dominant 'drum group'. Since the battle of Tit in 1902 when Lieutenant Cottenest decisively defeated the Kel Ahaggar, the French colonial administration built up the power and prestige of the Amenukal, then Moussa ag Amastenane, a Kel Rela with his home at Abalessa. This power was extended far beyond the Amenukal's original realm into the Kel Ajjer and Kel Air. It enabled a miniscule French administration to rule a vast area indirectly through the Amenukal. More modern Algerian social reforms and economic development have again drastically diminished the Amenukal's influence and prestige.

Touareg society is now breaking down quickly in both Algeria and Niger through a number of factors. Among these are: Algeria's socialist agrarian reform policies, economic development and the need to work for money on roads, construction projects and the uranium mine at Arlit. Compounding this discord was the 1968-74 drought which destroyed so many nobles' camels (the source of much of their wealth and authority). The drought forced more people into the labour market and into slum dwellings or 'bidonvilles' at places like Tamanrasset and Arlit. Many migrated south and in Nigeria today many Touaregs have permanent jobs as 'myguardis' or watchmen living on factory premises or next to people's houses as security guards. As such they are feared because they have been known to use their ferocious swords or 'takouba' on

Touareg women appreciate jewellery very much. This is a 'teraout' which is worn around the neck as a pendant especially by the Kel Ahaggar. It is made of pairs of decorated triangles of fine silver laminated and linked together with other similar triangles

Kel Ajjer Touaregs of the Djanet-Illizi area

Kel Gress Touaregs of the Zinder-In Gall area

intruders. As a minority group they have also recently suffered much persecution in Mali. Consequently many Kel Tademaket and Kel Adrar can be seen in Niamey virtually as refugees desperately trying to sell their swords and their characteristic red leather Mali trinket boxes.

Generally, descent in Touareg society is matrilineal or through the female line. Traditionally Touareg women have not been veiled, have owned slaves and livestock in their own right and have been the organisational focus of much social life. Much of this is in contrast to other Islamic societies, and has lead to many unfortunate interpretations about Touareg social life especially concerning 'women's lib' and sexuality.

The origin of the men's veil is still obscure despite numerous hypotheses. 'Tagelmoust' is a term reserved for the shiny indigo-dyed cloth worn usually only on ceremonial occasions. 'Khent' is the manufactured blue cloth worn for daily use. However, today the most common type of veil is the 'echchach': a white, black or dark blue manufactured cloth readily accessible in the shops of Tamanrasset (usually imported from Belgium). The women's headcloth is the 'ekerhei'.

Probably the most valid, readable and up to date account of Touareg life in English is by Jeremy Keenan **The Tuareg** (1977) Allen Lane-Penguin, London, even though it concentrates on the Kel Ahaggar. Much of the above information is derived from this book.

Toubou The negriod nomads of the Tibesti area of northern Chad. Essentially, there are two main groups with linguistic and cultural differences:
● Teda — who live in the villages of Chirfa and Seguedine (in Niger) and the northern Tibesti area of Chad.
● Daza — who live in the southern Tibesti and around Faya Largeau in Chad.
Toubou men can be distinguished by their comparatively unkempt turban.

A group of three Kel Gress Touaregs and their servant visit a market in a Sahel town. Note the sword carried by the man on the right

A group of Kel Ahaggar Touaregs standing in front of their Land Rover near Tit in the Hoggar Mountains. Note the differences in the way Touaregs from different regions tie their headcloths (Compare these Kel Ahaggar with the Kel Ajjer and Kel Gress in the previous photos)

Perhaps one of the best general works on the various peoples of the Sahara is R. Capot-Rey, **Le Nomadisme Pastorale dans le Sahara Français** (1942) Travaux de l'Institut de Recherches Sahariennes, Algiers. Also worth looking at is L.C. Briggs, **Tribes of the Sahara** (1960) Harvard University Press, Cambridge.

A Toubou nomad. They are very dark complexioned negroid people. Note the characteristically Toubou method of tying a very untidy-looking turban

Glossaries of useful words

Hausa
(See: Kraft, G.H. and Kirk-Greene, A.H., **Hausa, A Complete Working Course,** 1975, Hodder and Stoughton, London.)

Rankadidi = Greeting to someone you have great respect for.
Sanu = His reply to one person.
Sanunku = His reply to a group of people.
Barka d'azua = Welcome, respectful.
Lai'hya loh (sometimes: Lafia loh) = Welcome.
Nagadjia = Reply to welcome.
Sanu d'aiki = Hello, how is work?
Typical greeting procedure:
   Question: Sanu (or Sanunku)
   Response 1: Lai'hya loh
   Response 2: Nagadjia
   Response 3: Bagadjia
   Response 4: Enalai'hya
   Response 5: Naquana
   Response 6: Toh Mahdala
Toh, Mahdala = Okay; very good; I'm satisfied.
Nagode = Thank you.
Nagode quere = Thank you very much.
Toh = O.K.
Shikenah = Finished. Over. Don't want it.
De Kyao = Good or delicious.
Kao = Call (a person); or bring things.
Albasa = Onions.
Guro = Ockra.
Zafi = Hot.
Ruanzafi = Hot water.
Duka = All.
Sanyi = Cold.
Ruansanyi = Cold water.
Rua = Water.
Nowa = How much?
Yaro = Boy.
Gida = House.
Gidan = House of.
Abinchi = Food.
Shinkafa = Rice.
Gishiri = Salt.
Abambami = Blocks of Salt.
Shanu = Cattle.
Kyanwa = Cat.
Shaniya = Cow.
Tunkiya = Sheep.
Bunsuru = Goat.
Rakumi = Camel.
Azalai = Camel caravan.
Dantsako = Chicken.
Garu = Dog.
Ungulu = Vulture.
Itache = Wood.
Yishiwo = Sick.
Sannu sannu = Slowly.
Muza Muza = Quickly.
Hunkli Hunkli = Carefully.
Makerin farfaru = Silversmith.
Madara = Milk.

Zoh = Come.
Mallam = Koranic Teacher or polite term of address.
Alhaji = Man who has been on the haj to Mecca.
Gobe = Tomorrow.
Kori = Dried up oued, wadi, or river bed.
Fadama = Irrigated river bed.
Nama = Meat.
Kwai = Eggs.
Mutum = Man.
Mache = Woman.
Saddaqua = Alms giving.
Aiki = Work.
Hanya = Road.
Wanan = This, that.
Magida = Master.
Sarkin = Chief.
Kifi = Fish.
Kazua = Market.
Tafi = Impolite way to say, Go away!
Bature = European, or expatriate.

Daya = 1	Goma = 10
Biu = 2	Gomashadaya = 11
Oku = 3	Gomashabiu = 12
Hudu = 4	Ashirin = 20
Biart = 5	Ashirindadaya = 21
Shida = 6	Ashirindabiu = 22
Bokwai = 7	Ashirindaoku = 23
Takwas = 8	Ashirindahudu = 24
Tara = 9	Talatin = 30

Jaka = 1000 CFA
Sisi = 6 pence or 5 kobo
Sule = 1 shilling, or 10 kobo
Fam = £1 or N2
Toro = 3 pence
Rabi = Half
Naira = Naira or N
Kobo = Kobo or k
Akwai rua = Is there water?
Rua akwai = There is water.
Babu rua = There is no water.
Kao kudi = Give me money.
Babu kudi = No money.
Khai = Expression of surprise or of disgust.
Haba! = Expression of surprise.
Wallahi! = Expression of surprise.
Babu = No.
Bunka! (together with the thrusted fist and released five fingers) = Bastard!
   (This is the Hausa for a bad insult or swear word).
Wanan abinchi da kyao = This food is good!
Akwai Hausa? = Do you speak Hausa?
Kadunkadunk = Only a little.
Uhuh = No, negative, don't want it.

   A fairly long Hausa glossary has been given because, although Hausas live on the extreme southern fringe of the Sahara, they are traders and their influence is widespread throughout the southern half of the desert. Hausa is more widely spoken in the southern Sahara than Arabic or French. You will be able to speak Hausa to almost everyone as far north as Assamaka, Arlit, Gao, Iferouane, Chirfa, Seguedine, Dirkou, Bilma, Fashi, Agadez, etc. All government officials in Niger Republic will be able to speak Hausa as well.

Arabic
Acheb = Small plant that grows after the rain in the desert.
Adrar = Mountains.
Asma = Waiter.
Atai = Tea.
Barakeren = To make a camel kneel.
Basour = Tent on camels back, for women.
Barid = Post Office.
Ben = Son of.
Bint = Woman.
Boernoos = Moroccan type of cape, with a hood.
Bordj = Fort.
Bou = Short for, Father of, or owner of.
Caid = Tribal chief.
Cheche = Length of material wrapped around the head, for dust protection.
Chott = Salt lake.
Djebel = Mountain.
Djemal = Camel.
Djinn = Ghost.
Dokkali = Woven blanket, or saddle cloth made of colourful wool.
Douar = Encampment made up of tents.
El, Al = The.
Erg = Big sea of sand dunes.
Essence = Petrol.
Feche feche = Deep sand, with crust on the surface.
Foggara = Subterranean canals to take water to palmeraie.
Gandoura = Long white shirt like clothing, made of cotton.
Gara = Small rock standing in the plain.
Gassi = Valley between dunes.
Goum = Camel Racer.
Guerba = Water bag made from goat skin.
El Haji; Hadji; Alhaji = Man who has made the pilgrimage to Mecca.
Hammada = Flat stoney plain.
Haratinen = Dark skinned cultivators of desert oases.
El Jina = Friday.
Khadi = Judge.
Kahoua = Coffee.
Kasbah = Fort.
Kem? = How much?
Khalifa = Spiritual leader or chief.
Khobz = Bread.
Kouba = A small domed monument.
Ksar = Wall around a small town or a fortress.
Ksiba = Fort.
Labess = Hello (in Morocco).
Labass = Hello (in Algeria).
Lalla = Literally 'Holy Woman', or polite way to address a lady.
Ley = No.
Lil = Night.

Litham = Mask used by Tagui (male Touareg) to cover his face.
Ma = Water.
Mansour = Literally 'victor', or a polite way of addressing a man.
Marabout = Wise man.
Mehari = Racing camel.
Mey = Water.
Minaret = Tower of a mosque.
Mouse = Knife.
Mtaka = Fork.
Muezzan = Man who calls people to prayer.
Nam = Yes.
Nails = Leather sandals.
Nour = Light. (Deglet Nour = fingers of light. This is the name given to the
   succulent Souf dates).
Oued = River bed.
Ould = Son of.
Ouled = Children of.
Ramia = Sand.
Razzia = Robbing raid.
Reg = Flat plain of pebbles.
Roumi = Christians or non believers.
Sahra = Great desert.
Salaam = Greetings.
Sarouel = Wide trousers with gathered ankles. (Traditional for men).
Sbah = Morning.
Sebka = Salt lake.
Seguia = Irrigation canal.
Sidi = Sir, only used to a person of higher standing than oneself.
Sif = Top of dunes.
Souk = Small shops.
Taleb = Teacher.
Tassili = Limestone plateau.
Tobol = Tambourine.
Tobsi = Spoon.
Tric = Road or piste.
Zaouia = Monastery.
Zeriba = Reed hut.
Shokrah = Thank you.
Salaam al Laikoum = Greeting.
Al Laikoum salaam = Reply.
Al Djezir = Algeria.
Al Mahgreb = Morocco.
Common Arabic Numerals.

0	.	Sifr	12	١٢	Etnatashara
1	١	Wahid	13	١٣	Talathashara
2	٢	Zouje	14	١٤	Arba'ashara
3	٣	Tlata	15	١٥	Hams ashara
4	٤	Arba'a	16	١٦	Sett ashara
5	٥	Hamsa	17	١٧	Sab ashara
6	٦	Setta	18	١٨	Thamania ashara
7	٧	Seb'a	19	١٩	Tis ashara
8	٨	Thimaniya	20	٢٠	Ishrun
9	٩	Tesa'a	30	٣٠	Talat'in
10	١٠	Ashara	40	٤٠	Arba'in
11	١١	Hadashara	50	٥٠	Hamsin

60	٦٠	Set'in	100	١٠٠	Mia
70	٧٠	Sab'in	200	٢٠٠	Miat'in
80	٨٠	Thaman'in	1000	١٠٠٠	Alef
90	٩٠	Tis'in	2000	٢٠٠٠	Alfain

Tamahaq

Aba = Father
Abarequa = Road, piste.
Aguenna = Rain.
Aguelmane = Permanent lake in the rocks.
Ahal = Festivity.
Aman = Water.
Amise = Camel.
Anou = Well.
Arraw = Child.
Assukar = Sugar.
Eidi = Dog.
Emenir = Guide.
Enad = Artisan.
Asammid = Cold.
Eserer = Wood.
Guelta = Waterhole in the rocks.
Imrad = Slaves.
Ihadan = Night.
Ma n eket? = How much is it?
Tagella = Bread.
Tamat = Woman.
Taguelmoust = Touareg turban of cloth, sometimes impregnated with indigo.
Takouba = Touareg sword.
Tanezrouft = Desert within a desert.
Targui = Touareg man.
Targuia = Touareg woman.
Tarhlamt tessoum = Salt caravan.
Ténéré = Desert.
Tifinarh = Written Touareg script.
Tufat = Morning.
Ukas = Hot.

Toubou Greeting Sequence.

Kallaha kallahali? = Peace, is it peace.
Kallahi = It is peace.
Kallahalei = Let there be peace.
Kallahalei ge = Yes, let there be peace.
N'di mazo? = What have you heard?
Kallaha = Peace.
N'di durumi? = What have you seen?
Kallaha. = Peace.
(Toubou greetings sequence reproduced by kind permission of Rainbird Publishing Group, London, current holders of the rights to Norwich, J.J. **Sahara,** Longmans, London, 1968.)

8
Explorers and Conquerors

Today's intrepid wanderers who set out from London, Paris or Munich with 'trans-Sahara' blazoned across the sides of their VW Kombis and Toyota Land Cruisers are perhaps the modern equivalent of a long line of adventurers, rugged individualists and others needing to prove something. Since the early nineteenth century the Sahara has presented an irresistible challenge to people from Europe.

In 1805 Mungo Park managed against tremendous odds to explore much of the Niger River but died at Bussa in what is now Nigeria. The first crossing of the Sahara by a European expedition was the Denham, Clapperton and Oudney one in 1822-1825. Setting out from Tripoli amid much controversy, bureaucratic red tape and animosity between themselves, the group crossed via the slave caravan routes to Murzuk, Bilma and on to Kano and Sokoto. They achieved little in terms of widening man's knowledge of the Sahara and didn't even stake empire building claims. Clapperton died in a later expedition near Sokoto in northern Nigeria.

In response to the Geographical Society of Paris offering a ten thousand franc prize to the first man to enter Timbuktu and bring back a worthwhile account of his journey, René Caillié disguised himself as an Egyptian pilgrim and travelled from Sierra Leone to the fabled Timbuktu (the myth that it was the fabulously rich centre of the gold trade was still much believed) and then via Taoudenni to Morocco in 1828. Although it was quite an achievement, at that time it was slightly tarnished by the fact that he travelled with local trading caravans and in disguise instead of bearing the French flag. Yet without this disguise he would undoubtedly not have made it. Just prior to Caillié's journey the Scot, Gordon Laing, had led an expedition from Tripoli all the way to Timbuktu. Just south of In Salah he was badly cut up in a Touareg raid on his party and then after leaving Timbuktu for the return journey he was probably murdered and certainly never heard of again.

It was not until the German Dr Heinrich Barth in 1850 to 1855 took an expedition across the Sahara that any real achievements were made, apart from being 'first' like Clapperton and Caillié. Barth combined physical endurance with meticulous observation and dedicated scholarship over a five-year period in the Sahara and it is he who 'discovered' and mapped more of Africa than any other European explorers, even to the present time.

In 1860, a disciple of Barth's, Henri Duveyrier was commissioned by

A plaque erected over the entrance to the place where Gordon Laing stayed in Timbuktu in 1826. It reads:

"To the memory of
ALEXANDER GORDON LAING
2nd West India Regiment
The explorer who at the cost of his life
reached Timbuktu in 1826.
Erected in his honour by
THE ROYAL AFRICAN SOCIETY
in 1963"

The German explorer Heinrich Barth combined physical endurance with meticulous observation and dedicated scholarship in a marathon five year expedition across the Sahara in the 1850s (BBC Hulton Picture Library)

Napoleon III to conduct a reconnaissance mission into the Tassili N'Ajjer. After seven years in Africa he published the first full ethnography on people in the Sahara: **Les Touaregs du Nord.** With Barth and Duveyrier some of the exploration had now matured, moving away from pure adventure and into serious observation and enquiry.

However, Duveyrier's success coincided with an increased French interest in the Sahara which now became a challenge for France. There followed a series of sometimes disastrous military expeditions. In 1880-1881 Lieutenant-Colonel Flatters with ten officers and eighty-six Chaamba tribesmen from the El Golea area was despatched from Ouargla only to be led into a trap and massacred by Touaregs along with most of his men as they entered the

Hoggar region. A disaster to French pride, this debacle slowed French enthusiasm for the Sahara. However, less than twenty years later, in 1898, the Foureau-Lamy military expedition consisting of over 250 infantrymen equipped with machine guns set out from Ouargla. After more than a year just a handful of exhausted soldiers limped into Zinder. They had lost all their camels, abandoned most of their ammunition, many had died of disease and exhaustion and some had even committed suicide rather than continue their journey. To the French this expedition was a humiliating disgrace.

At the turn of the century an aristocratic Captain Laperrine was put in charge of operations in southern Algeria. Soon, with a series of desert trained camel patrols or 'méharistes' the French conquest of the Algerian Sahara began in earnest. First, In Salah was captured and the Tidikelt Touaregs subdued. In 1902 Lieutenant Cottenest with machine guns and Chaamba méharistes conquered the Kel Ahaggar Touaregs at the Battle of Tit.

Laperrine was not only a leader of men but he understood the desert. In the training of his méharistes the emphasis was not so much on discipline and perfection but rather on the understanding of the desert and how to survive in it while at the same time understanding the people who lived in it. Under Laperrine the French military subdued the Algerian Saharan but in many ways he also broke the spirit of the Touaregs by reducing them to a passive acceptance of French rule. The breakdown of Touareg society can be traced to conquests at the turn of the century.

However, almost as if in revenge and quite tragically the Sahara claimed Laperrine. He died of his injuries and thirst following an aeroplane crash near Tin Zaouaten in the southern extremity of Algeria in 1920.

There were many more explorers from Europe whose impact on man's knowledge of the Sahara and on history in the area vary considerably. Gernhardt Rohlfs and Gustav Nachtigal in the 1860s and 1870s, Erwin von Bary who in 1878 found traces of a former crocodile population in the Air, the Austrian Oskar Lenz who in 1880 retraced Cailliés footsteps, and the courageous Dutch woman Alexandrine Tinné who in 1869 was murdered by Touaregs south of Murzuk. There were many more: driven by an insatiable drive to challenge one of the most inhospitable and hostile environments devised by nature.

These challenges continue today. Crazy people cycle across, even jog across the Sahara (along the main Hoggar piste only) but perhaps the most courageous recent exploit was the attempt by Geoffrey Moorhouse to walk across in 1973. He didn't succeed but survived some of the same kind of treachery which killed some of last century's loners like Laing, Tinné and von Bary. The Sahara is still no place for the faint-hearted.

However, the motor vehicle has transformed travel in the Sahara. During the 1974 World Cup Rally a Citroen DS-23 was driven from Tangiers on the Mediterranean to Kano in Nigeria in less than three days. Just seventy-five years earlier it took the Foureau-Lamy expedition more than a year at the cost of more than 200 men's lives to do a similar north-south crossing.

Perhaps two of the last great 'go it alone' scientific explorers were Theodore Monod and R. Capot-Rey. In the 1930s and 1950s Monod travelled by camel extensively in the western Sahara and Mauritania making many archeological discoveries (notably the neolithic civilization at Tichitt). During the same period, Capot-Rey (with a wooden leg) explored southern Libya (where in the Murzuk Edeyin he discovered the oasis of Bahr el Doud with its few inhabitants who lived on worms dredged from a lake in the middle of the dunes) and made extensive studies of pre-historic sites in the Tibesti and Ennedi mountains.

Later scientific exploration has been largely confined to heavily sponsored

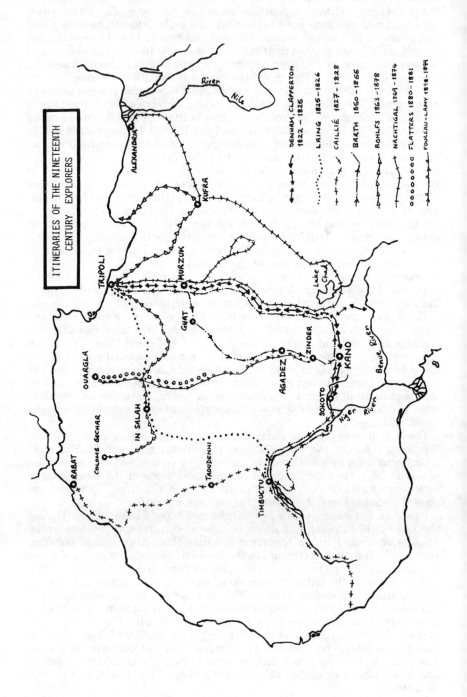

ITINERARIES OF THE NINETEENTH CENTURY EXPLORERS

DENHAM, CLAPPERTON 1822 - 1825
LAING 1825 - 1826
CAILLIÉ 1827 - 1828
BARTH 1850 - 1855
ROHLFS 1863 - 1878
NACHTIGAL 1869 - 1874
FLATTERS 1880 - 1881
FOUREAU-LAMY 1898 - 1899

River Nile
ALEXANDRIA
KUFRA
TRIPOLI
MURZUK
Lake Chad
GHAT
OUARGLA
ZINDER
KANO
AGADEZ
Benue River
IN SALAH
SOKOTO
Niger River
COLOMB BECHAR
RABAT
TRONDENNI
TIMBUCTU

expeditions like the 1959-1960 Berliet Expeditions. Today much exploration is done simply by detailed analysis of satellite photography. Major expeditions are usually only carried out when and where there is a need to confirm on the ground the findings of Multi-Spectral and Infra-red photography. This was much the case with the 1978 joint American-Egyptian Expedition to the Gilf Kebir and Jebel Uweinat. Funded by the Egyptian Geological Survey and the U.S. National Geographic Society, they had considerable support from the National Aeronautics and Space Agency. The financial demands of such scientific exploration in the Sahara today are clearly beyond the financial resources of the individual. However, with experience, perseverence and sound equipment and vehicle, the individual should not be deterred too much from carrying out research on a small scale. A good example of this can be seen in Dr Mark Milburn who has in the last decade made repeated journeys into the Sahara to conduct his own much respected studies of pre-historic tumuli and research into Touareg origins (see: Milburn, M. **Secrets of South Sahara,** 1979, Vantage, New York).

A 'Saint'

Vicomte Charles de Foucauld was born in Strasbourg in 1858 to a family well known in French nobility. Having lost his parents at an early age, when he was only sixteen he entered the army and trained as an officer at the prestigious St. Cyr academy. He served in Algeria but was generally lazy, lacking in perseverance, and pleasure loving. As a worthless, wealthy playboy, he was a dashing carefree officer. Given to throwing wild parties and insolence towards his superiors, he finally resigned his commission during a disagreement concerning his mistress and left the army in disgrace.

He then set out to explore the Maghreb disguised as a Jewish Rabbi. It proved to be a very difficult and quite humbling exploration. He had to endure tremendous hardship and suffer persecution as a Jew. It changed Charles de Foucauld. After a few years of training, in 1889 he entered a Trappist Monastery and spent the next seven years praying and in isolation. For him, his life hitherto had been dissipated; it was now full of concentration on prayer and repentance. In 1901 he entered the priesthood and travelled to the Sahara.

At Beni Abbes, a tiny oasis existing precariously on the edge of the Grand Erg Occidental, all by himself he built a hermitage and chapel which is still there today. The simplicity, poverty and humility of the chapel is quite beautiful. In Beni Abbes, de Foucauld did not convert anyone. Instead, he quietly set about buying freedom for slaves and working for charity. The fame of this 'marabout' — this holy man who seemed to live on love for his fellow men — spread far and wide across the Sahara. He became respected by everyone and was eventually persuaded by his friend Captain Laperrine to move to the Hoggar and work with the Touaregs.

In 1905 he walked from Beni Abbes to Tamanrasset, in spite of the fact that a camel was provided for him. An incredible feat — most of the journey was in summer, too. Once there, he built another chapel and soon, through his ministering and help, made friends with and was respected by the Touaregs; becoming counsellor and confident of Musa ag Amastan, the Amenokal of the Hoggar Touaregs. He of course learned Tamahaq and also compiled a massive French-Tamahaq dictionary.

However, despite his close relationship with the Touaregs, he was also very close to Laperrine, the French military governor of the Sahara. The inference has been made that de Foucauld was perhaps inadvertently used by Laperrine and the French authorities to help ease the pains of subjugation felt by

113

the Hoggar Touaregs. Nevertheless, he could not have been more respected by the Kel Ahaggar.

De Foucauld built another hermitage for himself high up among the volcanic peaks of the Hoggar at Assekrem. If one had to be alone and secluded for a long time there could not be a more magnificent place to be. It reinforces

Charles de Foucauld (BBC Hulton Picture Library)

114

in one's mind the impotence of man and is quite awe-inspiring. Yet, it was at this lonely hermitage that Charles de Foucauld was finally murdered late in 1916 by a Kel Ajjer Touareg raiding party; shot through the head at point blank range as he knelt in prayer. It was during World War I and the Turks, who ruled Libya at that time, had been trying to disrupt French rule in the Sahara by stirring up the Senoussi sect of the Kel Ajjer Touaregs in the Djanet and Ghat region. These Senoussi raiding into the Hoggar did not really know about Father de Foucauld and must have seen him as just another form of colonial oppression.

Today the successors to Charles de Foucauld carry on his unselfish and humble work in the Sahara. Inspired by his example, the order known as Les Petites Soeurs de Jésus operate a retreat in Father de Foucauld's hermitage and chapel at Beni Abbes. They minister to the poor of the oasis, help out in schools and subsist on their own vegetable gardens. In Tamanrasset they also work with the poor as well as in the hospital. These nuns make it their business while working with the poor and the distressed to experience for themselves the problems and harshness of life for the common people by living and working with them. For them this is preferable to isolating themselves from the real world by retreating into total seclusion and prayer. Thus little Sisters of Jesus can be found working in a clothing factory in Chicago or a vineyard in Italy or an old people's home in Melbourne and many other diverse places.

At the hermitage in Tamanrasset there are also some of Les Petits Frères de Jésus, two of whom live more or less permanently at the Assekrem hermitage. One of them, Father Jean-Marie, has been there for twenty-five years. He spends his time meditating, praying, writing a grammar book on Tamahaq and making weather recordings as well as receiving visits from Touaregs who need him. Today it would seem that the Petits Frères and the Petites Soeurs are only tolerated by the Algerian government either because or provided that they keep a low profile. But, in both Tamanrasset and Beni Abbes they are much respected and even venerated by the local people as well as by local officials. Should they ever have to leave Algeria, it would be a disaster.

9
Maps and Bibliography

1:4 000 000 Maps

One of the two best maps available is the Michelin 953 (formerly 153) **North West Africa** which covers the whole of the Sahara west of Egypt and the Sudan with surprising accuracy and reliability on a scale of 1:4 000 000 (10cm = 400km). The latest edition was published in 1982 (known as the 1983 or 10th edition) and nobody should travel in the Sahara without one. The Michelin 953 has a companion on the same scale, Michelin 954 (formerly 154) **North East Africa,** which covers Egyptian and Sudanese parts of the Sahara as well as Ethiopia, Somalia, Uganda and the north of Kenya. Michelin maps are available from the publisher of this book, Roger Lascelles.

The German KVRR **Africa North and West** (No 22-3) map covers an area similar to that of the Michelin 953 and is on the same scale. It is superb and an excellent alternative to the 953 as a motorist's map of the Sahara. It covers slightly more of Egypt and the Sudan than the 953. It is available from: Kartographische Verlag Reinhard Rybousch, Postfach 2105, D-6053 Obertshausen 2, West Germany. Also available from Roger Lascelles.

Bartholomew of Edinburgh also publish a good map of the Saharan region on a scale of 1:5 000 000 entitled **Africa North and West.** It has contours which both the Michelin and VWK maps lack but it is not intended primarily as a motorist's road map and so lacks the vital information that these other two maps give (e.g. distances, road surfaces, indications of facilities in towns, water availability, etc.)

1:2 000 000 Maps

The United States Defence Mapping Agency Topographic Center in Washington D.C. publishes a series of 1:2 000 000 maps covering the Saharan region. Road or piste and settlement details are totally unreliable. However, they are made from satellite derived information and so are very accurate and reliable in their coverage of vegetation and different desert terrains (e.g. ergs, oueds, parallel dunes, hammada, rocky mountain areas, etc.) The most useful ones for the Sahara are:

No.7 In Salah   (Most of Algerian Sahara)

No.8 Sabhah (East of Algeria and West of Libya).
No.12 Ouagadougou (All Malian Sahara and parts of Niger).
No.13 Ft. Lamy (All Nigerian Sahara)

They are available from The Aeronautical Department, Edward, Stanford Limited, 12-14 Long Acre, London, WC2E 9LP.

1:200 000 Maps

The most useful scale of map for navigation and as a general guide is 1:200 000. Small scales don't have the detail to enable one to stand next to the vehicle and positively identify features on the ground with those on the map. 1:200 000 maps have been produced of Algeria but are very old, and the most useful ones have all been sold a long time ago (e.g. the maps of the Djanet area.) However, it may still be worth trying the Institut Geographique National, 107 Rue de la Boetie, Paris VIII. The most useful map to use, to get south of Djanet and on to the balises to Chirfa and Bilma (the difficult Tiska area), is entitled **Djanet.**

For Niger Republic excellent and recent 1:200 000 maps are available from Service Topographique et du Cadastre, B.P. 250, Niamey (opposite the Ministry of Finance, near the old post office).

The most useful ones for the Ténéré crossing from Djanet to Bilma and Agadez would be the following: **Djado, Seguedine, Dirkou, Achegour, Bilma, Fashi,** and for a trip into Libya: **Dao Timni, Madama, Toummo,** and for a Bilma — N'giugmi crossing: **Dibella, Agadem, N'gourti.**

For Chad, also, excellent 1:200 000 maps are available (from I.G.N., L'Astrolabe, van Wijngaarden's and Daerr's — see addresses at the end of this chapter). For a journey to Timbuctu the most useful would be: **Timbouctou Est, Bamba, Gourma Rharous, Farit, Gao.** For Libya, 1:400 000 maps made between 1934 and 1940 by the Italians are available! There are no others available on Libya.

Approaches to the Sahara

Michelin produce excellent road maps of **Morocco 169** (1:1 000 000), **North Algeria and Tunisia 172** (1:1 000 000), and **Ivory Coast 175** (1:700 000)

There is a good **Road Map of Nigeria** at 1:2 000 000 published by the Nigerian Mapping Company, 22 Moor Road, Yaba, Lagos, Nigeria for N3.00. It also has rudimentary street maps of main Nigerian cities and towns, on the back.

Landsat Imagery

Probably the most effective guide to surface features and terrain in the Sahara are satellite photographs. Their clarity and detail are incredible and some are really beautiful, too. Negative and positive, black and white and colour transparencies are available at just under A4 size (30 x 21cm) from which superb detailed enlargements may be made. Satellite photos are ideal for gaining advance knowledge of remote areas of desert that one wants to explore. Catalogues and prices of Landsat photos are available from: EROS Data Center, U.S. Geological Survey, Sioux Falls, South Dakota, U.S.A. 57198. Chosen carefully, the right photos could prove invaluable and easily worth the US$20-30 they each cost.

117

Guide Books on the Sahara Area

1 Vaes, B. et alia. **Guide du Sahara** 1977 Hachette: Guides Bleus, Paris. An excellent guide with a lot of archeological and anthropological background as well as detailed route itineraries. It is very French oriented and does not include Libya. In French. In 1981 Polyglott published a German translation.

2 Daerr, K. and E. **Trans Afrique** 1987 Touring Club Suisse, Zurich. A very good selection of route descriptions covering the whole of the African continent. It is continually being updated as members of the Touring Club Suisse send back reports and new revised editions are published every few years. In French. A German edition is also produced as **Durch Afrika.**

3 Daerr, K. and E. **Trans Sahara** 1976 Globetrotter, Munich. A good source of information based on the authors' wide experience of many trips across the Sahara and the contacts they have made through their expedition equipment shop on the outskirts of Munich. Its route itineraries are limited. In German.

4 Tesch, B. **Afrika: Fuhrer fur Selbstfahrer** 1976 Globtrott Zentrale, Aachen. A comprehensive and reliable guide to the whole continent based on the author's personal experience and contacts made through the expedition equipment shop that he runs at Aachen near the Belgian frontier in Germany. In German.

5 Morgan-Grenville, G. **Cruising the Sahara** 197?. David and Charles, London. Good on vehicle preparation (even though it is very Land Rover oriented), driving techniques, survival, etc. but contains no information on routes or places.

6 Stevens, V. and J. **Algeria and the Sahara** 1977, Constable, London. Confined to the Algerian Sahara, it describes some routes but gives little useful practical information.

7 Stevens, J. **The Sahara is Yours** 1969, Constable, London. Similar to the previously mentioned book.

8 McElduff, C. **Trans Africa Motoring** 1975 Royal Automobile Club, London. The Sahara is only part of the book. Itineraries cover only the Hoggar and Tanezrouft routes, are lacking in detail and are now dated.

9 Crowther, G. **Africa on a Shoestring** 1983, Lonely Planet, Melbourne. This third edition is a considerable improvement on the first 1977 edition.

10 Sheldon, P. (Ed) **Fodor's North Africa** 1981 Hodder and Stoughton, London. Although it concentrates on the Mediterranean coastal areas, its coverage of some of the Sahara is very useful, particularly in Algeria and Tunisia.

11 Société Shell, **Guide du Tourisme Automobile au Sahara,** 1955, Shell, Algiers. It is interesting to compare touring the Sahara today with conditions in the 1950s. The French authorities used to exercise strict control over motorists then.

12 Eckbert, U. and W. **Algerische Sahara** 1984, Dumont Buchverlag, Cologne.

An excellent detailed guide with useful itineraries. It is confined only to the Algerian Sahara.

General Books on the Sahara

1 Weyer, H. and Lhote, H. **Sahara** 1980, Kummerly and Frey, Berne. A magnificently illustrated large 'coffee table' book which is also very readable. Helfried Weyer is an expert but aggressive photographer and Henri Lhote is perhaps the greatest living expert on the Sahara. Available in French and German editions.

2 George, U. **In the Deserts of this Earth** 1978, Hamish Hamilton, London. While not concerned only with the Sahara, it is nevertheless full of useful geological, ornithological, botanical and zoological theory and information. Available in German and English versions.

3 Gardi, R. **Sahara** 1967, Kummerly and Frey, Berne. A very readable general account of life in the Sahara by one of the foremost experts. Lovely photos. Available in English, French and German editions.

4 Swift, J. **The Sahara** 1975, Time-Life, Amsterdam. Part of a series on the world's wild places. Lovely photos and useful discussion of nature in the Sahara. English and German editions available.

5 Kazuyoshi Nomachi, **Sahara** 1978, Arnoldo Mondadore Editore, Milan. A beautifully illustrated photo-book by a sensitive photographer. Available in English and Italian versions.

6 Sabates, F. et alia **Les Raids** 1981, Editions Messine, Paris. An excellent account of the growth of motor rallies and marathons across the Sahara from the turn of the century to the present Paris-Dakar series. Beautiful photos. In French.

7 Newton-Keith, A. **Children of Allah** 1965, Michael Joseph, London. Account of life in Libya during the 1960s. Still useful for the Libyan Fezzan area.

8 Gardi, R. **Ténéré,** 1978, Benteli Verlag, Berne. Although beautifully illustrated, this book written by a Sahara expert is more than just a 'coffee table book'.

9 Melville, K.E.M. **Stay Alive in the Desert** 1980, Roger Lascelles, London. An excellent survival manual by a doctor with many years of practical experience in Libya.

10 Milburn, M. **Secrets of South Sahara** 1979, Vantage Press, New York. An absorbing account of years of private research into pre-historic tumuli and other remains in the southern Sahara.

11 Slavin, K. and J. **The Tuareg,** 1973, Gentry, London. A very readable account of contact made with the Touareg people (and others) over many years of professional work in the Sahara.

12. **Sahara 10,000 Jahre zwischen Weide und Wuste** 1978, Museen der Stadt Koln, Cologne. This is really an academic work. A magnificent collection of

papers by eminent authorities on many aspects of the Sahara including geology, fauna, flora, climate, irrigation, prehistory.

13. Sabine, T. **Paris-Dakar** 1984, Paris. A well illustrated book on the history and development of the annual Paris-Dakar Rally by its creator and promoter.

Accounts of Recent Journeys in the Sahara

1 Gallisian, C. **Croissière des Stables** 1977, Arthaud, Paris. A beautifully illustrated 'coffee table' book describing the 1977 west-east crossing of the Sahara by a team from the Saviem (now Renault) truck company. In French.

2 Shepherd, T. 'The Joint Services West-East Sahara Expedition', **Geographical Journal** No. 142 July 1976. Report on a military expedition.

3 Leonard, J. 'The 1964-1965 Belgian Trans Saharan Expedition', **Nature** Jan. 8 1966. Report on a Belgian Government expedition.

4 Hugot, H.J. **Missions Berliet : Ténéré et Tchad** 1962, Arts et Metiers Graphiques, Paris. Detailed scientific report on one of the most important major expeditions into the Sahara. In French.

5 Weyer, H. **Ténéré : Das Land Dort Draussen** 1979, Badenia Verlag, Berne. Beautifully illustrated account of a Daimler Benz sponsored expedition into the Sahara.

6 Wepf, R. **Heisser Sommer in der Sahara** 1979, Bubenberg Verlag, Berne. Another viewpoint of the same Daimler Benz expedition described by H. Weyer above. Dr. Reinholt Wepf is an amateur photographer and artist of considerable depth and talent. In German.

7 E. Baz, F. et alia 'Journey to the Gilf Kebir and Uweinat, SW Egypt, 1978' **Geographical Journal** Vol.143, Parts 1 and 2, 1979. Description of a joint American and Egyptian scientific expedition to the remote SW corner of Egypt.

8 Norwich, J.J. **Sahara** 1968, Longmans, London. An interesting description of a journey from Djanet to the Tibesti mountains.

9 Heseltine, N. **From Libyan Sands to Chad** 1960, Museum Press, London. A useful narrative of the Tripoli-Sebha-Tibesti-Faya Largeau-N'Djamena route.

10 Frison-Roche, R. and Tairraz, P. **50 Ans de Sahara** 1976, Arthaud, Paris. The stories of several trips deep into the Sahara by experts. In French.

11 Heussler, G. **Trans Sahara** 1978, Orell Fussli Verlag, Zurich. Account of a round trip by 4x4 Hanomag trucks through Mauritania, Mali, Niger and Libya. In German.

12 Moorhouse, G. **The Fearful Void** 1974, Hodder and Stoughton, London. The story of a brave attempt to walk across the Sahara from west to east.

13   Trench, R. **Forbidden Sands** 1978, Murray, London. An account of a journey by camel through the remotest parts of Mali to the infamous prison centre at Taoudenni.

14   Toy, B. **The Way of the Chariots** 1964, John Murray, London. Story of an attempt to trace the route of the so-called trans-Saharan chariot races.

15   de Bary, E. **Wanderungen im Tassili,** 1971, Orion-Heimreiter Verlag, Heusenstaumm, Germany.

16   de Bary, E. **Im Bauch des Sandes** 1971. Discussion of her many journeys into the Libyan Fezzan in the late 1960s. In German.

17   Gozzi, A. **Journey Across Free Sahara** 1977, Edizione Laudoni, Leguano, Italy. Description of a journey to the Western Sahara as a guest of the Polisario.

18   Green, E. **A Boot Full of Right Arms** 1975, Cassell, Sydney. The book of the 1974 World Cup Rally across the Sahara (only 5 out of 53 vehicles completed the trans-Saharan section along some of the Sahara's easier routes).

19   Ilous, J. and Hayat, P. **Gazelle** 1981, Arthaud, Paris. The story of two Paris-Dakar rallies in a 1926 Renault KZ car. In French.

20   Maude, H. **Out of the Sand** 1966, Odhams, London. The story of Lt. Col. Leclerc's campaign across the Sahara from Chad to Tripoli during World War II.

21   Kennedy-Shaw, W.B. **Long Range Desert Group** 1945, Collins, London. Complete detailed history of this special British army group which made many remarkable journeys across the remotest parts of Egypt and Libya during World War II.

22   Foster, M. 'By Camel Caravan' **Expedition** (WEXAS), Vol. VI, No. 3, 1976. Detailed and very useful description of a journey with one of the 'Azalai' caravans across the Ténéré from Agadez to Bilma.

23   Englebert, V. 'I Joined a Sahara Salt Caravan', **National Geographic,** Vol. 128, No.5, November 1965. Very useful article on another journey with one of the 'Azalai' caravans across the Ténéré.

24   Polk, M. 'Retracing Alexander's Footsteps' **Quest** April 1981. Account of a camel trek from Siwa Oasis in western Egypt to Cairo.

25   Paolinelli, F. 'Saharan Salt Trade Recovers', **Geographical Magazine,** December 1982. Excellent analytical account of a journey with the 'Azalai' caravans across the Ténéré during 1982.

26   Weis, W. **Die Piste ins Tibesti** 1971, Jugend und Volk, Vienna.

27   Monod, T. **La Caravane du Sel** 1978, Editions Denoel, Paris. Beautifully illustrated book on salt caravans by one of the foremost experts on the Sahara.

28 Sheppard, T. 'Lone Desert Ranger', **Expedition** (WEXAS), Vol. IX, No.1, 1978. Description of a journey in a single Range Rover from Timbuktu direct to Reggane.

29 Amberg, T. and G. 'Vom Acacus zum Edeyen Murzuk' and Lutz, L. 'Vom Air nach Libye', **Tours Magazine,** Sept./Oct. 1981. Journeys by Mercedes LG315 truck and VW-Bus respectively in the Ténéré and southern Libya. In German. (Available from Lutze-Verlag GmbH., Charlottenstrasse 44, 7000 Stuttgart 1, W. Germany.)

30 Crewe, Q. **In Search of the Sahara** 1983, Michael Joseph, London. The story of a recent journey across the Sahara, through West Africa to Dakar and thence on to Sudan and Egypt. A must for anyone going to the Sahara for the first time because it explains so effectively about human relationships in the desert and about bureaucracy in Saharan countries. Beautifully illustrated.

31 Ritter, H. **Caravanes du Sel** 1981, Arthaud, Paris. Originally in German, the author has written of first hand recent journeys on all the remaining salt caravan routes.

32 Asher, M. **In Search of the Forty Days Road** 1984, Penguin, London. An account of travels by camel in the desert area of the north-western Sudan.

33 Asher, M. **A Desert Dies.** 1986, Penguin, London. Experience of living and working in the north-east of the Sudan.

34 Asher, M. **The Impossible Journey** 1990, Penguin, London. The story of the first ever crossing of the Sahara from west to east entirely on foot. A magnificent achievement and, moreover, a journey only completed twice previously by heavily sponsored teams in powerful four wheel drive trucks and Land Rovers. The title is most appropriate.

35 Edwards, T. **Beyond the last Oasis** 1986, Oxford University Press, Oxford. An excellent account of a solo journey by camel from Timbuktu in Mali to Oualata in Mauritania through the Empty Quarter.

Probably thousands of people have written of their journeys in the Sahara. The author of this book has not seen every book or article but has seen many and those listed above are some that have been found useful.

Some Academic Works on the Sahara

Geology
1 Bagnold, R.A. **Physics of Blown Sand** 1941, Methuen, London. Detailed scientific work based on the Sahara.

2 Fabre, J. **Introduction à la Geologie du Sahara Algerien et des Regions Voisines** 1976, S.N.E.D., Algiers. Excellent reference book worth taking with you.

3 Cooke, R.V. and Warren, A. **Geomorphology in Deserts** 1973, Batsford, London. Book of general principles.

4 Grove, A.T. 'Geomorphology of the Tibesti Region' **Geographical Journal,** No. 126, 1960.

5 El Baz, F. 'Circular Feature Among Dunes of the Great Sand Sea, Egypt' **Science** Vol. 213, July 24 1981. A short analysis of the large El Baz meteorite crater in the Egyptian desert north of Djebel Uweinat.

Saharan Prehistory

1 Lhote, H. **The Search for the Tassili Frescoes,** 1959, Hutchinson, London. Narrative of the discovery of the rock art in the Tassili N'Ajjer in Algeria by perhaps the greatest expert on Saharan pre-historic culture.

2 Lhote, H. **Vers d'Autres Tassili** 1975 Arthaud, Paris. An expansion of the previous work. In French.

3 Lhote, H. **Les Gravures du Nord-Ouest de l'Air** 1970, A.M.G., Paris.

4 Lhote, H. and Columbel, P. **Gravures, Peintures Rupestres et Vestiges Archeologiques des Environs de Djanet.** 1979, Parc National du Tassili, Alger. Detailed description of some Tassili rock art.

5 Shaiboub, A. 'Libyan Rock Art' **Popular Archeology** February 1982. Article on ancient rock art in the Tadrart Acacous massif of southern Libya.

6 Hugot, H.J. **Le Sahara Avant le Desert** 1974, Hesperides, Paris. Excellent coverage of culture in the pre-desert Sahara by one of the foremost experts.

7 Hugot, H.J. and Bruggmann, M. **Les Gens du Matin, Sahara,** 1976, Bibliotheque des Arts, Paris. A magnificently illustrated book on pre-historic life and culture in what is now the Sahara. Much more than just a 'coffee table' book, it is a must for any Sahara enthusiast. In French and German editions.

8 Frobenius, L. **Ekade Ektab,** 1978 Verlagsanstalt, Graz, Austria. The authority on the pre-historic art of Libya. In German. (Originally published Leipzig 1937.)

9 Breuil, H. **Les Roches Peintes du Tassili** 1954, Editions Arts et Metiers, Paris. Description of the rock art originally re-discovered by Col. Brenans in the Ouad Djerad area near Illizi. In French.

10 Camps-Farbrer, H. **Matiere et Art Mobilier dans la Prehistoire Nord-Africaine et Saharienne** 1966, Editions Arts et Metiers Graphiques, Paris.

11 Hugot, H.J. **Recherches Prehistoriques dans l'Ahagger Nord-Occidental,** 1953 Editions Arts et Metiers Graphiques, Paris.

12 Tschudi, J. **Les Peintures Rupestres du Tassili N'Ajjer** 1956, Editions La Baconniere, Neuchatel.

13 Von Noten, F. **Rock Art of Jebel Uweinat** 1978, Akad. Druck und Verlaganstalt, Graz, Austria.

14 Maitre, J.P. **Contribution à la Préhistoire de L'Ahaggar** Published 1971 by Arts et Metiers, Paris for Centre de Recherches Anthropologiques, Préhistoriques et Etnographiques, Algiers. Several volumes.

15 Boaz, N.T. and Cramer, D.L. 'Fossils of the Libyan Sahara' **Natural History** Vol. 91, August 1982. Article on early hominid remains at Sahabi site in southern Libya.

16 Desmond Clark, J. **The Prehistory of Africa** (1970), Thames and Hudson, London. Excellent. The best overall coverage of prehistory in Africa and the Sahara.

17 Wendorf, F. et alia. 'The Prehistory of the Egyptian Sahara', **Science** Vol. 193, 9 Jul 1976.

Saharan Peoples

1 Keenan, J. **The Tuareg** 1977, Allen Lane, London. One of the best studies of the Hoggar Touaregs so far.

2 Lhote, H. **Les Touaregs du Hoggar** 1955, Editions Payot, Paris. An excellent coverage of Touareg society.

3 Creyaufmuller, W. **Mauren und Tuareg** 1980, Linden-Museum, Stuttgart. Well illustrated study of Touaregs and Maures. In German.

4 Griaule, M. and Dieterlen, G. 'The Dogon of the French Sudan' in Forde, D. (Ed.), **African Worlds** 1954, Oxford University Press, London.

5 Riesman, P. **Freedom in Fulani Social Life** 1977, University of Chicago Press, Chicago. A fascinating ethnography which studies Fulani people in Upper Volta.

6 Beckwith, C. and Van Offelen, M. **Nomads of Niger** 1983, Harry N. Abrams, New York. A coffe table book of a detailed ethnography of a group of the Fulani people known as the 'Wodaabe' in the Agadez region. Superb photography.

7 Capot-Rey, R.. **Le Nomadisme Pastorale dans le Sahara Francais** 1942, Travaux de l'Instituit de Recherches Sahariennes, Algiers. One of the best general works on the people of the Sahara. In French.

8 Briggs, L.C. **Tribes of the Sahara** 1960, Harvard University Press, Cambridge, U.K.

9 Akesker, R. 'Tibesti, Land of the Tebou' **Geographical Magazine,** No. 21, 1958.

10 Chapelle, J. **Les Toubous, Nomades Noirs du Sahara** 1982, Editions L'Harmattan, Paris. The best work on the Toubous of Northern Chad.

11 Kronenberg, A. **Die Teda von Tibesti,** 1958, F. Berger Vienna. In German.

12 Recherches sur la Zone Aride, **Nomades et Nomadisme au Sahara,** 1963 UNESCO Paris. A collection of essays.

13 Mercer, J. **Spanish Sahara** 1976, Geo. Allen and Unwin, London. One of the best sources on the Reguibat and other peoples of Western Sahara.

14 Perhaps the most reliable short guide to the people of the Sahara and the rest of Africa is Hiernaux, H. **The People of Africa,** 1974, London.

15 Those seeking detail may need to refer to the many arts of the still incomplete **Ethnographic Survey of Africa** edited by Forde, D. This series is published by the International African Institute, London and Paris, from 1950 onwards.

16 Capot-Rey, R. 'Nomadism in the Sahara' in Zartman, I.W. (Ed.) **Man, State and Society in the Contemporary Maghreb** 1975 Praegar/Holt, Rinehart and Winston, New York.

17 Bernous, E. **Touaregs Nigeriens** 1981, Editions de l'Office de la Recherche Scientifique et Technique Outre Mer, Paris. The most detailed and comprehensive work on the Touaregs of the Southern Sahara especially in Niger.

Flora and Fauna
1 Quezel, P. **Vegetation du Sahara** 1965, Paris. One of the authorities on Saharan vegetation.

2 Capot-Rey, R. **L'Afrique Blanche Francaise II: Le Sahara Francais** 1953, Presses Universitaires de France, Paris. A major authority on Saharan vegetation.

3 Vial, Y. and M. **Sahara Milieu Vivant** 1974, Hatier, Paris. An excellent field guide to the flora and fauna of the Sahara. Worth taking with you even if you cannot read French.

4 Serle, W. **A Field Guide to the Birds of West Africa** 1977, Collins, London. Excellent field guide to both sedentary and migratory birds of the Sahara and West Africa. Worth taking with you.

5 Schmidt-Nielsen, K. **Desert Animals : Physiological Problems of Heat and Water** 1965, Oxford University Press, London. A scholarly explanation of
adaptations to desert life — very useful to understanding survival in the desert.

6 MacFarlane, W.V. 'Survival in an Arid Land', **Australian Natural History** Vol. 19, No.1, Jan-March 1977. Very relevant to the Sahara.

7 Schmidt-Nielsen, K. 'The Camel : Facts and Fables', **UNESCO Courier,** Nos. 8 and 9. 1955.

Climate
1 Grove, A.T. 'Climate for Deserts', **Geographical Magazine** July 1977. Good discussion of desertification.

2 Grove, A.T. 'Man Gets His Deserts' **Geographical Magazine** August 1977. Also on desertification.

3 Farouk El Baz, 'When the deserts bloom again' **South Magazine,** January 1984. A more up to date view of desertification.

4 Biswas, R. and A.K. (Eds.) **Desertification,** 1980, Pergamon Press, New York. Associated case studies prepared for the U.N. Conference on Desertification at Nairobi in 1977.

5 Secretariat of U.N. Conference on Desertification (Ed.) **Desertification: Its Causes and Consequences,** 1977, Pergamon Press, Oxford. The papers presented at the United Nations Conference on Desertification at Nairobi in August and September 1977.

General
1 McGiunnes, W.G. et alia, **Deserts of the World : An Appraisal of Research into their Physical and Biological Environments,** 1970, University of Arizona Press, Tucson, USA. A massive and excellent reference book.

2 Cloudsley-Thompson, J.L. (Ed.) **Sahara Desert** 1984 Pergamon Press, London. One of a series about the physical and living environment. Contributors are all experts in their fields.

Historical Background

1 Fage, J.D., Gray, R. and Oliver, R. (Eds.) **Cambridge History of Africa** 1978 Cambridge University Press, Cambridge. (Eight volumes)

2 Ajayi, J.F. and Crowder, M. **History of West Africa** Vols I and II. 1971-1976 Longmans, London.

3 Ajayi, J.F. and Espie, I. (Eds.) **A Thousand Years of West African History,** 1965. Ibadan University Press, Ibadan, Nigeria. A very useful collection of essays.

4 Hargreaves, J. **West Africa : the Former French States,** 1967, Prentice-Hall, New York. A useful history.

5 Trimmingham, J.S. **History of Islam in West Africa** 1962, Oxford University Press, London.

6 Gardiner, B. **The Quest for Timbuctoo** 1968, Cassell, London. Historical background to early European exploration.

7 Saad, E.N. **Social History of Timbuktu** 1983, Cambridge University Press, Cambridge.

8 Last, M. **The Sokoto Caliphate** 1967, London.

9 Fage, J.D. **An Atlas of African History** 1978, London.

Classical Works

1 Barth, H. **Travels and Discoveries in North and Central Africa** 1857, Longmans, London.

2 Batuta, I. **Travels in Asia and Africa** (trans. by Gibb, H.R.) 1929, London. Originally written in mid-fourteenth century.

3 Caillié R. **Journal d'un Voyage à Tombouctou,** 1830, Paris

4   de Foucauld, C. **Reconnaissance au Maroc,** 1888, Paris.

5   Denham, D., Oudney D. and Clapperton, H. **Narrative of Travels and Discoveries in Northern and Central Africa in 1822, 1823 and 1824.** 1826, Murray, London.

6   Khaldun, I. **Histoire des Berbères** (trans. by de Slane, four volumes, Paris 1925-1926). Originally published in the late thirteenth century.

7   Lenz, O. **Tombouctou : Voyage au Maroc, au Sahara et au Sudan** 1888, Paris.

8   Leo, J. (Leo Africanus) **A Geographical History of Africa** 1600, George Bishop, London.

9   Nachtigal, G. **Tibesti : Die Entdeckung der Riesenkrater und die Erst-durchquerung des Sudan** 1978, Erdmann, Munchen. (First Published 1870.)

10   Richardson, J. **Travels in the Great Desert of Sahara** 1848, Bently, London.

11   Rohlfs, G. **Quer Durch Afrika-Reise Vom Mittelmeer nach dem Tchadsee** 1879, Leipzig.

12   Thessiger, W. 'Camel Journey to Tibesti', **Geographical Journal,** XCIV, 1939.

13   Vischer, H. **Across the Sahara from Tripoli to Bornu** 1910, Edward Arnold, London.

14   von Bary, E. **Sahara Tagebuch 1876-1877** 1880, Leipzig.

15   Douglas, N. **Fountains in the Sand** 1912, Martin Secker Ltd., London. An annount of travels in the desert areas of southern Tunisia before World War I.

16   Kennedy Shaw, W.B. **Long Range Desert Group.** 1989, Greenhill Books, London, (originally by Collins in 1945) The definitive work on the highly successful mobile fighting force which operated behind enemy lines in the Sahara during World War II.

Vehicles

1   Slavin, K. and J. and MacKie, G. **Land Rover : The Unbeatable 4x4** 1981, Gentry, London.

2   Robson, G. **The Land Rover : Workhorse of the World** 1976, David and Charles, London.

3   —, **A Guide to Land Rover Expeditions** 1974, British Leyland Publication No. R 1068/8.74 Solihull, Britain.

4   Jackson, J. **Four Wheel Drive Book** 1982, Gentry, London.

5   Sheppard, T. 'The Expedition Vehicle'
    Sheppard, T. 'Vehicle Maintenance on Long Haul Journeys'
    Glen, S. 'Overland Travel'
    Glen, S. 'Volkswagen Kombis'
    Glen, S. 'Below Deck : Shipping a Vehicle'
    Jackson, J. 'Land Rovers'
in Cranfield, I. (Ed.) **The Traveller's Handbook** 1982, Heinemann, London.
An excellent reference book packed full of useful facts, information and
addresses. Published every two years.

6   Fraenkel, P. **Overland** 1975, David and Charles, London. Book on
overland travel by Land Rover.

7   —, **Ici Commence l'Aventure** 1976, Citroen, Paris. A 30-page booklet
about overland travel by 2CV Citroen.

8   Glen, S. 'All about Kombis'**Overlander Magazine** Vol. 2, No. 3 1977.
Sydney, Australia. Care and maintenance of VW-Buses.

9   VW Public Relations Dept. **Instructions for Operating Passenger Cars
and Transporters in Tropical Climates (Z4)** Volkswagen Aktiengesellschaft,
Wolfsburg 1972. Recommended for VW owners.

10 King, C. **Four Wheel Drive Fundamentals** 1977, Haesner, New Jersey,
USA.

11 Hewatt, J. and T. **Overland and Beyond** 1981, Lascelles, London. Practical tips on overland travel by VW-Bus.

12 Taylor, J. **The Land Rover 1948-1984** 1984 London. Detailed catalogue of
all models produced to 1984. A Land Rover enthusiast's book.

Novels

There are some works of fiction that are surprisingly accurate in their por-
trayal of the Saharan environment and conditions, as well as being enjoyable
reading:

1   De Saint-Exupery, A. **Wind, Sand and Stars** 1939, Heinemann, London.
Semi-autobiographical, it is a novel about flying in the Sahara in the 1920s.

2   Bagley, D. **Flyaway** 1978, Collins, London. A fast moving thriller set in
the Tassili and Ténéré.

3   Wren, P.C. **Beau Geste** 1924, John Murray, London. Set in imaginary
places that could well have been the Hoggar and Agadez early in the nineteenth century, or even Timbuctu.

4   Also by P.C. Wren and set in the Sahara are: **Beau Ideal** and **Beau
Sabreur** both published by John Murray, London, 1928.

Keeping Up To Date

To keep up to date on events and changes in the Sahara some useful publica-
tions are:

1 **Keesings Archives** — a weekly guide to world events country by country. Found in most public libraries.

2 **Tours Magazine** a German travel magazine which frequently has articles by people who have just made journeys through the Sahara. Published bi-monthly by Lutze-Verlag GmbH, Charlottenstrasse 44, 7000 Stuttgart 1, West Germany.

3 **Auto Verte** a French off-road motoring magazine which frequently has articles on the Sahara as well as on off-road vehicles. Its coverage of rallies like the Paris-Dakar is always excellent. Available from: Auto Verte, 15/17 Quai de l'Oise, 75019 Paris.

Both these magazines have classified advertisement sections which are useful for locating used vehicles which could be suitable for expeditions into the Sahara and to make contact with other people seeking travelling companions for journeys in the Sahara.

It would also be worthwhile joining a club of Sahara enthusiasts. Two of these are:

153 Club,
94 Sebright Road, Barnet, Herts., EN5 4HN.

La Rahla,
4 Rue Coetlogan, 75006 Paris.

Both have very useful monthly letters.

Bookshops

There are few bookshops that have a really decent selection of books on travel in Africa and on the Sahara in particular. Perhaps the best are:

Artou-La Librairie du Voyageur,
  8 Rue de Rive, Geneva. (Tel: 022/21 45 44)

L'Astrolabe-La Librairie du Voyageur,*
  46 Rue de Provence, 75009 Paris. (Tel: 285 42 95)

Daerr Expeditionservice GmbH.,*
  Theresienstrasse 66, D-8000 Munchen 2. (Tel: 089/282 032)

Hof's Expeditionsservice,
  Rustengasse 7, A-1150 Vienna. (Tel: 85 71 01)

Travel Book Shop Gisela Treichler,
  Seilergraben 11, CH-8001 Zurich; (Tel: 01/2 52 38 83)

G.L.A.F. Kartcentralen,
  Vasagaten 16, 111-20 Stockholm.

Jacob van Wijngaarden,
Geografische Boekhandel, Overtoom 136, 1054 HN Amsterdam. (Tel. 020 121901)
Closed Mondays.

*These two bookshops have a mail order service.

10
Place Names In Arabic

In some countries road direction signs are either in Arabic only or the alternative romanised script has been scratched or painted out by self-righteous vandals. This is particularly the case in Libya and in parts of northern Algeria. Therefore the following list of place names has been included to help those faced with signposts in Arabic only and not knowing which road to choose.

Abalessa	أبالص
Adrar	أدرار
Aflou	أ فلو
Alexandria (El Iskandariya)	الاسكندرية
Algiers (Alger, El Djezair)	الجزائر
Assekrem	أسكرم
Bechar (Colomb-Bechar)	بشار
Benghazi	بنى عباس
Beni Abbes	بنى نازى
Cairo (El Qahira)	القاهرة
Centre Ville	وسط المدينة
Djanet (Fort Charlet)	جنات
Djelfa	الجلفة
Egypt	مصر
El Oued	الوادى

Ghardaia	غرداية
Ghat (Rhat)	قات
Giza (El Gizeh)	الجيزة
Hassi Messauod	حسى مسعود
Hirafok	هرفوك
Ideles	أدلس
Illizi	إلـبزى
In Guezzam (Ain Guezzam)	عين كزام
In Salah (Ain Salah)	عين صالح
Khartoum	الخرطوم
Ksar el Boukhari	قصر البخاري
Kufra (El Kufra)	الكفرة
Laghouat	الأعواض
Libya	ليبيا

Typical of the sort of problem that the person who cannot read Arabic may have to face in the Sahara. Initially, the authors took the piste on the left. After 30 km it fizzled out at an abandoned oil drilling site. This meant returning and taking the right hand piste to Illizi — a waste of 60 kilometres worth of precious fuel

131

Maghreb (El Maghreb, Morocco)	المغرب
Mauritania	هوريتانيا
Medea	المدية
Moulay Lahcen (Moulay Hassan)	مولاى الحسن
Murzuk	مرزوق
Oran	
Ouargla	غرادية
Port Sudan	لورتسودان
Reggane	رقان
Sebha	سبها
Sidi bel Abbes	سيدى بنى عباس
Sudan	السودان
Tamanrasset (Fort Laperine)	تمنراست
Targhit (Tarhit)	تاغيت
Tazrouk	طزرولو
Timimoun	تيميمون
Tit	تيت
Tripoli	طرابلس
Tunisia (Tunis)	تونس

11
Tour Companies Operating in the Sahara

Since about 1974 the Algerian government has severely restricted the operations of foreign tour companies in favour of its own state-run organisation. Mauritania stopped tours of its northern interior because of the war involving the Polisario guerrilla movement, though at least two tour companies have recently been permitted to have limited operations in that country. Libya, with its fundamentalist regime, has tended not to encourage tour operators but persistent, sensitive and discreet companies should not be deterred. The Tibesti region of Chad has been the scene of bitter fighting for many years now and is still dangerous. Thus the only really convenient places left for foreign tour operators are Tunisia, Mali, Egypt, Sudan and Niger (though the latter has recently imposed restrictions).

Apart from price, duration, and the places visited, perhaps the most important point to consider, is how many people are accommodated in a Land Rover (most operators use them). It is not the most comfortable of vehicles, at the best of times, but some operators have been known to squeeze eight people into a LWB station wagon; usually quite an ordeal.

In Britain, especially, there are several trans-African operators, usually using 4x4 trucks. There are also occasional fringe operators, who have left truck loads of young people stranded in In Salah, Agadez, and other less pleasant spots further south. If contemplating a Trans-African tour, you should book through Trail Finders Ltd., 46 Earls Court Road, London, W8 6EJ, England, a large booking and information organization which financially guarantees the security of people booking overland tours through them.

There are a considerable number of groups operating in or through the Sahara. Some are short-lived fly-by-night affairs, while others are known for their inefficiency, rudeness to clients, overcrowding in vehicles and inability to ever stick to schedules. The following is a list of tour operators which have been in existence for many years now and have demonstrated their reliability and worth:

Altour (Office National Algerien du Tourisme)
25-27 Rue Kheilifa Boukalfa, Algiers.
Only a stone's throw from the ferry terminal. There are also offices in:
Germany: Taunusstrasse 20, 6 Frankfurt/Main.
France: 28 Avenue de l'Opera, 75002 Paris.

Belgium: 36 Rue de la Montagne, Brussels.
Britain: 35 St. James's Street, London SW1.
Tamanrasset: Tahat Hotel.
This is the offical agency through which most tours taking place within Algeria must be booked. It is expensive, and you benefit if you speak quite good French (or Arabic). In the Sahara they concentrate on two regions: the Hoggar and the Tassili. Their tours usually take place in chauffeur/guide driven Land Rover and Land Cruiser station wagons. Including meals, the price per day (1983) is 438DA per person in a party of four. A party of two would cost 1,248DA per person per day. Some of the tours operating out of Tamanrasset are:

1 Tam. — Iamane — Assekrem (3 days)
2 Tam. — Assekrem — Hirafok — Tazrouk — Tam. (4 days)
3 Tam. — Assekrem — Hirafok — Mertoutek — Tazrouk — Tamekresset — Tam. (6 days)
4 Tam. — Abalama — Tagara — Oufkit — Tamekresset — Tam. (6 days)
5 Tam. — Assekrem — Ideles — Serouenout — Djanet (6 days)
6 Tam. — Assekrem — Ideles — Serouenout — Ft Gardel — Sendelene — Djanet — Erg d'Admer — Talertheba — Tazrouk — Tam. (9 days)

They will also do excursions to order.

From Djanet organised trips into the Tassili are always available (see itinerary section on Djanet).

With perseverance it is also possible to organise camel tours out of Beni Abbes and Timimoun through Altour (November to March).

Ashraf-Reizen
Bijltjespad 4, 1018 KH Amsterdam, Holland.
Dutch company with tours across the Sahara and in West Africa.

An amazing sight: a Rotel Tours bus and 'hotel' trailer at Agadez. However, it was accompanied by six wheel drive Magirus-Deutz tow truck

Avventure nel Mondo
Via Cino da Pistoia, 7, 00152 Roma, Italy.
Specialising in ambitious tours deep into more remote areas of the Sahara in Algeria, Niger, Mali and Mauritania.

Baobab Travel
Delftseveerweg 31b, 3134 Je Vlaardingen, Holland.
A Dutch company with tours across the Sahara and into Mali.
Mercedes 4x4 trucks.

Encounter Overland
271 Old Brompton Road, London SW5, England.
Usually operating transcontinental tours, they do have 3 and 4 week Sahara tours into Algeria and Tunisia.
Bedford 4x4 trucks.

Exodus Travels
All Saints Passage, 100 Wandsworth High Street, London SW18 4LE, England.
Usually operating transcontinental tours.
Bedford 4x4 trucks.

Guerba Expeditions
Stokehill Farm, Erlestoke, Devizes, Wiltshire, England.
A newish company with a good reputation. They offer several trans-Saharan tours originating and terminating in Dakar, Accra and Tunis. Also have tours specialising in Mali, Senegal, Sudan, Kenya and Egypt as well as trans-Africa.
Bedford 4x4 trucks.

Jerrycan Expeditions
Rue du Stand 53, 1204 Geneva, Switzerland.
An efficient operator with tours specialising in Mali, southern Algeria, and Mauritania as well as trans-Sahara.
Land Rovers.

Lama-Expedition GmbH
Schone Aussicht 16, 6000 Frankfurt/Main, Germany.
A very efficient company which specialises in in-depth tours to the remoter parts of the Egyptian SW (e.g. Jebel Uweinat), Sudan and Ethiopia.
Unimogs and Gelandewagens.

Mike Foster
40 Sunningdale Close, Chapel St. Leonards, Lincolnshire, PE24 5TL, Britain.
A very small company run by a Sahara expert and specialising in tours to remote areas of the Sahara.
Land Rovers.

Sahel Expeditions
Aucombe, Horningsham, Warminster BA12 7JN, England.
Specialists in mixed desert, river, marsh, and mountain Land Rover tours of 2-4 weeks in the Sahara, especially in Mali and Mauritania.

Temet Voyages
Expeditions Sahelo-Sahariennes, B.P. 178, Agadez, Niger Republic.
Reasonably priced tours of the Ténéré and Air.
Range Rovers and Land Rovers.

Weyer-Foto-Flug International
Schulgasse 6, 633 Wetzlar-Nauborn, West Germany.
Conducted photo-safaris which sometimes take place in parts of the Sahara.

Rotel Tours: Das Rollende Hotel
50 Herrenstrasse, 8391 Tittling/Passau, West Germany.
Luxury buses which tow large trailers containing sleeping quarters — rolling hotels. They have tours into the Sahara.
Mercedes buses.

Luxus Hotelbus Reisen
Schwarzbrunnweg 4, 895 Kaufbeuren-Neugablonz, West Germany.
Similar to Rotel above.
Mercedes buses.

In France there are companies and clubs which have guided 'raids' or tours into the Sahara where you take your own vehicle along with a group of other participants in their vehicles. The organisation provides insurance, ferry and hotel bookings, as well as a support truck which carries a mechanic, spare parts and most of the jerrycans. Three such organisations are:

Raids Septentrion,
Francois Deldique, 95 Rue des Martyrs, 59113 Seclin.

Guilde Européenne du Raid,
Jean-Marc Cognot, 11 Rue de Vaugirard, Paris 75006.

Club Auto Verte 4x4
52 Rue Guynemer, 92400 Courbevoie.

Tours are also from time to time organised by or on behalf of groups of Sahara-buffs like The 153 Club and La Rahla. These are usually of an adventurous nature into more remote areas of the sahara. Contact addresses are:

The 153 Club,
97 Thornlow Road, W. Norwood, London SE 27, England.

La Rahla,
4 rue Coetlogan, 75006 Paris, France.

It should also be pointed out that in some Saharan oases there are small tour companies operated by local people e.g. Agence Tim Beur in Djanet, Atlantide Tours in Agadez and the Hotel Taghit. Some are not only good value but offer courteous attention and very personalised tours.

Vehicle Hire

It is very difficult to find vehicle hire companies which will allow you to take one of their vehicles out of Europe and into the Sahara. Large deposits are usually required and the actual hire costs are high too. For example, late in 1981 the authors arranged to hire a petrol Land Rover station wagon in Britain for use in the Sahara for £150 per week plus £263 for two months of insurance.

Some companies which have four-wheel drive vehicles for hire and will accept arrangements for their uses in the Sahara are:

Four by Four Hire Ltd.
113 Walnut Tree Close, Guildford, Surrey, GU1 4UG, England. Tel: (057 62) 3334.
Land Rovers and Range Rovers.

Manfred Zeller GmbH.
Expedition Gelandewagenvermietung, 6800 Mannheim 1, West Germany. Tel: (0621) 24124.
Toyota Land Cruisers.

A tour group camp site in the middle of spectacular Saharan scenery (Photo by courtesy of Guerba Expeditions)

Location Tout-Terrain Chabert.
Chemin de la Glacière, 06200 Lingostieres — Nice, France. Tel: (93) 29 83 16.
Range Rovers, Land Rovers.

Knook's Automobielbedrijf B.V.
1442 PV Purmerend, Flevostraat 66-70, Holland. Tel: (02990) 27257/34141.

12
Visas and Vaccinations

Algeria
No entry for citizens of South Korea, Malawi, South Africa, Taiwan and Israel, or any holders of passports with visa or entry stamps from these countries.

West Germans are strongly advised to obtain a double entry visa in Germany before departure. The second entry dates should correspond with any expected return journey through Algeria. West Germans are not infrequently kept waiting several weeks in Niamey, Lagos, or Douala, probably only to have their application finally turned down. If arriving in Algeria from the south, ensure that you will conform to Algerian regulations; a return trip to Niamey, from Djanet, across the Ténéré, could be most unwelcome.

Trans Sahara travellers in both directions are required to have a valid certificate of inoculation against yellow fever (except infants under 12 months).

Consulates: London, Paris, Bonn, The Hague, Brussels, Stockholm, Berne, Rabat, Tokyo, Abidjan, Accra. Lagos, Niamey, Oujda, Tunis, Douala, Tripoli, Rome, Bamako, Dakar, Cairo, Washington.

Burkina Faso (formerly Upper Volta)
Passport holders from South Africa will be refused entry.

Consulates: London, Paris, Bonn, Brussels, Washington, Bamako, Accra, Abidjan, Monrovia. (No consulate in Niamey.)

Chad
Because of troubles in the north of the country, special authorization is required from the Ministry of the Interior for travel within Chad outside the immediate environs of N'Djamena. Enquire at a Chad Consulate. Travel in the north (at the time of writing) is virtually impossible as there is still a simmering war going on and the dangers of being killed in cross fire or as a spy cannot be underestimated

Consulates: Paris, Bonn, Brussels, Lagos, Khartoum, Washington.

Egypt
No entry for citizens of Taiwan, South Africa, Yemen P.D.R. (South Yemen), and Libya.

For most nationalities visas are required (exceptions are Algeria, Bahrein
138

Ghana, Guinea, Jordan, Kuwait, Malta, Mauritania, Morocco and other Arab countries). While obtaining a visa before departure for Egypt minimises delays on arrival, it is possible to have a visa issued upon arrival at Cairo airport but this facility is not available to arrivals by land or sea. Visas are generally valid for one week (no matter what length of time you applied for it to be); which means that you have to register at the Office of Foreigners in Cairo within this time. If the stay is for less than seven days, then this formality is not necessary.

If you arrive at Alexandria with a right hand steering vehicle, this may require a two-day trip to Cairo and back with a lot of fast talking with transport authority officials to get the necessary permission to drive your car on Egyptian roads.

All tourists' foreign registered vehicles have to be issued with Temporary Tourist Egyptian number plates. This takes time and sometimes monetary assistance is needed to speed things up.

Consulates: London, Paris, Brussels, The Hague, Bonn, Copenhagen, Stockholm, Canberra, Nairobi, Khartoum, Addis Ababa, Tripoli, Rome, Berne, Athens, Beirut, Amman, Lagos, Kano, Algiers, Tunis, Rabat, Washington, Ottawa.

Libya
No entry for citizens of Israel, South Africa, or holders of passports bearing visa entry stamps from those countries. West Germans must have a visa issued in Bonn, and nowhere else. The first few pages of passports and health certificates must carry an Arabic translation. If you have a British passport, this may be done free at the Passport Office in London. However, any Libyan consulate will give the name and address of an accredited translator. If you arrive by air at Sebha from Niger then a visa may be issued on arrival. However, at the time of writing no such flights operate.

All tourists' foreign registered vehicles have to be issued with temporary tourist Libyan number plates. This is done at the first frontier post that one encounters. The plates are surrendered upon departure from the country. It would be most advisable to have a Carnet de Passages for a visitor's car and it is essential for all drivers to have International Driving Permits.

In view of the diplomatic crisis between Britain and Libya during 1984, British passport holders are advised to consider very carefully when planning to visit Libya. It might be worthwhile to consult the British Foreign Office about the current state of affairs. Within Libya, consular matters involving British citizens are now handled by the Italian Embassy (legal advice, visits in jail, repatriation, passport loss, etc.). However, despite this political crisis, the individual who is considerate and temperate is usually treated with respect and often kindness in Libya.

Consulates: Rome, Paris, Berne, Bonn, Algiers, Tunis, Rabat, Lagos, Cairo, Niamey, Agadez and Canberra.

Mali
Visas are not obtainable from French Consulates. Sometimes the visa is for seven days only and entry must be on a specified date.

Consulates: Paris, Bonn, Lagos, Abidjan, Accra. Monrovia, Niamey, Dakar and Brussels.

Mauritania
Travel in the extreme north may be restricted.

Consulates: Paris, Algiers, Rabat, Abidjan, Dakar, Lagos and Bamako.

Morocco
No entry for holders of Israeli or South African passports. Entry for all nationalities can be refused on the grounds of dress or appearance.
Consulates: Bonn, Madrid, Algeciras, Algiers, Oran, Nouakchott, Dakar, Lagos, London, Paris, and The Hague.

Niger
French Consulates no longer issue visas for Niger. Swiss nationals must obtain visas from the consulate in Paris.
Consulates: Paris, Bonn, Algiers, N'Djamena, Lagos, Kano, Cotonou, Accra, Abidjan, Brussels and Bamako.

Nigeria
The Consular section in London is usually very crowded. It is possible to obtain a visa elsewhere e.g. Niamey where service is quick, helpful and pleasant. Nigerian officials may wish to see the Carnet de Passage and count your travellers cheques before issuing a visa.
Consulates: London, Paris, Brussels, The Hague, Bonn, Berne, Rome, Canberra, Washington, Ottawa, Algiers, Niamey, Accra, Cotonou, N'Djamena, Yaoundé, Rabat.

Sudan
No entry for Israeli and South African passport holders. Sudanese Consular officials may wish to see your Carnet de Passage, count your travellers cheques, and even require a letter from the bank guaranteeing you for US$500. Special permits are required for travel in southern Sudan. Enquire at a Sudanese consulate.
Consulates: Cairo, Asmara, Addis, Ababa, Nairobi, Kampala, N'Djamena, Lagos, London, Washington.

Tunisia
No entry for Israeli or South African passport holders. Travel in the southern part of Tunisia requires a special permit (obtainable from the Governor at de Medenine), as this is a restricted military zone. Without this authorisation, entry into Tunisia from In Amenas (in Algeria to the south) will be refused. Enquire at a Tunisian embassy.
Consulates: Rome, Tripoli, Benghazi, Annabi, Algiers, Paris, Marseille, London, Bonn, Lagos, Rabat, Cairo, Washington, Ottawa, The Hague. (No consulate in Niamey.)

Foreign Consulates in the Sahara Region

Australia: Algiers, Lagos, Accra, Cairo.
Austria: Algiers, Lagos, Kaduna, Tunis.
Belgium: Algiers, Niamey, Lagos, Tunis, Rabat, Dakar.
Britain: Algiers, Tunis, Rabat, Lagos, Kaduna, Dakar, Niamey (honorary only), Abidjan, Khartoum, Cairo.
Canada: Algiers, Tunis, Rabat, Lagos, Cairo.
Denmark: Algiers, Tunis, Rabat, Lagos, Abidjan, Cairo.
France: Algiers, Tunis, Rabat, Oran, Lagos, Niamey, Cairo, Tripoli, N'Djamena, Ouagadougou, Bechar, Abidjan, Nouakchott, Dakar.
Ireland: Lagos.
Italy: Rabat, Algiers, Tunis, Tripoli, Cairo, Lagos, Kaduna, Abidjan.

Netherlands: Rabat, Algiers, Tunis, Tripoli, Cairo, Lagos, Ouagadougou, Abidjan, Dakar.
New Zealand: Accra.
Norway: Rabat, Algiers, Tunis, Cairo, Lagos, Abidjan, Dakar.
Sweden: Rabat, Algiers, Tunis, Cairo, Lagos, Abidjan, Dakar, Niamey.
Switzerland: Rabat, Algiers, Tunis, Cairo, Lagos, Abidjan, Dakar.
U.S.A.: Rabat, Algiers, Tunis, Tripoli, Cairo, Khartoum, N'Djamena, Lagos, Niamey, Ouagadougou, Bamako, Abidjan, Nouakchott.
West Germany: Rabat, Algiers, Tunis, Tripoli, Cairo, Khartoum, N'Djamena, Lagos, Niamey, Ouagadougou, Bamako, Abidjan, Dakar.

If you need the address of your embassy or consulate while in a foreign city, it is best to ask at banks, information offices, etc. or look it up in the telephone directory. In Algeria, telephone directories are in Arabic, so this presents special difficulties. Here are some addresses in Algiers.

Australia: 60, Boulevard Colonel Bougara, El Biar.
Austria: Logement 55, Cite Dar el Kef, Rue Shakespeare, El Mouradia.
Belgium: 1 Rue Abdelkim el Khettabi.
Britain: 7 Chemin des Glycimes.
Canada: 27 bis Rue Anjou.
Denmark: 23 Boulevard Zirout Yousef.
Egypt: Chemin Abdel Kadar Gadouche, Hydra.
Finland: 2 Boulevard Mohammed V.
France: Rue Larbi Alik, Hydra.
Germany (W): 165 Chemin Sfinda.
Germany (E): 12 Rue Payen, Hydra.
Ghana: 62 Rue Parmentier, Hydra.
Greece: 38 Rue Didouche Mourad.
Italy: 37 Chemin Cheikh Brahimi, El Biar.
Libya: 15 Chemin Cheikh Brahimi, El Biar.
Morocco: Rue B. Amani, Air de France, Bouzareah.
Netherlands: 23 Boulevard Zirout Yousef.
Niger: 12 Rue Ali Cherif, El Biar.
Nigeria: 27 Ali Boufelgued.
Spain: 10 Rue A. Azil.
Sweden: 4 Boulevard Mohammed V.
Switzerland: 27 Boulevard Zirout Yousef.
U.:S.A.: Villa Mektoub, 4 Chemin Brahimi, El Biar.

However it is advisable to obtain a list of addresses of your country's legations, in the area, before departure. N.B. For New Zealanders, the nearest embassies are in Accra and Rome.

General
Where there is no official representation, British Consular officials will look after the interests of Canadians, Australians, New Zealanders, Nigerians, Indians, Irish, etc. (e.g. visits while in jail).

There are Israeli consulates in Niamey, Nairobi, Lagos and Cairo.

Consular officials at embassies are usually totally unsympathetic towards people stranded with insufficient funds. Do not expect helpful treatment.

Above all guard your passport. You cannot leave a country without it and a lost one takes an eternity to replace, especially if you are in a country where your nation is unrepresented. It is preferable to travel with two passports, even though illegal in most cases, but don't let frontier officials see that you have two.

Health Certificates

Endless hassles can result from inadequate International Health Certificate records. Cholera vaccination is valid for only six months, and yellow fever for ten years. However make sure no inoculation period is due to end while you are in a Saharan country. For example, on entering Algeria from the south, if your cholera vaccination has three days to go, passport officials will make sure you have another one. In some places e.g. Sokoto in Nigeria, it is preferable to have your own needle for vaccination, as the local ones have been used many time before and are not only blunt but also carry great potential for infection, especially hepatitis. Most local doctors will be quite understanding when you provide your own needle.

Make sure the dates in the certificate are to internationally agreed standards, e.g."7 November 1980" not "7.11.80" and also not the American style "11.7.80". Similarly make sure all figure sevens have the European style cross through them (7) so that they are not confused with the European style figure (1).

On return to Europe, Australia, or North America from Saharan countries you may need to update cholera and yellow fever vaccinations to avoid quarantine. (U.S.A. no longer insists on cholera vaccinations.) Morocco, Algeria and Tunisia require no health certificates if arriving from Europe. However, if arriving from Mali, Niger, Nigeria, Burkina Faso, etc. up-to-date cholera and yellow fever vaccinations are required. Similarly, if arriving from Niger, at Tamanrasset, the Algerian officials will sometimes insist that you go to Tamanrasset hospital and have a malaria test, before they will process your passport. Niger, Nigeria, Mali, and Burkina Faso require both main vaccinations and may refuse to issue a visa without valid certificates.

It is also in your own interests to have up-to-date typhoid, polio, and tetanus inoculations before travelling to Saharan countries. An injection of gamma globulin which gives four to six months protection against infective hepatitis, is also worthwhile, especially in the Sahel area. Even currently rare diseases like diphtheria, and typhus could be contracted, and prove disastrous, in the Ténéré for example.

	Algeria	Burkina Faso	Chad	Egypt	Libya	Mali	Mauritania	Morocco	Niger	Nigeria	Sudan	Tunisia
West Germany	Yes	Yes	No	No	Yes	Yes	Yes	Yes	No	Yes	Yes	No
U.S.A.	Yes	Yes	Yes	Yes	Yes	Yes	No	Yes	Yes	Yes	Yes	No
Switzerland	No	Yes	Yes	Yes	Yes	Yes	No	Yes	Yes	Yes	Yes	No
Sweden	No	No	Yes	Yes	Yes	Yes	No	No	Yes	Yes	Yes	No
Norway	No	No	Yes	Yes	Yes	Yes	No	No	Yes	Yes	Yes	No
New Zealand	Yes	Yes	Yes	Yes	Yes	Yes	No	Yes	Yes	Yes	Yes	Yes
Netherlands	Yes	No	Yes	Yes	Yes	Yes	No	Yes	Yes	Yes	Yes	Yes
Japan	Yes	Yes	Yes	Yes	Yes	Yes	No	Yes	Yes	Yes	Yes	No
Italy	No	No	Yes	Yes	Yes	No	No	No	Yes	Yes	Yes	No
Ireland	Yes	Yes	Yes	Yes	Yes	Yes	No	Yes	Yes	Yes	Yes	No
France	No	No	No	Yes	No	No	No	No	Yes	Yes	Yes	No
Denmark	No	No	Yes	Yes	Yes	No	No	No	Yes	Yes	Yes	No
Canada	Yes	Yes	Yes	Yes	Yes	Yes	No	Yes	Yes	Yes	Yes	No
Britain	No	Yes	Yes	Yes	Yes	Yes	No	No	Yes	Yes	Yes	No
Belgium	Yes	No	Yes	Yes	Yes	No	No	No	Yes	Yes	Yes	No
Austria	Yes	Yes	Yes	Yes	Yes	Yes	No	Yes	Yes	Yes	Yes	No
Australia	Yes	Yes	Yes	Yes	Yes	Yes	No	Yes	Yes	Yes	Yes	Yes

Yes = Visa required. No = Visa not required.

Nigerians need visas for Algeria, Mali, Tunisia, Burkina Faso, Morocco, and Libya, but not for Niger.

Ghanaians need visas for Algeria, Mali, Burkina Faso, Morocco, Libya but not for Tunisia and Niger.

Quick Reference Visa Guide

13
Banks and Mail

Algeria

There is only one bank in Algeria, the Banque Nationale d'Algerie. There are branches in the Saharan area at: Tamanrasset, Adrar, Ghardaia, Laghouat, Bechar, Hassi Messaoud, Ouargla, Touggourt, El Oued, Biskra, Djelfa and of course at Algiers, Oran, Annaba, Blida, Tlemcen, and the frontier post near Oujda. New branches have recently been opened at Djanet, Ain Salah and El Golea.

Hours are usually: 08.30 to 1300 and 1600 to 1700 Saturday, Sunday, Monday, Tuesday, Wednesday, but the morning session till 12.00 only, on Thursday. All banks are closed on Friday.

There is a foreign currency blackmarket in Algeria, but the risks of ruining a trip are too great to make it worthwhile. On entry to Algeria you have to fill in a currency declaration form. This must be retained and surrendered on departure from Algeria. Travellers cheques and foreign cash must be exchanged at BNA banks (and some hotels) only. It is essential to have the bank fill in the amount and stamp the form. If you cannot produce all the money you are supposed to have, at the frontier, your departure will be delayed by considerable haggling and may involve the police. Many Customs posts are able to exchange foreign cash, (especially Deutsche Marks, French and Swiss Francs) but not travellers cheques, for the purpose of motor vehicle insurance (see Chapter on Vehicle Documents).

Foreign tourists are allowed to bring in and out of Algeria up to 50 Dinars in cash. In fact, Algerian dinars can be bought at a very favourable rate from major banks in Europe. A big saving on holiday expenses can be made by smuggling in more than 50 DA. However, the risk is considerable and the decision to do it a personal one.

Recently it became compulsory for tourists entering the country (other than by air) to change 1,000 dinars' worth of foreign currency per person at the frontier. This could make a visit to Algeria quite expensive, especially if there were more than two people travelling in the one vehicle and only transiting across to Niger or Mali in only two or three days.

If you have a lot of spare dinars when you leave the country, bank officials at the frontier (e.g. near Oujda, and the Oran and Algiers ferry terminals) can exchange some of them for foreign currency, on the basis of a sliding scale depending on how long you have been in Algeria.

In Britain, as in France, Netherlands, Belgium and Germany, the National Girobank has recently extended its 'Postcheque' service to include Algeria. People with a National Girobank current account (i.e. cheque account) and a cheque guarantee card, may obtain books of five Postcheques. Each cheque can then be used at post offices in other reciprocating countries to draw local currency of up to the equivalent of fifty British pounds. Two cheques can be cashed each day. There is no charge at the point of exchange but one's account in Britain is debited fifty pence for each cheque cashed. This service now includes Algeria but it may be difficult to use at remote Saharan post-offices.

Libya

Up to 20 dinars may be imported and exported. There is no restriction on the amount of foreign currency exported by visitors, provided that it was declared on arrival.

Mali

There is no restriction on the importation of Mali francs or foreign currency provided they are declared on entry. There are banks at Bamako, Mopti and now at Gao. At the start of 1985, Mali joined the CFA West African currency zone and thus started using CFA francs.
(Note: 100 CFA francs = 200 Mali francs = 2 French francs. This is a fixed rate which does not fluctuate with international money markets.)

Mauritania

The ougiya is equal to 5CFA on a fixed rate.

Niger and Burkina Faso

As with most former French African countries, Niger and Burkina Faso (formerly Upper Volta) are members of the ''Communauté Financière d'Afrique''. There is no restriction on taking in foreign currency and CFA francs. In fact, CFA francs can usually be bought at a slightly more favourable rate in Europe, except in France where the rate is fixed at 50 CFA to 1 French Franc.

If travelling into Niger via Djanet or Libya, it is essential to take at least sufficient CFA francs to buy fuel at Dirkou or Bilma.

If leaving Niger for Algeria, dinars can be bought at about half the official rate in Agadez, but there are risks involved.

Both old and new CFA notes are in circulation.

Two banks operate in Niger and Burkina Faso: the BDRN and BIAO. In Ouagadougou, Bobo Dioulasso, Niamey, Zinder and Tahoua there are branches of both, but only one of the two at Birni N'Konni, Tahoua, Maradi and Agadez.

Nigeria

Nigeria's Central Bank will not repatriate its own currency. It is illegal to import or export naira. All foreign exchange dealings must be through a bank. Consequently, there is a lucrative black market for foreign cash and travellers cheques within Nigeria among Nigerians and expatriates. In an attempt to stem the black market, tourists are required to declare all their foreign currency, on arrival and departure. Any difference must be accounted for by receipts from banks.

Nigerian Customs are very strict about the currency regulations and it is as well to ensure that your personal currency documents are in order. Make sure that Customs give you a currency declaration on arrival.

Outside Nigeria, naira can be bought from some banks and other sources for much less than the official exchange rate, especially in neighbouring countries and in cities like London, Beirut and Cairo. In Zinder, street money-changers are not hard to find. They also buy your surplus naira at a shocking rate. When buying naira outside Nigeria ensure the notes you buy are the current issue.

Unfortunately, there are no facilities for changing surplus naira back into foreign currency before leaving Nigeria.

Transmission of Funds

If you find yourself stranded without sufficient money, it can be sent to you, from your home country, in several ways.

1. Through Banks
You can write to your bank and have them send you a bank draft. This involves using the mail system. Therefore, post two letters several days apart to make sure that at least one arrives safely. Your bank then posts a draft (just like a cheque) to you (ask for it to be sent registered airmail) in the currency you specify. Remember that usually the banks in the country you are visiting will exchange your draft only for local currency.

Alternatively, you could try to rely on banks using their telex systems. This would only really be helpful in sophisticated places like Niamey, Tunis or Abidjan. Even then, you could normally only do it if your bank has direct links with the bank in the country you are visiting (e.g. BIAO in West Africa has close links with the Banque Nationale de Paris in France; Union Bank of Nigeria is linked to Barclays Bank in Britain). All this of course depends on whether the telex system is functioning at the time.

Finally, you could use the American Express system. Money is sent by telegram from one American Express office overseas to an American Express office in the country you are visiting. This is a very expensive but reliable method, but still relies on the mail system to instruct the bank. Moreover, the money is always paid out in local currency, and in the Saharan area there are no American Express offices, the nearest ones being at Douala, Lagos, Cotonou, Dakar, Tunis, Tangier, Rabat, Casablanca, Cairo, Tripoli and Nairobi.

2. Through the Post Office
Between France and French speaking West Africa is a good cable money order system ('mandats'). You can have money sent from a small town in France to Agadez Post Office in five days. Registered letters (in French, 'recommandé') are suitable for only small amounts, but are reliable.

Travellers Cheques and Cash

Generally, in all countries in the Saharan area, travellers cheques can be cashed only in banks. It is therefore advisable to take a considerable amount in well known currencies and in cash, e.g. French and Swiss francs, Deutsche marks, and U.S. dollars, (though the latter has been unstable in the last few years).

However, for safety reasons the bulk of your money should be in travellers cheques preferably in a strong currency like Swiss francs, or Deutsche marks.

Mail

There are satisfactory Poste Restante services in the following towns: Niamey, Zinder, Agadez, Kano, Sokoto, Tamanrasset, Ghardaia, Djanet, and the big cities on the Mediterranean coast.

However, letters are frequently sorted according to the first letter of your name. Ask people writing to you not to use your full first name, as this will be confused with your surname. Similarly, avoid the use of a title like Mr., Mrs., Miss, or Ms. Here is an example:

Bloggs, J.
Poste Restante,
Niamey,
Republique du Niger.

It is preferable to write your name thus on a piece of paper and hand this to the post office clerk, when collecting mail.

In some cases mail is kept for only a few weeks and then returned or even destroyed. So people writing to you must know fairly accurately when you will arrive.

American Express operate clients' mail services at all their offices. To use this you must know the addresses of the different branches, and have each envelope labelled 'Clients Mail'. The advantage of this service is that mail will be returned if it is not collected.

Some nationalities have diplomatic legations which will receive and hold their nationals' mail. Australians are among those that don't.

14
Vehicle Documents

Ownership

Essential: Any ownership papers, or any official document which states not only that you are the owner but also the country of registration, the registration number, chassis and engine numbers. In Britain this is known as a 'Log Book'; in France, Algeria, Tunisia, Niger, as a 'Carte Gris'; and in Nigeria as a 'Motor Registration Book'. For Australian registered vehicles the annual state 'Certificate of Registration' is quite valid, but you should type in bold letters across the top the word 'AUSTRALIA'. Similarly with a New Zealand registered vehicle, the 'Certificate of Registration' should have 'NEW ZEALAND' typed across the top. Officials in Saharan countries don't know of the existence of Australia or New Zealand, let alone Queensland or Wellington.

If the vehicle is borrowed, or a hired one, you must have a letter of authority to use it, typed and with at least one official looking stamp on it.

Carnet

Properly known as 'Carnet de passages en douane.' This is a booklet of tear-out pages issued for one year (renewable) by motoring associations in most countries (e.g. NRMA and RACQ in Australia, AA in New Zealand, AAA in U.S.A., ADAC and A.V.D. in Germany, A.A. and RAC in Britain). It enables one to take a car temporarily into a country without paying import duty or lodging a deposit with Customs. But motoring associations will issue them only if a bank guarantee is provided. The amount a bank has to guarantee varies with the age and type of the vehicle, and also with the countries you expect to take your car into. This can be very demanding on bank managers, e.g. for a 1974 Range Rover taken to Nigeria the British A.A. required a guarantee of £7,250 or 150% of its 1978 British market value, and the Carnet was limited to West Africa only. It would have been higher if Kenya, Egypt or South Africa had been on the itinerary.

In Britain there is a way around this by taking out an insurance indemnity policy with one of two insurance companies each nominated by the A.A. and RAC. The RAC's company is R.L. Davidson and Co. Ltd., (1 Devonshire Square, London, EC2M 4SY). Their premium is 10% of the guarantee required. The A.A.'s company is Alexander Howden Ltd., (22 Billiter Street London, EC3M 2SA); their premium is 3%. These fees are small for an old 1968 VW-Bus, but for a new Range Rover would be astronomical.

The Australian Automobile Association requires a bank guarantee amounting to 300% of the value of the vehicle, which could be AUS$30,000 for a VW Kombi and much more for a Range Rover.

If your vehicle is registered in New Zealand, a carnet could be easier to arrange. For example, the A.A. in Auckland issued a carnet with a 'world wide' validity to the owner of a 1973 VW-Camper for a bank guarantee of only NZ$6,000 (less than 100% of the car's market value), but it had to be (and was) New Zealand registered.

In Germany the ADAC will issue a carnet for a refundable deposit of 1000 DM and an administrative fee amounting to 180 DM. This carnet is valid for all Saharan countries requiring it, including Nigeria, and is also valid for India. However, the vehicle must be registered in Germany (this also includes oval tourist 'z' plates).

For Dutch-registered vehicles a carnet can be issued by the A.N.W.B. on receipt of a deposit of 100% of the current used car market value of the car or a bank guarantee.

The carnet works like this. On entry to, say, Nigeria, the right and left hand coupons of one page are signed, dated and stamped. The centre coupon is left untouched at this stage, but the right hand one is detached and retained by Customs. On leaving Nigeria, both remaining coupons are signed, dated and stamped, but the centre one is torn out and kept by Customs. It is essential that you ensure Customs do this properly. If you leave

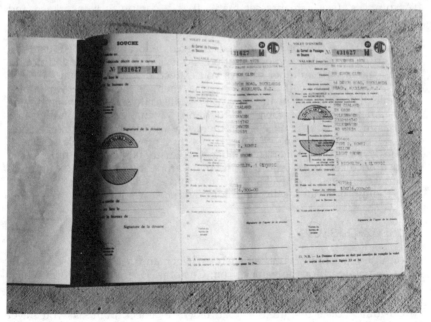

A 'Carnet de Passages en Douane' is like an international passport for the vehicle. Seen here opened to reveal the two coupons to be removed by Customs officials upon entering and leaving a country. Officials must also stamp the butt on the left each time a coupon is removed. Note: some Saharan countries do not require a 'Carnet'

a country with the centre coupon still in the carnet booklet you will be likely to lose much, or all, of the amount your bank has guaranteed for you.

Carnets are not required for Morocco, Algeria, Tunisia, Libya, or Niger, but are necessary for Nigeria. In fact, the Nigerians may not even issue a visa unless you have a carnet. Niger Republic officials may ask if you have one, and if you say you have one they will want to stamp it. But if you don't let them know you have one they will let you continue. If you enter Algeria from the south do not ask Customs to process your carnet. If you do, you will have great problems having the exit coupon accepted in the north.

If you sell your car in a country where you used your carnet on entry, Customs must sign, stamp and detach the centre coupon when import duty has been paid.

Insurance

Campbell Irvine Ltd., of 46 Earls Court Road, London W8 6EJ sell comprehensive and full third party insurance policies for limited periods (e.g. one or two months) that give coverage for Morocco, Algeria, Tunisia, Libya, Egypt, etc. but only as far as 20° latitude north. Coverage ceases south of this point. But this does give 'Green Card' cover for Europe, Morocco and Tunisia.

In addition there is compulsory frontier insurance for tourists entering Algeria. This is a third party personal liability insurance only. It is sold at all frontier posts in the north of Algeria, Adrar and Djanet, but at Tamanrasset it is up to you to go to the office of the 'Societé Algerienne d'Assurances' (see Tamanrasset map). It is a compulsory insurance and there are roadblocks in the north of the country where police check on insurance.

This insurance cannot be extended. A separate local insurance must then be taken out for a three month period. So it is important that you do not under-estimate the number of days you expect to stay in Algeria.

For Niger Republic, Mali and Nigeria there is no frontier insurance available. If you wish to insure, you will be able to do so only in major towns e.g. Niamey, Bamako, Zinder, Sokoto, Kano, Katsina, and only on the same basis as local residents. In Nigeria there are a great many insurance companies, and despite some of their names they provide a reliable service.

If on arrival at the Nigerian frontier, the Customs officials require to see an insurance certificate, show them your European Green Card and quote its serial numbers. This will satisfy them and enable them to let you pass, even though it is not legally valid for Nigeria.

Laissez-passer

Upon entry to some countries such as Niger and Mali a 'Laissez-passer' must be obtained for the vehicle from Customs. It is merely a form which states the details of the vehicle such as its numbers, make and name of owner. A small administrative fee is charged for it and it has to be shown to Customs, Police or Sureté at road blocks or check points as you travel through the country.

Resale

In Algeria, not only is import duty very high, but also a licence to permanently import the car is required, involving much bureaucracy and corridor walking.

Often one meets people in the Sahara with cars they hope to sell in West Africa, usually old Peugeots or VW-Buses. This used to be easy but there are pitfalls. For example, all the official paperwork that has to be chased from office to office over several weeks, and consequent accommodation costs can ruin you.

In Niger Republic it is now illegal to sell a temporarily imported vehicle unless the owner has been resident for two months. During 1978 the bottom dropped out of the used Peugeot and VW-Bus market in West African countries, partly as a result of world economic trends. Consequently prices have fallen to near European equivalents, even if you find a buyer, once you have paid the import duty. An exception to this is probably the Range Rover which has a Mercedes-like prestige.

From the point of view of import duty Nigeria can be one of the easiest countries, provided your vehicle fulfils certain conditions. All cars over 2500 cc are prohibited imports. Other cars have to have import licences and duty ranges from 50 to 200% depending on the engine size. However, the money realised from the sale of the vehicle, in Nigeria, cannot be exported, and the bureaucracy involved in paying the duty can take literally months. To many Westerners the system of 'dash' in Nigeria (small bribes to speed things along) is abhorrent, but it is a very effective system when handled in the right way. Importing a car therefore can be a very quick and simple matter if you hire a customs clearing agent who is small enough to know how to handle each official at each stage, e.g. Godwin of Eastern (O'seas) Agencies Ltd., 10 Fagge Road, P.M.B. 3251, Kano. (See Central map, Itinerary 22.)

Other Documents

Nigeria requires an International Driving Permit, and Customs will also ask to see an insurance certificate (it doesn't really matter about its validity or geographical coverage, so long as it has a number).

Algerian Customs issue a temporary vehicle importation permit on entry. This is valid usually for three months and **must** be surrendered on exit.

Unless it is obvious, do not admit to having travelled through Morocco, as this invites a very thorough time-consuming search of your vehicle (for hashish).

Some Niger officials ask to see an International Driving Permit.

Shipping from West Africa

Avoid Lagos and Port Harcourt as the congestion is extreme. There is a roll on/roll off ferry service from Dakar to Europe (see Chapter 28). It is also possible to ship your vehicle by ordinary cargo ship from Abidjan to France. Similarly, one can air-freight vehicles from Nigeria to Europe at very reasonable rates. (Airlines offer special concessions to fill empty freight planes on the return journey to Europe.)

Above all, when shipping a vehicle, watch it like a hawk. Fit extra locks to doors, and chains and padlocks to cupboard doors, and if it is a VW-Bus fit a makeshift plywood partition behind the front seats to seal off the rear section. Remove hub caps, mirrors, radios, etc.

Motor Vehicle Plates

The International Convention on Motor Traffic (1949) specified international signs or ovals to be fitted to the rear of vehicles visiting countries other than the original country of registration. These plates should **not** be used to indicate the nationality of the vehicle's occupants but the vehicle's country of registration. Thus, Americans travelling in Europe and the Sahara in a British registered vehicle with a USA oval sticker on the back are inviting trouble from the authorities. For this reason the authors, despite their own Australian nationality, have travelled in Europe and the Sahara at various times in vehicles with genuine international ovals that have included AUS, GB, NZ, and WAN. Police in some countries, such as Austria, Spain, Finland, Algeria, Tunisia, and Nigeria, have stopped the authors at various times to check on the validity of the international oval.

The following are international oval symbols for countries in the Sahara and West Africa:

Algeria	DZ	Libya	LAR
Benin	DY or RPB	Mali	RMM
Burkina Faso	HV	Mauritania	RIM
Cameroun	CAM	Morocco	MA
Chad	TCH	Niger	RN or NIG
Egypt	ET	Nigeria	WAN
Gambia	WAG	Senegal	SN
Ghana	GH	Sierra Leone	WAL
Guinea	RG	Sudan	SUD
Ivory Coast	RCI or CI	Togo	TG
Liberia	LB	Tunisia	TN

The following is information about some of the registration plates used in some Saharan countries:

Algeria — DZ
The final pair of numerals denotes the provincial or Wilaya code. Sometimes this is the final pair on the top line of a square plate.

01	Adrar	17	Djelfa
02	El Asnam	18	Djidjelli
03	Laghouat	19	Setif
04	Oum el Bouachi	20	Saida
05	Batna	21	Skikda
06	Bejaia	22	Sidi bel Abbes
07	Biskra	23	Annaba
08	Bechar	24	Guelma
09	Blida	25	Constantine
10	Bouira	26	Madea
11	Tamanrasset	27	Mostaganem
12	Tebessa	28	Msila
13	Tlemcen	29	Mascara
14	Tiaret	30	Ouargla
15	Tizi Ouzou	31	Oran
16	Algiers		

Normally these plates are black numerals on a white or yellow reflective background. Temporary tourist plates have red numerals on a white background. Diplomatic and consular plates are black on a green background. Plates of vehicles belonging to foreign technical personnel are yellow on blue, though white numerals on a green background are also used.

Mali — RMM
Normal plates are white on black, government plates are black on red, diplomatic are black on green and temporary tourist plates are red on white.

Egypt — ET
Egyptian plates are in both Arabic and Roman script. All temporarily imported vehicles must carry Egyptian temporary tourist plates. These are issued by customs on arrival at the border or a port. All plates indicate a code for the class of vehicle (e.g. PRIVE = private cars, TAX = taxis, CH = temporary tourist) and a code for the place of issue:

ALX := Alexandria		GZ = Giza	
ASN = Aswan		IS = Ismailya	
C = Cairo		SIN = Sinai	

Libya — LAR
Plates are technically in both Arabic and Roman script but nowadays more usually in Arabic only.
White on black = motorcycles and cars
White on blue = taxis, buses and temporary tourists
White on green = diplomatic
Black on white = government
Black on yellow = trucks

Morocco — MA
Normal plates are white numerals on a black background and Al Maghreb in Arabic. Foreign residents (e.g. US military personnel) have black on yellow. Diplomatic plates are white on blue.

Niger — NIG or RN
French style plates with white on black and two letters indicating the town or region:

AZ = Agadez	NY = Niamey	
DO = Dosso	TA = Tahoua	
MI = Maradi	ZR = Zinder	

Nigeria — WAN
Usually black number plates with white letters and numerals. There are two series: old and new, but in each the letters indicate the town of registration:

Some of the old series:	
Lagos	LA to LZ LAA to LAZ
Kano	K,KN,KNB,KNC,KNF
Kaduna	KA,KAB,KAD
Katsina	KT
Sokoto	S,SO,SK
Zaria	Z,ZA
Gusau	G,GS,GSA
Argungu	A
BirninKebbi	B,BK
Jos	PL,BP,BY,BYA

Some of the new series:	Lagos	LA	numerals	A
	Kano	KN	"	K
	Kaduna	KD	"	K
	Katsina	KD	"	T
	Sokoto	SO	"	SA
	Zaria	KD	"	Z
	Gusau	SO	"	G
	Argungu	SO	"	A
	BirninKebbi	SO	"	B
	Jos	PL	"	J

Senegal — SN
French style plates with white on black for the normal series. Diplomatic plates are black on green. Foreign technical personnel are red on white. The final numeral indicates the district:

1 = Dakar
2 = Casamance
3 = Diourbel
4 = St. Louis

5 = Senegal oriental
6 = Sine Saloum
7 = Thies

Tunisia — TN
The normal series are usually black with white lettering and do not indicate the district or town. Diplomatic, foreign technical personnel, and temporary tourist plates are black on white. On all plates 'Tunisia' is included in Arabic.

15
Les Raids et Les Rallyes

The first vehicular incursions into and across the Sahara earlier this century were very major expeditions. Being generally exceptionally well prepared for, success was almost guaranteed. The first major vehicle expedition into the centre of the desert was a Fiat one in 1920. Led by a General Naville, the 28 Fiat trucks covered the 3,000 kilometres from Algiers to Tamanrasset and back in only 28 days. Its progress across the desert went as smoothly and efficiently as a well-planned military operation. The expedition carried 70 men and 40 tonnes of equipment — which also included three portable 32 metre high (100 ft) radio masts.

The first true crossing of the Sahara was a Citroen expedition lead by Haardt and Audouin-Debreuil in 1922-1923 using five special half-track trucks or 'autochenilles'. At each stage provisions and fuel were waiting for the team. The crew wore riding boots, jodhpurs, sports jackets, ties and pith helmets. They were also armed with rifles — the French Foreign Legion had still not yet fully subdued the Touaregs and 'rezzous' or raiding parties still harassed desert travellers. In addition, the Citroen team carried the first trans-Saharan mail on their 20 day crossing. This is one third of the time it would have taken to do the same journey by camel.

In 1923 a Renault expedition (officially the Mission Gradis-Estienne) of seven men and three cars each with six dual wheels (4x6) travelled from Colomb-Bechar across the Tanezrouft to Bourem on the Niger River near Gao in just seven days. They continued across the Niger to Cotonou on the coast. By this stage intense rivalry had developed between the two giant French car makers, each vying for the attention of the world's press for yet another spectacular transcontinental expedition.

Citroen stuck doggedly to its half-track technology while Renault promoted six wheels instead, and in 1924-1925 they mounted their Croisière Noire. Eight half-track Citroen trucks were used on a massive expedition of 20,000 km which crossed the Sahara via the Tanezrouft and then made its way through the Congo to East Africa, the Rhodesias, Cape Town and finished up in Madagascar. This expedition was re-enacted by a group of Frenchmen in three Peugeot-Dangel 4x4 cars during 1980-1981.

Later in the 1920s major crossings of the Sahara and the rest of Africa became fairly commonplace. In 1925-1926 a husband and wife team (M. et Mme. Delinguette and their mechanic) took eight months to travel all the

156

Vehicles of the 1922-1923 Haardt and Audouin-Dubreuil expedition encounter Touaregs south of Ain Salah. This was the first true crossing of the Sahara by motorised vehicles, in this case by half-track Citroen 'autochenilles' (Photo by courtesy of Andre Citroen S.A., Paris)

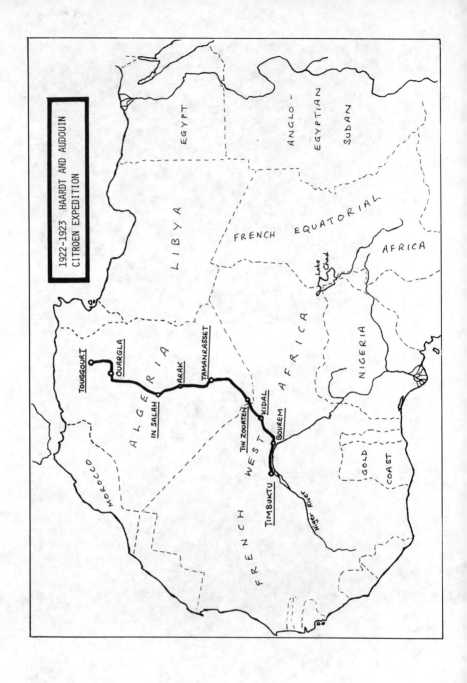

1922-1923 HAARDT AND AUDOUIN CITROEN EXPEDITION

EGYPT

ANGLO-EGYPTIAN SUDAN

LIBYA

FRENCH EQUATORIAL AFRICA

Lake Chad

NIGERIA

ALGERIA

TOUGGOURT
OUARGLA
IN SALAH
ARAK
TAMANRASSET
TIN ZOUATEN
KIDAL
BOUREM

FRENCH WEST AFRICA

MOROCCO

TIMBUKTU
Niger River

GOLD COAST

158

way to Cape Town.

The first solo crossing of the Sahara by car was by George Estienne in 1926 in a 6cv Renault touring car. He drove across the Tanezrouft to Bamako and back to the Mediterranean in just 36 days. His car was similar to the 1927 model Renault KZ Gazelle, which successfully took part in the 1979 and 1980 Paris-Dakar Rallies driven by Philippe Hayat.

The 1930s and 1940s saw a decline in interest in these major 'raids' into Africa. The world was pre-occupied with depression and war. Nevertheless, war was the stimulus for a most impressive trans-Saharan expedition. In 1941 Lt.-Colonel Leclerc set out north from Fort Lamy on the shores of Lake Chad with a column of 400 Free-French and British troops and 55 battered old trucks. They passed through Faya Largeau to the major Italian fortress at Kufra in southern Libya — a distance of some 2,000 km across desert which is 'unknown' even today. They then captured the fortress in spite of being out-numbered two to one. Leclerc's small band continued their expedition across the Sahara in a series of Touareg-like 'rezzous' or raids on the Italians. Ultimately they joined up with the British and Montgomery's Eighth Army at Tripoli — an amazing feat. They literally had to fight their way, out-numbered, for 4,000 km across the world's largest and most arid desert. Moreover, they had almost no logistical support from their base in Chad, had to use a motley collection of obsolete trucks and jeeps and they were always greatly outnumbered by their foes. Lt.-Colonel Leclerc (actually Philippe de Hauteclocque) led an expedition that far outshines any other in the Sahara this century in terms of its achievements against such odds (see Henry Maude, **Out of the Sand** 1966, Odhams, London.).

It should be noted, too, that Leclerc was accompanied by groups of British and New Zealand troops from Cairo. These men, known as the Long Range Desert Group (or L.R.D.G.), were led by Major (later Brigadier) R.A. Bagnold and in 1940-1941 they specialised in secret motorised forays deep into Italian controlled Libya. These involved crossing the vast Western Desert, Kalansho and Rebiana Sand Seas, areas never before crossed by man. Moreover, they did so in two wheel drive Chevrolet trucks (see W.B. Kennedy-Shaw, **Long Range Desert Group,** 1945, Collins, London). Bagnold, a geologist based in Cairo, carried out pioneering research into the physics of sand movement. During the 1920s and 1930s he had conducted many motorised research expeditions into the vast lunar landscape of western and southern Egypt, northern Sudan and southern Libya. Forty years later, in 1978, a joint Egyptian-American Universities expedition found Bagnold's vehicle tracks and campsites in the Jebel Uweinat and Gilf Kebir areas unmarked by the elements and time, as if they were made the previous day.

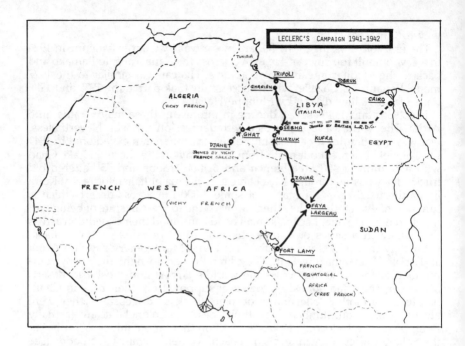

The development of commercial rallies

In the 1950s interest in the Sahara returned. In 1950 a rally organised by a French group called Les Amis du Sahara, the French magazine *L'Action Automobile* and the Touring Club de France set out from Algiers to Cape Town, Like the early Redex Round Australia Trials and the East African (or Coronation) Safaris, it attracted a mixed group of essentially amateur adventurers in very standard street cars — often just the family car was used. In fact it was won by a Delahaye Jeep and in this and later trans-African rallies in 1953 and 1959 vehicles like the Peugeot 203 and Volkswagen Beetle quickly established a reputation for strength and reliability.

By 1961 professional drivers began to dominate. The law sponsored Rallye Mediterranée — Le Cap saw intense competition between the Mercedes and Citroen factory teams who employed famous grand prix drivers like Olivier Gendebien, Paul Frere, Karl Kling and Lucien Bianchi. Indeed, between Ain Guezzam and Agadez across open sandy desert with no marked road or track Karl Kling's Mercedes 220 averaged just over 120 km/h and at times was cruising at 160 km/h! However, with a guerrilla war in Algeria, chaos in the Congo and other political problems in the new countries of Africa, this was the last attempt at a trans-African rally. Instead, the professionals and the massive factory involvement were diverted to more localised events like the East African Safari and the Bandama Rally (in Ivory Coast) which had become highly sophisticated media events.

The amateur adventurer didn't have much opportunity until the 1974 London-Kano-Munich World Cup Rally. Yet the trans-Saharan sections proved so tough that of 71 starters only five cars finished the rally: a Citroen DS23 followed by three Peugeot 504s, and a Jeep CJ-6 was fifth. Yet, the Saharan sections were along regular and commonly used tourist pistes. The winning Citroen DS23 was driven by amateurs who were veterans of the round Australia trials of the 1950s: Andre Welinski, Ken Tubman and Jim

160

Two-wheel drive Chevrolet trucks of the British Long Range Desert Group outside Siwa Oasis in Egypt during 1942. The L.R.D.G. carried out many courageous raids against the Italians and Germans hundreds of kilometres behind enemy lines deep into Libya across vast areas of dunes in uncharted sand seas. Part of the L.R.D.G. joined up with Col. Leclerc's Free-French forces in a successful campaign right across the Sahara from Chad to Tripoli (Photo by courtesy of the Imperial War Museum)

Reddiex. They carried their own tools, spare parts and equipment with them and were not backed up by truckloads of mechanics and equipment from the factory.

In December 1975 the first of the French trans-Saharan rallies took place: the Cote d'Ivoire — Cote d'Azur, from Abidjan to Nice. It was followed by another in December 1976 which even took vehicles across the Ténéré from Agadez into Libya. By this time marathons and long distance rallies were starting to become big business for promotional entrepreneurs.

In December 1978 Thierry Sabine, a veteran of the Cote d'Ivoire-Cote d'Azur rallies, Le Mans 24 Hours, and a former marketing and public relations student, organised the first Paris-Dakar Rally. Promoted by a soft-drink manufacturer, this was the first of a series of spectacular promotional extravagances. Nominally open to the rank amateur, they attracted vehicle and component manufacturers to such an extent that the costs of a realistically competitive vehicle became enormous. The publicity to be gained from a car's, motorcycle's or truck's victory in the rally meant that manufacturers competed in an orgy of spending on development and team preparation.

Suddenly, western promotional circuses have been unleashed on the simple and poverty-stricken villagers and nomads of the Sahara and Sahel. These are simple people who could never hope to buy a Range Rover or a Yamaha 500XT. Yet the harshness of their environment is exploited quite

161

callously as droves of swashbuckling mechanics, journalists, television film crews, tourists and competitors descend upon villagers en route. It seems cruel to inflict some of the most extrovert and self-interested people in our western society upon these simple, honest but naive and gullible people. Surprisingly, some quite left-wing Saharan governments openly collaborate in the organisation of these events. Occasionally, villagers have been killed by rally cars (as in 1982).

With the intense competition between manufacturers, these rallies no longer present much opportunity for the amateur — the Paris-Dakar is big business. Nevertheless, the Paris-Dakar has become a sort of proving ground for new ideas and products. The four wheel drive Renault R20 with its turbo-charged engine which won the 1982 event was superb technologically. Yet, just because a Renault R20 won, it does not follow that one should prefer it to a Land Rover, a Land Cruiser, a VW Kombi or a Citroen 2CV when choosing a suitable expedition vehicle. On the contrary, a once-off win for so sophisticated a car cannot prove a vehicle's suitability, no matter how much manufacturers may use this for advertising. However, the consistent high placings by Yamaha 500XT motorcycles in so many events must prove something.

The Paris-Dakar Rally has become what is probably the toughest rally in the world. Lasting over 20 days and across 10,000 km of Saharan and Sahelian pistes it is a major test of stamina and endurance for men and vehicles alike. In the 1982 event, the under 10 tonne truck class was won by Georges Groine, Thierry de Salieu and Bernard Malferiol in a Mercedes Unimog U1700 (above). They repeated their success in 1983 in a 4x4 Mercedes 1936AK truck (Photo by courtesy of Daimler-Benz A.G)

Results in the First Eight Paris-Dakar Rallies
● 1979

All vehicle categories mixed
1. Neveu, Yamaha 500XT
2. Comte, Yamaha 500XT
3. Vassard, Honda XR500
4. Genestier, Range Rover

● 1980

Cars
1. Kotulinsky/Luffelman, VW Iltis 4x4
2. Zanirdi/Colesse, VW Iltis 4x4
3. Marreau/Marreau, Renault R4-Sinpar 4x4

Motorcycles
1. Neveu, Yamaha 500XT
2. Merel, Yamaha 500XT
3. Pineau, Yamaha 500XT

Trucks
1. Atouat/Boukrif/Kaoula, Sonacome 6x6
2. Heu/Delobel/Versino, M.A.N. 14T 6x6
3. Bouzid/Daid/Mekhelef, Sonacome 6x6

● 1981

Cars
1. Metge/Girou, Range Rover 4x4
2. Cotel/Corbetta, Volkswagen-PRV 4x2
3. Briavoine/Deliaire, Lada Niva 4x4

Motorcycles
1. Auriol, BMW R80/GS
2. Bacou, Yamaha 500XT
3. Merel, Yamaha 500XT

Trucks
1. Villette/Gabrelle/Voillereau, ALM Acmat 4x4
2. Briy/SalouPau, Ford Transcontinental 6x6
3. Groine/deSavlieu/Malferiol, Mercedes Unimog U1700 4x4

● 1982

Cars
1. Marreau/Marreau, Renault R20 Sinpar 4x4
2. Briavione/Deliaire, Lada Niva 4x4
3. Jaussaud/Briere, Mercedes Gelandewagen 280GE 4x4

Motorcycles (over 500cm3)
1. Neveu, Honda 550XR

Motorcycles (under 500cm3)
1. Maitrot, Honda 250XR

Trucks (under 10 tonnes)
1. Groine/Saulieu/Malferiol, Mercedes Unimog U1700 4x4
2. Laleu/Langlois, Mercedes Unimog U1300 4x4
3. Villette/Gabrelle/Voilereau, Acmat ALM 4x4

Trucks (over 10 tonnes)
1. de Rooy/Straetmans, DAF N2800 6x6
2. Thijssen/Duysters, DAF N2800 6x6
3. Avoyne/Landais, Leyland Marathon

● 1983

There were many different classes but first into Dakar among the cars, motorcycles and trucks were:

Cars
1. Ickx/Brasseur, Mercedes Gelandewagen 280GE 4x4

2. Trossat, Lada Niva 4x4
3. Metge/Girou, Range Rover 4x4
Motorcycles
1. Auriol, BMW R80 GS
2. Drobecq, Honda 550 XR
3. Joineau, Suzuki DR 500
Trucks
1. Groine/Saulieu/Malferiol, Mercedes 1936 AK 4x4
2. de Rooy/Rogenband/Perry, DAF 3300 6x6
3. Avoyne/Deblandre/Dierl, MAN 20280 6x6
Trucks (under 10 tonnes)
1. Henriksson/Bernhardsson, Volvo C3 4x4
● 1984
Cars
1. Metge/Ickx/Kussmaul, Porsche 911 4x4
2. Zaniroli, Range Rover 4x4
3. Cowan, Mitsubishi Pajero 4x4
Motorcycles
1. Rahier, BMW R100
2. Auriol, BMW R100
3. Vassard, Honda XLR 600
Trucks
1. Laleu/Durce, Mercedes-Benz 1936 AK 6x6
2. Bonera/Grass, Mercedes-Benz Unimog U1700 4x4
3. Gabrelle/Voillerau, MAN 20 320 8x8
● 1985
Cars
1. Zaniroli/Da Silva, Mitsubishi Pajero 4x4
2. Cowan/Syer, Mitsubishi Pajero 4x4
3. Fougerouse/Jacquemar, Toyota FJ60
Motorcycles
1. Rahier, BMW R100
2. Olivier, Yamaha XT 600
3. Picco, Yamaha XT 600
Trucks
1. Capito/Capito, Mercedes-Benz Unimog U1700 4x4
2. De Rooy/de Saulieu, DAF F330 4x4
3. Strohmann/Capito, Mercedes-Benz Unimog U1700 4x4
● 1986
Cars
1. Metge/Lemoyne, Porsche 959 4x4
2. Ickx/Brasseur, Porsche 959 4x4
3. Rigal/Maingret, Mitsubishi Pajero 4x4
Motorcycles
1. Neveu, Honda NXR 750
2. Lalay, Honda NXR 750
3. Balestrieri, Honda NXR 750

The 1986 event was brought to a total stop for 24 hours at Gourma Rahrous in Mali when it was learned with torment and sadness that the organiser and driving force behind every Paris-Dakar to date, Thierry Sabine, had been killed. During a search for lost competitors, his helicopter crashed into a sand dune killing all five people on board instantly.

1984 was the first time that the winning car arrived at Dakar before the leading motorcycles. In the last three Paris-Dakars it took the winning vehicles twenty days to complete the 10,000 kilometres of the rally. Taking into account the period of over 24 hours used up to cross the Mediterranean by ferry, this has meant that distances of over 550 km per day had to be maintained. Thus in 1982, for example, the winning motorcyclists had to keep up speeds of close to 160 km/h (100 mph) in the sand and rocks of the section between Tit and Timeiaouine in southern Algeria: an incredible pace in those conditions and sheer torture for men and their machines. With the speeds and intense competition involved it is little wonder that in the 1982 event three people were killed (a bystander, a competitor and a journalist).

In 1983, a total of 389 vehicles set out from Paris. The 10,000 kilometres over twenty days proved so tough and punishing for men and their machines that only 60 vehicles managed to cross the finishing line at Dakar. The people who win these races are supermen with endurance and stamina derived only from a long term dedication to winning. The Paris-Dakar makes the American Baja 1000 and Mint off-road races look like week-end picnics.

For those interested in warm-up events just prior to the Paris-Dakar, there are the Paris-Tunis Rally (long sections in the Tunisian Sahara) and the Rallye d'Algerie (from Algiers to Tamanrasset). These rallies are held in October and November each year and organised by the Touring Club de France and the Federation Automobile Algerienne respectively.

The lateral routes

Most rallies and expeditions across the Sahara have tended to make north-south or south-north crossings. However, an east-west or west-east crossing not only involves travelling two and a half times the north-south distance but also requires that one travel along very few established pistes. In fact, for most of the distance in any lateral crossing one has to blaze one's own trail intersecting the main pistes only briefly. Thus, the Sahara has never been crossed by motorised vehicle from east to west and only twice from west to east. Until 1989, it had never been crossed in either direction

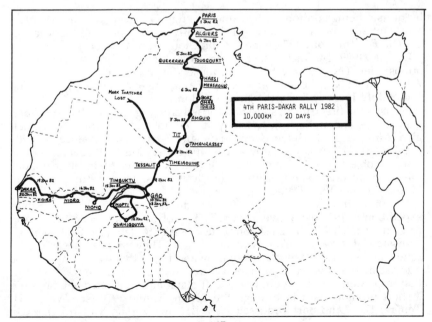

The victorious works BMW motorcycle team for the 1984 Paris-Dakar Rally together with one of their 980 cm³ BMW R 100 enduro bikes. From left to right: Raymond Loizeux, Gaston Rahier (winning motorcycle), Hubert Auriol (second motorcycle and winner of the 1981 and 1983 events also on a BMW) Note the large six-wheel drive MAN seven tonne support truck which accompanied them with mechanics, tools, spare parts, lubricants and fuel (Photo by courtesy of BMW AG Presse, Munchen)

by human beings on foot or by camel, though Geoffrey Moorhouse made a valliant attempt in 1973 in which he nearly lost his life (see Moorhouse, G. **The Fearful Void** 1974, Hodder and Stoughton, London.).

During 1989 Michael Asher and Mariantonietta Peru achieved the impossible! They vindicated Moorhouse's courage and did walk the 7,245km from Nouakchott to the Nile, an amazing feat. (See Asher, M. **The Impossible Journey** 1990, Penguin, London.)

Perhaps the first true west-east motorised crossing was the 1964-1965 Belgian Trans-Saharan Expedition led by M. Petiniot and sponsored by the Belgian Ministries of Defence and Foreign Affairs (see **Nature** Vol.209 Jan 8 1966). This was primarily a scientific expedition with several serious research objectives. With a team of twelve men in three Mercedes Unimogs they kept to established pistes as much as possible by setting out from Morocco rather than Dakar.

The other true west-east crossing was the Saviem Croisière des Sables expedition in 1977 using five Saviem TP3 and two Saviem SM8 four wheel drive trucks. This is the most complete crossing to date (see Gallissian, C. **Croissière des Sables** 1977 Arthaud, Paris). They pioneered some new routes and erected a few balises but, by and large, this was a promotional exercise by the Saviem truck manufacturer. At the time there was competition from Mercedes Benz but this didn't materialise until two Unimogs did a short promotional trip through the Ténéré in mid-1978 (see Weyer, H. **Ténéré, Das Land dort Draussen** 1979, Badenia Verlag, Karlsruhe).

166

The four-wheel drive air-cooled Porsche 911 car that won the 1984 Paris-Dakar Rally driven by Rene Metge and Dominique Lemoyne travelled at speeds in excess of 180 km/h during some open desert sections. Three such technologically superb but specially constructed and very expensive cars from the Porsche factory were supported by a team of mechanics in two accompanying eight wheel drive MAN ten tonne trucks loaded with spare parts and other equipment. Other manufacturers provided similar support for their vehicles in this rally (Photograph by courtesy of Werkfoto Porsche, Stuttgart)

Another major west-east expedition was a British Joint Services one led by Tom Sheppard in 1975. Not a true Sahara crossing because it made extensive use of made up roads in areas well to the south of the desert in Niger, Nigeria, Chad and the Sudan, it nevertheless did pioneer a crossing of the Mauritanian Empty Quarter (Majabet el Koubra). Using four 1-tonne V8 Land Rovers, there were several scientific objectives as well as a military training role and the proving of a then new design of Land Rover (see **Geographical Journal** Vol 142, Part 2, July 1976).

With the Sahara occupying an area greater than Australia or the United States (excluding Alaska) and with this area being the most arid on earth (all of it receiving less than 100mm of rain a year), it is no wonder that its full width has been crossed by so few. Even the Antarctic has been crossed more times. Perhaps the Sahara is the last great challenge left on the earth's surface for man. It will be a remarkable occasion when a man finally walks across, west to east or vice versa.

Finally, probably the most important vehicle expeditions into the Sahara were the two Berliet missions in 1959-1960. Sponsored jointly by the Societé des Automobiles, M. Berliet, the University of Algiers and the Museum of Ethnography and Prehistory at Bardo (Algiers), they not only pioneered new pistes in the Ténéré and Tibesti regions but they conducted research on a scale hitherto unknown. They used nine six-wheel drive Berliet trucks, five Land-Rovers and a Bell helicopter. Details of their fascinating research,

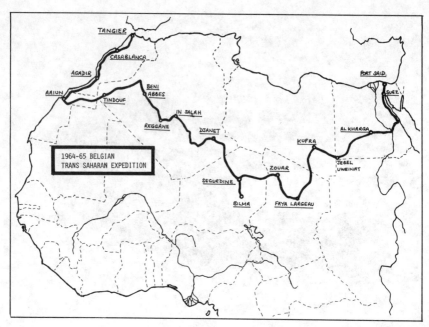

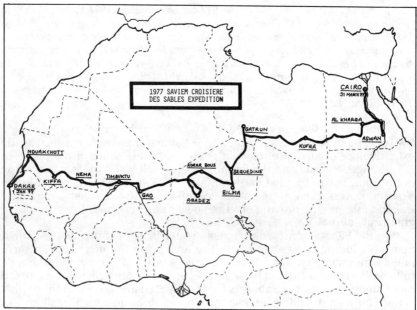

especially into Saharan prehistory, can be found in Hugot, H.J. **Missions Berliet Ténéré et Tchad,** 1962, Arts et Metiers Graphiques, Paris. Anyone intending to travel in the Ténéré would be well advised to track down a copy of this book.

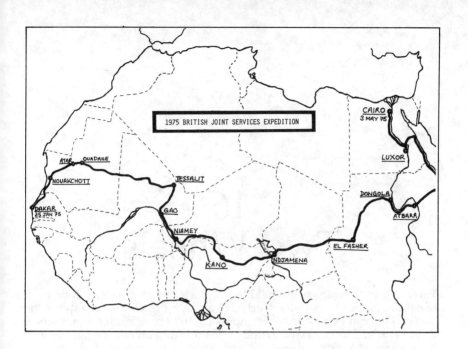

16
Two Wheels

Travelling in the Sahara by trail bike, and a support vehicle, can be most rewarding. One can park the truck, or van, take off, and really explore the desert. One can go places either impossible to impractical for a four wheel drive vehicle. One can explore, find prehistoric rock art never before viewed by modern man, visit villages and wells far from the beaten track, and find places of magnificent beauty and solitude. With this type of versatility and independence, a whole new world of Saharan travel opens up.

A real drawback is the limited range and load capacity of a trail bike. A support vehicle large enough to carry fuel, spares, and possibly even the motorcycles themselves, is essential. This adds tremendously to the overall running costs of trail bike travel in the Sahara, and also requires a big capital outlay on a suitable support vehicle.

One way around this support vehicle problem is to take an Enduro bike. These have nearly the 'go anywhere' versatility of trail bikes and yet they are built for long distance rough track racing without a support vehicle.

However, to take an Enduro bike across the Sahara, some modifications are vital. An enlarged fuel tank has to replace the existing one. It has to be especially made and should be able to hold at least 30 litres. A carrier rack has to be especially constructed to carry not only personal gear like sleeping bag, cooking implements, food, clothing, spare parts, tools, spare oil, etc. but also 30 litres of petrol, 20 litres of water, and two spare tyres. The petrol and water has to be carried in steel jerrycans. All told, this is quite a weight, but every bit of this fuel, plus what is in the tank, would be needed between Tamanrasset and Agadez.

The following is a brief description of just some of the many potentially suitable motorcycles:

Yamaha 500 XT
In many ways an ideal vehicle for a trans-Saharan journey, it has a big four stroke single cylinder 500cm^3 motor with long stroke characteristics that, while producing only a modest 29kW, give it tremendous low r.p.m. torque. It is strong and simple: built to be reliable rather than sophisticated. Its simplicity makes major repairs en route a possibility for the rider without professional mechanical training. Unladen it weighs 145kg.

The latest version, marketed as the XT600 'Ténéré', has the Yamaha

'Monoshock' single shock absorber rear suspension and is fitted with a large 30 litre fuel tank giving a range of about 500 km.

BMW R80GS
A powerful and fast bike with the same flat twin four stroke 980cm³ motor that powers the BMW 100RT road bike but detuned for a leisurely unstressed 44kW and an excellent torque range. In true BMW fashion it has a drive shaft. At 175kg unladen, it is a heavy bike for this size.

Honda XR500
A single cylinder four stroke 550cm³ motor developing merely 29kW, it is fast and reliable. Unladen it weighs only 140kg.

Smaller engined motorcycles like the Honda 250XR, Husqvana 250, Yamaha 250XT and DT175, KTM 240, and Kawasaki KDX175 are equally suitable. However, preference should be given to choosing larger engined bikes because with the massive loads that have to be carried, often through deep sand for long distances, there is a need to minimise stress in order to achieve long term reliability. There is no breakdown service or repair shop around the next corner.

It should be pointed out that while 'Enduro' bikes like those already mentioned are most suitable, the availability of spare parts especially in Saharan and Sahel countries is likely to be non-existent. In these countries, generally only small street 50cm³, 90cm³ and 125cm³ Japanese bikes are sold. The highly specialised components of an Enduro bike like shock absorbers, chains, forks, wheels, spokes, tyres, etc. are just not available. Makes like BMW, MotoGuzzi, Husqvarna, KTM and Ossa are completely unknown.

Travelling on two wheels puts you very close to the elements especially the wind, the dust and the sun with the resulting dangers of sunburn, dehydration, salt loss and heat exhaustion or even heat hyperpyrexia.

A well equipped Yamaha Enduro bike at Agadez. Note the enlarged fuel tank and the heavy load the bike has to carry

Particularly on the fringes of the desert, there is a continual danger of hitting a startled camel, a scatter-brained sheep or a perverse donkey. This in turn may bring you into volatile contact with local people. On two wheels you are more vulnerable to hostile villagers, aggressive truck drivers or crowds of cheeky urchins. It takes a special kind of person to travel on two wheels and yet keep his cool at all times.

The rider must pay attention to servicing details that maintain the bike's reliability. Timing is crucial to prevent overheating, and frequent attention to the air cleaner is vital. Similarly, a frequent check must be made on spokes, (e.g. every evening).

The bike has to carry its rider and all the load over terrible corrrugations, across feche feche, and through deep sandy ruts. Power and speed are essential (e.g. averaging 70-80km/h from Assamaka to Agadez). This rules out the small Enduro bikes (e.g. the Yamaha DT 175 even with its strong 'Monoshock' frame), and the rough conditions will make reliability and stability very difficult for a normal road bike.

Many normal road bikes do make it across the desert, and this is a tribute to the fortitude of their riders, but the Enduro bike is built for rough conditions. As such, it is capable of taking the rider off the beaten track, in conditions almost impossible for a road machine, and yet with the greatest of ease. In other words, the normal road bike is confined, really, to the main Hoggar route from In Salah, Tamanrasset, Agadez to Kano, and then with difficulty.

As considerable speed is needed to pilot the bike across some of the worst stretches of desert, quick judgement of conditions, and precise control are essential. In deep sand keep full power on but keep only very light control over the handlebars. Nevertheless, sooner or later the rider will come off. A bike loaded up for a desert crossing is extremely heavy. A fully laden BMW with 50 litres of petrol, 20 litres of water, spares, tools, clothes and camping gear could weigh in at up to 300kg! One person alone could die trapped under his fallen bike, unable to lift it off himself. This is the biggest danger of travelling by motorcycle. A partner on a similar bike is virtually essential if big risks are to be avoided.

With these kinds of loads particular attention should be paid to the preparation of the suspension. Not only should heavy duty shock absorbers be fitted (e.g. those by Ohlin or Koni) but their settings should be carefully monitored. This also applies to the Yamaha 'Monoshock' elements. To protect the chain against rapid wear caused by sand, an O-ring chain should be fitted. Many manufacturers make these (e.g. Chaingang); they have little rubber rings incorporated in each chain link which have a self cleaning function. Double thickness tubes (e.g. those made by Barum of Czechoslovakia) should be fitted because the constant pinching of the tubes on rocks causes tubes to deteriorate rapidly.

Pedal Power

Every year it seems people set out to pedal across Africa. The locals in the major oases that are strung out across the Sahara invariably consider these intrepid cyclists quite crazy if not demented. Generally, these rugged individualists do actually make it. However, crossing the Sahara, they virtually have to stick to the main Hoggar piste. Even so, it is impossible for a cyclist to carry enough water to last him for even one of the shorter hops between oases (e.g. the 400 or so kilometres between El Golea and Ain Salah). The cyclist has to resort to begging or borrowing water from passing motorists.

A cyclist will have to be prepared to carry many spare tubes and tyres and to spend many long hours pushing his heavily laden bike through deep sand in blazing hot sun or blinding dust laden wind: feats requiring quite considerable endurance and stubborn courage.

The bike should have a strong trustworthy frame (not butt welded) heavier than a racing bike's, and be fitted with steel rims (for strength and repairability). Spokes should be the best quality available (e.g. 12 gauge double butted) and built to only moderate tension, not tied and soldered. Spoke breakage has to be catered for. Thorn proof tyres should be used (solid foam type). The saddle should be the most comfortable leather one on the market. All gear should be carried in panniers but care should be taken not to carry too much weight up front as this makes steering sluggish, tiring and difficult to handle in sand. On the other hand, the rider should carry as little as possible — let the bicycle carry the load — but protect yourself from dust, wind and sun.

Isao Nakaburo of Hiroshima City, Japan, setting out across Africa and seen here in the terrible Tademait Plateau. Note that he is well protected from the elements and lets his bicycle carry the load

17
Choice of Vehicle

All too often, choice of vehicle is guided by subjective factors like style, image, and patriotism. The Sahara is no place for poseurs. Practical considerations like space, fuel economy, power, strength, budget, availability of parts and mechanical expertise, must dictate the final choice.

Two-wheel or four-wheel drive?

The main trans-Saharan pistes are easily crossed by sound well-maintained two-wheel drive vehicles like Citroen 2CVs, Volkswagen Kombis and Peugeot 504s. These pistes are the Tanezrouft from Adrar to Gao, the Hoggar route from Ain Salah to Tamanrasset, Agadez and Zinder, and the route from In Amenas to Illizi, Djanet and Tamanrasset. Nevertheless, sections of them are incredibly rough and quite a punishment for the vehicle. Getting bogged in sand several or many times is almost inevitable. Distances are immense between refuelling points and vast quantities of fuel, water, spares and recovery gear must be carried. (For example, it is 1500 km between Adrar and Gao.) The difficulties, dangers and logistic problems that have to be faced on these routes are considerably greater than travelling Australia's 'Gunbarrel Highway' and Birdsville Track or an overland trip through Asia (all of which the authors have done). Nevertheless, a sensible two-wheel drive vehicle should have no serious problems on these main pistes. Of course, a London taxi, a 1937 Austin, a Fiat 500 or a Vespa scooter are just not suitable. During the mid-seventies two Australians were foolhardy enough to take a very tired old DAF saloon car across the Hoggar route. They made it, but luck was on their side. They should really have been ashamed of their feat. Not only did they unnecessarily risk their lives but, had they broken down, they would have made themselves a liability on other travellers kind enough to give assistance — most unfair in an already trying situation.
　　Yet people experienced in Saharan travel have taken two-wheel drives into incredible places. For example, a German from Freiburg has travelled through the Mandara Sand Sea in southern Libya in his Volkswagen Kombi. A University of Arizona research team in 1978 used Volkswagen 181s to travel to and explore the Jebel Uweinat area of southwestern Egypt. Heavily overladen two wheel drive Fiat and Mercedes trucks from Libya cross the

174

Typical of the two-wheel drive Fiat, Berliet, MAN and Mercedes trucks which cross the Ténéré regularly between Agadez in Niger and Sebha in Libya. Grossly overloaded, trucks like this Fiat are driven across literally thousands of kilometres of soft sandy desert: a feat only possible after many years of desert driving experience. They often travel at night with a man running ahead with a hand held torch for many kilometres in particularly difficult sections. In this photo, taken at the edge of the Ténéré near Adrar Azzaouager, the truck has stopped for prayers and breakfast. It is an arduous journey for the passengers as up to fifteen of them have to ride on top of the load in the dehydrating sun as the truck lurches along.

A patrol of the British Army's Long Range Desert Group at rest somewhere in the Sahara in May 1942. These Chevrolet trucks with only two-wheel drive were used very successfully throughout the war in remote very sandy areas such as the Kalansho and Rebiana Sand Seas (Photo by courtesy of the Imperial War Museum)

Ténéré regularly. The late proprietor of the Agadez Camping frequently drove to Bilma at high speed in his Peugeot 404. It is also impressive to see a VW-Bus exploring the Oued Indebirenne near Djanet, terrain normally reserved for Unimogs. In the early 1940s the Long Range Desert Group, manned largely by British and New Zealand troops, made several crossings of the Kalansho and Rebiana Sand Seas in Libya using two wheel drive Chevrolet trucks heavily laden with weapons, fuel and supplies. In these cases there are several factors of crucial importance. Some are: driving technique, experience in the desert, ability to 'read' the sand, very low tyre pressures and knowledge of the vehicle.

The main advantage of four-wheel drive vehicles is that they offer one the prospect of less digging. Four wheel drive and low range gears give the vehicle tremendous traction and are a real asset in difficult conditions. However, driving across soft sand requires flotation rather than traction. This is achieved by increasing the contact area between the vehicle and the ground thus distributing its weight over a greater surface area. The usual methods for obtaining flotation for the vehicle are use of minimal tyre pressures and/or specialised sand tyres. Thus good flotation can be achieved with a two-wheel drive vehicle.

Yet, when driving in sand, it is also necessary to minimise the amount of torque applied to the driving wheels in order to prevent them digging into the sand. This can be achieved by using a gentle right foot on the accelerator

A 1940s Delahaye jeep seen in Tamanrasset on its way across the Sahara in 1981. Powered by a four cylinder petrol engine, it has front and rear independent suspension controlled by transverse torsion bars

This 1950s Dodge Powerwagon was recently still giving faithful service at Tahoua in Niger Republic. Generally, taking old vehicles into the Sahara is an unnecessary risk

pedal and a relatively high range of gears. Four-wheel drive vehicles have an advantage in that they are able to spread the torque needed to drive them forward through four wheels instead of just two, thus lessening any tendency for the driven wheels to dig into the sand. (Perhaps the ultimate set-up might be four-wheel drive with an automatic transmission controlled by a torque converter but this would add to the vehicle's complexity and reduce its reliability in the desert.)

Nevertheless, much depends on how the vehicle is handled and the experience of the crew. The notorious 'sea of sand' between Ain Guezzam and Assamaka at the Algeria-Niger border along the main Hoggar trans-Sahara route has ensnared many a Land Cruiser or Land Rover for hours while carefully driven VW-Buses and Peugeots have done it unscathed in minutes.

On the other hand, to explore remote areas like the Djado Plateau, the Mauritanian Empty Quarter or to pioneer new routes in the Ténéré, in relative safety and with a minimum of hard work, at least two sound and well-equipped four-wheel drive vehicles are essential. Moreover, they should have a proven record for robustness and reliability, should be equipped with this in mind and should be big enough to carry adequate supplies of fuel, spares, water and food. If the authors were incredibly rich and planned to travel in the Sahara for several months including travel to rarely visited areas, they would probably choose between a Mercedes Benz Unimog U1300 or a Steyr-Puch Pinzgauer 710. Both vehicles are almost unstoppable. The Unimog is a powerful diesel and is well known in every Saharan country. The Pinzgauer is smaller, technically superb with advantages like independent suspension and an air-cooled petrol engine, but it is unfortunately rarely seen in the Sahara.

Generally two-wheel drives are cheaper than 4x4's: for the price of a basic new Land Rover one could have a new Volkswagen Kombi (bus) fully converted as a campervan and equipped for the Sahara plus about U.S.$2000 in spending money. Often two-wheel drives have more room (especially for sleeping in) and are more comfortable to ride in. Usually two-wheel drives are more economical: a Range Rover needs to carry an absolute minimum of 14 jerrycans of petrol to cross the Ténéré while a Volkswagen Bus would need only 9. There is no denying the Range Rover's superb performance in sand. Yet, with much perseverance, a correctly driven and well equipped

A 1954 Hanomag A-L 28 four-wheel drive ex-military ambulance seen at Tarhit, Algeria. Although very strongly built to last, this vehicle could turn a Saharan holiday into a nightmare should it break down. Spares are virtually impossible to obtain nowadays for Hanomags. The dual rear wheels are a hindrance in sand

This Citroen ID19 carcass once served faithfully as a Parisian taxi for many years and hundreds of thousands of kilometres. In its retirement it was loaded up, taken to the Sahara and driven to exhaustion. It expired near Arak and has subsequently been cannibalised

VW will make it. Inevitably, whatever one prefers in a vehicle, something has to be compromised.

Also of paramount importance is a vehicle's reputation and proven ability in the Sahara for strength, reliability, spares availability and local bush mechanics' knowledge of it. (For even if you are an expert mechanic, you still might need help in Bilma or Gao.) Therefore it is preferable not to take a Holden Kingswood or a Nissan Patrol.

The condition of the vehicle

Very old vehicles are often just not up to the stresses and strains of Saharan travel. (Though amazingly some ancient Land-Rovers and Peugeot cars can occasionally be seen, ponderously battling and rattling along some of the major pistes at the hands of their Touareg or Arab owners.) In Tamanrasset during 1981 an ancient 1955 Austin Gypsey 4x4 was still in daily use and in immaculate condition. The authors met a Frenchman with a 1940s independent suspension Delahave jeep crossing by the Hoggar route. A 1926 Renault KZ car completed the 1980 and 1981 Paris-Dakar rallies — testimony that cars were built much stronger fifty years ago. Nevertheless, generally speaking, very old vehicles are an unnecessary risk in an already risky situation. In choosing a vehicle one should aim to minimise those risks. One's life may depend on one's vehicle.

Do not be influenced by tales of the numbers of VW-Bus and Peugeot carcasses seen abandoned between Tamanrasset and Agadez. These are, in fact, some of the most suitable vehicles to take along the main trans-Saharan pistes. But many people buy cheap, old, rusty and very tired ex-delivery vans and ex-taxis, and expect them to survive the harshness and heat of the Sahara with inadequate preparation, little maintenance and a full load. Some are lucky. These old cars are popular because they have lots of room, are cheap, and are supposed to be easy to sell in West Africa.

The Sahara is dangerous and vehicle destroying. Corrugations in Australia are mere ripples compared to those of the Sahara; vast seas of 'bull-dust' have to be crossed at speed; cavernous ruts have to be ploughed through; and sooner or later the loaded vehicle will have to jump over or into great

177

trenches, usually without warning. Because human life will depend on it, the car has to be very strong and has to survive such treatment for several weeks. The Australian Mallee Desert Rally and the American Baja 1000 are good fun for long week-ends but the Sahara is serious. There is often no chance of rescue. The right choice of vehicle is vital.

Petrol or diesel?

Usually diesel vehicles offer superior fuel consumption. A four cylinder diesel Toyota Land Cruiser will use only as much fuel as a VW Kombi. Diesolene is also safe to carry; unlike petrol which is lethal after being shaken about in hot jerrycans on a roof rack across the Tanezrouft at outside temperatures of 50°-60°C (120°-140°F). Diesel engines are simple in that they have no points, coil, condenser or distributor to go wrong; though they do have fuel injectors which should not be abused. Diesels generally lack the power of the equivalent petrol engine. Fuel availability varies: Agadez may have run out of petrol but not out of diesolene for a week, or vice versa. However, diesolene is usually cheaper than petrol especially in Algeria and Nigeria.

Air cooled engines

These (e.g. Volkswagen, Pinzgauer and Magirus-Deutz) have big advantages of not having a radiator to go wrong, a water pump to seize up and pipes to split. Moreover, water for the vehicle does not have to be carried. Yet, an oil temperature gauge is essential as the engine oil has to function as a coolant as well as a lubricant.

Dual rear wheels

If possible, avoid taking a vehicle with dual rear wheels. Usually, only trucks are fitted with these on the load carrying rear axle. There are two main disadvantages associated with dual wheels:
1. Sand tends to build up between and in front of the wheels. This acts

This old Mercedes 406D van is typical of so many vehicles brought to the Sahara. Exhausted and very rusty after many years of service delivering goods in Germany, it was bought cheaply by a romantic young couple who set out for West Africa without spares, jerrycans, sand ladders or a shovel and precious little money. Such people tend to become a liability and play on the kindness of others

In contrast, this fifteen-year old Land-Rover, photographed near Abalessa in the Hoggar region, has spent all its life in the Sahara and is still suitable for Saharan travel. Its engine, transmission and suspension are in good condition and parts and expertise are available at every major oasis. Note the Michelin Xs sand tyres, the air-filter pre-cleaner, the folding sand ladder, the jerrycans for petrol and oil, and the 'Guerba' goatskin water bag hanging from the roof rack

as a brake on the progress of the truck and can cause it to become stuck in sandy conditions.

2. The tyres on dual wheels cannot be deflated effectively to increase flotation for travel across sand. If the tyres are deflated they rub against each other. The resultant overheating would quickly cause tyre failure.

Caravans

Campervans (or motor caravans) are wonderful to travel in because home is always there with its bed, cupboards, cooker, sink, mosquito netting and privacy. However, for the Sahara they should be small compact vehicles that can be extracted from sand independently with sand ladders and without too much digging on the part of the crew. Large two-wheel drive campervans almost invariably need a tow or lots of other voluntary manpower to be extracted from sand even along the main Hoggar north-south trans-Saharan piste. Thus, one should normally rule out large two-wheel drives like the Mercedes 406D, 307D, the Toyota Dyna and the Volkswagen LT from even the main Tanezrouft and Hoggar trans-Saharan routes (though some do get through). Even in smaller vehicles the furniture can add unwanted weight and unproven conversions can fall to pieces on the piste. German 'Westfalia' conversions are very strong and light.

Caravans or trailers are almost an intolerable liability. With a powerful 4x4 (e.g. Chevrolet Blazer or Range Rover) it is possible to do the Tanezrouft or Hoggar route to Agadez with one. But, the pounding received by a trailer will usually cause it to break up. The large semi-trailers that the state truck operators use in Algeria and Niger are incredibly strong and heavily built. Moreover, (in contrast to large trucks in Europe), on the rough piste corrugations, those in the Sahara have tandem rear axles that are designed to 'tramp'. This means that only bulky solid items like sacks of dates or steel pipes can be expected to survive intact. Thus, even a caravan with suspension built for the Sahara is in danger of having all its contents break up.

Suspension systems

Four-wheel drive vehicles vary tremendously in the suspension systems available and choosing the right vehicle for travel in the Sahara should take these into account.

The simplest system consists of a pair of beam axles each comprising an axle casing enclosing a set of differential gears in the centre and a drive shaft (or 'half-shaft') on either side linking the differential to the wheels, the whole axle being supported and connected to the vehicle chassis by leaf springs at either end. Drive to the rear wheels from the gear-box is via a propeller shaft. A transfer case is used to take power along another prop shaft to a similar front axle. This system can be made very strong, is cheap to build and usually simple to repair. It is not too different from the suspensions on nineteenth century bullock carts. Almost invariably vehicles with this system have a hard bumpy ride and their roadholding is generally inferior. The bumps or shocks felt by one wheel are passed to the opposite wheel and also up to the chassis. Traction can also suffer as the vehicle bounces easily and it is difficult to build vehicles with leaf springs that have a very long vertical wheel travel. Very rough terrain may leave the vehicle stationary with two diagonally opposed wheels spinning freely in the air.

However, three of the world's most successful four-wheel drives, the Jeep,

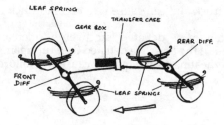
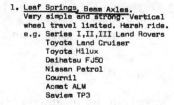

1. <u>Leaf Springs, Beam Axles.</u>
Very simple and strong. Vertical
wheel travel limited. Harsh ride.
e.g. Series I,II,III Land Rovers
Toyota Land Cruiser
Toyota Hilux
Daihatsu FJ50
Nissan Patrol
Cournil
Acmat ALM
Saviem TP3

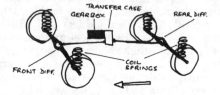

2. <u>Coil Springs, Beam Axles</u>
Simple and strong. Good vertical
wheel travel. Soft ride.
e.g. Mercedes Gelandewagen
(which also has two locking
differentials)

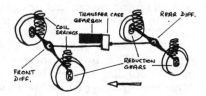

3. <u>Coil Springs and Reduction Gears</u>
All advantages of coil sprung
suspension. Reduction gears on
portal axles increase ground
clearance.
e.g. Mercedes Unimog
Volvo C202 and C303 are
similar but leaf sprung
(Unimogs and Volvos also
have locking differentials)

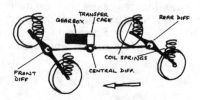

4. <u>Coil Springs and Three Diffs.</u>
Simple strong suspension and
sophisticated drive train :
permanent four wheel drive.
Central differential prevents
transmission wind up and main-
tains traction if one pair of
wheels slips. Central diff is
lockable.
e.g. Range Rover
1-10 Series Land Rover

the Land Rover and the Land Cruiser, have this simple bullock cart suspension. Part of their success lies in their simplicity and relative cheapness. This is a definite asset in the Sahara.

Generally, coil sprung four-wheel drive vehicles have better vertical wheel travel characteristics enabling them to cope more effectively with very rough terrain without losing traction. The two axles are better able to articulate and to allow all wheels to follow the terrain. This is one of the assets of a Range Rover compared to a leaf sprung Land Rover or a Land Cruiser but, in on road driving, coil sprung vehicles are usually more prone to body roll when cornering. The Mercedes Gelandewagen, although fitted with coil springs, does not roll as much as a Range Rover because it has a stiffer suspension set-up and is not capable of so much vertical wheel movement. This would theoretically cause it to be a worse performer in very rough conditions because like many leaf sprung vehicles its wheels may not be able to follow the terrain as well and it would become stuck while one or more wheels spin freely in the air depriving the other wheels of their driving torque. Mercedes have overcome this problem by fitting lockable differentials to the Gelandewagen, thus giving it a distinct advantage over the Range

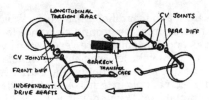

5. Torsion Bar Independent
Simple and strong springing which
allows for the sophistication of
fully independent wheel movement.
This is an asset to roadholding
but does not allow great vertical
wheel travel.
e.g. Fiat Campagnola
(which has longitudinal
torsion bars)

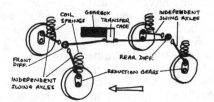

**6. Independent Coils & Reduction
Gears**
Simple, strong and perhaps the
most sophisticated suspension.
Add reduction gears, two locking
diffs and one has just about the
ultimate combination.
e.g. Steyr Pinzgauer

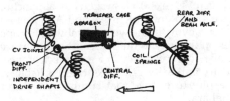

**7. Coil Springs, Independent Front
and Three Diffs**
Basically a refinement of the
Range Rover system with indep-
endent front suspension.
e.g. Lada Niva
Peugeot-Dangel
(Lada has lockable diff.)

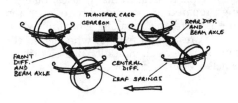

8. Leaf Springs and Three Diffs
Basically similar to Toyota
Land Cruisers and early Land
Rovers but with constant four
wheel drive. Central diff has
limited slip function on Jeeps
but on Land Rovers central diff
is lockable.
e.g. Jeep Quadra-Trac
Chevrolet Blazer
Land Rover V8 1979-1983

Rover in the rough.

Independent suspension systems would seem to offer an alternative method of solving the problem of getting every driven wheel to follow the terrain. However, one of the problems of independent systems has often been an inability to design them with a lot of vertical wheel movement for off road use. Many attempts have been made. For example, early Austin Gypseys, Delahaye jeeps, and the successful wartime four wheel drive Volkswagen Schwimmwagen. They all had transverse torsion bars similar in principle to those on the VW Beetle and Bus. Today the Fiat Campagnola uses longitudinal torsion bars to spring front and rear wheels independently as is the case with the front wheels of the modern Mitsubishi Pajero and Express, the Isuzu Trooper and KB41, and the Datsun 720 pick-ups. However, none of these is quite as effective in really rough off-road conditions as the coil sprung beam axles of the Gelandewagen, Unimog and Range Rover (and now also the new coil-sprung Land Rovers).

Perhaps the ultimate four-wheel drive suspension system for rough off-road conditions is that employed in the Steyr-Puch Pinzgauer. With four-wheel independent suspension controlled by coil springs, it also has tremendous vertical wheel movement and its front and rear differentials are lockable. Reduction gears at each wheel dramatically increase ground clearance too.

However, Gelandewagens, Unimogs and Pinzgauers are very expensive vehicles. The person contemplating buying a vehicle especially for travel in the Sahara has to resolve for himself the question of whether the extra cost of a more sophisticated vehicle is warranted not only in terms of capital outlay but also in terms of reliability, repairability and whether it will get him safely to where he wants to go and back again. Exploration of the massive sand seas in eastern Libya and western Egypt would be preferable in a Unimog but a Toyota Land Cruiser would be admirably suitable for travel on the pistes of the Hoggar Mountains, an area where the extra cost of the Unimog could not normally be justified.

Some vehicles are built stronger and heavier than others and most four-wheel drives are built to take a much more punishing life than most two-wheel drives. Yet it is quite surprising how flimsy some of the small 4x4 pick-ups are. This is in marked contrast to the strength of some two-wheel drives like the VW-Bus and the Peugeots. Recently, a number of four- wheel drive versions of sophisticated front wheel drive cars have appeared on the market. Among these are the Subaru 4x4, Citroen Visa 4x4, Volkswagen Passat Synchro 4x4, Audi Quattro 4x4, Toyota Tercel 4x4, Renault R18 4x4 and Alfa Romeo 33 4x4. These cars may be excellent for rallying in the wet and snow in Europe or for negotiating icy Alpine passes on the way to the ski resort but they are not really built for Saharan conditions. Their relatively low ground clearance, long overhangs and especially their complexity can make them a liability. Also, it would seem to be such a pity to expose that sumptuous velour upholstery to the rigours of the Sahara.

The fact that a vehicle has four-wheel drive should not be taken as an indication that it would be suitable for the Sahara. In many cases, taking a suitable two-wheel drive and being prepared for occasional hard work and to adapt to desert driving techniques is preferable to taking some four-wheel drives. With some justification, there are Sahara experts who regard the use of four-wheel drive vehicles in many cases as an indication of their drivers' ignorance of how to handle a vehicle in desert conditions.

18
Survey of Potential Vehicles

Aro 4x4
These are Rumanian made four wheel drives.

The 100 and 101 are small 1300cm³ four-wheel drives with a transfer case and independent suspension. The mechanicals are based on the Dacia, a licence-built Renault 12.

The 240, 243 and 244 are short wheel base Land Rover sized four-wheel drives with leaf springs, beam axles and a transfer case. They are available as a 2 door soft top, 2 door hard top, 2 door pick-up or as a 4 door station wagon. Engines vary from market to market. It is usually sold with a 4 cylinder 2500cm³ petrol engine and sometimes with 4 cylinder Daihatsu or Peugeot petrol and diesel engines. It is built under licence in Portugal as the 'Portaro'.

All Aros are unknown in the Sahara, though WAATECO in Nigeria have sold them.

Citroen 2CV
2 models: 4 door saloon or 2 door panel van, each available with two engine sizes: 450 cc (2CV4) and 600 cc (2CV6). Air cooled front wheel drive and with very light body. Although not having very great ground clearance, they have big 15 inch wheels which, coupled with engine weight over the drive wheels, give good traction in sand. They are available with double air cleaners, stronger rear suspension, reinforced chassis, and extra engine protection. The public relations department of Citroen produces a very useful booklet on preparing 2CVs (and other Citroens) for rally and off-road use called "Ici commence l'aventure..." (S.A. André Citroen, quai André Citroen 133, Paris XV, France). The 2CV is also produced with a very lightweight, glass reinforced plastic body, known as the Mehari, which is also available from the manufacturer with four-wheel drive. This 4x4 Mehari is identified by the spare wheel mounted on the front bonnet.

Two of the biggest advantages of the 2CV are its cheap price and its economy (5.8L/100km or 50 mpg). It is also very well known in all the Saharan countries. Citroen 2CVs have been taken across the Ténéré but, despite their robustness and simplicity, normally they should be confined to the two main trans-Saharan pistes.

A French company, Voisin Tout Terrain (38220 Livet, France), specialises in converting the 600cm³ (2CV6) model to four-wheel drive. It has a transfer case with low range and drive through the rear wheels can be engaged while on the move.

Agents in the Sahara region:

Algeria : SONACOME, Algiers, Oran, Bechar, Adrar, Tamanrasset, Ghardaia.
Niger : S.E.A.N., Niamey.
Nigeria : it is unknown here.
Mali : Ets. Vezia, Bamako.

Citroen DS & CX

A DS won the 1974 London-Kano-Munich World Cup Rally but in the hands of Citroen experts and enthusiasts. These cars have one big advantage: a pneumatic suspension which can be raised to give tremendous clearance. Other advantages are engine weight over the driven wheels, 15 inch wheels, and the ability to power their way through problem sections of piste. However, they are very complicated vehicles rarely seen outside Algiers, Tunis or Niamey.

Agents as per the 2CV, though the DS has been sold in Nigeria through S.C.O.A., the Peugeot dealers.

Chevrolet Blazer

The U.S. equivalent of the Range Rover, though noticeably bigger all round — its rear is big enough to sleep in. There is a choice of petrol engines ranging from a 4.1 litre six to a 6.6 litre V8. It has live axles with coil springs and is full-time four-wheel drive (i.e. three differentials) like the Range Rover. Generally, it is unknown in the Sahara region, although the U.S. Agency for International Development uses them in Niger.

Cournil

A small French company, founded by Bernard Cournil in 1946, started off by modifying World War II Jeeps for agricultural use. Today the company, Société SIMI S.A. of 4226 St. Germain-Laval, France, produces a limited number of its own unique short and long wheel base four-wheel drive vehicles.

Cournils are very conservatively simple and austerely equipped. They have beam axles supported by leaf springs, a four speed gearbox (no synchromesh

A cheap but simple and well equipped Citroen 2CV. Note the perforated steel planking mounted with the shovel and spare wheel above the rear window. Properly maintained, this car would take its occupants safely and inexpensively across the main trans-Saharan pistes

The French Cournil is a simple and robust four wheel drive. A license-built Portuguese version is also available in many countries and is made by UMM of Lisbon

on first gear), a transfer case and a limited slip differential at the rear. Hard and soft top versions are available on both wheel bases and there is a choice of three four cylinder engines:

2.3 litre Peugeot Indenor diesel
2.0 litre Renault petrol
3.6 litre Saviem diesel

Cournils are also made under licence in Portugal by Unixo Metalo Mecanica Lda., Rua des Flores 71, DTo Lisbon, and fitted with a Daihatsu or a Peugeot diesel engine.

Generally, Cournils are unknown in the Sahara area.

Daihatsu 4x4

A small conventional leaf sprung beam axle Japanese four wheel drive about the size of a Lada Niva. It is virtually a scaled down short wheel base Toyota Land Cruiser.

It is sold in some countries as the Daihatsu Taft and the Toyota Blizzard. Originally marketed as the 1000cm^3 petrol engined F10, it is now available as the F20 with a 1600cm^3 petrol motor, the F50 with 2500cm^3 diesel motor and a longer wheel base pick-up, the F55 with a 2500cm^3 diesel.

A new re-styled but basically similar version was introduced in 1984 using the same short wheel base chassis: the F70 Rocky with 2000cm^3 petrol or a 2800cm^3 diesel motor.

Daihatsus are available in Germany, Holland, France and Britain but are generally unknown in the Sahara region.

Fiat Campagnola

Available with two-wheel bases and in each case in hard and soft top form. The Campagnola has a 2 litre petrol engine (2.4 litre diesel optional), five speed gearbox, rear limited slip differential, four wheel drive and a transfer case (two wheel drive is via the rear wheels), 16 inch wheels and the sophistication of independent suspension at all four wheels controlled by longitudinal torsion bars. Slightly smaller than a Land Rover or a Land Cruiser, they are not infrequently brought to the Sahara by tourists.

Since 1983 Fiat have produced a four wheel drive version of their diminutive Panda car. Developed by Steyr-Puch in Austria, normal drive is via the front wheels with the rear wheels being engaged for all wheel drive.

Fiat agents in the Sahara region are:

Nigeria   : Incar Ltd., Kano and Kaduna.
Mali   : Ets. Vezia, Bamako.

Ford Transit

A V4 engined, rear wheel drive, panel van of Kombi size. Lacking independent suspension, it does not do well in corrugations. Its front axle is particularly low and vulnerable when negotiating sandy ruts. Unknown in Algeria and Niger, however, it is very popular as a taxi in Nigeria, in Sokoto and Zaria. Australian models are available only with straight six 'Falcon' engines.

A German company, Autobus Rao GmbH of Hammerschied Gasse 1-12, 7312 Kerchheim-Teck, W. Germany, produces a 4x4 version of the basic Transit. It has the approval of Cologne and the TUV (German vehicle approving authority).

Ford agents in the area:

Nigeria   : Allens Ltd., Kano

Isuzu KB40 and KB41

A small four cylinder four wheel drive pick-up to rival the more successful Toyota Hi-Lux. It has independent torsion bar front suspension and a leaf sprung beam or axle. Available with petrol or diesel motors. Sold as the Bedford KB41 in Britain, Holden KB41 Rodeo in Australia, Chevrolet KB41 Luv in the USA, and Isuzu KB41 New Rodeo Big Horn (!) in Japan.

An attractive and comfortable station wagon version sold variously as the Isuzu Trooper or Holden Jackaroo is also available.

The KB40 is the superseded body style for the pick-up. Isuzus are unknown in the Sahara.

Jeep

The Jeep CJ5, CJ6, CJ7 and CJ8 are very 'macho' short wheel base four-wheel drives with powerful engines ranging from a 3.8 litre six to a 5 litre V8. The CJ7 is available with automatic transmission and sophisticated 'Quadra-Trac' central limited slip differential (full-time four-wheel drive). However, like so many other smaller four-wheel drives, it lacks load space for a long Sahara trip. It also consumes a lot of fuel and is unknown in the Sahara and West Africa. It is sold in Europe with a 2.7 litre Perkins diesel engine. The CJ5 is licence built in Japan by Mitsubishi and in India by Mahindra.

At the end of 1982 Jeep introduced their new 1-tonne truck, the J10. It has a much longer wheelbase and choice of petrol or diesel six cylinder engines but without full-time four wheel drive.

The Jeep Cherokee and Wagoneer are similarly much larger 2 and 4 door station wagon vehicles and with much more room. They are available with 3 and 4 speed manual transmissions as well as the full-time four-wheel drive 'Quadra-Trac' automatic gearbox. There is a choice of large capacity six and V8 petrol engines.

In 1983 Jeep introduced new smaller versions of the Wagoneer and Cherokee known as the XJ with a choice of 2.5 litre 4 cylinder and larger 6 cylinder motors.

However, Jeeps are largely unknown throughout the Sahara region.

Lada Niva

A small Russian made two door station wagon which is virtually a miniature Range Rover with coil springs, beam rear axle, 16 inch wheels, permanent four-wheel drive and a central lockable differential. Its 1600cm³ engine is a Fiat-derived motor used also in Lada saloons. Front suspension is independent.

It is widely used in the Sahara region by tourists because it is a sound vehicle for the desert (especially sand) and is very cheap: during 1986 it cost only 56,000FF (incl. 33.3% VAT). It is also economical to run and has earned itself a good reputation in desert rallies.

It is sold in Niger, Nigeria and Tunisia but **not** in Algeria (where spares are a problem). Agents:
Nigeria: WAATECO, Sokoto, Kano, Kaduna.

Peugeot Indenor diesel engine conversions are carried out by: Ets. Periquet, Zone Industrielle, 55400 Etain, France. Tel (29) 87 02 78.

Land Rover

Probably the most widely used four-wheel drive vehicle in the world, the Land Rover is still 'King of the Sahara', although its supremecy is being seriously eroded by the Toyota Land Cruiser. Its chassis strength is unsurpassed; it is familiar to all bush mechanics; its alloy body panels can be rapidly stripped from the chassis; and second hand or cannibalised spare parts are available in most large oases.

Until recently, there have been two basic British made chassis available on the civilian market: the 88 inch short wheel base and the 109 inch long wheel base. Each was available with cab only, soft top, light truck, panel van, and station wagon bodies (all with 2 side doors except for the long wheel base station wagon which has four). 109 inch models became available with an optional 2.6 litre six cylinder Rover engine in 1966 (with overhead inlet and side exhaust valves). There were also 109 inch and 110 inch forward control models produced from 1966 to 1972.

From 1974 to 1978, a lightweight 88 inch Land Rover was produced for the military market. Designed to be carried by helicopters into the field of battle, it was stripped of all but the essentials. Yet, it was never available on the civilian market although some are now increasingly available through army surplus merchants. Similarly, from 1974 to 1978 a 101 inch forward control Land Rover was manufactured which had the Range Rover's V8 engine mounted centrally as well as its three differential full-time four-wheel drive transmission but with leaf instead of coil springs.

During 1980 this concept was introduced to the 109 inch Land Rover models which became available with the V8 motor in front, three differentials and constant four-wheel drive but with only leaf springs and drum brakes. In Australia this three differential model also became available with a slightly more powerful 3.9 litre four cylinder Isuzu diesel engine.

Early in 1983 the new 1-10 Series was introduced. With a slightly longer wheel-base (110 inches), these vehicles have a wider track and flared wheel arches, a one-piece windscreen, revised dashboard, front disc-brakes, coil springs front and rear, and the Range Rover's 3-differential permanent four wheel drive system. This has put the Land Rover into the sophisticated 4x4 league with the Lada Niva, Range Rover, Unimog and Gelandewagen. It is now technologically more advanced than its main rivals: Nissan Patrols, Mitsubishi Pajeros, Toyota Land Cruisers and Hi-Lux vehicles. It should perform better, too, especially in sand, but the Japanese vehicles' simplicity, price and after-sales, back-up could still prove to be the new Land Rover's undoing in the Sahara region during the next few years.

During 1984 the 90 Series Land Rover was introduced. This is essentially a short wheel base version of the full-time four-wheel drive 1-10 Series with a wheel base of 93 inches. Wind-up windows also became available on all Land Rovers.

The Lada Niva is a highly successful yet sophisticated Russian four-wheel drive. This one is air-conditioned and is registered in the Wilaya of Tamanrasset

A British Army 101 inch forward control Land Rover. It has the V8 petrol engine of the Range Rover placed amidships and like the Range Rover also has full-time four-wheel drive

187

Three engines are currently available on British models:
4 cylinder petrol (very reliable and well known all over the Sahara)
4 cylinder diesel (simple, economical, reliable but relatively unknown)
V8 petrol engine which is available only in models with the Range
Rover's sophisticated permanent or full-time four-wheel system.
1-10 models are available with very useful five speed gearboxes (ten forward
speeds altogether, including low range).

Fuel Consumption		
Motor	Asphalt Roads (factory figures)	Ténéré Sand
4 cyl. petrol	15L/100 km (19 mpg)	25-30L/100 km (11-9 mpg)
4 cyl. diesel	9.5L/100 km (30 mpg)	18L/100 km (16 mpg)
6 cyl. petrol	19.5L/100 (14.5 mpg)	24-27L/100 km (12-10 mpg)

Spanish made Santana Land Rovers are available in short wheel base (88 inch), long wheel base (109 inch) and 2 tonne forward control versions. The 109 inch and 2 tonne vehicles come with six cylinder diesel or petrol engines and wind-up windows.

Land Rovers are also assembled in CKD kit form in over twenty countries and therefore differences do exist, such as in the case of Spanish Santana vehicles, Australian vehicles with Isuzu diesel engines, and South African models with six cylinder Leyland petrol motors.

Heavy duty springs and shackle pins should be fitted and spare front and rear springs and shackle pins carried. Some Land Rovers are prone to breaking rear axles especially if they have heavy right footed drivers or if larger engines have been fitted. These vehicles have semi-floating rear axles, whereas in the case of 109 inch LWB Series III models (late 1971 onwards) the axles are of the fully floating Salisbury type and do not snap so readily.

Great care should be taken not to overload a Land Rover as this will drastically shorten its service life often resulting in structural failure to the bulkhead, windscreen supports and roof structure. A long wheel base vehicle should be loaded with less than one tonne including the weight of a roof rack and jerrycans of fuel and water. Land Rovers are just about the most suitable vehicle for the Sahara but to overload one is to stress it and court disaster. A major chassis crack or broken axle could put your life in jeopardy in the middle of the Ténéré. (Of course overloading any vehicle will have similar consequences.)

Land Rover diesel engines have superior economy and should last longer than petrol motors. However, 6 and V8 engines don't have to work quite so hard in sand. In really bad sand ridges at right angles to the direction travelled, Tom Sheppard in British Army 6 cylinder vehicles managed only 50L/100km (5.7 mpg).

4 and 6 cylinder Land Rovers have four speed gear boxes which can be in either high or low range, and either can be in two or four- wheel drive. There are no differential locking facilities. Overdrive and free wheeling front wheel hubs are useful and economical extras. V8, 90 Series and 1-10 Series vehicles are full-time four-wheel drive vehicles (with four-wheel drive permanently engaged) and have three differentials, the centre one being lockable. The British high capacity pick-up (HCPU) version has tremendous potential. Introduced early in 1982, its chassis is strengthened to carry 1300kg compared to the normal 1000kg capacity. It is available with all three engines.

The 90 Series Land Rovers introduced in 1984 are virtually a short wheel base version of the sophisticated 1-10 Series. The County model shown here is the top of the range with luxury features which include wind-up windows and other creature comforts

The four door station wagon version of the 1-10 Series Land Rover introduced first in 1983 with coil springs, front disc brakes, permanent four-wheel drive, revised dashboard and a one-piece windscreen

A tremendous range of optional equipment is available e.g. de luxe front seats, tropical roof, heavy duty suspension, power brakes, oil cooler, raised air intake, laminated windscreen, long range fuel tanks, swivel housing gaiters, high altitude carb. jets, etc. British Leyland publish a booklet: 'Optional Equipment for Land Rover Series III' and another: 'A Guide to Land Rover Expeditions' with useful advice and lists of suggested extra tools and spares.

Manufacturers' addresses:
Land-Rover Ltd., Lode Lane, Solihull, England, B92 8NW.
Metalurgica de Santa Ana S.A., Avenida de Manoteras 6, Madrid 334, Spain.

Agents in the Sahara region:
Algeria — SONACOME; Algiers, Oran, Bechar, Adrar, Tamanrasset, Ghardaia, Touggourt.
Niger — Niger Afrique; Niamey.
Libya — Gordon Woodroffe Ltd; Tripoli.
Nigeria — BEWAC; Kano, Kaduna, Jos, Lagos.
Mali — Manutention Africaine; Bamako.

A Dutch company, Knook's Automobielbedrijf B.V. (66-70 Flevostraat, 1442PV Purmerend near Amsterdam) specialises in preparing Land Rovers and Range Rovers for expeditions. They are the main importers of these vehicles to the Netherlands and by prior arrangement are prepared to give a refund on unused spare parts returned to them after a Sahara expedition. Similarly, they will, if discussed with them before departure, air freight urgently needed spare parts to any airport in the Saharan region that is served by scheduled airlines.

Range Rover
Now in production since 1970, the Range Rover has become synonymous with affluence and opulence. Unfortunately, this has led to a rich man's toy reputation. In fact it has a lot going for it. Its General Motors designed alloy V8 will, if treated with respect, last over 200,000 km (about 125,000 miles) before needing a decoke and valve grind. Similarly, transmission and

suspension will last even longer. Many of the body panels are 'Birmabrite' (an aero-space derived aluminium alloy) and so will not rust and are more readily panel beaten than aluminium. Production has not kept pace with demand so that prices of used models are high. Generally, a Range Rover is a sound investment.

The Range Rover is one of the best vehicles for the sand dunes of the Bilma Erg even with a full load and 18 full jerrycans, provided that tyre pressures are very low (1.0 kg or 14 psi up front and 1.2 kg or 17 psi for the rear). However, on corrugations it can be quite hair-raising, unpredictably losing its tail end (lower the rear tyre pressures to lessen this tendency). Its fuel consumption is phenomenal. Across the Ténéré from Djanet to Bilma and Agadez it will average 28-26L/100 km (10-11 mpg). Consequently, a lot of payload space is used up with jerrycans. Moreover, even empty it is not long enough to sleep in. No matter which material is used, the seats are a positive incentive to sweat. One of its biggest detractions is the way the interior fittings, lining, door handles, etc. don't seem to be able to stand up to the rough conditions of the Sahara: almost daily something drops off, jams or breaks.

Unfortunately, Michelin XS sand tyres cannot normally be fitted to a Range Rover as they are relatively high profile tyres and would rub inside the wheel arches.

The four door version introduced in 1981 has the same wheel base, internal and external dimensions as the two door model. Consequently there are no advantages in terms of space, load carrying ability and road-holding. From 1983 the Range Rover became available with a five speed gearbox. For 1989 the third central differential was replaced by a new Borg Warner viscous coupling unit.

Slow down if oil temperature approaches the red: distortion and cylinder head cracking could result. Don't allow oil pressure to stay too high for too long: this can interfere with bearing lubrication and camshaft bearings are not replacable (new engine!!) The oil pressure relief valve has different settings. Fit a pair of rubber bonnet straps: the existing mechanism is inadequate. Be careful of the vulnerable exhaust pipe under the gearbox when negotiating deeply rutted tracks. Roof racks must have large 'feet' to be mounted on the not very strong alloy gutters, and in Germany a roof rack may not be fitted unless an interior roll bar or cage is installed.

A 1980 model Spanish made Santana Land Rover. Note the one-piece windscreen and wind-up windows

During 1981 a four door version of the Range Rover was introduced. The Range Rover is permanently in four-wheel drive, is a superb vehicle in sand and is much revered in many parts of the Sahara

190

Generally Range Rovers are beautiful to drive, but the gear box must not be rushed. Power steering is a pleasure. A petrol tank guard is absolutely essential (not standard equipment), and flame guards above the exhaust system help keep the floor cooler. An overdrive is a worthwhile extra if a lot of motorway driving is done. Rear coil springs should be fitted to the front and heavy duty springs to the rear. A sagging rear end can be a problem with a heavily laden vehicle in spite of the 'Boge Hydromat' ride levelling unit fitted to all vehicles. An oil cooler would only be necessary if long distance fast driving was contemplated in hot countries with good bitumen roads (e.g. Australia, Nigeria, Saudi Arabia). There are at least eight operational Range Rovers in Agadez (usually hidden behind mud walls) whose owners will invariably stop tourist Range Rovers and ask to buy parts. Range Rovers have wide wheel rims. Consequently it is very hard to 'break' tyre beads when repairing a puncture (especially with M + S tyres). It can be done with much hard work but it pays to carry 2 spare wheels. Also, 205-16 tyres can be impossible to obtain in Saharan countries (including Nigeria).

Range Rovers are assembled from CKD kits by Jaguar-Rover Australia Pty Ltd, (Box 59, Liverpool, Sydney 2170).

For Range Rover vehicle and parts distributors in the Sahara region see Land Rover section.

Land Rover Discovery

In September 1989 Land Rover announced a new model: the **Discovery.** In terms of price and equipment it slots in between the Land Rover and the Range Rover. Designed to compete in price with the Mitsubishi Pajero (Shogun in Britain) and the Isuzu Trooper, it is marginally bigger than them and technically superior, with coil springs and a central lockable differential as per the pre-1989 Range Rovers.

Initially available in three door form only, a five door version was released during 1990. It shares the Range Rover's 100 inch wheel-base and successful 3.5 litre General Motors originated V8 engine but the entirely new 4 cylinder 2.5 litre diesel is Land Rover's own design : the 200Tdi with direct injection and turbo. It has the same wide 16 inch pressed steel wheels as the Range Rover and, with an outside mounted spare wheel, it has considerably more room in it for passengers and equipment than the more up-market and luxurious Range Rover.

In terms of price, size and technical advantages the Discovery promises to be an admirable vehicle for the Sahara.

Agents: as for Land Rover and Range Rover.

Mercedes Benz Unimog

Just about the ultimate 'go anywhere' vehicle but with two major drawbacks: price and fuel consumption.

For the price of a new U1300 Unimog (cab and chassis only!) you could have at least three Volkswagen campervans or two Land Rovers. Yet, you could almost leave your sand ladders behind! On the other hand, the authors once accompanied a 2.2 litre six cylinder 404 Unimog which consumed petrol at the rate of 70L/100km (4mpg) across the Bilma Erg!

However, older petrol Unimogs can be fitted with modern diesel motors which increase their reliability and improve fuel consumption (e.g. C.G. Hoes, Postfach 448148, D2800 Bremen 44, W. Germany).

Usually available new only as an open load carrying truck, living quarters have to be specially built onto the back and this structure cannot be connected to the cab because of the tremendous flexibility designed into the chassis. Large 20 inch car type wheel rims can make puncture repairs very

A Mercedes Unimog 404 of 1950s vintage at Tamanrasset. A rugged ex-German army vehicle with a go-anywhere ability second to none. These older Unimogs had fuel inefficient and less reliable six cylinder petrol engines. This one has been roughly repainted to cover its original military camouflage colour scheme because military uniforms and camouflaged vehicles are illegal for civilian use in many Saharan countries

One of the latest U1300 Unimogs at Agadez. Very inexpensive to buy, they give tremendous security when used to travel in remote parts of the Sahara. Note the pre-cleaner for the engine air intake (near right front door) and the perforated steel planking (P.S.P.) strapped to the side. These tyres are unfortunately Continental mud and snow tyres, and designed to dig through mud and snow, not to float over sand

difficult, especially with the standard tubeless M+S tyres fitted to new vehicles. The old 404 six cylinder Unimogs need to have a larger radiator installed if they are to travel in the Sahara during May, June or July; otherwise, one is reduced to travelling between 4 a.m. and 11 a.m. only when conditions are cooler.

Unimogs are generally very reliable vehicles and give tremendous security in the more remote parts of the desert. Parts common to other Mercedes vehicles are widely available in main centres of all Saharan countries. The six cylinder diesels share the same OM352 series engine as Mercedes Benz 1413/1448 trucks and tractors which are known and used throughout the Sahara.

There is an excellent book on owning and maintaining Unimogs : 'Unimog typ 404 als Wohnmobil' available from Pritz- Globetrotter-Ausrustungen, 17 Schmiedgasse, 8390 Passau, W. Germany. It has a good section on fitting diesel engines to old Unimogs. Also in Germany, there is a strong Unimog enthusiasts' club : Unimog Interessen-gemeinschaft, 7 An den Birken, 5307 Wachtberg.

Currently seven basic models are available with various wheel base and diesel motor combinations. All have beam axles, coil springs, reduction gears at each wheel and lockable (not l.s.d.) differentials:

Model	Cylinders	Capacity	Power
U600	4	2404cm³	38kW
U800	4	3780cm³	53kW
U900	6	5675cm³	64kW
U1100	6	5675cm³	70kW
U1300	6	5675cm³	92kW
U1500	6	5675cm³	110kW
U1700	6	5675cm³	123kW

The U1300, U1500 and U1700 have a more modern cab design, a wider track, higher clearance, more sophisticated cab and power assisted disc brakes on all four wheels. The four cylinder models are available with 18 inch wheels. Older ex-German army 404 Unimogs are available reconditioned from Sea-Mar Diesel Ltd., Great Yarmouth, Britain and from Geo-Service, 35 Industriestrasse, 7521 Hambruckën, W. Germany.

Agents in the Sahara region:

Algeria   : SONACOME, Algiers, Oran, Adrar, Bechar, Ghardaia,
            Tamanrasset.
Niger   : S.E.A.N., Niamey.
Nigeria   : Leventis Motors, Sokoto, Kaduna, Kano, Jos, Maiduguri.

Mercedes Benz Gelandewagen

The Mercedes G-type or Gelandewagen (cross-country car) was developed jointly and is manufactured jointly by Daimler-Benz A.G. and Steyr-Daimler-Puch A.G. in the Steyr factory at Graz in Austria. In most countries it is marketed as a Mercedes Benz but in some as a Steyr-Puch.

First released in 1979, the Gelandewagen was hailed as the first real competition for the Range Rover. It is available in two wheel bases (2.40m and 2.85m). Like the Range Rover it has beam axles and coil springs and is fairly sumptuously equipped and expensive to buy. Unlike the Range Rover, it is not equipped with permanent four-wheel drive but instead has the conventional system of engaging the front axle when four-wheel drive is required. Yet, its two differentials can be locked. In many circumstances, a possibly better system than the Range Rover's.

As yet they are usually brought to the Sahara by tourists though they are sold as prestige vehicles in Niger. They are fitted with water cooled four cylinder (petrol and diesel), five cylinder (diesel) and six cylinder (petrol) engines which are also available in Mercedes saloon cars. Thus spare parts are available only in main cities such as Algiers, Tunis, Niamey and Kano, and then for the saloon car models sold in those countries. They are also sophisticated engines (especially the fuel-injected twin overhead camshaft six) and major repairs are likely to require specially trained mechanics. However, they are very robust vehicles and their reliability has never been disputed.

Gelandewagens are bigger than most photographs would initially indicate: the long wheel base model being as long and higher than a Volkswagen Kombi. There are five basic models on the two wheel bases:

2.400m SWB soft top
2.400m SWB hard top station wagon
2.400m SWB hard top panel van
2.850m LWB hard top station wagon
2.850m LWB hard top panel van

They all have 16 inch car type wheel rims.

The Gelandewagen is also made under licence in France for the French army as the Peugeot P4 and is equipped with four cylinder Peugeot petrol and diesel motors (an excellent combination for Africa!), but unfortunately not yet available to the public.

Agents in the Sahara region:

Algeria   : SONACOME, Algiers, Oran, Bechar, Adrar, Ghardaia,
            Tamanrasset.
Niger   : S.E.A.N., Niamey.
Nigeria   : Leventis Motors, Sokoto, Kano, Kaduna, Jos.

A Mercedes Gelandewagen station wagon at El Golea. The tyres are unfortunately for mud and snow, not sand. The bull-bar mounted on the front bumper bar is largely unnecessary

A four-wheel drive Mitsubishi L300 Express van. It has the same mechanicals, drive train and suspension as the Mitsubishi Pajero or Shogun. A potentially useful vehicle but its effectiveness is marred by a low ground clearance and vulnerable suspension components, gearbox and fuel tank

Mitsubishi Forte or Express
Sold as the Mitsubishi Express in Australia and in the USA as the Dodge Power Ram, it is almost identical in technical specifications to the Isuzu KB41: four cylinder front water-cooled engine, four-wheel drive with transfer case, rear leaf springs and front torsion bar suspension. Unknown in the Sahara. A station wagon version of the Forte or Express known as the 'Pajero' is available with short and long wheel bases and 2 and 4 doors respectively as well as four cylinder petrol and turbo-diesel motors. It is sold in the USA as the 'Mantero' and in Britain as the 'Shogun'. Although still relatively unknown in the Saharan region, a Pajero was first in the 1985 Paris-Dakar Rally and Pajeros took the manufacturers' team prize in the 1983 event.

Mitsubishi also produce a four-wheel drive version of their forward control L300 Express van and minibus which has similar engines, drive train and suspension components to those of the Pajero.

Nissan 720 F
A small four cylinder pick-up very similar to the Isuzu KB41 and Mitsubishi Forte in mechanical and suspension and diesel versions as well as a four door double cab model. Unknown in the Sahara.

Nissan Patrol
Sometimes marketed under the Datsun name. In 1980 a completely face-lifted Nissan Patrol was released in two door short wheel base and in long wheel base (4 door station wagon and 2 door pick-up) form. A new 4 speed all synchromesh gearbox and six cylinder diesel motor was added to the specification which retained the old straight six petrol engine as an option. Otherwise, it is an old fashioned basic four wheel drive vehicle with leaf springs, beam axles and a transfer case.

Turbo six cylinder diesel engines and front disc brakes became options during 1983. Short wheel base Patrols are built under licence in Spain by the Ebro truck company and fitted with four cylinder licence built Perkins diesel engines.

194

In 1988 the Nissan Patrol station wagon was consierably upgraded with a wider track and coil sprung suspension with options of automatic transmission and locking differentials, making it a formidable off-road vehicle.

Nissan Patrols are unknown in the Sahara although they have been on sale in Nigeria.

Peugeot 404, 504 & 505

These Peugeots (not the smaller front wheel drive models) are probably the most popular cars in virtually every African country with an unsurpassed reputation for their strength, reliability and ability to survive continuous abuse. Bush mechanics everywhere know how to fix a 'Peejotte'. The success of these cars lies partly in their simplicity as well as their after sales back up. Spares and expertise are available in all main Saharan oases and main towns all over West Africa. There are usually old Peugeots to cannibalise from in most towns. However, it is advisable not to take a petrol fuel injection model because of its complexity. The 504 and 505 are assembled in CKD kit form in Kaduna in Nigeria.

Some saloons and station wagons have live rear axles and coil springs. Larger engined saloons have independent coil sprung rear suspension. All Peugeot 404 and 504 pick-ups or 'plateaus' have live rear beam axles and simple semi-elliptic leaf springs. All front engine-rear drive Peugeots have McPherson strut independent front suspension.

These Peugeots lack the weight of an engine over the driven wheels and so must be driven at speed in sandy areas, for example: 110 km/h (69mph) across the Ténéré.

Peugeot 404s come with 1.6 litre petrol and 1.9 litre diesel motors. The 504s come with 1.6 litre, 1.8 litre and 2.0 litre petrol engines and 2.0 litre, 2.1 litre and 2.3 litre diesels. No limited slip differential is available, though a specialist French company makes very successful four-wheel drive versions of the 504 station wagon and pick-up. These Dangel-Peugeots have a central differential system, permanent four-wheel drive, high and low range and 16 inch wheel rims. In France during 1986 the petrol Dangel-Peugeot 504 pick-up cost 95 000FF (incl. 17.6% VAT) and the petrol Dangel-

The four-wheel drive Mitsubishi Pajero (or Shogun or Montero in some countries) is available in two and four door station wagon forms. It shares engine and drive train components with the Mitsubishi Express and has had some success recently in the Paris-Dakar Rally

A Peugeot 404 pick-up or plateau from Niamey. Note the P.S.P., the jerrycans, equipment boxes and the wire mesh grille fitted to the front to prevent grass seeds from fouling the radiator. A most suitable vehicle for the main pistes. Peugeot 404, 504 and 505 cars, station wagons and pick-ups are used all over Africa

Peugeot station wagon cost 135 000FF (incl. 33.3% VAT). Diesel versions cost more. The Peugeot factory co-operates with Dangel to produce these conversions which are available only on new cars.

Dangel-Peugeots have been in production since 1978 and large numbers of them have demonstrated their reliability by finishing in every Paris-Dakar Rally to date. Address:

Automobiles Dangel S.A., B.P. 01, 68780 Sentheim, France.

Agents in the Sahara region:

Algeria : SONACOME, Algiers, Oran, Bechar, Adrar, Tamanrasset, Ghardaia.

Niger : C.F.A.O., Niamey, Zinder, Maradi.

Nigeria : R.T. Briscoe, Kano, Zaria, Kaduna, Maiduguri.

Renault 4

A small water cooled front wheel drive 4 cylinder saloon (5 doors) or panel van (3 doors). It is very strong, reliable and a simple vehicle with a reputation for surviving abuse. Some of its disadvantages are its small wheels (especially on corrugations) and its low ground clearance. It is sold in France with an 800cm³ motor and elsewhere with an 850cm³ engine which is now available in 1000cm³ form. Like the Citroen 2CV, it scores on its simplicity, its economy and the fact that it is well known. However, like the 2CV, its use should normally be confined to the Hoggar and Tanezrouft pistes.

An open glass reinforced plastic bodied version is available known as the Rodeo. A French company, SINPAR of rue d'Arsonval ZL, 69680 Chassieu, France, produces 4 x 4 conversions of the saloon, panel van and Rodeo. A SINPAR Renault 12 won the Cote d'Ivoire — Cote d'Azur Rally outright in 1976.

Late in 1982, Renault introduced a four-wheel drive version of the R18 station wagon. Like the Subaru and Toyota Tercel 4x4, this is a comfortable front wheel drive family car with the option of also engaging the rear wheels. The R18 4x4 uses the same transmission system as the Volkswagen Iltis and has an extra low fifth gear rather than a transfer case and a whole low range. It is available with petrol or diesel motors. Like the Subaru and Tercel 4x4, this is not an off-road vehicle. It is basically an on-road car with

A Dangel-Peugeot 504 pick-up. These vehicles have a central differential system with permanent four-wheel drive. The Dangel system is also available for the Peugeot 504 and 505 station wagons which are fairly frequently seen in the Sahara (Photo by courtesy of Automobiles Dangel)

A Renault R4 at the Agadez Camping. These reliable, economical and hard working little vehicles are taken across the main pistes but they have small wheels and low clearance

196

built-in optional four-wheel drive for assistance in icy slippery conditions.
    Renault agents in the Sahara region:

Algeria   : SONACOME, Algiers, Oran, Bechar, Adrar, Tamanrasset,
               Ghardaia.
Niger   : Niger, Afrique, Niamey.
Nigeria   : Leventis Motors, Sokoto, Kano, Jos, Kaduna.
Libya   : N'Ga Renault Libya Ltd., Tripoli.
Mali   : Manutention Africaine, Bamako.

Steyr Haflinger

Very small, light, forward control 4x4 vehicle with 650cc air cooled rear
engine. It has four swing axles with drop spur gear hubs and coil springs.
This
combination of light weight, long travel independent suspension, 45°
degree approach and 40° departure angles, high clearance and individually
controlled differential locks gives the Haflinger an all terrain ability far
superior to most modern 4x4s.
    It has a top speed of only 75 km/h (47 mph) unladen, but this is compen-
sated for by a miserly 9.4L/100 km (30 mpg). Its tiny two cylinder 4 stroke
engine is very reliable and capable of prolonged hard work. Unfortunately
Haflingers are no longer in production, and spares are a big problem.
Relatively unknown in the Sahara, though a search in Zinder, Niger Republic, should produce several to cannibalise from.

Steyr Pinzgauer

Same basic formula as the remarkable Haflinger: a four-wheel drive with
independent swing axles, locking differentials, light weight, forward control, excellent clearance, only on a larger scale and with a 2.5 litre air-cooled
4 cylinder petrol engine placed amidships behind the front axle. The four-
wheel drive version (the 710 Series) has a one tonne payload and a top
speed of 105km/h on the highway, yet it still uses only 15L/100km (19mpg)
on the piste. Potentially the ultimate Sahara vehicle. Unfortunately, it is
very expensive and generally unknown in the Sahara. It is also available
with six-wheel drive (the 712 Series).

Subaru FWD Leone

A small two and four door four-wheel drive Japanese saloon, station wagon
and pick-up. Currently available with 1600cm³ and 1800cm³ motors and
with or without a transfer case for low range. Two-wheel drive is via the
front wheels (as per Citroen 2CV Voisin) and four-wheel drive engages the
rear wheels also. It has a flat water-cooled 4 stroke engine. They are not
really an off-road vehicle but are good for asphalt or gravel roads rendered
difficult by ice or mud. There is an optional suspension mechanism to raise
or lower the vehicle to change the ground clearance.
    Unknown in and not recommended for Saharan conditions.

Suzuki

A diminutive two door but simple four-wheel drive with beam axles, leaf
springs and a front water-cooled engine. Available with hard top, soft top
or cab and tray.

Model	Years	Engine
LJ50	1973-1978	3 cyl. 600cm³ two stroke
LJ80/LJ81	1978-1981	4 cyl. 800cm³ four stroke
SJ30/SJ31	1981-	4 cyl. 800cm³ four stroke

The Austrian Pinzgauer, seen here with the Swiss army, is potentially one of the most suitable vehicles for travel in really remote areas of the Sahara. It is also available as a closed in station wagon or van

The Suzuki SJ30 or SJ410 four-wheel drive in its long wheel base form

The LJ80 replaced the LJ50 with a slightly wider track and a very small four stroke engine. The SJ30 series replaced the LJ80 in 1981 with a slightly wider and more stylised body. All models have been sold variously as the Jimny or Sierra.

Two stroke models especially are not noted for a long engine life and the vehicles are very lightly built. However, Suzukis have 16 inch wheels, a good reputation for sand travel and frugal fuel consumption. They are cheap to buy new but have been on sale only in Niger and Nigeria in small numbers.

During 1983 a long wheel base SJ30 Suzuki became available on some markets.

Toyota Tercel 4x4
A small family car with front wheel drive and the option of selecting four wheel drive. It does not have a transfer case. Like the Subaru and Renault R18 4x4, it should not be regarded as an off-road vehicle but an on-road car with optional 4x4 drive for increased traction for roads which are icy or slippery. Unknown in the Sahara region.

Toyota Hi-Lux 4x4
A four-wheel drive version of the popular Hi-Lux two- wheel drive pick-up. Like the Land Cruiser, it has a very basic four-wheel drive system of two beam axles and leaf springs. Normally driven in two-wheel drive, four-wheel drive can be in high or low range. It also has split truck type wheel rims which make for easier puncture repairs. It is widely used in East Africa and Libya, Niger and Tunisia but in 1986 was not yet being distributed in Algeria.

Available with a 2.0 litre single overhead camshaft four cylinder petrol engine or a 2.2 litre four cylinder diesel, the Hi-Lux comes in three basic forms:
2 door cab and chassis only
2 door cab and well-side pick-up truck body
4 door double cab well-side pick-up truck body

Late in 1983 the Hi-Lux range was given a styling face-lift, a five speed gearbox and front disc brakes. In 1984 an additional model was introduced: a two door five seat station wagon. In 1989, with a further face-lift, a four-door station wagon became available together with independent torsion bar

The popular Toyota Hi-Lux pick-up. This four-wheel drive is used increasingly in many African countries. Available with a five speed gearbox, diesel or petrol engines, and single or double cab form as shown here

The biggest threat to the Land Rover's supremacy is the Toyota FJ45 pick-up seen here at Beni Abbes in Algeria. Now widely used throughout the Sahara. Note the pre-cleaner for the engine air intake and the Bridgestone V-Steel Jamal sand tyres

front suspension. This station wagon version of the Hi-Lux is sometimes sold as the "4-Runner".

Toyota agents in the Sahara region:

Algeria : SONACOME, Algiers, Oran, Bechar, Adrar, Tamanrasset, Ghardaia, El Oued, El Golea.

Niger : C.F.A.O., Niamey, Zinder, Maradi.

Nigeria : R.T. Briscoe, Kano, Zaria, Kaduna, Maiduguri.

Toyota Land Cruiser

The Land Cruiser has supplanted the Land Rover in Australia and East Africa but in the Sahara it still has to do so convincingly. It has earned a reputation for strength and reliability that is derived substantially from its simplicity, being a basic four-wheel drive with no sophisticated gimmicks. In the main cities of the Saharan countries it is generally cheaper, and spares availability and after sales service are often superior to those of the Land Rover. Unlike the Land Rover, it has an all steel body which cannot be so readily disassembled from the chassis. It is also much more prone to rust (not, of course, in the Sahara!).

A Toyota FJ60 station wagon at Beni Abbes. Note the air pre-cleaner and the sand tyres

The Toyota Land Cruiser FJ70, one of a new range of Land Cruisers introduced in 1985. This particular model has broken new ground for Toyota in that it is equipped with coil instead of the more traditional leaf springs

Model availability varies from market to market but generally there are four different wheel bases and various engine and bodywork options:

Wheel-base	Model	Engine	Body Options
2.285m (SWB)	BJ40/FJ40	Diesel 4 Petrol 6	Hard and soft top
2.430m	FJ42	Diesel 4	Hard and soft top
2.950m (LWB)	HJ45/FJ45	Diesel 6 Petrol 6	Hard and soft tops, steel tray, cab-chassis
2.730m	HJ60/FJ60	Diesel 6 Petrol 6	Station wagon
2.700m	FJ55	Petrol 6	Station wagon (superseded)
2.310m (SWB)	BJ70/FJ70	Diesel 4 Petrol 4	Hard top, soft top and fibreglass top
2.600m	BJ73/FJ73	Diesel 4 Petrol 4 Diesel 6	Soft top and fibreglass top
2.980m (LWB)	HJ75/FJ75	Diesel 6 Petrol 6	Hard top, pick-up with steel tray, cab-chassis

The Achilles heel of Land Cruisers (especially those built during 1975 and 1976) has been the weakness of the alloy transfer case. From 1973 a four speed gearbox was introduced and in 1975 Land Cruisers were built with fully floating axles. However, they still have a very simple leaf sprung suspension front and rear. All models are currently available with all synchromesh dual range gearboxes and disc-brakes on the front wheels.

Early in 1985, Toyota released a new range of Land Cruisers designed to replace the BJ40/FJ40, the FJ42 and the HJ45/FJ45 models but not the HJ60/FJ60 station wagons. They have a completely re-styled body, less austere interior and a five speed gearbox. The long wheel base models are also available with an optional 90 litre extra fuel tank giving a very useful total fuel capacity of 180 litres. All models retain the simple leaf springs, beam axles and transfer case system of the earlier range although the short wheel base models now have the availability of coil instead of leaf springs as optional extra. (This option provides a softer suspension but increased vertical wheel travel which should improve its rough off-road capability.)

During 1990 Toyota introduced a new range of their Land Cruiser station wagon models, known in the trade as the HZJ80, HDJ80 and FJ80 or "80 series". They are all fitted with coil springs. Bottom of the range models have a transfer case but the top models are available with four wheel disc brakes and a central differential and thus full-time four wheel drive. The central differential is lockable and a limited slip differential is available for the rear. A range of six cylinder engines is available depending upon the market they are sold in, such as diesel and turbo diesel, and carburettor petrol and fuel injection petrol. They are also potentially quite sumptuous and luxurious vehicles now, with options such as plush carpeting and seats, sound systems, electric windows, mirrors and sun-roof and central locking doors, a massive array of instruments and, of course, air conditioning.

Motor	Fuel Consumption Asphalt Roads (factory figures)	Ténéré Sand
6 cyl. petrol	17L/100km (17mpg)	24L/100km (12mpg)
6 cyl. diesel	12L/100km (24mpg)	21L/100km (13mpg)
4 cyl. diesel	10L/100km (28mpg)	20L/100km (14mpg)

These figures will of course vary with terrain and driving style. However, six cylinder petrol engine vehicles are notorious for their fuel consumption when cruised at more than 80 km/h. The five speed gearbox available from 1983 on FJ60 and HJ60 station wagons should be of some help in reducing this. Petrol versions of all Land Cruisers sold in the USA and Australia have power robbing and fuel sapping exhaust emission controls fitted.

On short wheel base models (BJ40 and FJ40) especially, extra leaves in the rear springs are advisable if heavy loads of fuel and water are to be carried. In some markets laminated windscreens are not standard: they are essential in the Sahara. Short wheel base Land Cruisers can, like the 88 inch Land Rover and the Range Rover, be quite hair-raising on corrugations. Hard top models have glass reinforced plastic roofs mounted on the gutter. This can cause problems in successfully mounting roof-racks. Roof-rack feet need to be long or travel the full length of the gutter. Better still, roof-racks need to be chassis mounted. (See chapter on 'Vehicle Preparation and Equipment'.)

Depending on which market they are sold in, diesel Land Cruisers are available with 12 or 24 volt electrics. 24 volt systems are preferable as they provide more reliable starting in cold climates.

Limited slip differentials for both front and rear axles are available as after market accessories. Some l.s.d. brand names are: TrueTrac (Detroit Automotive Inc.), Gov-Lock, and Dual Drive-Selectro — all are American and available from:
Differentials Pty Ltd., 91 Riley Street, Sydney, Australia 2010.
Warn Equipment S.A., 28, rue Dorian, 42703 Firminy/St Etienne, France.

Toyota make their own front and rear l.s.d. which are available from: Toyota Racing Development, 18425 S Western Avenue, Gardena, California 90248, USA.

The Russian UAZ 469 is a very simple four-wheel drive but not noted for its reliability

The Russian UAZ 452 van and minibus are 4x4 versions of a rather archaic two-wheel drive vehicle

A fully locking differential is available as an after market accessory from: Altair Aviation Pty, Ltd., Church Road, Menzies Creek, Melbourne, Australia 3159. Normally, if a Land-Cruiser (or any other basic four-wheel drive vehicle) is stuck across a ditch with only two diagonally opposite wheels on the ground, it would have to be rescued by another car. A locking differential will allow all power to go to the wheel (or wheels) still on the ground and not to be sapped up uselessly in a wildly spinning wheel. A locking differential does this much better than a limited slip differential. (Mercedes Gelandewagens and Unimogs, and Steyr-Puch Pinzauers have locking diffs.)

Ideally, a Land Cruiser should be fitted with the optional air intake precleaner or an additional alternative aircleaner such as a Donaldson (from Nova-Handels) or a Tecafiltre (from Tecafiltres S.A.) See page 220 for addresses.

Toyota agents in the Sahara region:

Algeria   : SONACOME, Algiers, Oran, Bechar, Tamanrasset, Adrar, Ghardaia.
Niger   : C.F.A.O., Niamey, Zinder, Maradi.
Nigeria   : R.T. Briscoe, Kano, Zaria, Kaduna.

UAZ 4 x 4
The 469 is a four door soft top conventional four-wheel drive with beam axles, leaf springs and a transfer case. Quite unsophisticated and very basic, it has a four cylinder 2500cm³ petrol engine. It has synchromesh on third and fourth gears only. Generally unknown in the Sahara (except in Egypt and Libya where the military use them) but tourists, especially from Italy, do bring them.

The 452 is based on the 469 but with a van/bus body and similar proportions to a Volkswagen Kombi (but there the similarities end!).

Agents in the Sahara region:
Nigeria   : WAATECO, Sokoto, Kano, Kaduna.

Volkswagen Iltis
Developed by the Audi-NSU section of Volkswagen, the Iltis is a descendant of the old DKW Munga introduced to the German army during the 1950s and 1960s. Released only during 1979, the Iltis won the first and second places in the 1980 Paris-Dakar rally.

It has a 55kw 1700cm³ version of the Golf/Passat water-cooled engine driving the front wheels. By selecting four-wheel drive the rear wheels are brought into action. There is no transfer case but an extra low fifth gear instead. Suspension is independent with wishbones controlled by transverse leaf springs. The Iltis is only available as a soft top and without fixed doors. Unfortunately, its price is prohibitive making it more costly than a Range Rover or a Mercedes Gelandewagen. It has good clearance, 16 inch wheels and, although it is still unknown in the Sahara, has already earned an enviable reputation as a true all terrain vehicle.

Iltis production in Germany came to an end in 1983. It was an expensive vehicle. However, production under licence in Canada is continuing.

Volkswagen Type 2 Bus or Kombi
The Volkswagen Type 2 (known also as the Kombi or Bus) has for many years been one of the most widely used vehicles in the Sahara. The police and the army use them all over Algeria, they are used as taxis in Niger and Nigeria, and by tourists everywhere. Consequently, it is relatively easy to find spare parts and wrecks from which to cannibalise. Genuine new German spare parts can be obtained from backstreet Ibo traders in Nigerian towns for

First generation Volkswagen Type 2. The authors' 1966 Nigerian registered double cab Kombi was extremely useful: with seats for six as well as a tray long enough to sleep in fully stretched out. Also, with the engine weight over the driven wheels and reduction gears it had a tremendous traction. Main external distinguishing features of first generation vehicles are split windscreen and varying rear wheel camber

Second generation Volkswagen Type 2. The authors' 1973 Australian assembled Kombi has travelled more than 360,000 km around Australia and through its centre, twice across the Sahara, and overland from Europe through Asia to Australia

ridiculously low prices. However, it should be stressed that the new water cooled petrol and diesel engined Type 2s are unknown in the Saharan region.

The VW's ability to survive misuse (up to a point), carry heavy loads over rough terrain economically, and provide the privacy of a mobile home, are some of the factors which make it so popular. Its independent suspension gives it stability on corrugations and directional precision on deep sandy ruts when negotiated at speed. Early pre-1968 models with rear swing axles were risky in fast cornering, yet these rear drop axles gave them superior traction to today's models. However, modern VW Buses fitted with the optional limited slip differential (VW Option M 220) can go places that will astound many 4 x 4 drivers.

The VW Type 2 has been in production since 1949 with independent torsion bar suspension and a flat four alloy air-cooled petrol engine. There have been thousands of detailed changes since then. The early Type 2 Kombis had a split windscreen, kingpin front suspension, rear swing axles and reduction gears.

The 1968 models were the start of the second generation Kombis with a full width windscreen, ball-joint front suspension and constant camber rear suspension with four constant velocity joints.

The 1980 models were the first of the third generation with an entirely new body and coil springs at all four wheels. Not having the strong torsion bar axle beams of the earlier models the third generation Kombi has yet to prove its robustness in Saharan conditions. Nevertheless, it has been sold in large numbers in Nigeria since 1980 — a good indication of its hardiness.

For 1983, European third generation Type 2s were sold only with the water-cooled in-line diesel engine from the Golf and a totally new flat water-cooled 'boxer' petrol engine. These models are quickly recognised by the extra grille at the front for the radiator.

In 1985 Volkswagen, in co-operation with Steyr-Puch, introduced a four wheel drive version of the third generation water-cooled Type 2 Bus. The system used is unique and potentially very effective in slippery conditions

Third generation Volkswagen Type 2. Introduced for 1980 with the successful air-cooled rear engine formula but with coil sprung instead of torsion bar suspension. They are currently only available with water-cooled petrol and diesel engines. The four-wheel drive Synchro version shown here was introduced during 1985 (Photo by courtesy of Volkswagenwerke A.G)

in that drive to the front wheels is engaged automatically as soon as the rear wheels begin to lose traction. Also, various underbody components of these new four-wheel drive third generation vehicles which were previously vulnerable, like the spare wheel, fuel tank and gearbox, have now been relocated or given extra protection and ground clearance has been improved even further. However, it will be some time before these sophisticated vehicles are commonly seen in the Saharan region.

Kombis marketed in many African countries such as Algeria, Egypt and Togo are of Brazilian manufacture and are a hybrid mixture of first and second generation models in terms of suspension, mechanicals and bodywork.

Volkswagen publish a pamphlet entitled: 'Group Z4: Instructions for Operating Passenger Cars and Transporters in Tropical Climates'. Not only does this give useful advice, but it also lists all the options available for VWs e.g. low compression motor, by-pass oil filter, twin air cleaners, oil bath and cyclone air filters, high altitude jets, limited slip differential, heavy duty shock absorbers, gearbox and sump protection plates, laminated windscreen, and other items.

Air-cooled engines are ideal for the Sahara as one does not have to carry water for the engine and there are no hoses to split, radiators to leak or get clogged with dust, mineral deposits, or grass seeds, as well as no water jacket to become choked by sediment and mineral deposits. However, much of the success of a Saharan journey in an air-cooled VW will depend on how it is maintained. There are four basic areas of maintenance that are vital to an air-cooled VW's survival (and perhaps that of its crew) in the Sahara:

1. If driven fast on bitumen roads, or if just driven in the central Sahara, oil temperature will get close to 127°C (260°F), the permitted maximum. Slow down if it reaches this temperature and allow it to cool down. Similarly, when the oil temperature is high do not stop and immediately switch off. In this case, oil temperature will actually increase, with the danger of cracking a cylinder head. Instead stop and allow the engine to idle for ten to fifteen minutes or until oil temperature descends to 105°C (220°F). Air cooled VW engines run coolest when idling. The best check on this is to fit a VDO oil temperature gauge in place of the dipstick with the dial mounted on the dashboard.

2. Similarly tappets or valve clearances should be checked every 2-3,000 km in the desert. Not only will this minimize the chance of burned valves, but it will also let you know when a valve stem is stretching and likely to drop. When a valve drops it goes with a bang and usually sends bits and pieces into the opposite combustion chamber. An immediate halt is essential if disastrous damage to cylinder head, piston crown, and bearings is to be avoided. The engine must be removed and dismantled on the spot.

3. The third vital point of VW maintenance is inspection of the air cleaner daily. A rear engined vehicle is exceptionally vulnerable to dust. The standard European, American, or Australian air cleaner on VWs is inadequate for prolonged desert use. 1600cm³ Buses should have oil bath cleaners or the air cleaner with the precleaning 'cyclone' stage (VW option M153). Big engined twin-carburettor Buses should have the M153 option (VW part no: 029 129 607A) air cleaner or a two stage one like the American Donaldson or the French Tecafiltre. If the air cleaner is neglected dust will enter the combustion chamber causing rapid valve and piston ring wear and finally bearing seizure through abrasion or lack of oil.

4. The fourth point is to ensure that timing and dwell angle (contact point gap) are correct, otherwise overheating will result with cracked cylinder heads, block distortion and valve failure.

If these four maintenance points are adhered to rigorously and frequently, your Bus should not let you down in the Sahara, provided that the engine is in good condition before departure. Old engines should be checked for bearing, piston ring, oil pressure relief valve, and valve guide wear before departure.

Suspension, brakes and electrics will look after themselves with normal maintenance but do not overload the front of the Kombi. With first and second generation vehicles this will lead to premature torsion bar spring breakages and finally a danger of front axle ball joints being violently ripped from their recesses; (and probably a bad accident). Driving with the rear engine lid open allows dust to be sucked in as well as hot air already expelled from the engine's cooling system.

A protector plate for the front of the gearbox is highly recommended, as is the removal of the front anti roll bar at the beginning of the journey (it will soon become bent and therefore totally useless otherwise). With third generation vehicles, remove the spare wheel and its cover from under the cab and store it inside the car. Mounted under the front it decreases ground clearance and will get fouled up on the rocks and the centre hump of wheel ruts. Also on third generation vehicles, the petrol tank, mounted under the floor in the centre, is extremely vulnerable. It **must** have a steel plate welded underneath it between the two main longitudinal chassis beams. Care should be taken to protect the point where the gear selector shaft enters the front of the gearbox. These third generation VWs also need additional precautions taken against dust in the engine bay: use duct tape around the front of the engine compartment and seal off the flap covering the oil filter cap.

Carry a couple of concertina emergency push rod tubes just in case (made by Scat and Empi in USA). Pop top campers should have VW Option M 073: plate fitted under the chassis to give necessary torsional strength after a hole has been cut in the roof. Big 1700, 1800 and 2000 engines are not seen much in Saharan countries but the similarly engined VW 411 was sold in Nigeria.

Generally, Kombis should be kept to the main pistes but the pistes between Reggane and Ain Salah, Tamanrasset and Timieaouine, and Djanet and Tamanrasset, would also cause no problems.

Agents in the Sahara region:

Algeria : SONACOME, Algiers, Oran, Bechar, Adrar, Tamanrasset, Ghardaia.
Niger   : S.O.N.I.D.A. and S.C.O.A., Niamey, Maradi, Zinder.
Nigeria : Mandilas Ltd., Sokoto, Kano, Jos, Zaria, Kaduna, Maiduguri.
Libya   : Arrahila Co. Ltd., Tripoli.

Volkswagen Type 1

The Type 1 includes the 181 Safari or Kurierwagen, the Beetle, and the Igala; all of which have similar (but not identical) chassis and varying versions of the upright fan flat four air-cooled engine.

The 181 four door open soft top 'jeep' is based on the World War 11 'Kubelwagen'. Until 1973 it had rear swing axles with drop axles and reduction gears, which gave it great clearance and traction. Later models have the more sophisticated 4 constant velocity joint rear suspension common to the 1302 and 1303 Beetle. Both are available with limited slip differential (option M220), as well as most of the tropical extras listed in the VW booklet (Z4). Being a soft top it cannot easily be fitted with a roof rack. Otherwise it should be treated with the same understanding recommended for the Bus (above). It has been sold in Algeria, Niger and Nigeria. The 181 has also been used in very remote parts of Egypt (Jebel Uweinat) by the University of Arizona for a long term research project.

The current Brazilian made Volkswagen Type 2 is used widely in Algeria and some other West African countries. It is a mixture of first and second generation vehicles with the second generation front but with the first generation's king pin front suspension, hinged side loading doors and small side and rear windows (This particular one is registered in Togo)

The Volkswagen 181 is well suited to travel throughout the Sahara, especially the models with reduction gears. This one is registered in Niamey

The Volkswagen Iltis is a modern front engined water cooled four-wheel drive with an outright victory in the Paris-Dakar Rally to its credit and tremendous potential, but with a price tag that has made it uncompetitive

A Volvo G202 Laplander. This one has been fitted with fat wheels and a very neat 'pop-top' roof making it an excellent compact campervan which also has a four-wheel drive and locking differentials

The Beetle is similar to the 181 but of course with a totally different body. The suspension is not quite as robust and ground clearance not so high. However, Beetles frequently cross the Sahara along the two main pistes. Brazilian Beetles assembled in Nigeria and Egypt have the earlier more simple swing axle rear suspension rather than the more modern CV-joint type. For a time between 1977 and 1981 a four-door version of the Brazilian Brasilia was assembled in Nigeria as the Igala. It is basically a Beetle but with a modern hatchback body with lots more room. They have been much used in Nigeria as taxis.

Apart from the 181, Volkswagen Type 1 cars should be confined to the two main pistes.

Agents in the Sahara region: as for VW Bus.

Volvo C303, C304
(Military designation: 4140 and 4141 respectively.) The Swedish equivalent to a Unimog, it is a forward control 4 x 4 vehicle with the B30 six cylinder petrol engine of the old Volvo 164 saloon cars. With minimal overhangs, excellent clearance, chassis strength, reduction gears and locking differentials, it can go anywhere just about. It does not have coil springs on its beam axles like the Unimog but has the more simple leaf springs. It is available with cab and chassis only or a very useful five door station wagon body with plenty of room for bunks, cupboards, etc.

The C303 has a 1.0 tonne payload ability and the C304 can carry 1.5 tonnes. It is, however, little known in the Sahara and another drawback is its fuel consumption which averages about 23.5L/km (12mpg) on the piste, though it is advisable with an optional 272 litres fuel tank. It is also very expensive. A six-wheel drive version is available.

Volvo C202 Laplander
(Military designation: L3314). A smaller scaled down version of the C303/C304, it has the four cylinder B20 series petrol motor of the 144 and 244 saloon cars but similar drive mechanicals and suspension to the bigger C303 and C304. It can carry a 0.75 tonne payload. It also is regrettably unknown in the Sahara.

Larger Trucks

Renault TP3 (formerly Saviem TP3)

A large Unimog sized 4 x 4 van with front, water cooled, 4 cylinder motor and high/low ranges, Very simple suspension with leaf springs. Available as petrol or diesel. Its high clearance and simplicity, coupled with widely available parts and expertise make it an ideal Saharan vehicle. However, like the Unimog it is slow and uncomfortable; it lacks some of the sophisticated advantages. They are used extensively by armies in Algeria, Niger and Mali. It is easy to find old examples to cannibalise from.

Slightly larger Renault four-wheel drive trucks of four and eight tonne payload capacities are also available: the TRM 2000 and the SM8.

During 1977 a team of four TP3s and three Saviem SM8 four-wheel drive trucks (now also marketed under the Renault name) became the first vehicles ever to cross the Sahara from west to east.

Agents in the Sahara region:

Algeria : SONACOME, Algiers, Oran, Bechar, Adrar, Tamanrasset, Ghardaia.
Niger : Niger Afrique, Niamey.
Nigeria : Leventis Motors, Sokoto, Kano, Kaduna, Maiduguri.
Libya : N'Ga Renault Ltd., Tripoli.
Mali : Manutention Africaine, Bamako.

Magirus-Deutz

German Magirus-Deutz trucks are used by the military in Algeria, Niger and Tunisia. They are available in 4x4 or 6x6 drive form with beam axles and leaf springs. They all have bonneted front air-cooled diesel engines of various sizes.

SONACOME

This state owned Algerian company produces Berliet trucks under licence. They also make their own SONACOME six-wheel drive bonneted truck based on Berliet chassis and drive train components but with 8 cylinder Deutz air-cooled diesel engines. An excellent desert vehicle. A team of two

The Renault Saviem TP3 is widely known throughout the Sahara. A very useful campervan, this Italian registered van, seen at Arak in Algeria, has Michelin Xs sand tyres but the jerrycans fitted below the floor could create a ground clearance problem

A six-wheel drive Magirus-Deutz truck used as a support vehicle for a German tour company. It has a large air-cooled diesel engine

of these SONACOMEs competed in the 1980 Paris-Dakar Rally and finished first and third in the truck section.

SONACOME spare parts and expertise are available in every major Algerian oasis.

Berliet

Now owned by Régie Renault, Berliet trucks are easily the most widely used trucks in most Saharan and West African countries, and have been so since the 1940s. In 1959 and 1960 it was a team of Berliet trucks which pioneered and established pistes in the remote Ténéré-Tibesti areas of Chad, Niger and Algeria (accompanied by some Land Rovers). New Berliets now carry the Renault name. Spares and expertise are available in virtually every major oasis.

Bedford

Four-wheel drive Bedford trucks, especially ex-British army models, are much favoured by British based trans-Africa overland tour companies such as Encounter Overland and Guerba. These companies take large quantities of spare parts and tools with them and usually a member of the crew is a Bedford expert. When Bedfords break down in the Sahara it is necessary to be totally self-contained for Bedfords are completely unknown in all Saharan countries and spares would have to be obtained from Britain or perhaps France (there is a slim chance that some parts could be obtained in Nigeria). By contrast, spare parts and mechanical expertise for other equivalent size and performance four-wheel drive trucks like the Mercedes 911, the Renault/Saviem TP3 and SM8, the Fiat 75, and the Berliet L64, are available in virtually every major town in Algeria and in the larger centres in other countries in the Sahara and West Africa.

The rather rounded split windscreen 4 ton RL and RS Bedfords were in production from 1952 to 1969. The squarish one piece windscreen 4 ton MK Bedford went into production in 1962 and in 1977 was supplemented by the 8 ton TM. They are all forward control leaf sprung beam axle four-wheel drive trucks, without reduction gears or locking differentials. A variety of 6 cylinder diesel and petrol water-cooled engines is available. They all have 20 inch split rim wheels.

Bedford four-wheel drive trucks have been popular with British trans-Africa tour operators. This well equipped truck is one of the MK series (Photo by courtesy of Guerba Expeditions)

The French Acmat ALM 4x4 is one of the few vehicles specifically designed and built for the Sahara desert (Photo by courtesy of Christopher F. Foss)

Agents in the region:
Nigeria   : Niger Motors Ltd., Kano.

Volkswagen LT 28 and VW-Man Trucks

Usually the VW LT series of vans and light trucks are a bit too big for comfortable travel even on the main trans-Saharan pistes. However, a German company specialises in making a very useful Volkswagenwerke and TUV (German motor vehicle approval authority) approved a four-wheel drive version of the LT which compares favourably with the Renault/ Saviem TP3. The company, Sulzer Fahrzeughbau (Viedemannstrasse 2, 8901 Konigsbrunn, W. Germany) has only a limited production at present. This 4x4 LT has two differentials, leaf springs and conventional beam axles, a five-speed gearbox, a transfer case, and 16 inch wheels as well as a six cylinder diesel motor. It is considerably cheaper than a Mercedes Unimog.

In production at the Volkswagen factory at Hanover is the VW-Man range of small trucks. Among these Volks-Man trucks available now is the 10.136 G Range: 4x4 trucks built with a simple leaf sprung beam axle suspension, varying carrying capacity up to 10 tonnes and powered by six cylinder VW diesel engines.

Mercedes Benz

Like the Berliet, Daimler-Benz trucks are used all over the Sahara and West Africa. They are also assembled in Nigeria from Brazilian made CKD kits. The 4x4 LA911B five tonne truck is used by the Nigerian, Tunisian and Niger armies. Spares and expertise are widely available.

A six-wheel drive air conditioned Mercedes-Benz bus used by the state run long distance bus company (SNTV) in Algeria in the more difficult areas of the Sahara. Note the Michelin XS sand tyres, the pre-cleaner for the engine air intake and the perforated steel plating stored on the roof rack in case the bus becomes bogged in sand. The rear axles have single and not dual wheels at each end, as dual wheels tend to be a liability in sand. The flexible partition between the cab and the main passenger section is necessary to the tremendous twisting that the chassis is capable of in the rough conditions

M.A.N.

M.A.N. trucks and buses can be seen in use all over Algeria. M.A.N. trucks are also in use in most other Saharan and West African countries. Spares and expertise are quite widely available.

Acmat 4x4 ALM

The French company Ateliers de Construction Méchanique de l'Atlantique based at Saint-Nazaire build a 2.5 tonne truck especially for Saharan conditions. It was first developed in the late 1950s and adopted by the French Foreign Legion. It is still little known in Europe or even in its native France but is used especially for long range desert patrols by the French military as well as the armies of Morocco, Senegal, Chad and Burkina Faso.

An excellent desert vehicle, it has a simple beam axle and leaf sprung suspension, a four speed gearbox, transfer case and is powered by a Ford 589E six cylinder water-cooled 4.9 litre petrol engine developing 92kW at only 2800 rpm, or a 5.8 litre six cylinder Perkins diesel developing 88kW at 2800 rpm. Standard equipment includes two 100 litre fuel tanks and a 200 litre water tank. They are available with three different wheelbases and there is also a six wheel drive version.

There are many other potential vehicles available in different parts of the world. Moreover, since the first edition of this book was published, the variety of four wheel drive vehicles sold around the world has expanded dramatically. The vehicles considered so far are perhaps the most likely to be taken by tourists and others visiting the Sahara. Though this does not rule out others, travel in the Sahara is risky and fraught with hazards. Use of an unknown or unproven vehicle only increases the risks involved. The Sahara is dangerous and one of the vital factors which could lead to a disastrous expedition or even death is wrong choice of vehicle.

The two most widely used vehicles in the Sahara: the Berliet truck and the Land Rover

211

19
Vehicle Equipment and Preparation

Suppliers

In Australia and U.S.A. there are off-road equipment shops in most towns, but in Britain and mainland Europe there are only a few outlets that sell the type of equipment suited to fitting out a vehicle for travel in the Sahara. The following is a list of some of the places in Europe. They all sell equipment like jerrycans, roof racks, sand-ladders or perforated steel plating, air cleaners, tyre pumps, tents, roof rack tents, shovels, water purifiers, etc., in addition to normal outdoor and camping gear:

Daerrs Expedition Service, Theresienstrasse 66, D-8000 Munchen 2, Germany. Tel: 089/282 032. One of the best supply and equipment shops. They are Sahara specialists and also sell a large range of travel books. Well worth the extra distance to Munich. They have catalogues and a mail order service.

Safari Quip, 13a Waterloo Park, Upper Brook Street, Stockport SK1 3BP. Tel: 061 429 8700. Also one of the best supply and equipment outlets especially for the Sahara and Africa. They also have a good stock of relevant books and maps. They will send you their catalogue of equipment and operate a mail order service.

Syro-Depot GmbH, Zur Eisernen Hand 25, D-6109 Muhltal-Traisa (near Darmstadt just south of Frankfurt) Tel. 06151 147794. They also sell a large range of travel books and are campervan specialists. Will send a detailed catalogue.

Bernd Woick, Spaichinger Str. 31c, 7000 Stuttgart 75. Tel. 0711/473080. They also sell travel books and maps, and will send their catalogue.

Magasin Globe Trotter, 150 Route de St. Julien, 1228 Plan des Ouates, Geneva. Tel. 022/944747, Catalogue available.

Map-Home, 220 quai Stalingrad, 92130 Issy-les-Moulineaux, France. Tel. 558 55 77. Apart from selling equipment for a Saharan journey, they will specially prepare your vehicle.

Compagnie Européenne de Distribution, BP 247, B1 de la Liane, 62204 Boulogne-sur-Mer, France. Tel. 21/92 00 22. A large variety of vehicle equipment available. Land and Range Rover specialists.

Nice Off-Road Center, 107 avenue Cyrille Besset, 06100 Nice, France. Tel. 93/82 19 77. Wide variety of vehicle equipment available. Specialists in off-road preparation of VWs.

In most European cities there are many shops specializing in camping gear, but very few that can sell you items essential for a trans-Saharan motor journey. In Britain it is virtually impossible to track down and buy p.s.p. (let alone the aluminium variety). In fact there is only one shop in Britain which sells sand ladders, and that is the one listed above. In Holland there seems to be none.

There are also a few places that specialize in fitting out vehicles with heavier springs, roof racks, overdrives, etc. Here are some British addresses:

Quest 80, Abbey Farm, Holton-Cum-Beckering, Lincoln LN3 5NG. Tel: 673/ 858 274. Specialists in Land Rovers, Discoveries and Range Rovers.

Carawagon International Ltd., Thames St., Sunbury-on-Thames, TW16 5OR, (Tel. 85205). Specialists in 'pop-top' caravan conversions on Land Rovers.

In Holland there is:

Knook's Automobielbedrijf B.V., Glovostraat 66-70, 1442 PV Purmerend. Tel. 02990-27257/34141. Specialists in Land Rovers, Range Rovers and Jeeps.

Advice on Travel in the Sahara

There is, however, someone who is prepared to give free experienced advice on travelling in the Sahara and in West Africa as well as on vehicle preparation for it. He is: Pieter Kersten, Palmstraat 79, Amsterdam, Holland. (Tel. 020/252556). A real authority on the Sahara, the ebullient Pieter Kersten is fluent in Dutch, English, German, French and will welcome the

The two most commonly used and most practical tools for sand extraction: perforated steel plating (p.s.p.) and sand ladders. A pair of either is absolutely essential for safe travel in the Sahara. The p.s.p. shown is the much lighter aluminium variety whereas the sand ladders are made of galvanised steel. A long handled shovel is also tremendously useful as it enables one to dig sand out from underneath the vehicle relatively easily

213

opportunity to give restrained and practical advice. Alternatively, the authors would also welcome the opportunity but unfortunately live a long way from the Sahara. However, we will respond promptly to any letter sent to: Box 711, Aitkenvale, Townsville, Australia 4814. (Tel. 077/793 368).

Equipment

Sand ladders and p.s.p.

Excellent, light, galvanised sand ladders are sold by Brownchurch Components. Their only disadvantage is that they tend to get buried. Steel perforated steel planking is also excellent, and best for use with big trucks as it doesn't get buried easily, nor does it bend easily. For lighter vehicles like VW-Buses, Land Rovers and Range Rovers, aluminium p.s.p. is probably the best: it doesn't get buried easily and is lighter than steel p.s.p., also it doesn't get quite so hot to hold. It should be cut in half lengths. It is expensive though; Daerrs sell it pre-cut in half lengths. A fibreglass moulding of p.s.p. has been produced, which is effective for a while, as it is light, doesn't get buried easily, and is never hot; but it soon begins to crack and tear, and is treacherous on the hands.

Do not bother with other methods of sand extraction. Lengths of wide canvas belting, even with bits of steel 'dexion' angle iron bolted to them, are light and easy to handle, but in deep sand they are all too often like ordinary sacks: the wheels just pull them in and throw them out the back. You need a very strong material virtually to build short artificial roads to ride on. So far, only steel sand ladders and p.s.p. can do this satisfactorily. For 'Bull Bags', winches and sand anchors see Chapter 22 Driving in the Sahara.

The galvanised sand ladders and half length p.s.p. referred to above fit very neatly on a roof rack, across the width of the vehicle. On Kombis, Land Rovers, Range Rovers, Unimogs, Land Cruisers, they do not exceed the overall width. Safari Quip and Quest 80 sell very neat little brackets that enable one to carry them at the side of a Land Rover, suspended from the roof rack. However, sand ladders and p.s.p. should always be held down with strong but easily twistable wire. To stop them rattling tie them down with strips of old inner tube.

Jerrycans

Never carry petrol in plastic jerrycans! Firstly, petrol can react with plastic and cause it to disintegrate slowly. Secondly, plastic jerry cans are not strong enough to contain the tremendous expansion that takes place when petrol, very hot and shaken up, changes to gas. They swell up and crack, allowing gas to escape. Any naked light or static electricity will cause an instant explosion: a tragic end to a Saharan holiday.

The best jerrycans are the steel 20 litre (4.4 gallons) ones originally designed for and used by Rommel's Afrika Korps in World War II. They gave the Germans an initial advantage over the British, who were unable to carry petrol as safely in Saharan conditions. The British soldiers called them 'Jerry' (their nickname for the Germans) cans. These jerrycans are made of two pieces of pressed steel welded together along a single seam, giving them strength to contain the tremendous pressure built up by the expanding petrol vapour as the can is shaken violently all day in 50°C heat, on a roof rack. Because of this pressure, never open a hot jerrycan quickly. The petrol inside could be boiling and a fountain of it will spurt out several feet into the air! Although a proper jerrycan will not swell up like a balloon,

Two brand new steel petrol containers.
Left is the US Army style wide mouthed
container or 'merrican' and on the right
the more common 'jerrycan'

When nothing else is available, two full
jerrycans may be used as a safety
precaution in case a jack fails. These two
cans are supporting the VW Kombi

as a plastic one will, it will swell slightly, though perhaps not noticeably. Therefore, when placing jerrycans on a roof rack in the cool morning do not pack them tightly. You must allow room for expansion. For example, with eight of them standing up on a roof rack, there must be space for nearly one more, early in the morning. By mid-day they will be tightly packed. If you don't do this, either the roof rack, or the jerrycans have to give.

Most jerrycans have a date pressed in them. New ones are expensive. However, you will see old Wehrmacht ones dated 1940, with swastikas on them, still in use in the Sahara! The important thing is to renew the rubber seals before using old ones. The old seals can be easily prised out with a screwdriver and new ones pressed into the lid, with your fingers. Leaking jerrycans are frustrating and dangerous. Also, old jerrycans should be washed out with petrol, to get rid of the paint, water, oil or any other contaminants, and to check for leaks. Enroute, it is very difficult to get leaking jerrycans welded up, at places like Tamanrasset or Agadez, because of the obvious danger. (The French for 'to weld' is 'souder'.) One way to avoid leaks developing is to prevent jerrycans bouncing up and down. Tie them down firmly, and put them on part of the rack that has a plywood floor, so that they don't chafe against the metal bars.

Wide spout U.S. Army 'Merricans' with screw-on lids do not seal as well as the original design and don't pour as well. Generally, do not be afraid to stack or store a jerrycan on its side. If the seal is good it will not leak. If the seal is faulty it will leak standing upright as well.

Jerrycans can always be sold all over the Sahara, and they fetch higher prices there than in Europe. If you arrive on the edge of the Sahara with insufficient jerrycans, they can be bought at two places, at least: at the roadside stall between Touggourt and Square Bresson in N.E. Algeria and at stalls outside the supermarket, opposite the Family House Hotel, in Agadez, Niger.

When pouring from the jerrycan to the petrol tank, ensure that the static electricity has been dissipated by touching a metal part of the car, and the ground, at the same time.

Pouring spouts which clip over the mouth of the jerrycan are available from most supply shops. Flexible metal funnels should be avoided as they dribble all over the place, and always seem to leak. They also need an extra person to hold them, while you pour. Long cranked but fixed funnels seem to be best, especially if they have fine gauze to prevent dirt being poured

Burnt out VW Kombi at Moulay Hassan. Do not put petrol in plastic containers

into the petrol tank.

A very neat syphon cap that can be attached to the mouth of the jerrycan and connected to the carburettor by hose, is available from Daerrs. It would be most useful in the event of a petrol pump failure or complete inability to use the petrol tank. It is also worth taking a little hand-squeeze operated plastic syphon. These are available at most accessory shops in Germany, and avoid your getting petrol in the mouth.

Metal jerrycans are available with a special inner lacquer, expressly for drinking water. If used they should be clearly marked 'WATER' and even painted a different colour to the petrol ones (customarily, white is the colour for water jerrycans). However, plastic jerrycans are generally quite a bit cheaper, and suitable for drinking water. Translucent ones are specially good as you can tell at a glance how much water is left. A can that has once contained petrol or diesolene is almost impossible to clean out satisfactorily for drinking water purposes no matter whether it is of plastic or metal.

Petrol jerrycans mounted on the front or rear bumper bars can be dangerous in even a small accident.

Extra Fuel Tanks

On some vehicles, especially Land Rovers and Unimogs, it is possible to fit extra fuel tanks under seats, or between chassis members. An advantage is that one can fill up where fuel is cheap, and travel thousands of kilometres without having to pay duty, or empty jerrycans of fuel. This is not a problem at frontiers within the Sahara as distances are so great between fuelling points, that Customs have to ignore such finer details; but on entry to Morocco from Algeria, for example, it could be a problem.

Shovels

An essential piece of equipment; preferably it should have a large blade about a foot or more across for shovelling large quantities of sand. It should also

216

A good cranked metal funnel is necessary to refuel some vehicles, using a jerrycan

Jerrycans mounted safely on the side of a Toyota Land Cruiser. Note the padlocks and chains to prevent theft

have a long handle, so that it can reach right underneath the vehicle. A small army-type folding shovel is also useful for toilet trips.

Tow Rope
Even if you feel you will never use it, you may wish to help some other vehicle, whose occupants have not bothered to bring one, or to extend the length of his rope so that you can pull him, from outside a soft patch. It should preferably be a 1cm diameter steel cable spliced and thimbled at both ends and about 20m long. You should also have at least two 2 tonne galvanised shackles. It can also be used to draw water from a well.

Spare Wheel Position
If your vehicle has a spare wheel mounted under the rear it should be removed and carried inside the vehicle, on the roof rack or mounted on the side, front bonnet or rear door. Underneath the rear its cradle will become damaged on ruts and the spare wheel may be difficult to remove or it could drop off. It will often slow your progress through deep sand. This particularly applies to vehicles like the Toyota Land Cruiser FJ60 station wagon, the Datsun MQ Patrol station wagon and some Peugeots.

Roof Racks
Roof racks are often an annoying necessity. On the good roads of Europe you hardly notice you have one, even when fully loaded up. On Saharan pistes, even an empty roof rack can fall to pieces. Here are some guidelines.
   It must be strong and rigid.
   It should have a plywood floor to stop items falling on the roof, and to minimize chafing.
   Avoid putting heavy items on it, as this makes the vehicle top heavy and can destroy gutter rails.
   Preferably store full jerrycans inside the vehicle.
   Don't connect a roof rack that is fixed to the roof or gutter to the chassis, especially on Land Cruisers and Land Rovers. The body and chassis flex differently and something would have to give.
   Don't connect a cab mounted roof rack on a Unimog to the rear load compartment. The chassis twists that are designed to occur would wreck the roof rack.
   The 'feet' at the bottom of the roof rack legs should be as long as possible, preferably following the entire length of the guttering, in order to distribute the load. If not, it may be impossible to open doors on a

Land Rover station wagon after a while.

Secure all objects on the roof rack so that they don't bounce off, or chafe.

Use lengths of small chain and padlocks to tie around jerrycans, spare wheels, shovels, etc. so that they cannot be easily stolen.

Remember that some ferries charge considerably more if the vehicle is over a certain height (e.g. 'Dana Corona').

A roof rack with a plywood floor can be a very pleasant and secure place to sleep: away from scorpions and thieves. 'Air Camper' folding roof rack tents are sold by Daerrs and Brownchurch Components. They are expensive.

Windscreens

Do not go without a laminated windscreen. It is essential, and consists of two untempered pieces of glass stuck together with a thin sheet of plastic. It is compulsory for all vehicles sold in the U.S.A., and is always an option when buying a new car elsewhere. It will not shatter into thousands of pieces like a normal tempered windscreen, when hit by a stone. It will usually 'star' or crack very slightly on the outside layer only. Although it costs more than an ordinary windscreen, it can become pock-marked with hundreds of stone 'hits' before it becomes useless (equivalent of literally hundreds of normal windscreens).

With a laminated windscreen you do not need elaborate stone guards. In fact, the cost of a satisfactory stone guard is probably more than the extra cost of a laminated windscreen.

Winches

Electric, hydraulic, or hand operated winches are generally an unnecessary extra load in the Sahara. They are usually not much use for unbogging a

A Toyota FJ55 Land Cruiser station wagon with a cage type roof rack. Mounted on a roll-cage structure fixed to the chassis, this roof rack does not touch the roof or the gutters and so avoids all the problems of gutter fixed racks

218

vehicle from sand (see Chapter 22, Driving in the Sahara), but could be used to advantage for righting a rolled vehicle or extracting one from a rocky gully or pulling one up a slip face of a dune. But, in each case other improvisations could suffice.

12 volt electric winches capable of pulling 3 tonnes range from UK£250 upwards and can flatten a battery in four minutes. Power take off winches are even more expensive, from UK£400 upwards.

Among the hand operated winches available, the French made 'Tirfor T 16' is relatively compact, capable of pulling 2.5 tonnes, but is expensive and fairly heavy, about 18kg. The Japanese equivalent, the 'Elephant Looper', is a bit cheaper but it has 1.5 tonne limit. The American 'Hi Lift' jack (which 'walks' up its own stand) can be used as a slow but very effective winch, capable of pulling 3 tonnes, or for its designed purpose as a jack. It weighs about 8kg.

For the amount of use one would get out of a winch, it would not be an economical proposition, and never really an absolute necessity.

Bull Bars
Opinion varies considerably on the efficacy of erecting these heavy bars (known variously as 'roo-bars', 'bush-bars' and 'crash-bars') on the front of the vehicle to protect it on impact with livestock and other animals.

A strong well designed 'bull-bar', mounted on the front of a large vehicle with a chassis, can do just that. They are particularly suited to heavy trucks and will enable such a vehicle to come off unmarked after hitting a camel. Land Rovers have protruding front chassis members to which a 'bull-bar' can be mounted, but so often flimsy, badly stressed structures only make the damage to the vehicle worse.

For the chassis-less vehicles like Peugeots and 2CVs, it is extremely difficult to design an effective one, particularly as it must be cantilevered forward from some part of the vehicle, near the radiator. This is true, too, of the VW-Bus, but there is even more danger here, in that the 'bull-bar' cantilevered out front will add excessive weight to the front of the vehicle, especially with a spare wheel mounted to it. This will excessively compress the front suspension even before the car is driven on the piste.

There is also a very real danger on saloon cars like the Peugeot 504 and on vehicles like the VW Kombi that their designed progressive crumple rate on impact will be interfered with. Some 'bull-bars' are mounted to a VW Kombi front axle, at the existing axle bolts. This, too, is dangerous as these bolts are tapered. Interfering with them in this way will leave them permanently loose and the axle could shift.

A 'bull-bar' is always expensive, and for this reason too, only after careful consideration should one decide to attach one.

Other Protection
A Volkswagen Kombi should have a steel plate attached to the rear torsion bar tube with U-bolts to protect the front of the gearbox. Other normal road cars should have sump guards fitted. Usually these are standard equipment on models destined for tropical lands. A Land Rover sump is protected by the front axle, but be careful if negotiating rocky slopes.

If heading into places like the Parc du ''W'' or further south into Africa, wire mosquito netting could be placed across the grill to prevent the radiator becoming choked with grass seeds.

Air Cleaners
Extra, more effective air filtration may be necessary on some vehicles. British

A 1600cm³ Volkswagen Kombi engine fitted with the optional M-153 air cleaner for use in very dusty conditions. Note the plastic bowl of the 'cyclone' pre-cleaner stage (VW part no: 211 129 904)

Leyland sell an optional high mounted additional filter for Land Rovers. Usually, the existing filtration, or air cleaning system should be retained, adding an extra 'cyclone' filter to it to pre-clean the air of heavier particles before it enters the normal filter.

Volkswagenwerke produce an optional special two stage filter for big engined twin carburettor VW Kombis (VW Option M153 and part number 029 129 607A). However, the oil bath air cleaner used on 1972 model 1700cc engine VW-Buses is perfectly adequate provided it is inspected and cleaned frequently. Tropical models of the small engined 1600cc VW-Bus either have a large oil bath air cleaner or, more recently, a two-stage cyclone and paper element air cleaner (VW Option M153 and part number 211 129 904). Both these air cleaners are perfectly adequate, provided they are attended to frequently. Rear engined vehicles are especially prone to dust problems and need constant vigilance.

Excellent accessory air cleaners with a pre-cleaning cyclone stage are made by 'Donaldson' (USA) and 'Tecafiltre' and are available from Nova-Handels AG, Josefstrasse 84, Zurich 8031, Switzerland and Tecafiltres S.A., BP 32, 93230 Romainville, France, respectively. 'Donaldson' air cleaners are also obtainable from Chardonnet Division Motorac, B.P. 205, 93 003 Bobigny, France. Both brands are available for a variety of engine sizes.

With all vehicles watch that the plastic hose leading from the air cleaner to the carburettor, or from one air filter to the other, does not get fractured.

Oil Filters

Standard on most vehicles, they are only a rarely seen option on the small engined VW-Buses. They are an advantage in ensuring long crankshaft and bearing life, especially in the desert. An alternative is to fit a 'Frantz' oil filter. This is an American by-pass unit that uses toilet rolls as the filtering medium,

A two stage Donaldson 'Cyclopac' air cleaner mounted to the front of a Toyota Land Cruiser

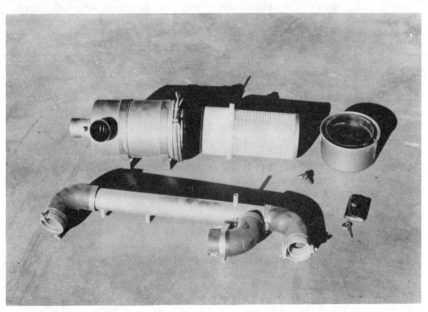

A Donaldson 'Cyclopac' air cleaner which is marketed with these special adaptors for second generation twin carburettor Volkswagen Kombis

and can be easily fitted to any vehicle. (Manufactured by Sky Corporation, Stockton, California 95206, USA.)

Oil Cooler

Land Rovers and Range Rovers need oil coolers if cruised fast on bitumen roads in the Sahara and in places like Nigeria. Brownchurch Components sell them and they are easy to fit. Air cooled VWs have satisfactory coolers, but fitting a larger one would help tremendously. However, beware that it doesn't lower oil pressure too much.

Reevco (1135 Sixth St., Berkley, California 94710) produce an excellent external oil cooler for the big type 4 VW-Bus. However, their external cooler for the small engined bus (1600cc) is totally unsuitable for the Sahara as it hangs beneath the engine in a most vulnerable and dangerous position.

Second Battery

This is essential if travelling alone, and if running a fridge. Batteries can give up with collapsed cells, without warning. A pair of jumper leads should be carried too. You might inadvertently flatten a battery or you might need to help someone else.

Shock Absorbers

Land Cruisers, Land Rovers, Unimogs and Range Rovers have good big, adequate shock absorbers, provided that they are in good condition. It would be an advantage to fit heavier duty shock absorbers to Peugeots, Citroens, Renaults, etc. On many overseas specification Volkswagens (e.g. Australia, Nigeria, etc.) heavy duty shock absorbers are standard. They should be fitted if not already present. Alternatively, heavy duty versions of other makes like Gabriel, Koni, or Bilstein could be fitted, though they are twice the price of the normal heavy duty Boge brand and last the same time.

Beware of fitting shock absorbers with assister coil springs around them. The spring can dislocate itself and rub against the shock absorber, wearing a hole in the casing, and causing it to leak badly.

Tyres

Do not fall into the trap of assuming that the Sahara will wreck your tyres anyway, so why not take old ones, especially as you need smooth tyres for the sand. Tyres can make the difference between a pleasant, enjoyable Saharan trip and a frustrating, tiring and hazardous ordeal. You must have the right tyres, and they must be in the best condition possible at the outset.

In the Sahara tyres should be a special combination: capable of providing good flotation in sand, and of withstanding sharp stones and rocks on the hard piste. Mud and snow tyres can do the latter well, but they will only dig in sand (unless pressures are dangerously low). Generally, therefore, M + S tyres should be avoided, as they will cause more work than necessary.

There are three good, purely sand tyres: the Dunlop Sand Tyre, the Sumitomo Sand Tyre SC 705, and the Bridgestone Alligator. They are balloon cross-plies designed specifically to float rather than provide traction. The first two have almost no tread, apart from a few shallow longitudinal grooves which run the full circumference of the tyre. The third one has large but flattened lumps on it rather like an almost bald Goodyear G800. They are high pressure tyres perfect for sand, but are not good on gravel roads and are lethal in the wet. They are available in 15 inch and 16 inch sizes for Land Cruisers and Land Rovers, and are most popular with Libyans who operate Land Cruiser 'taxis' between Sebha and Agadez across the Fezzan and Ténéré.

Sand tyre: Dunlop   *Sand tyre: Michelin XS*

Two tyres which are a satisfactory combination but with the emphasis on stony terrain rather than sand, are Goodyear High Milers and Michelin XY; both being steel braced radials and reasonably priced.

Perhaps the most common tyre in the Sahara on every vehicle from giant Kenworth Trucks to Land Cruisers is the Michelin XS. It is a steel braced radial with the emphasis on flotation in sand work. It is just about the best tyre for the desert. (Though it is very slippery in wet weather in Europe.) The Japanese equivalent of the Michelin XS is the Bridgestone V Steel Jamal, with a tread pattern, nearly identical. Unfortunately neither is available for wheel sizes smaller than those of the Land Cruiser (7.00 x 15). So for Peugeots, VW-Buses, Citroen 2CVs, and Renault 4s, one has to settle for the nearest equivalent. Generally, this seems to be the Michelin ZX and XZX; a relatively smooth tread steel braced radial (available also in 8-ply reinforced versions).

Ordinary cross-ply tyres are now a thing of the past in the Sahara. Steel radials no longer have problems with soft sidewalls, provide flotation in sand, adhesion on bitumen, and double the mileage of cross-plies.

New tyres are often very difficult to find in the Sahara (especially for Peugeots and VWs), and always two or three times their cost in Europe. Therefore, set out with the best possible tyres; you can always sell them at a profit if you have too many.

Because of the rough treatment received, tubeless tyres should not be used in the Sahara. They will lose air gradually, and can suffer from sudden deflation if a wheel rim gets slightly buckled. Because the bead grips the rim so tightly it can be very difficult to 'break the bead' when repairing a puncture. They are also virtually impossible to pump up without a tube in them unless a high pressure garage pump is used.

Tyre Pumps
Foot operated pumps tend to become ruined by sand. They are also slow.

Hand operated pumps tend to be equally slow. However one make of hand pump is very fast and requires little effort: the 'Kinsman' pump (made by Econa Parkamatic Ltd., Drayton Rd., Shirley, Solihull, B90 4XA, U.K.). It is available with single or double barrels and the authors' single barrel version takes about 270 strokes to pump a VW Kombi tyre to 2.1 kg/cm² or around 8 strokes for each 1 p.s.i. The German Schraeder company produce a pump operated by removing one spark plug and inserting a pump apparatus in the motor. This is very quick and effective. It does not pump petrol gas or exhaust into the tyre. It should not be used on air cooled VWs because the plugs are relatively inaccessible and there is an ever present risk of damaging a plug hole thread.

Because variations to tyre pressures are vital to travel in the Sahara, two tyre gauges should be taken, in case one gets lost, or broken. Probably the best Gauge is the Michelin one.

Puncture Repair Kits

The best puncture repair kit is the German Rema 'Tip Top' brand. It uses a vulcanising glue. It is most important that the instructions are carried out to the letter, especially removing the cellophane paper and 'stitching' the patch. 'Tip Top' patches are widely used throughout the Sahara and have largely replaced the old 'Hot Patch'.

Oils

Oils are expensive in Niger, Morocco and Tunisia. In Algeria and Nigeria they are cheaper than anywhere in Europe (except cutprice lines in Britain) and of good quality with 20W50, 40, 30 and 30-40 widely available. SAE 90 hypoy gearbox oil is also widely available and cheap in Nigeria and Algeria. Automatic Transmission Fluid for Range Rover power steering can be almost impossible to find anywhere. If your vehicle has a limited slip differential

Puncture repair kit and tools. Note the simple but effective tyre levers, the talcum powder, the spare valves and the large rubber mallet

224

it will be necessary to take along a supply of the LS-90 oil that is required for LSDs. Supplies of this oil are rare.

In Algeria oils are sold in sealed one and two litre cans (Naftilia is the brand) but in Nigeria oil sold in four and five litre cans should be checked to see that the lid has not been previously opened and part of the contents removed or substituted.

Petrol

In Nigeria, there is usually only one grade despite pump labels. In Niger, Super is usually available only in Niamey. Generally, in the heat of the Sahara it is preferable to buy Super if you can, especially for VWs. If the petrol is of too low an octane rating, it may contribute to overheating. To be safe, specify Super.

Some Octane Ratings		
Country	Normale	Super
Algeria	90	97
Morocco	87	96
Tunisia	87	95

In most places, if fuel is not available, ask around locally. It may be necessary to wait only a few days for supplies to arrive. In Nigeria, despite the country being a major oil exporter, it is sometimes necessary to queue for hours either waiting for it to arrive or to wait for the electricity supply to come on again. The cheaper petrol coupon system for tourists has been discontinued in Morocco since 1979.

Increasingly, petrol engined vehicles sold in Europe require unleaded fuel. This poses two serious problems for Sahara travellers. Firstly, use of leaded fuel in these vehicles can lead to timing and overheating problems and valve and piston failure. Secondly, the orifice for the petrol tank may be too small to accept a leaded fuel pump nozzle.

Diesel

Diesolene is cheaper than petrol in most Saharan countries. One advantage of diesolene is that, if you run out on the piste, it is often no trouble for a passing truck to sell (or even give) you 50-60 litres as he is usually carrying so much in his massive tanks anyway. Usually, petrol powered vehicles have barely enough for themselves let alone spare fuel to sell to someone else. On the other hand, a town may have run out of diesolene while there is plenty of petrol (or even vice versa).

Fuel Filters

All diesel engines have fuel filters in order to protect their sensitive fuel injection systems. Take plenty of spare filter cartridges or elements. If your petrol engined car doesn't have a fuel filter, fit one of the small cheap disposable ones half way along one of the flexible fuel hoses. Take some replacements, too. Fuel on sale throughout the Saharan region invariably has a lot of fine dust in it which quite quickly clogs up filters.

Wheels

In the Sahara there is little point in fitting fancy wide rimmed or magnesium alloy wheels. Initially, there would be a slight advantage in the wide wheels assisting flotation on sand. But, with the tough conditions the vehicle has to endure, they would put unnecessary long term stress on the wheel bearings; just slightly increasing the risk to human life. Also, wide rims can make tyre removal more difficult. Cast alloy wheels are a risk because of the danger of breaking them on rocks, whereas the standard steel rims can always be temporarily bent nearly true again. Generally, they are an unnecessary expense in an already expensive and risky game.

A second spare wheel is not usually necessary if you are prepared to repair your own punctures. (Not so difficult, once you've got the hang of it.) Carrying only one spare wheel is also a considerable saving in weight and space. However, one should carry a second spare tyre and tube.

If however you have a Range Rover, a second spare wheel with tyre fitted is essential. Alone in the bush or desert, it is nearly impossible to 'break the bead' on the standard Range Rover wheels, which have a slightly wider than normal rim. This is especially difficult with Michelin 205 x 16 M+S tyres. The same applies to Unimogs, when equipped with mud and snow tyres.

Some Other Items
- Spare ignition keys.
- Warning triangle. (Use large rocks, stones and branches, too.)
- Fire extinguisher. (BCF type for use with petrol and electric fires.)
- Mat, or small canvas sheet, to use for lying under the vehicle when working on it.
- Safety glasses to protect your eyes from sand particles when working under the vehicle.
- 'Swarfega' or other hand cleanser.
- Towelling seat covers to make smooth plastic seat surfaces much more comfortable.

20
Vehicle
Maintenance

In the desert the climate is so fierce and distances so great that one's life can depend entirely on one's vehicle. Not only must one have a suitable vehicle in good working order, but the owner or driver **must** know how to carry out routine maintenance and be prepared to carry out improvised repairs.

Manual
Even for a trained mechanic, a prerequisite is a manual for the vehicle. Not only does a manual explain procedures, but it also gives specifications for things like tappet settings, timing, dwell angle, etc. If major repairs beyond the scope of the owner, were necessary in Agadez or Djanet, the manual would be an invaluable help to the local mechanic, giving him details of cylinder head torque and tightening sequences, firing order, tear down and reassembling procedure, etc.

Two suggested suppliers of good manuals for vehicles commonly used in the Sahara are: Motor Books and Accessories, 35 St. Martin's Court, London, W.C.2 (among the theatres east of Leicester Square) and Daerrs Expedition Service, Kirchheimer Strasse 2, D-8016 Heimstetten (near Munich).

Probably the best manuals for Land Rover and Range Rover are those published by British Leyland, even though they are expensive. Volkswagen of America publish an excellent manual for VW-Buses. For Land Cruiser, probably the best is published by Chilton Book Co., Radnor, Pa 191089, U.S.A. If you buy a new Land Rover on tourist delivery in England there are, from time to time, Land Rover maintenance courses well worth attending (at the Rover Company's Service Department in Solihull).

Regular Servicing
Before the vehicle leaves for the Sahara it must have been regularly serviced and checked for some time.

The desert will stress the suspension, steering, transmission and engine, close to, or over the manufacturer's limits. For example, it is no good taking a VW-Bus that has not had its valve clearances checked and adjusted for 50,000 km. Even if one checks and resets them just prior to setting out, that long period of neglect will certainly have begun to weaken and stretch the exhaust valve stems. In the heat and in the middle of a long stretch of feche feche, a valve could drop into the combustion chamber and cause untold damage, just when it can be least afforded. This applies to many other parts of all vehicles, and is the main advantage of taking a brand new vehicle.

In the desert itself one must maintain a strict service schedule. Change engine oil and filters when they are due for it. Grease the suspension at regular intervals. In some cases, like the tappets (valve clearances), it pays to increase the normal servicing frequency. In this way one could be fore-warned of a valve breaking and be able to choose the time to repair it. The normal servicing frequency for air-cleaners should most certainly be increased, to every day if necessary, depending on how dusty conditions are. Nothing can make an engine wear out more quickly than to allow the carburettor to suck in great quantities of dust.

Daily Inspection

Every day without fail there **must** be a vehicle inspection routine. This will enable you to see, for example, that a shock absorber is leaking, and to do something about it before it gives up completely and damages the rest of the suspension, or causes premature tyre wear. You will see that the exhaust pipe has lost a securing bolt and is about to drop off. You will know to top up the engine oil before it is too late.

Suggested items that should be inspected every day (depending on the type of vehicle):

Radiator water level.
Security of radiator cap.
Fan belt (tension and cracks).
Spark plug leads.
Air cleaner hoses.
Engine oil level.

Dust can be a problem with rear engined vehicles. However, regular (usually daily) checking and cleaning of the air cleaner will ensure that the engine continues to function efficiently despite the dusty conditions. Here two well-maintained VW-Buses race through a mass of fine bull dust

Check under motor for leaks.
Check gearbox for leaks.
Shock absorber shackle pins and bushes.
Check shock absorbers for leaks.
Check steering damper.
Brake hoses near the backing plate.
Look for signs of brake cylinder leaks.
Look for holes in the exhaust system.
Check tyre pressures.
Notice any damage under the vehicle.

This daily inspection is necessary as part of a routine overall programme of ensuring your vehicle's and your survival in the desert. It also ensures that you are not a liability on others.

Overloading

Be very careful not to overload your vehicle. Long wheel base Land Cruisers, Land Rovers and VW-Buses are designed to carry a payload of up to one tonne (including passengers). To exceed this is to stress one's vehicle and court disaster. The vehicle will become bogged in sand much more easily and extraction will be correspondingly more hard work. Vehicle stress will initially show itself through broken springs and torsion bars, shock absorber mounts, increased punctures, a labouring and overheating motor and, finally, major fractures of chassis rails. In fact, in the Sahara it is preferable to travel with one's vehicle as lightly loaded as possible.

Spare Parts

The spare parts taken will vary with the type of vehicle. They will also vary according to how one interprets the idea that spare parts add unwanted weight and therefore are likely to stress the vehicle, so that one of its components will fail, making the spare parts necessary! This can be true, but it is necessary to strike a balance between weight, price, potential need, and ability to improvise. It should also be remembered that spare parts can fetch high prices in towns like Agadez, Bamako and Djanet, especially for Land Rovers and Range Rovers, and VW-Buses:

1. Land Rover 4 cylinder

Left and right rear half shafts. (axles)
Hub oil seals.
Complete rear spring.
Main leaf for front spring.
U-bolts, nuts and shackle pins.
Spring bushes.
Shock absorber bushes (upper and lower).
Petrol pump.
2 fan belts.
4 spark plugs.
Distributor cap and carbon brush.
Rotor arm.
Complete decoke gasket set.
Condenser.
2 contact breaker point sets.
Ignition coil.

Water pump and gasket
Jubilee clips (large enough for radiator hoses).
Can of Holt's 'Radweld' and steel wool.
Inner and outer hub bearings.
Clutch slave cylinder repair kit.
Brake master cylinder repair kit.
Speedometer cable.
Valve spring.
Exhaust and inlet valves.
Pin for clutch operating shaft.
Headlight bulb.
Indicator, side and brake bulbs.
2 spare tyres.
2 radial tubes and 4 valves.
For diesels only:
    3 fuel filters.
    2 heater plugs.

229

Starter and generator brushes.
Upper and lower radiator hoses.

2. Range Rover
2 or 3 petrol filters.
Perol pump (electical or mechanical)
Ignition coil.
Condenser.
Distributor cap.
Distributor carbon brush.
8 plugs.
4 contact breaker points.
Upper and lower radiator hoses.
Water pump and gasket.
2 Fanbelts.
Power steering belt.
Starter motor brushes.
Upper and lower shock absorber brushes.
Jubilee clips.
Accelerator cable.
Speedometer cable, and T-junction.

2 injector and sealing rings.

Air cleaner elements, at least six.
Brake master cylinder kit.
Set of brake pads (8).
Clutch slave cylinder kit.
Dust seal for tie rod ends.
Headlight bulb.
Side indicator, and brake/rear light bulbs.
4 brake hoses.
Can of Holt's 'Radweld' and steel wool.
Can of 'Gun Gum' and muffler repair kit (for exhaust manifold).
2 radial tubes.
2 spare wheels, with tyres and tubes fitted.
4 tube valves.
500 ml ATF fluid for power steering.

Shock absorbers can be a constant problem. Preventive care like wiring up the nuts on the shackle bolts can stop them coming undone

The left shock absorber has lost its rubber bush. The right one has had its lower mounting point break open. These are just some of the more common problems encountered with shock absorbers in the incredibly punishing conditions of the Sahara

3. Volkswagen Kombi Bus

Exhaust valve (sodium filled)
Valve spring.
2 emergency push rod tubes.
Push rod.
Complete decoke gasket set.
Petrol pump.
Petrol filter (accessory).
4 oil filter elements (accessories).
2 fan belts.
2 contact breaker points.
Distributor cap.
Distributor cap carbon brush.
Barrel and piston with rings.
Main bearing seal.
4 plugs.
Ignition coil and condenser.
Regulator.

Accelerator cable.
Clutch cable.
Speedometer cable.
Clutch release bearing and lever.
Shock absorber bushes.
Front and rear shock absorbers.
Steering damper.
Set front wheel bearings
 (inner and outer)
Headlight bulb.
Indicator, dim and rear/brake
 light bulbs.
Left and right rear torsion bars.
2 radial tubes and 4 valves.
2 spare tyres, but only 1 spare
 wheel is necessary.

There should be sufficient gearbox and engine oil, brake fluid, and grease to last the journey (though oils are good and cheap in Algeria).

English — French Car Parts Words List

General

| Body | Carrosserie |
| Chassis | Chassis |

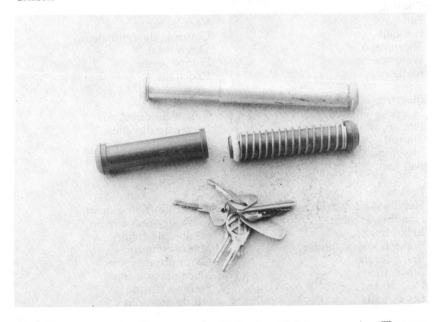

Two different types of replacement pushrod tubes for a Volkswagen engine. These are designed for emergency use in that the cylinder head does not have to be removed in order to fit one

Windscreen	Pare-brise
Pulley	Poulie
Nut	Ecrou
Bolt	Boulon
Lock nut	Contre ecrou
Locking washer	Arretoir
Speedometer	Compteur
Speedo cable	Flexible de tachymetre
Distance recorder	Compteur kilometrique
Gasket	Joint
Hose	Durite
Bumperbar	Pare chocs

Fuel System

Carburettor	Carburateur
Needle valve	Pointeau
Float	Flotteur
Throttle valve	Papillon
Accelerator jet	Gicleur de pompe
Slow idle jet	Gicleur de ralenti
Main jet	Gicleur d'alimentation
Float chamber	Cuve à niveau constant
Fuel pump	Pompe à essence
Fuel line	Canalisation
Fuel gauge	Indicateur de niveau, jauge
Fuel tank	Reservoir
Petrol cap	Bouchon de reservoir

Cooling

Fan	Ventilateur
Fan belt	Courroie de ventilateur
Thermostat	Thermostat
Water pump	Pompe à eau
Radiator	Radiateur

Steering

Steering wheel	Volant de direction
Pitman arm	Levier de direction
Tie rod	Barre de connexion
Steering column	Colonne de direction
Ball joint	Rotule

Brakes

Handbrake lever	Levier de frein à main
Handbrake cable	Cable de frein à main
Brake hose	Flexible de frein
Brake master cylinder	Maitre-cylindre
Brake lining	Garniture de frein
Brake shoe	Machoires de frein
Disc brakes	Freins à disque
Set of pads	Jeu de machoires

Ignition

Glow plug	Bougie de prechauffage
Spark plug	Bougie

Distributor	Allumeur
Contact points	Jeu de contacts, rupteur
Rotor arm	Rotor de distributeur
Condenser	Condensateur
Coil	Bobine d'allumage
Ignition switch	Contacteur d'allumage
Battery	Batterie

Electrical

Fuse	Fusible
Starter motor	Demarreur
Solenoid	Solenoide, Bendix
Armature	Induit de demarreur
Carbon brush	Balai
Generator	Dynamo
Regulator	Regulateur
Alternator	Alternateur

Transmission

Clutch	Embrayage
Clutch plate	Disque d'embrayage
Release bearing	Butée d'embrayage
Pressure plate	Plateau de pression
Clutch master cylinder	Pompe d'embrayage
Clutch slave cylinder	Servodébrayage
Push rod	Tige de poussoir
Gear box	Boite de vitesses
3rd gear	Pignon de la troisième vitesse
Propellor shaft	Arbre de transmission
Universal joint	Cardan de roue
Ball bearings	Roulement à billes
Differential	Diferentiel
Axle casing	Corps de pont
Limited Slip Differential	Differential autobloquant
Crown wheel and pinion	Couple conique
Wheel hub	Moyeu de roue

Suspension

Rear axle	Pont arrière
Spring	Ressort de suspension
Rubber bush	Coussinet en caoutchouc
Leaf spring	Lame de ressort
Shock absorber	Amortisseur
Anti roll bar	Barre de stabilisateur
Universal joint	Cardan de roue
C.V. joint	Joint homocinetique

Motor

Engine mounting	Tampon
Dipstick	Jauge d'huile
Oil filter	Filtre à huile
Piston	Piston
Piston ring	Segment
Gudgeon pin	Axe de piston
Conrod	Bielle

Bearing	Coussinet
Crankshaft	Vilebrequin
Flywheel	Volant
Inlet valve	Soupape d'admission
Exhaust valve	Soupape d'echappement
Valve Guide	Guide de soupape
Valve spring	Ressort de soupape
Cotter pins	Bagues d'appui
Rocker	Culbuteur
Rockershaft	Axe de culbuteurs
Push rod	Tige de culbuteurs
Push rod tube	Couvercle de tige
Camshaft	Arbre à cames
Valve cover	Couvercle de culasse
Cylinder head	Culasse
Cylinder block	Bloc-cylindres
Oil seal	Bague d'étarchéité
Manifold	Collecteur
Oil cooler	Radiateur d'huile
Water pump	Pompe à eau
Wheel	Roue
Spare wheel	Roue de secours
Jack	Cric
Tube	Chambre à air
Tyre	Pneu
Patch	Rustine
Puncture	Crevaison
Leakage	Fuite
Fracture in tyre	Dechirure
Wheel rim	Jante

Tools

Socket spanner	Clé à tube
Crescent spanner	Clé plate
Spanner	Clé
Screwdriver	Tournevis
Pliers	Pince
Hammer	Marteau
Torque spanner	Clé dynamométrique
Phillips screwdriver	Tournevis cruciforme
Ring spanner	Clé à oeillet
Socket	Douille
Tyre lever	Demonte pneu

Tools for the Vehicle

Special auxiliary equipment like jerrycans, sandladders, shovels, funnels, etc. are covered in the chapter on Vehicle Equipment and Preparation. Tools needed to work on the motor or suspension do vary from vehicle to vehicle, although there will be basic types of tools needed for every vehicle. As a representative sample here are lists of tools recommended for a Range Rover and a Volkswagen.

A 'Hi-Lift' jack can lift more than three tonnes. Always chock the wheels to prevent the vehicle rolling as the jack lifts it and ensure that the jack is resting on firm ground. When working under a jacked up vehicle do not rely on the jack to prevent the vehicle falling and killing you

Left: One must be prepared to carry out one's own vehicle repairs in the desert. This land Rover is having its front suspension attended to (Photo by courtesy of Ida and Pieter Kersten)

1. Range Rover

Set of AF ring spanners
Set of AF open ended spanners
Set of AF sockets, including a
  ratchet and extension
Assorted large sockets e.g.
  27mm, 32mm (or equivalent)
Breaker bar (or 'T' bar) for
  large sockets
2 tyre levers
Large, medium and small flat
  screwdrivers
Large, medium and small
  Phillips screwdrivers
Ball joint remover
Large wheel puller
Steel hammer
Pair insulated long nose pliers
Pair insulated ordinary pliers.
Pair of vice grips (Mole-wrench)
Pair of multi-grips
Large adjustable spanner
Dwell angle meter/rev. counter
Small electric test light
Torque spanner (essential for
  alloy engines)

Set of feeler gauges
Flat metal file
Small round file
Hand drill and bits
Metre long length of ¾" steel
  pipe (spanner & 'T' bar
  extension)
1.5 tonne hydraulic jack
2 blocks of wood (about
  6x5x25cm) useful when
  jacking the car.
Roll of strong duct tape
Empty ½ litre can for pouring oil.
Insulation tape
Grease gun
Hack saw
Plug spanner
Pair of jumper leads
Tin of assorted nuts, bolts,
  screws, washers, etc.
(N.B. some export Range
  Rovers have some metric
  components, such as track
  rod ends).

2. Volkswagen Kombi Bus

Set of metric ring spanners
  (8 to 19mm)
Set of metric open ended
  spanners (8 to 19mm, also
  27mm)
Set of metric sockets (10 to
  19mm) ratchet and extension
Large sockets especially 27, 32,
  36, 46mm.
Adapter and breaker bar ('T'
  bar for large sockets.)
Set of Allen keys, metric.
Splined key socket for CV
  joints.
Large, medium and small flat
  screwdrivers.
Large, medium and small
  Phillips screwdrivers.
Track rod ball joint remover.
Large wheel puller.
Pair insulated long nose pliers.
Pair uninsulated ordinary pliers.
Pair vice-grips (Mole-wrench)

Small test light
Set of feeler gauges
Flat metal file
Small round file
Empty ½ litre can, for pouring oil
Plug spanners
Hand drill and bits
Roll of strong duct tape
Metre long length of ¾" steel
  pipe (spanner and 'T' bar
  extension)
1.5 tonne hydraulic jack
2 blocks of wood (about
  6x5x25cm) useful when
  jacking up the car.
Hack saw
Grease gun
Insulation tape
Gearbox plug spanner (male
  hexagon)
Assorted taps and dies
  (especially 10mm tap)
Tin of fine and coarse valve

Pair multi-grips
Steel hammer
Large adjustable spanner
Torque spanner (essential for
alloy engines)
Dwell angle meter/rev. counter

grinding paste
Suction cup valve grinder
Tin of assorted nuts, bolts,
screws and washers, etc.
Pair of jumper leads.

Basic Fault Finding

Your vehicle won't start despite the fact that the starter motor works and turns the engine. Don't persevere and flatten the battery. There are two basic tests that should be carried out in order to isolate the problem:

1. Electrical
a.   Switch on the ignition.
b.   Pullout the distributor end of the main high tension lead between the coil and distributor.
c.   Take the distributor cap off and push it to one side.
d.   Remove the rotor arm or button.
e.   Hold the distributor end of the main high tension lead about a centimetre away from a steel part of the engine block.
f.   With the other hand, flick open the distributor points and let them close.
This should show a strong blue spark jumping from the end of the lead to the engine block, indicating that the electrical ignition system is okay, and that one should look for a petrol problem. A weak red spark indicates a faulty coil or a faulty condenser. Replace one or both with your spares.

2.   Petrol
a.   Remove the air cleaner.
b.   Look into the throat of the carburettor while you operate the accelerator pump.
If a spray of petrol is seen, then the fuel supply system is okay. If not, try some of the following further tests, preferably in this order:

3.   Are you sure you haven't run out of petrol?
4.   Check the fuel filter (if fitted). This could be clogged with fine sand, fluff, leaf particles or even water. Replace or clean it. (If there was water in it, put a cupful of methylated spirits into the petrol tank next time it is filled. This will break down any water lying in the bottom of the tank.)
5.   Check that the fuel pump is operating by removing the carburettor end of the fuel supply line that goes from the fuel pump to the carburettor and seeing if petrol is pumped out at a good rate when the starter is operated. A mechanical fuel pump is most likely to have a fractured or weak diaphragm. Replace it, or in some cases a new pump must be fitted. An electric pump may be just too hot. Wrap a wet cloth around it for a minute or two and remove it. If this doesn't bring it back to life then replace it with your spare. (An electric pump ticks as it operates.)
6.   Check the float chamber of the carburettor by undoing the retaining screws. See if there is fuel in the chamber. It may have fuel in it but be clogged up with sand, but more than likely it is empty or only partially full and the float needle valve is jammed. Unscrew it and clean it or replace it: it may have sand particles stuck in it.

If the car has been standing for a long time (several weeks or more), fuel may have all drained back to the petrol tank. In that case, remove the air cleaner, pour half a cup of petrol down the carburettor throat and it should start. If the engine only runs for a few seconds repeat the process two or three times.

These basic electrical and fuel supply checks will not be relevant to more complex systems: e.g. transistorised ignition and electronic or mechanical fuel injection. This highlights the need to come to the Sahara with a standard commonly used vehicle without complicated and sophisticated functions.

Other Improvisations
1. Your starter motor does not work and you cannot push-start your vehicle because the ground is too flat, it is bogged in sand, or for some other reason. There is still a way of starting it:
(a) Jack one of the powered wheels off the ground. (Both wheels in the case of vehicles with a limited slip differential.) Wedge a couple of stones around the opposite wheel so that the raised side of the car does not fall off the jack when the car starts.
(b) Select second gear.
(c) Switch on the ignition.
(d) Turn the jacked wheel as far back as possible. Then, very firmly and quickly spin the wheel forwards, hard. This action will crank the engine. As soon as it starts, slip it into neutral in order to avoid the possibility of the shuddering from the engine causing the car to fall off the jack. One has to put it into neutral as soon as possible and if one is alone it would be best to jack and crank the powered wheel on the driver's side.
This procedure would not normally be possible with a Range Rover or other full-time four wheel drive vehicles, nor with automatic transmissions. Part-time four wheel drives should be in two wheel drive, high range, and not have any differential lock engaged. Of course, if your car can be started with a crank handle, it is preferable to do so.
2. A leaking and damaged radiator can be repaired with 'Radweld', marketed by Holts and by Shell. If the hole is big, then pack it tightly with steel wool prior to pouring in 'Radweld'.
3. A split or holed petrol tank can be temporarily prevented from leaking by rubbing a cake of soap into the crack or hole, and smearing the soap all around. If necessary, repeat frequently. Mixing fine sand with the soap helps it bond.
4. If the coil spring on the front suspension has 'jumped out' because a strut has lost its retaining bolt, patience and hard work can fix it. Remove the coil spring. Compress it by lowering the jacked up car on to it. Then, while it is compressed, tightly bind up the spring with lots of wire. Jack up the car again and instal the wired-up spring over its strut. Bolt up the strut again, and one by one, cut the wires that compress the spring.
5. If a fuel line is irreparably damaged, a petrol tank incurably leaking, or a petrol pump is not working, then a jerrycan set up higher than the engine and connected to the carburettor by a plastic hose will do the job of supplying the motor with fuel. However, it will need constant vigilance and careful driving. Wire or tape the jerrycan to the roof rack or onto the bonnet.
6. If a Volkswagen-Bus (1968 to 1971 models) has broken its engine carrier, the whole transmission and power unit will drag on the ground. Drill or knock two holes in the floor above the engine compartment and use your steel tow rope to wire up the engine into its normal position. You can continue for thousands of kilometres like this.
7. If one of two vehicles in convoy has a non-functioning generator or alternator, swap batteries every hundred kilometres.
8. If one wheel has a badly leaking brake cylinder, don't let it continue to waste fluid and ruin the linings. Isolate the offending brakes by tightening wire around the brake hose; or, cut the metal brake tube, bend the end over

and crimp it tight with a pair of vice grips.

9. If you have an oil temperature gauge and feel that the engine is getting too hot, stop and allow it to cool down by switching off, or in the case of an air-cooled engine allow it to cool by idling. If you are too late and it is showing signs of seizure, like loss of power and knocking, switch off to prevent any further damage from being done. You may decide to dismantle the engine to investigate, or repair it. If there is a partial seizure remember that six cylinder engines can be run on four cylinders, and a flat air cooled VW engine will run on three! To isolate a cylinder; remove the con rod and the piston and disconnect the spark plug; close the valves by removing the push-rods, or rocker arms. You must seal the disconnected cylinder; and to avoid a disastrous explosion you **must not** allow the plug to operate.

10. In a VW, you are travelling along. The motor is hot. There is a loud explosion from the engine. Switch off immediately. Chances are that you have 'dropped' a valve. (Usually through overheating, incorrect tappet settings, or worn valve guides.) You must switch off instantly to minimize further damage to the combustion chamber, piston and remaining valves. When dismantling the engine, remove both cylinder heads, as the force of the explosion, when the valve 'dropped', will have sent pieces of valve through the inlet manifold to the opposite cylinder.

11. If a conrod has broken and pushed a hole through the block, disconnect that cylinder, as outlined above. Then, use any sheet of metal to cover the hole, e.g. flattened tin can. Drill holes in the block and use Araldite and self-tapping screws to hold the cover in place, over the hole. This will work for a time.

12. When changing engine oil, save old oil. You might open your can of new oil and find that it is water contaminated, or the can has been wrongly labelled. If you have let the old oil straight out of the sump onto the ground you may regret not having saved it. Also, old oil is perfectly good for use in an oil bath air cleaner. It can make quite a saving if the air cleaner oil has to be changed every day.

13. Chewing gum is often a useful item to have on hand; to extract a nut or washer that has fallen down a hole, to seal a hole up against dust and water penetration, to hold something in place, and to insulate.

14. If your vehicle has broken a set of leaf springs, a coil spring or torsion bar, tie or wire up an inflated tube and tyre between the axle and the chassis. Preferably the wheel rim should not be included. Instead, an inner rubber liner as found on split rim wheels should be inserted inside the tyre before the tube is inflated. This combination will quite effectively serve as a temporary spring for hundreds of carefully driven kilometres and will minimise structural damage to the vehicle. Avoid placing the tyre too close to the exhaust system, brake lines and exposed rotating drive shafts, CV-joints and universal joints.

15. If an air cooled VW engine has developed a major and rapid oil leak, and upon inspection you find it to be a split oil cooler; this is usually a sign that one or both of the oil pressure relief valves has jammed closed. A new oil cooler has to be fitted; although binding the damaged one up with lots of wire and Araldite will work for a while. However, the jammed oil pressure valve **must** be dislodged. The only way to do it is to use a 10mm tap to extract the thimble-like pieces of metal. (On engines after 1969 there are two.) Either new valves should be fitted, or the old ones cleaned up with sand paper before being installed. Remember, too, that the problem of jammed oil pressure relief valves is usually caused by wear or distortion through overheating or a combination of both. They might jam again soon after reinstallation.

16.　If an aircooled VW engine has a damaged or leaking pushrod tube (a major danger in the ruts or 'ornières' of the Sahel), it may be easily remedied by fitting a concertina pushrod tube (available at most non-agency but specialist or enthusiast VW shops and garages). To do this, jack up the car on the damaged side, to avoid any further oil loss. When the engine has cooled remove the tappet cover, and unscrew the two rocker shaft retaining nuts simultaneously. Remove the rockershaft and pull out the push rod from the damaged tube. Bend out the damaged tube and replace it with the emergency concertina type. (This can be a permanent fixture as it is an improvement on the original.) Do up the rocker shaft nuts to the correct torque setting; top up with oil and drive on. Check the tappets the following morning.

17.　If you have a diesel engine and find it impossible to obtain fuel, a satisfactory temporary substitute is kerosene (paraffin in Britain), mixed with a little oil. The mixture should be 100 parts kerosene to one part engine oil. The oil serves as a lubricant for the injector pump.

18.　If you have a bent track rod, remove it (preferably with the correct ball joint extractor tool), and hammer it straight, on a rock. If you leave it bent, not only will you have accelerated abnormal tyre wear, but in deep sand there is a very real danger of rolling!

19.　Remember that if a four-wheel drive vehicle fitted with free-wheeling hubs breaks a front half shaft, it can continue in rear two-wheel drive and with the hubs in the free-wheel position. Without free-wheeling hubs, it would be necessary to remove the broken half shaft from the axle, as well as the front propellor shaft. If a rear half shaft is broken, it should be removed together with the rear prop. shaft and the vehicle driven home in 'four-wheel drive'; in other words with only the front wheels driving. If a Range Rover or Land Rover with three differentials jams itself into the 'Diff Lock' position, remove the front prop shaft and continue cautiously in rear-wheel drive only (it is a shocking car to drive like this).

20.　If you have a pre-1980 VW-Bus, remove the front anti-roll bar before you leave the asphalt road. It will only get buckled on ruts and rocks, and will even cause you to become bogged when it drags in the sand, slowing you up. Re-install it when you return to the asphalt.

21.　Sometimes the Range Rover's standard wheel spanner is just not strong enough to remove the wheelnuts: it just bends. The only alternative is a 27 mm socket and strong breaker or 'T' bar.

22. It is very hot and you are bogged. You switched off your Range Rover's engine while you dug and laid sand ladders. You then found you couldn't start it again. The electric fuel pump may be hot and suffering from a vapour lock. Climb underneath and wet it with a very damp cloth. This will usually cure the problem.

23.　Finally, never trust other people's work on your car; no matter whether it is a 'bush mechanic' in Tamanrasset or a large main dealer in Germany, France or Britain. Always inspect the work done on your car afterwards. Your vehicle may be the cause of your death in the Ténéré but it won't affect the mechanic who was careless in London or Munich. Sometimes a 'bush mechanic' doesn't mind if the customer looks over his shoulder supervising, especially if he helps the process along with the occasional cigarette or can of orange juice.

Puncture Repairs

Punctures are almost an inevitability on any journey into the Sahara. Once you understand the mechanics of how a tyre fits a wheel rim and have had a little practice, puncture repairs can become a relatively quick and painless operation. Being able to repair your own puncture allows you to travel with only one spare wheel: a considerable and important saving of weight and space. A second spare tyre and several spare tubes should be carried nevertheless.

To remove the tyre case from the wheel rim it is first necessary to release the tight grip between the inner edge of the tyre (the bead) and the outer rim of the wheel. This is 'breaking the bead' and can be really difficult. One way around the problem is to lay the punctured wheel on the ground and drive over the sidewall of the tyre, thus pressing the tyre bead away from the wheel's outer rim. Alternatively, lay the wheel on the ground and jack up the car with the foot of the jack on the side wall of the tyre. This should take the bead away from the rim. Sometimes it is necessary to repeat this procedure with the other side of the wheel. You are then able to set to with the tyre levers.

Tubeless and 'mud and snow' tyres can be particularly stubborn for breaking the bead. The same applies to some wide rims. Avoid bringing them to the Sahara for this reason. Of course 'breaking the bead' is not a problem with Toyota Land Cruisers and other vehicles with truck type split rims: a simple lever system is used to split the outer rim and remove it from the wheel

Thorns are very big and strong in the Sahel and southern Sahara. Do not park under acacia thorn trees. Thorns break off and become embedded in the outer rubber of the tyre tread. No immediate puncture occurs but after several hours or even days later with the constant flexing of the tyre in motion, the piece of thorn gradually works its way inwards until it punctures the tube. Such punctures usually start with only a slow leak. When repairing this sort of puncture check to see that several thorns have not been the cause of air loss. It may also be necessary to use a pair of pliers to extract thorns from the tyre casing

242

'Breaking the bead' by jacking the vehicle up on the tyre

'Breaking the bead' by driving over the tyre

altogether.

Always be prepared for unforeseen emergencies when working on a jacked up vehicle. The author's life was saved by a jerrycan placed under the car when the ground on which the jack was standing caved in and the jack collapsed.

When a puncture in a tube has been repaired, do not forget to run your hand around the inside of the tyre case to feel for any protruding thorns, nails or wire. If your steel belted tyre has begun to show the wire cords, discard it as these wires will quickly give a tube multiple punctures.

When driving always be suspicious of any hint of squeamishness in the car's handling especially off the asphalt. Driving only a hundred metres at speed on a flat tyre can wreck the case totally. In the desert it doesn't pay to run out of tyres.

1. After 'breaking the bead', use tyre levers to prise the tyre bead up and over the wheel rim. At the outset, ensure that the tyre bead on the opposite side of the wheel is well depressed into the wheel rim cavity. You cannot start to prise the tyre bead over the rim until this happens

2. When the complete tyre bead has been lifted over the wheel rim, pull out the tube, find the puncture and repair it. Feel inside the tyre case for the offending nail, thorn or other object and remove it

3. Replace the tube and make sure the valve is well seated and not pulled to one side. Using a tyre lever, prise the bead back over the wheel rim. Note how the author is standing on the opposite side of the tyre to ensure that it lies well inside the wheel rim. This is essential to getting the last bit of tyre bead over the rim. (Talcum powder can be sprinkled inside the tyre case to minimise friction between it and the tube)

4. As the tyre pump is fitted to the valve, grip the valve stem with a pair of pliers to prevent it slipping inside the wheel. It pays to keep sand out of this whole puncture repairing process: hence the sheet of cardboard seen in these photos

21
Camping Equipment

The type of gear taken for cooking, sleeping, relaxing and sheltering in, is very much a personal choice, depending on how one wants to do it and, of course, budget. However, here are some tips on the merits or demerits of just a few camping items.

Campervans
Sometimes known as motor homes, motorized caravans, or campmobiles, these have the big advantage of enabling you to sleep and eat in the privacy of your own vehicle. They also give the added sense of security of taking your own home with you, rather than the very temporary expedient of camping. One doesn't realise it at first, but after living and travelling for two months in the back of a Range Rover, one longs for the comfort and homeliness of a Volkswagen Campmobile.

Preferably camper conversions should have furniture made of marine plywood rather than particle board, as it is stronger, more durable, lighter and not prone to disintegration if wet. If you do not wish to do the job yourself, two of the better van conversion specialists in Germany are Campingbusse Simek (Baslerlandstrasse 6, D-7800 Freiburg) and Franz Knobel und Sohne KG (Postfach 540, D-4832 Wiedenbruck) both of which manufacture the official VW sponsored 'Westfalia' conversions. There are other very effective specialists in Britain such as Devon Conversions (Sidmouth, Devonshire EX10 9HA) and Motorhomes International (Leighton Buzzard, Bedfordshire). However, the authors have had experience of some other conversions in the Sahara which were absolutely shocking in the way they fell to pieces (e.g. one made at a small town in Essex, England).

Avoid big American style conversions. They have lots of space and other home comforts but their fuel consumption, weight, low clearance, and size make them totally unsuitable for a Saharan journey off the bitumen. Yet some people insist on trying to bring them. If you feel you need the extra space of a big vehicle, then a Mercedes Benz Unimog, or even a big MAN 4x4 truck with living quarters in the back would be much more suitable. But the initial investment in the vehicle cab and chassis, plus the special conversion, would be extremely high, even before you started to pay for the astronomical running costs. However, a specialist Italian coach builder, Grand Erg Linea Cirani (Via Dante 19, 20039 Varedo — Milano) Manufacture superb and

246

luxurious camping conversions based on the rugged four wheel drive chassis of trucks like MAN-Meccanica, Renault TP3, Fiat 75 PC and Mercedes Unimog U1700.

Generally, the small Mercedes vans and LT Volkswagens converted to campers are also too big and cumbersome. They will cause their owners untold hard work and anxiety even on a simple journey like that from Tamanrasset to Agadez. The optimum size seems to be that of the air-cooled VW Kombi and the Ford Transit, though the latter have problems with a very low front axle. This size is big enough to live in. It is big enough to carry food, water, spares, stove, fridge, beds, clothes, extra fuel, sand ladders, and two people in comfort, yet still remain economical to run, small enough to negotiate narrow streets, and light enough to make debogging less frequent and easier.

High Roof
A high roofed version is good to stand up in, and gives extra storage but is more expensive on ferries, and has more wind resistance, pushing up fuel consumption and making the engine work harder and hotter thus shortening its life and increasing the risk of mechanical failure.

'Pop Tops'
For extra head room a fibreglass 'Pop Top' seems ideal. However, on some vehicles the hole cut in the roof has actually weakened the structure of the vehicle. The ordeal in the Sahara will almost certainly cause structural failures and cracks in the body chassis: failures that would not normally occur if the vehicle spent its life in Europe. As an example, all 'Pop Top' Volkswagen conversions must have 'VW Option MO73' built into the vehicle when the conversion job is done. This is a pair of pressed steel beams that are welded

The ultimate motorcaravan for the Sahara. The Grand Erg Linea Cirani range of luxurious camping vehicles are built on the chassis of large all-terrain four-wheel drive trucks like the Mercedes Unimog, Renault TP3 and, as shown here, MAN-Meccanica (Photo by courtesy of Grand Erg SRL, Milan)

The authors spent a cramped night in the back of their Range Rover while the family in the Volkswagen enjoyed the homely comfort of their campervan

A Series IIA Land-Rover station wagon with a 'Dormobile' conversion. A good compromise

into the roof structure after the hole has been cut but before the new roof lining is put in. It is included as standard on all 'Westfalia' conversions and many, but not all, British conversions. Unfortunately, most Australian conversions do not have it, and experience has shown that the chassis develops cracks in the Sahara. The same sort of precautions must be taken with other vehicles, like the Ford Transit and the Bedford CF vans.

An advantage of the fibre glass 'Pop Top' roof is that its white colour and the extra insulation involved make the car considerably cooler to travel in.

'Pop Top' conversions of Land Rovers are done by Serle Carawagons Ltd., (Thames Street, Sunbury, 'middlesex, UK) and by Dormobile Ltd., (Tile Kiln Lane, Folkestone, Kent, UK). The roof is not an integral part of the structure of the Land Rover and so cutting a hole in it doesn't affect the chassis. Both conversions of Land Rovers are robust and well used by overland travellers. Carawagon also do a 'Pop Top' conversion of the Range Rover but this increases only the head room and is not long enough to fit a bed upstairs.

Air Camper
Sleeping on a roof rack can be most pleasant: cool and away from thieves,

An efficient and strong camper conversion of a new 1-10 series Land Rover by Carawagon Ltd. of London. It has an all metal pop-top extending roof which is light and durable. (Photo by courtesy of Carawagon Ltd)

A Toyota Land Cruiser with a special campervan body built on to it. Note the 'pop-top' roof and the louvre windows at the rear

A well equipped second generation Volkswagen campervan. Note the large shovel, the galvanised steel sand ladders, the jerrycans, and the shower bag hanging from the roof rack

A series IIIA Land Rover station wagon fitted with a 'Syro' folding roof rack tent: a recipe for a cool pleasant night isolated from thieves, spiders and scorpions (Photo by courtesy of Ida Kersten)

spiders and scorpions. 'Air Camper', 'Syro' and 'Goelette' folding roof rack tents are available from Daerrs, Brownchurch Components, Syro-Depot, and Globetrott-Zentrale. (For addresses, see Chapter 19.)

Storage

One of the big advantages of taking a camper is that you have lots of cupboards to store things in. Unfortunately, some campers put too much emphasis on seating rather than storage, e.g. Devon 'Caravette' and Westfalia 'Helsinki'. On the other hand, cupboards must be light and strong and firmly mounted inside the car.

Water Tank

On many campervans the water tank is mounted underneath the floor and is most vulnerable off the asphalt highway.

Toilets

Generally a portable toilet is not necessary in the Sahara. A small folding shovel and a roll of paper will do. However, there are occasions when one would be most appreciated, for example, it's Friday in Algeria and you have no dinars left. You just missed the bank yesterday. You have no petrol. You have to camp right in the centre of the village or town. You have very bad diarrhoea and there are people everywhere! Cougar (U.S.A.) manufacture a self contained chemical portable flush toilet: 'PortaPotti 44'. It can hold 13 litres (3 gallons) of waste, and the chemical 'Aqua Kem' is biodegradable. It is also odourless. This could be invaluable in the above circumstances. The 'PortaPotti' range is marketed in Britain by Thetford Products Ltd., Nuneaton, Warwickshire.

Ventilation

Front opening quarter vents in the front doors are sometimes most appreciated and are optional on VW-Buses, as are a pair of fans built into the flow-through ventilation system. However, sometimes in the Sahara the outside air is so hot that it is preferable to have the quarter vents closed. A small 12 volt fan mounted in the rear compartment of a camper van could be pleasant.

A third generation Volkswagen Type 2 with a 'Westfalia' campervan conversion

Opening louvres fitted to a campervan have many advantages. You can sleep locked inside the car and yet have the windows open to allow a draught of fresh air through. They can remain open in the rain and, if also fitted with gauze, will not allow mosquitoes in

250

Washing

A sink is not really necessary in a camper travelling in the Sahara, as washing up can easily be done outside, in a plastic bowl which can also be used for body washing.

In Australia and U.S.A. an excellent solar heated shower is marketed; ideal for the Sahara in winter, when a warm shower may be more pleasant than a cold one. It is a four litre plastic bag with transparent and black plastic sides and a short hose with spray nozzle attached. You hang it up and, depending on the outside temperature, within an hour the water in the bag has been heated sufficiently to provide a hot shower.

Windows

Fresh air is often essential when sleeping inside a vehicle in the Sahara. The best type of windows are the louvred ones. Hehr International Ltd. of California make excellent louvres which are standard on the Westfalia conversions and virtually just pop into place once the side windows have been removed from a VW Kombi. They have mosquito gauze on them and because they are louvred they can be left wide open even in the heavy rain still allowing a draught of fresh air (essential south of the Sahara). They are available through all official VW spare parts outlets (VW Part No. 231 069401).

Radio

It is very easy to lose contact with the outside world while travelling this lonely desert. But sometimes out there you do wonder whether World War III has started or what is happening in the latest cricket test series. To keep in touch occasionally an ordinary car radio will not do: a short wave radio is just about essential. With one of these the world is yours.

Excellent news services emanate from the BBC World Service, Deutsche Welle, Radio Netherlands, Voice of America and even Radio Australia! You can also hear the views of Radio Peking, Radio Moscow, Radio Nigeria, the Vatican Radio, Radio R.S.A., and All India Radio: all in English too. Many smaller portable transistor radios have SW bands, but they don't have the fine tuning or reception of really good short wave radios like the Grundig Satellit 2000, the Sanyo RP 8880, and the National 48. Alternatively, Bosch and Blaupunkt make very satisfactory short wave car radios.

Refrigeration

A fridge is not necessary. More often than not it is a waste of space and needless extra weight. There are other ways of getting cooler water (a wet towel wrapped around a plastic jerrycan) and of keeping films and medicines cool (See Photography chapter). Nevertheless, Electrolux of Sweden produce a range of small 3 way caravan fridges (Model RAM 24B) that operate on either L.P. gas, 12 volts DC, or 240 volts AC. Engel of Germany produce cool-box size fridges in either 12 or 24 volts DC. They are very robust and available from all major camping equipment shops. However, much lighter and cheaper are the new dry operating thermoelectric 'Peltier Effect' fridges made by Koolatron Industries (56 Harvester Ave., Batavia NY 14020, USA; 230 Bayview Drive, Barrie, Ontario L4N 4YB, Canada; and 409 Sussex St., Sydney 2000, Australia). A product of American aerospace technology, this light weight 'Koolatron' fridge has recently revolutionised camping refrigeration.

A Grundig Satellit portable radio. A good short wave radio is just about essential as it allows one to keep up to date with world events and with crises that may affect one's journey in the Sahara, such as coups, currency fluctuations, fuel supply problems, border closures, earthquakes, etc

Two simple-to-use camping stoves and their fuels. On the left is the Optimus petrol stove and a jerrycan of regular petrol. On the right is the Bluet Camping Gaz stove which uses small cartridge gas cylinders. Both fuels are easy to obtain in much of the Sahara

Cool Boxes or Eskies

Usually insulated boxes will not lower the temperature inside but will prevent it becoming as hot inside as it is outside. If a cool box is left open during the coolest part of the night and closed up for the day at sunrise, it will do its job well. The more often it is opened, the less effective it will be. Much of its effectiveness also depends on its sealing. Among the good robust and generally effective cool boxes are those made by 'Camping Gaz' in France (24/28/32 litres), 'Ezetil' in Germany, and 'Coleman' in U.S.A. but there are many more on the market. There are two effective methods of reducing the temperature inside the box: adding 'Kuhl-Akku' tablets (made in Germany) to a small plastic container of water, or using the French made sealed plastic bag of chemical 'granules' which when compressed, start a chemical reaction and freeze. Unfortunately each of these can be used only once, and a long trip through the Sahara might call for many.

Attaching a canvas water bag to the front bumper bar looks good but is actually quite wasteful of water. Although producing good cool water the amount lost through evaporation, in order to cool the water, can be more than 50% in a 12 hour period. The same applies to a goatskin 'Guerba'.

Lights

Fluorescent lights inside a car use hardly any current and give a bright light for reading etc. For outside use, Bosch produce a good fluorescent light on an extension lead which clips to the car's battery. There are also self-contained battery operated portable units.

Kerosene (paraffin in U.K.) pressure lanterns made by 'Cougar' and 'Coleman' (U.S.A.) and 'Tilley' (Britain) are a good investment because kerosene is available practically everywhere and is cheap. They give a very bright light and are totally portable. A good supply of replacements mantles should be carried.

One problem with outside lights is that in Sahel areas they attract insects which in turn can attract many scorpions.

Trunks

If you don't have a campervan, then three or four water and dust proof

A cold winter's morning in the 'cram- cram' country of the southern Sahara near In Abangarit in Niger

aluminium trunks are ideal for carrying clothes, food, bedding, tools, etc. in. They can be used as tables or seats while camping and stored neatly inside the vehicle, or on the roof rack while travelling. They will also serve as excellent suitcases while travelling on public transport and will last much longer than ordinary suitcases.

Mattresses
Lengths of foam plastic serve well as mattresses inside a station wagon like a Peugeot or Range Rover and outside on the ground. They are lighter and less bulky than folding campbeds. However, camp beds do keep you away from the ground and from any scorpions and hunting spiders that might be there.

Stools
Camp stools should not have legs that will sink into soft sand easily. An alternative to camp stools and a camp table are jerry cans.

Stoves
Gas, kerosene or petrol? Gas is clean and reliable, and comes in several forms. Refillable gas bottles cause problems because they can be difficult to refill without the correct adaptors.

International Camping Gaz disposable cartridges are widely known throughout the Sahara and can be bought at Agadez, Bechar, Djanet (at petrol station), El Oued, Ghardaia, In Salah, Kano, Nefta, Niamey, Tamanrasset, Touggourt, Tozeur, Sokoto, Zinder. Principally the C-200 model (190 grams) are sold.

Kerosene stoves are a bit of a nuisance because they must be started with methylated spirits and one must carry kerosene (paraffin in Britain). Wick stoves are too slow to be practical. So choose a type which is pressurized. The fuel is available in many places. Also it is wise to carry plenty of prickers.

Petrol has the advantage that if you use a petrol vehicle you will already be carrying the fuel and need not carry any extra fuels like gas, kerosene and methylated spirits. However, these stoves are not as clean as gas stoves. The Swedish Optimus range has neat, folding compact stoves (some include

253

saucepans). These sets are not cheap, but from the space and weight point of view they are very handy.

Firearms
Guns should not be taken under any circumstances. If you are found with a gun in any Saharan or Sahel country big trouble with the police, and probably detention and deportation will follow. Most African countries are overly sensitive about so called 'mercenaries' and minor officials can over react. Unlike in Australia or U.S.A., there is usually never a need to defend yourself in Africa (Nigeria is an exception; armed robbery is fairly common in the south). If you were in the position where you had to, a fire extinguisher and a tyre lever would be useful.

Other General Items
Metal bucket for wells (not plastic, which cannot be persuaded to tip, sink and fill with water as easily as a good galvanised bucket).
Synthetic rope strong and long enough (10 metres) to lift a bucket of water from a well.
Rope for use as washing line.
Large plastic bowl for washing in (bodies, clothes, dishes, vegetables).
Torch, with spare batteries.
Sleeping bags.
English/French dictionary.
Pocket calculator (invaluable for currency conversions, distance and fuel calculations, finances, etc.)
An alarm clock.
Matches and a can opener!

Please bury your rubbish

An Italian caravan club visiting parts of the Algerian Sahara, seen here at Kerzaz.
These cumbersome vehicles were not able to leave the asphalt El Golea and
Timimoun. The problems caused by a caravan or larger motor-caravan in the Sahara
far outweigh any advantages

22
Driving in the Sahara

A prerequisite for travel in the Sahara is a fit vehicle, in good working order. It must be suitable: good ground clearance, robust suspension, suitable tyres, and a reliable motor. Four wheel drive locking differentials, and limited slip differentials are extra advantages, that are essential in some situations. Sand ladders or perforated steel planking (P.S.P. — aluminium or steel) are essential, as is a large shovel.

Your vehicle must not be overloaded, for this not only strains motor and suspension but also hinders your progress on all types of surfaces.

Asphalt
Watch out for sand drifts on the road. Hitting a pile of sand at speed can severely damage suspension and could cause you to roll.

A section of the new asphalt road near Arak in Algeria, badly washed out by flash floods. The water that did this damage could have washed a fully-laden Land Rover hundreds of metres away

Typical of long sections of the new road to Tamanrasset which became badly broken up shortly after it was completed

If, as a result of flash floods, there is water across the road at a Oued it could conceal holes literally metres deep where the road has been washed away. If the water is flowing, check its speed and depth by trying to walk

257

through it. If there is any danger of a person being washed away there is even more danger of a vehicle being tipped over and washed down the Oued by the current. If you can walk through you will be able to locate boulders or sand banks hidden by the muddy water.

Long stretches of once beautiful new asphalt roads have deteriorated rapidly in some parts of the Sahara. This has occurred on the road from the Mediterranean coast to Sebha in Libya and more recently on the new road from Ain Salah to Tamanrasset in Algeria. Usually it is a result of faulty construction resulting from poor survey work or the use of inappropriate or insufficient foundation material.

In these circumstances it becomes impossible to use the broken up asphalt road for many kilometres at a time. Traffic soon establishes miriads of pistes on either side of the former road with deep ruts or ornières and terrible corrugations. This can transform a two-day journey into a long frustrating ordeal because for hours one is never able to get into top gear. One just has to plod along with a resigned patience. Trying to speed up the journey will only stress you and the vehicle and possibly damage suspension components.

On the long open stretches of asphalt watch the oil temperature gauge, especially on Range Rovers and Volkswagens. If necessary, cruise at a slower speed. It is better to be late than to overheat the engine and then have it die on you later in a lonely erg just because you were impatient on the asphalt.

Corrugations

Tole ondulée, Wellblech, wasboard or corrugations; they all mean the same thing: thousands of transverse ripples parallel to one another across a dirt road. They are caused by cars and trucks travelling at speed on gravel roads and even hard sections of flat desert. Usually the only way to travel on corrugations is to build up speed to at least 70 km/h (45 mph) when they are effectively smoothed out. You can cruise all day like that. This is fine in East or Central Africa or in Australia but in the Sahara the corrugations are at times so big that it is impossible for any vehicle (other than very large trucks) to accelerate up to 70 km/h. The only alternative is to painfully and slowly pick your way through the rocks, ruts and deep sandy patches on either side of the road. This makes progress very slow indeed. You just have to be patient.

If you find a section of road where you think you could accelerate up to

Even though you may see no vegetation there are still camels 'grazing' out there! Camels do silly things when startled by cars and they can do an awful lot of damage to the front of any vehicle

If there is water across the road where it crosses a Oued, be careful because it could conceal badly washed away sections of road, large boulders and sand banks

258

70-80 km/h, remember that the pumping action of the corrugations heats tyres dramatically. Therefore, lower tyre pressures (preferably when cold), to avoid blowouts:

Surface	Bitumen	Corrugations
Land Rover	Front 1.9kg, Rear 2.6kg	Front 1.6kg, Rear 2.0kg
VW-Bus	Front 2.0kg, Rear 2.0kg	Front 1.2kg, Rear 1.6kg
Range Rover	Front 1.8kg, Rear 2.1kg	Front 1.4kg, Rear 1.6kg
Land Cruiser	Front 1.8kg, Rear 3.0kg	Front 1.2kg, Rear 1.6kg

The same pumping action affects shock absorbers and can wreck them in a few minutes through overheating. If fitted with Bilstein gas stiffened shock absorbers, your suspension will become far too hard and there is a danger that you will crack cast suspension members.

Corrugations can be quite hair-raising in some short wheel base vehicles like Range Rovers and SWB Land Cruisers, giving them a tendency to lose their tail end without warning. Unimogs also tend to slide around a lot but VW-Buses and Peugeots are very stable on them.

They also shake the vehicle so much that you think all the doors will fall off. You certainly shorten your vehicle's life by trying to travel on them at speed. Corrugations require patience.

Sand and Sand Dunes
Driving in sand requires special techniques generally learnt through experience.

Tyre pressures should be lowered considerably. It is quite an experience to be in an ordinary VW-Bus stopped before a vast sea of deep, soft sand, and know for certain that it will never get across. Then to lower tyre pressure far below the normal minimum and just cruise across to the other side with

Piste near Arak in Algeria. Note the size of the corrugations seen in the lower portion of the picture. The VW Kombi in the lower left corner gives an indication of scale

259

A sandy section of piste requiring quick, correct decision making and precise fast driving. If you have doubts, falter, slow down or take the wrong approach angle, your vehicle will become bogged

A giant Kenworth truck used for oil drilling preparations in Algeria. With these massive sand tyres this truck will exert less pressure on the sand than a man

no problem at all. In such a case it is necessary to pump up the tyres once safe on hard ground again. However, in large areas of soft sand like the Bilma Erg you can leave the tyre pressures right down for several days.

Surface	Asphalt	Sand
Land Rover	Front 1.9kg, Rear 2.6kg	Front 0.8kg, Rear 0.8kg
VW-Bus	Front 2.0kg, Rear 2.0kg	Front 0.6kg, Rear 0.6kg
Range Rover	Front 1.8kg, Rear 2.1kg	Front 1.0kg, Rear 1.2kg
Land Cruiser	Front 1.8kg, Rear 3.0kg	Front 0.8kg, Rear 1.2kg

The type of tyre is also important in sand. For Land Rovers, Land Cruisers, and Unimogs the Michelin XS is the most popular sand tyre. It also has the capability of surviving well on hard and rocky surfaces. For Land Cruisers

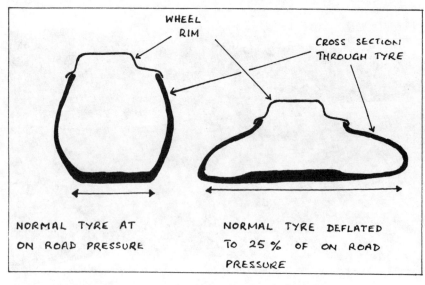

The advantage of deflating tyres for driving across sand: for the deflated tyre, the surface area in contact with the ground is more than doubled, thereby increasing its flotation on sand

260

Vehicle tracks in the Ténéré. Note the soft patches. Travelling in these conditions requires deflated tyres and preferably specialised sand tyres. It also requires a very gentle right foot on the accelerator pedal in order to minimise the amount of torque produced by the vehicle and thus reduce the tendency for the driven wheels to dig into the sand. The aim in these conditions should be to get the vehicle to float on the sand

A major dilemma: a steep hill and deep soft sand which is mixed with sharp basalt rocks. One needs the traction of a low gear to get up the steep slope but also the flotation and minimal traction of deflated tyres: together they can be counter productive. Also, the sharp rocks are extremely hazardous for deflated tyres. This photo was taken while crossing an escarpment near Fashi in the middle of the Ténéré

and Land Rovers, Dunlop and Sumitomo each produce a smooth balloon tyre purely for sand use. For Range Rovers, Peugeots and VWs normal radial ply tyres have to be used at very low pressure. Normal cross-ply tyres are not supple enough for sand.

In sand, gentle driving is necessary. Too heavy use of the accelerator will cause the wheels to dig rather than float on the sand. Often in soft sand you should not use the brakes; rather allow the car to coast to a halt. It is always easier to drive into the low sun, as the shadows highlight soft patches, ripples and previous tracks. With the sun behind you, the view can be totally uniform making it impossible to see the type of surface previous tracks have been through. Moreover, in big ergs with the sun behind you there is an ever present danger that you may not see a steep slope or slip face of a dune ahead, and consequently roll the vehicle. Therefore, in these conditions drive slowly and cautiously.

If you should accidentally go over the edge of a slip face, do not brake or turn. This will only dig in the nose of the vehicle and cause it to cartwheel down to the bottom. If anything, it would be preferable to accelerate and ride it out. It is in this kind of terrain that everybody in the car needs their seat belts on.

When crossing other vehicles' tracks keep in mind that they have broken a thin crust and created a soft patch that may slow you right up, causing you to lose momentum and get bogged.

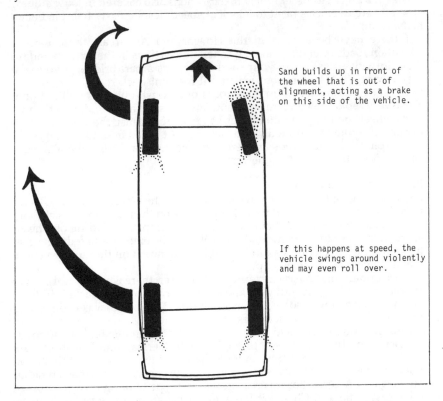

Sand builds up in front of the wheel that is out of alignment, acting as a brake on this side of the vehicle.

If this happens at speed, the vehicle swings around violently and may even roll over.

If a tie rod or track rod becomes bent on rocks, the front wheels will be out of alignment. The consequences could be disastrous when you encounter deep sand and have to drive through it fast

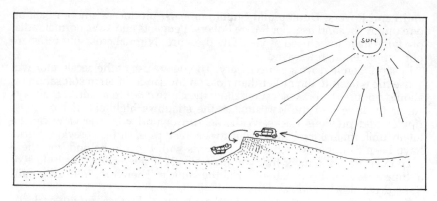

In the Mountains

On some mountain routes there are rocky, twisting and sometimes very rough roads.

The Iherir road could be a trap. A vehicle could get in but then find it very difficult to get out. The gradient is about 15-18% and covered with big loose rocks. The low range of 4x4 vehicles is very useful, but only VW-Buses with the big engine and a limited slip differential should attempt it.

The final ascent to Assekrem is 18-22% and is also covered in loose stones. Low powered vehicles need to take it at speed despite nasty hair pin bends halfway up.

If there have been rains in the Hoggar and Air areas, these narrow mountain roads often have deep washed out sections in them. Stop and fill them in with rocks or use your sand ladders as a part bridge. If you take it slowly you'll get there, but watch out for bent track rods.

If you bend a track rod on large rocks or in wash-outs this will not only cause very rapid uneven tyre wear but, later, in sand areas and with the two front wheels pointing in different directions, it can cause the vehicle to pull to one side quite unexpectedly and violently. At speed in sand the car could easily roll. When track rods are bent, remove them and bend them straight again with a hammer on some rocks.

Procedure for Convoys

Before starting out decide the travelling order for the vehicles each day. Don't vary this. The leader should try to keep an eye on the following vehicle, and if he gets too far ahead he should wait. If he gets impatient and shoots ahead, abandoning the slower vehicle, there is always the embarrassing danger that he might have a major breakdown and be dependent on the slower vehicle when it eventually catches up.

More important, unless strict order is kept then there is a very real danger that sooner or later nobody will know whether the other vehicle is in front or has broken down some distance behind. This could waste time, and precious fuel in fruitless searches.

Citizen Band radios are ideal for convoys as one can remain in continuous contact with other vehicles. Although Dutch, German and British sets are limited by their power output, in the Sahara's wide open spaces this should not cause too many problems for a convoy. The big problem is that CB radios are illegal in Algeria. For this reason the best type to bring is the combined broadcast radio and CB set: it looks more like an ordinary radio. Remove the microphone, and store it with your tape recorder. However, exercise discretion in its use; it can be a good tool if used properly.

IN RUTS, DRIVE WITH ONE SIDE UP AND ONE SIDE DOWN.

Ruts
In French, 'ornières'; they are two deep parallel trenches either in soft sand or hard dried up mud. The centre hump can cause big problems for low clearance vehicles: either the hard centre hump crashes against exhaust pipes, differentials and sump guards, or in the case of soft sand, the bottom of the vehicle eventually sits on the centre hump while the wheels spin freely. In both cases it is best to drive with one wheel on the centre hump and the other in a trough. Sometimes the vehicle slips off and gets bogged. Then you have to dig away the centre hump underneath the vehicle to allow the weight of the vehicle to sit on the drive wheels. Then lay sand ladders, dig away the hump for several metres ahead of the vehicle and try to drive out and get one wheel up on the hump again.

Bigger engined vehicles (Range Rovers and Land Cruisers) can power their way through these 'ornières', provided their underneaths are well protected. With less powerful Peugeots, 2CVs and VWs it is necessary to go through at speed with the vehicle bucking and jumping madly using sheer momentum to get through while at the same time trying to keep one wheel up and the other down. All this can be hard work for the driver, and both he and the passenger(s) must have their seat-belts on.

It is advisable that front seat occupants wear seat belts all the time. Conditions can be tough and the front passenger, especially, can be injured from bashing against the interior of the vehicle.

Getting Unbogged in Sand
Stop before the wheels begin to dig. You will quickly learn to depress that clutch pedal at the very moment when forward momentum ceases and digging momentum begins. The alternative is to create lots of work for yourself by allowing the wheels to spin and dig the car down in the sand, forcing you to dig it out again. If lightly bogged in a two wheel drive vehicle, just dig away a little sand in front of the rear wheels; put a sand ladder (or p.s.p.) in front of each rear wheel. Drive up onto the sand ladders and use them as a short piece of artificial road to give the vehicle a run and sufficient momentum to get through more sand. To get out of a large stretch of soft sand it may be necessary to use the sand ladders several times.

With 4x4 vehicles, if lightly bogged, put the sand ladders in front of the front wheels; engage four wheel drive and drive out. As the rear wheels pass over the sand ladders they will also have a little bit of hard 'road' to grip onto.

If you allowed the vehicle to get bogged deeply, it will be necessary first to dig sand from underneath the vehicle so that the body will be able to sit on the suspension rather than the sand. Then you can lay the sand ladders or p.s.p. This is the only way you will get the wheels to grip the sand ladders and ride up onto them. Remember always to keep the front wheels in the straight position, as turning them acts only as a brake, just when you need as much forward speed as possible.

In principle, attaching sand ladders with a rope to the rear of the car so that, after debogging, the car pulls them along behind, sounds good. You

Sandy 'ornières' (ruts) in the dry season

Sandy 'ornières' in the wet season, six months later

A Range Rover deeply bogged: a lot of hard work. Note that the chassis and axles are resting on the sand and all four wheels are able to spin freely without moving the vehicle at all. The vehicle's weight must be on the wheels and not the sand before you can expect it to move onto the sand ladders (or psp)

Range Rover 'correctly' bogged: the driver has declutched and stopped before the wheels have begun to dig. It is now only a quick two minute job to get the vehicle moving again

don't have to walk back and collect them. In practice, however, the drag is too much for a VW-Bus or 4 cylinder Land Rover and may cause you to get bogged again. Also, more often than not the sand ladders get buried by the weight of the vehicle and to have them attached will either break the rope or bring the vehicle to a sudden halt, bogged again.

It may be suggested that one could use a winch to pull one's vehicle out. For three reasons a winch is impractical. First, the time and effort spent in erecting a sand anchor may as well be spent digging and laying sand ladders. Second, usually when one has become unbogged it is necessary to keep going for a long distance without stopping to get past a particular soft patch. If the front of the car is attached by cable to a sand anchor this is not possible. Third, winches are expensive.

In Australia and in France a 'Bull Bag' or 'Cric Air' is available. This is a large bag attached to the car's exhaust tail pipe and blown up like a balloon by the motor's exhaust. It is a very strong bag and very effective for jacking up a vehicle. It has been suggested that it be used instead of digging a vehicle out and then just placing the sand ladders under the wheels. However, if deeply bogged in the sand it would be necessary to dig out a place to put the 'Bull Bag', and it would have to be in a place well away from a hot engine or exhaust: in the case of a VW virtually impossible. So you may as well dig anyway. If you stopped in time, of course, there is no need to dig or use a 'Bull Bag'.

Another theory is that one need not bother digging the vehicle out. Instead, one should jack up the vehicle using a large flat piece of timber as a base for the jack. Then put the sand ladders underneath the wheels, and drive off. Especially with a two-wheel drive vehicle, the jack gets in the way of sand ladders. If one has got bogged 'properly', i.e. declutched before the wheels dug, then very little digging is needed. If one is deeply bogged, then a combination of jack work and digging may be necessary, but one cannot avoid digging. Moreover jacking up the vehicle in deep, soft, sand is a slippery, unstable and hazardous business, really to be used as a last resort, no matter how big the plank of wood supporting the jack is. Generally there is no escaping the need to dig.

Feche Feche

This is fine soft deep sand with a thin crust on it. As you drive across it, your vehicle continuously breaks the crust, but keeps going, through sheer momentum, breaking more crust as it goes. If you go too slowly you become bogged. Being bogged in real feche feche is no joke as the small run provided by the sand ladders is often insufficient to build up enough speed and momentum to keep going. If you see feche feche ahead you try to avoid it. If you suddenly run into it you must try to keep going as fast as you can. This may be for many kilometres in third and second gears causing risks of overheating your motor. Of course, the lower your tyre pressures the better, but there is no simple way out of feche feche. Either your car gets through or you have a lot of digging and sand ladder laying to do.

Sand Storms

On the edges of the Sahara sand storms usually precede the rains in June/July in the south or October/November in the north. Visibility can be reduced to the windscreen only. You just have to stop. The wind is also very strong and everything must be well battened down (including pop-top roofs on campervans). Sometimes the storm ends with cool refreshing rain which is a tremendous relief after the intense heat which builds up before a storm.

At other times in the Sahara, strong winds pick up the sand and con

1. *This VW Kombi has become bogged on an ornière. The chassis is resting on the crest between the two ruts and the rear wheels spin freely*

2. *Sand underneath the vehicle has to be dug out so that the weight of the car is on the wheels and not the sand crest. It is hard work but the car will not move until its weight is on the wheels and not the sand*

3. When digging is complete place the sand-ladders (or psp) in front of the rear wheels

4. Before driving off, it may be advisable to dig away some of the sand crest in front of the car for some considerable distance to enable it to gain enough speed to climb up into the 'one side up and one side down' position again

Inevitably someone has to remain behind to retrieve the sand ladders and shovel. It may be more than a kilometre before the vehicle is able to stop on more stable ground

siderably reduce visibility for days on end. It is sometimes worth covering the front of your vehicle with grease so that it doesn't lose its paintwork and so that the headlights are not sand blasted opaque.

During the Harmattan season in January, February and March the strong dry wind can pick up great clouds of dust that force you to stop. There is a very real danger of a head-on collision in these circumstances, especially in Niger.

23
Water and Water Purification Methods

Using Water

For tourists it can be surprising to discover the importance of water conservation as it exists in the Sahara. In the desert local inhabitants have had to adapt to its scarcity and have long since realized its full value. This seems to be something tourists find hard to do. Use water sparingly and for essential purposes only; wash only when it is practical and wash clothes and dishes in a very sparing fashion.

Wells

It is sometimes possible to obtain water from local wells but to do this it is necessary to have a long (minimum 10 metres) rope and a strong (preferably metal) bucket. There is a great skill to flipping the bucket over, down the well to catch the water and draw it up. The rope should be very strong and plaited. Many wells are very deep and depth varies considerably from season to season and year to year. Therefore, the longer the rope the better.

Sometimes local inhabitants will offer to draw water for you and it is impolite to refuse their offer. They are very clever with the bucket and will have your containers filled in a very short time. A small gift will show them your appreciation. If this is not possible, then thank them warmly.

For desert peoples water is such an essential commodity that it is almost sacred. It is therefore best to ask if you may take water from the well in a town or when many herdsmen are surrounding a well in an isolated region. Water is not wasted by these local people and wasting water is something they cannot comprehend. Wells are treated with great care and concern and are never contaminated by washing nearby or allowing animals to fall into them. Respect this custom of keeping the water safe and don't wash hair, bodies, or clothes nearby where the water could run into the well and spoil the water.

Consumption

In the hot summer months it is feasible to drink over 6 litres a day and, even in January, 2 litres is not an unusual daily intake. Water which has been purified cannot do any harm. So drink as much as you want and remember that you need 6 litres a day in summer and about a third of that in winter.

272

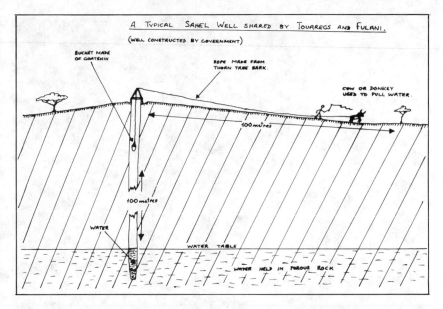

A TYPICAL SAHEL WELL SHARED BY TOUAREGS AND FULANI.

(WELL CONSTRUCTED BY GOVERNMENT)

BUCKET MADE OF GOATSKIN

ROPE MADE FROM THORN TREE BARK.

COW OR DONKEY USED TO PULL WATER.

100 metres

100 metres

WATER

WATER TABLE

WATER HELD IN POROUS ROCK

Health problems could result from insufficient water intake and salt intake should be balanced accordingly. Even if you are not thirsty it is as well to begin the morning with a couple of cups of water and continue to drink all through the day and before bed at night. Usually, in summer any less than 6 litres per day will cause mild dehydration, the symptoms of which are: concentrated urine, irritability, bad headaches, and constipation. With increased dehydration, headaches worsen and fever symptoms develop. This is the so-called 'sunstroke'. As dehydration reaches its final stages kidneys cannot function and one becomes delirious; death follows.

Storage Water
On leaving town, taking as much water with you as possible is important, even if the next water supply is very close. Water should be used first for survival and second for comfort. Washing cooking utensils, clothing and bodies should be considered less vital for survival. Calculate on the basis of 6 litres per person per day plus an extra few litres for cooking and washing dishes and bodies. Then allow for delays or emergency. Carry the maximum possible. For example, for two people for four days, it would be necessary to carry a minimum of 65 litres or 3 x 20 litre jerrycans and one 5 litre container full. Guerbas made from goat skin and canvas water bags can lose most of their water in a period of 24 hours, through evaporation. This may produce cool water but it is wasteful. An alternative is to wrap a plastic jerrycan in wet sacking cloth and keep the jerrycan in the coolest place possible. This also produces cool water but with minimal loss through evaporation.

Purification Methods

From the time you leave home it is worth considering the purity of the water. On arrival in North Africa it is definitely unsafe to drink untreated water. The water in the Saharan region has often been contaminated and is therefore a great risk to your health and well being, unless adequate measures are taken.

273

Although people cannot drink as quickly as these thirsty camels, one ought to drink about six litres of water a day in the Sahara

Some people argue that immunities can build up if one exposes oneself to disease-carrying bacteria but it is vital to remember that immunities take a long time to build up. Thus this policy is impractical on a journey of a couple of weeks or months. There are several ways of purifying water to make it fit to drink, and no matter which is chosen it is important to keep up filtration or purification.

Listed below are some of the many methods of filtration and purification, their place of manufacture, where they can be purchased, the method used, their effectiveness, weight, disadvantages and a brief comment about each product. All these factors need to be considered before a choice is made.

Sterotabs

Made in Britain and available from the Boots chain of chemists in that country. Sterotabs are very effective. One to three tablets should be added to a litre of water which should then be shaken and left to stand for thirty minutes. A bottle containing 100 tablets weighs approximately 200g. There are two disadvantages with this method, the first being that dirty water still looks dirty after sterilization, the second being a slight taste of chlorine after water has been treated.

Micropur MT20, MT1 and MT1000

These products are Swiss made and available from camping equipment shops in France, Germany and Switzerland. MT20 comes in a pack of 20 tablets and one tablet is used per 20 litres. Treated water should then be shaken and left to stand for about an hour. MT1 comes in a pack of 100 tablets and one tablet is used for each litre of water. MT1000 is a powder available in 100g packs. One gram of powder is added to 100 litres (the pack contains sachets of 1g each) and then the water must be shaken and stirred and left for twelve hours.

These products are all extremely safe. Once again, though, the disadvantage is that water colour is not changed. On the other hand, Micropur does have the advantage of leaving no taste in the water. Each packet weighs about 200-350g. They seem to be expensive but are extremely practical for those travelling for long periods of time through the Sahara. The MT100 is especially good for large parties.

Iodine

This is widely available everywhere in the western world and is usually inexpensive. Because it is liquid, it is difficult to carry. It also leaves a taste in the water and it does not help to make the water look cleaner. It weighs about the same as water per litre. The biggest disadvantage is that it is dangerous in large quantities. One drop in half a litre will kill bacteria but if too much is used iodine will do you a lot of harm because it is actually poisonous in large doses. Using iodine is therefore impractical when so many other safer methods are available.

Katadyn Filter Pump

This filter pump is Swiss made and available from Swiss, French and German camping shops. Two sizes are available and both use filters made of porcelain, which are easily cleaned and long lasting. A cleaning brush is included when you buy a filter.

The large filter (Model KFT) stands about 1m high and weighs around 3kg. The small filter (Model TF) is about half the size and a third of the weight. Both are extremely safe. They do not add an unpleasant taste and do remove the dirt as well as the bacteria. They are expensive but pay for themselves,

The larger Katadyn model KFT filter/pump. These Swiss Katadyn filters are extremely safe, do not add any unpleasant taste to the water and they remove not only dirt but also bacteria. Although expensive, a Katadyn filter would soon pay for itself in terms of peace of mind and good health

in terms of peace of mind and are a really worthwhile investment for those going on a long journey, or those who travel widely and frequently.

Safari Filter Pump
This is available from Brownchurch Components of London, (full address Chapter 19), and is made in Britain. Price varies according to the model chosen. Four different models are made. The smallest and cheapest is the 'Tourist Filter' which is fully portable. The others are free standing and wall mounted models. The filters cannot be cleaned as they are fully disposable. They weigh about the same as the Katadyn range filters. The tourist model is quite cheap, but the price of several replacement filters should be taken into account. They are very safe, do not add any unpleasant taste, and remove the dirty colour from the water. For long journeys they are definitely practical.

Recently some new water filters have appeared on the market. One, made by Walbro Water Purifiers, 1451 East Main Street, Ventura, CA 93003, USA (used by NASA in manned satellites). It weighs only 100g and is the size of a coffee mug but will last for only 400 litres or 105 US gallons. The other new filter is the Filtron Camp 3000 marketed by Sachs Motor Service, The Maltings, Tamworth Road, Ashby-de-la-Zouch, Leicestershire, LEG 5PS, UK.

The Sachs Filtron water filter kills bacteria and microbes electrostatically. Powered by small penlight batteries, it is handy for small quantities of water

277

Filter Papers

These are manufactured by Katadyn in Switzerland. They must be used in conjunction with tablets or an electric filter as they are insufficient by themselves. The water is poured through and dirt only is removed. They are very worthwhile for those who find the colour of the water off-putting yet prefer to use tablets or the electric filter. They cost 20DM for a packet of 20, and weigh about 100g.

Sachs-Filtron

This is an electric filter which runs on 4 small 1.5 volt batteries. It is German made and available from camping and electrical stores in that country. It kills bacteria through electrolysis, but it is unable to cope with heavy dirt and so may be used with the Katadyn Filter Papers. It is very small and compact, weighing only about 500g. It is very safe. Its biggest disadvantage is that it can be used for only small amounts of water at a time. It is, therefore, very practical for those going on a short journey, in a small party, and using paper filters as well. The greatest advantage is that the 1.5 volt batteries this filter uses are fairly widely available and can be bought en route in many towns in Niger, Mali, Algeria and Nigeria.

Water is precious to desert nomads. A well scene south of Agadez

24
Photography

For many, a trip across the Sahara is the adventure of a lifetime. It is essential to record it photographically, to bring back memories of lovely sights, hard work, friends, etc., no matter how bad a photographer you are.

Officialdom
Take care not to photograph police or military vehicles, police stations, military stations, or frontier posts, or even a policeman on point duty. Oil and gas installations in Algeria are also subject to a ban on photography. In Mali and Nigeria you need permission to take photographs. In Mali this is simply a matter of going to the police at Gao, Mopti, Timbuctu or Bamako with your camera, filling out a form and paying the set fee of 5,000 Mali francs (1984). This permit is then supposed to be valid throughout your visit to Mali.

In Nigeria, officially you have to get permission from the State Ministry of Information in each state capital (e.g. Kano, Kaduna, Sokoto, and Maiduguri): a difficult task as it must be a written application. At least make sure that nobody objects when photographing people in Nigeria.

People
When photographing people try to avoid paying for it with money or gifts. It is better to persuade people to let you photograph them by being friendly, jovial and open about it. This certainly makes the whole process less mercenary and also makes it easier for others who come after you.

Often there is open hostility to photographers even from children. Sometimes they throw sand and dust into the air in the hope that it will spoil the photos. Adults often regard photography by tourists as an invasion of privacy and for some the camera may even represent an evil spirit who tries to capture a little of their soul or life force. Great care and diplomacy should be taken to avoid offending local people. It is frequently possible to develop a rapport and then have their active co-operation as photographic subjects. This may take some time and may not even be successful enough to get their approval to be photographed but it is preferable to the methods of some professional photographers who have aggressive domineering approaches to the people they photograph.

One should avoid the temptation to allow nomads and other simple people along the way to look through the viewfinder of one's camera.

Doing so may well dispel fears of the camera being an evil spirit but it is one of the quickest ways to contract conjunctivitis or even more virulent, painful, and potentially disastrous eye diseases that could cause blindness.

Format
35mm is the most practical, especially with cassettes of 36 exposures. 35mm films are available more often than other sizes and the cameras made for them are usually sufficiently sophisticated and at the same time compact and robust. 110 films usually don't stand up to enlargement as well as larger sizes. 6x6 films really give excellent results but are more cumbersome and bulky to handle and protect.

Camera Type
Again 35mm cameras seem to be most versatile, especially single lens reflex models with through the lens metering. They are quick to handle, relatively compact and generally reliable and more robust. 110 pocket cameras don't usually have the facilities to photograph the Sahara at its best. Large format cameras, while giving excellent results, don't have quite the 'point and press' capability of the 35mm SLR.

However, the camera taken should be simple and robust rather than expensive and sophisticated. Some electrically operated 35mm SLR cameras can really let you down when a bit of microcircuitry goes wrong. It should at least have the possibility of being manually operated in an emergency.

Lenses
The usual standard 35mm SLR lens is in the range of 50 to 55mm. This lens is ideal for normal use. Some of the magnificent panoramas in the Sahara, however, need a wide angle lens. 24mm lenses seem to distort a little too noticeably. Perhaps the best compromise wide angle lens is one with a focal

"No photo!" Often there is open hostility towards photographers, even from little children

length of about 30 to 35mm. To make street scenes more interesting and especially for portrait work of local people, a telephoto lens of about 110mm is ideal. For spectacular sunsets and for emphasizing the magnitude of Saharan scenery 200 to 300mm telephoto lenses are more suitable.

Accessories
A skylight filter should be left permanently on the standard 50mm lens to protect it and slightly reduce glare. It would also pay to have one on each of the additional lenses. Strong polarised filters can give a lovely blue glow to hazy skies but they often also give an artificial brightness to some photographs. A tripod can be extremely useful in low light conditions or for delayed action shots. A lens puffer-brush is necessary and should be used frequently.

A flash unit is not very often used but sometimes can be used to great advantage inside buildings (e.g. to show an Agadez silversmith working at his forge) or outside when you want to avoid shadows on faces when there is backlighting (e.g. people working in the salt ponds at Bilma). It is also useful to take a light-proof black bag to change films that have become stuck, jammed or broken, in the camera.

Movie Cameras
For 8 and Super 8 films not to be jerky and amateurish requires great skill. 16mm movie film will provide more pleasing results, but at considerable difference in cost. Some people erect camera mountings on the car dashboard. So often the ride on the piste is so rough that the filmed result is a complete disappointment. In some instances local people object to movie cameras being used but don't mind still cameras as much.

Video Cameras and Video Recorders
Dust is perhaps the biggest problem. Carry your video gear in dust-proof photographic equipment cases. For any lengthy trip in the Sahara it would be wise to be equipped to recharge your video power pack from the car's batteries.

Remember that the PAL system used in Britain, Germany, Holland, Australia and other countries is incompatible with the Secam system used in France, Algeria, Tunisia and Morocco. Thus, if your camera records on the PAL system, then the video cassette you shot in the Sahara cannot be screened on Secam television sets. In a few cases, video recorders are equipped with an adaptor which enables them to record tape for either system (but not both).

With video equipment you will look professional to many people in Saharan countries. This could cause hostility in countries like Algeria and Mali if it was discovered that you had not received official accreditation from their Ministries of Information.

Polaroid Cameras
A simple black and white instant picture camera can be a tremendous asset especially for potentially troublesome officials, or in winning over villagers to the idea of being photographed.

Films
Black and white photography often requires more creative activity than colour. And, of course, there is a big difference in price. Also, black and white films are more resistant to heat, and offer better scope in terms of emulsion speed and grain.

If your choice is colour, then you still have to choose between negative (print film) and reversal (slides or diapositives) film. It is worth noting that from diapositive film really excellent enlargements on paper can be achieved by using 'Cibachrome' positive paper and chemicals; and that Kodak make excellent quality 10x8cm prints by machine from 35mm slides.

The faster the emulsion speed, the grainier the result. This is particularly the case when using a telephoto lens in low light conditions. A compromise has to be reached. For example, Agfa CT18 with an emulsion speed of ASA 50 is a relatively fine grain film, but in low light conditions you will need a slower shutter speed and wider aperture than you would with an Agfa CT21 which has an emulsion speed of ASA 100 but a less fine grain. At times, it can be most frustrating having a slow emulsion film in the camera, when there is a spectacular sunset or you meet some beautifully adorned and made up Fulani men in the streets of Agadez at dusk.

Agfa slide or diapositive film tends to bring out richer blue skies which make desert photographs so attractive. However, the authors have found after many years of living in tropical climates that Agfa slides disappointingly fade completely to a misty blue after eight to ten years whereas all Kodachrome slides of similar age are still crisp and brilliant.

Film Protection

Temperatures can get very high in the Sahara, especially in summer, when they will generally stay over 40°C all day. It would be a real let down to arrive back in Europe and find all your lovely photos have faded to wishy washy colours. If you have a fridge in your vehicle put the films in it, but it is essential that they are in an air tight container, preferably with sachets of silica gel in it also. Humidity is a bigger enemy of film emulsions than heat. If you don't have a fridge, an insulated cool box or 'esky' will do satisfactorily if the lid is left off during the cool night and replaced firmly at first thing in the morning and not opened again all day. A very effective method is to put films in a plastic bag inside a large empty tin (a milk powder tin for example). Wrap the closed tin firmly with a couple of wet cloths (tea towels are useful). Re-wet the cloths two or three times a day. Keep the tin in the coolest place in the vehicle. This method is very effective. In the Ténéré, shade temperatures were over 46°C every afternoon, but the temperature inside the tin was never more than 23°C. The films survived well. Care must also be taken not to leave your camera in the sun, or in a hot glove box, or next to the hot transmission tunnel. Store it wrapped up inside a sleeping bag in the morning, to provide insulation against the midday heat.

Buying Films

Bring all your films with you from Europe. Films sold in Tamanrasset are invariably of East European origin and not stored in cool conditions. Elsewhere in the Sahara region it is virtually impossible to get colour films except at the photographic shop in Niamey (see Niamey section) and at the bookstall of the Central Hotel in Kano. It is worthwhile taking a minimum of fifteen 36 exposure colour films with you.

Batteries

Do not forget to take two spare camera light meter batteries. These are generally unobtainable in the Sahara (except at the one shop in Niamey), and it is most frustrating to have a metering system give false readings because of a run down battery.

Lens Brush

Dust is the biggest single problem. It is impossible to protect a camera from it completely. Perhaps the best way would be to use an underwater camera, but even then dust gets in when changing films and lenses. Inevitably some photos will have dust scratches on them and often aperture selector rings etc. do not function properly because of dust particles. The only answer is to go over your camera, almost daily, with a bellows lens brush. Do so every time you change a film.

General

Continually check your camera to see that your emulsion speed setting is correct, especially if you are using different films during your journey. Nothing is more annoying than to arrive home and find that all of your photos are over or under exposed because you neglected to set up your camera properly. It is too expensive, time consuming and exhausting to do the whole trip again just to have a second attempt at the photos.

Finally, the Sahara is an incredibly beautiful place. Do not be in such a hurry that you stop, take the photo and immediately drive on. After you've taken your photo spend a little more time to admire the view and take in the desert's awesome beauty.

25
Camel Caravans

Before colonial rule there were extensive and well used trade routes across the Sahara. Commodities taken to and fro across these great distances varied considerably: dates, salt, slaves, gold, copper, bronze, spices, porcelain, carpets and cotton cloth. It was along these trade routes that Islam was spread from the Middle East and North Africa to the Black empires of West Africa. It was also along these routes that conquerors came: the Berber Almoravids from the southern Maghreb conquered Ghana in 1076 and in the sixteenth century the Moroccan King, El Mansour, took over the Songhai Empire

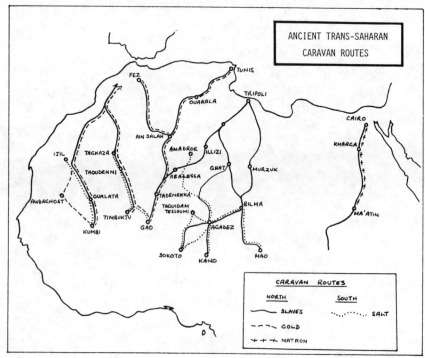

ANCIENT TRANS-SAHARAN
CARAVAN ROUTES

CARAVAN ROUTES

NORTH   SOUTH

———— SLAVES   ·············· SALT

– – – GOLD

+ + + NATRON

following the Battle of Bourem in 1591. Prior to both these conquests, the Garamantes of northern Libya had, during the third and fourth centuries BC, continually conducted raids across the Sahara to 'Ethiopia' and as far south as the Niger River. Rock engravings in many different parts of the present Sahara Desert bear testimony to their raids by horsedrawn chariots. Indeed, there is a strong possibility that the Roman centurion, Cornelius Balbus, went on some of these chariot raids and even to Niger.

However, the Sahara was a much more humid place then. Today, it would be impossible for pack-horses and horses pulling chariots to cross the Sahara Desert. About 400 BC the first camels were brought to Egypt from Asia. They proved to be ideal for the increasing aridity of the Sahara and were probably a factor in increasing trade and contact between the Sahel belt to the south of the desert and the states of the Maghreb and Mediterranean coast.

Throughout this time the Touaregs used to control the rights of passage of these long distance caravans. No caravan could proceed unmolested without paying tribute in kind to the various Touareg groups along the way (and to other desert peoples like the Chaambas, the Senussi and the Reguibat). If tribute was not paid a raid or 'rezzou' could be expected, often with disastrous consequences. Essentially, this is what happened to Lt. Colonel Flatters in 1881. He and his party of 90 (11 Frenchmen, 45 Arabs, 30 Chaambas and some Iforas Touaregs) were practically all massacred in the Amadror region of the Hoggar.

European colonial rule, which came late in the nineteenth century, severely retarded this trans-Saharan caravan trade. The French and Italians conquered and suppressed these desert people and the French and British in West Africa did the same with the important trading states of the Sudanic belt. They set up frontiers and attempted to control travel. They directed trade to coastal ports largely because the produce of these colonies now went to industrial Europe. The European powers justified their restrictions through the need

A camel caravan sets out for the salt mining oasis of Bilma. The camels are loaded up with manufactured goods and millet to exchange for salt

to 'civilize' and to stamp out the slave trade.

Today some of the ancient caravan routes are still used but increasing desertification, the advent of motorised transport and construction of asphalt roads have combined to curtail caravan traffic considerably. It may not be too long before no more camel caravans travel into the Sahara. Some of the routes still used are:

Bilma-Agadez

Every year between September and February the 'Azelai' takes place. Several caravans set out across the desolate and totally sandy Ténéré from Agadez for the salt extraction oasis of Bilma. Each caravan consists of between 50 and 100 camels, the combined resources of several camel herd owners who are usually of Touareg, Hausa or Kanure origin. On the outward journey they largely carry fodder for their camels but also a few other items to trade in Bilma (such as pots and pans, perfume, tobacco, herbs and kola nuts). It takes between two and three weeks to reach Bilma across the vast sandy and totally vegetationless Ténéré. Apart from short rests at wells in places like Tazolé, the Arbre du Ténéré and the oasis of Fashi the regime is one of a forced march. The caravan starts each day shortly after sunrise and walks non-stop at a fast pace until about 10 p.m., when the camels are unloaded, hobbled and the attendants sleep. On the march, groups of 10-20 camels walk strung together in lines. Most attendants walk at the head of their group of camels. If a man is delayed at all (e.g. to go to the toilet), he has to run to catch up.

The caravan spends about a week in Bilma, resting the camels while the team buys salt in pillars or circular slabs. The return journey to Agadez is conducted at a similarly hard and fast pace.

Some caravans on the Bilma-Agadez run may carry no salt at all on their return journey to Agadez, just dates, for both Bilma and Fashi are major date

A lone Kel Ahaggar Touareg traveller and his camels at Arak in Algeria. Note the traditional camel saddle on the animal nearest to him

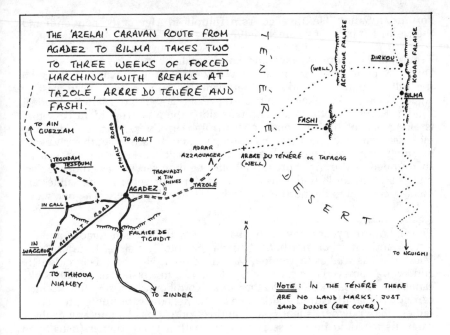

THE 'AZELAI' CARAVAN ROUTE FROM AGADEZ TO BILMA TAKES TWO TO THREE WEEKS OF FORCED MARCHING WITH BREAKS AT TAZOLÉ, ARBRE DU TÉNÉRÉ AND FASHI.

NOTE: IN THE TÉNÉRÉ THERE ARE NO LAND MARKS, JUST SAND DUNES (SEE COVER).

growing centres in the region.

Sometimes caravans also travel between Bilma and Nguigmi near Lake Chad. This is particularly difficult because of the need to negotiate hundreds of large parallel dunes which prevent a direct passage, whereas on the Bilma-Agadez route the caravans travel in the valleys between the dunes. In spite of there being no landmarks and no vegetation, no compass is carried. They know the dunes well despite the constant movement. Nevertheless, the men in the caravan business respect and fear the desert and avoid taking unnecessary risks. The forced march approach to each trek is out of necessity. Delays only increase the chances of running out of water and this means almost certain death.

For perhaps the best coverage of the Agadez-Bilma 'Azelai' see Mike Foster's beautifully illustrated article in **Expedition,** Vol VI, No.3, 1976 (a WEXAS bi-monthly magazine), and Franco Paolinelli's 'Saharan Salt Trade Recovers' in the British **Geographical Magazine** of December 1982.

Recently, a combination of protective legislation by the Niger Government and high fuel prices has given the 'Azelai' some respite in face of competition from motorised trucks. How long this will last is an open question.

Caravans operating on some of the other routes adopt similar procedures (e.g. forced march) to those used on the 'Azelai' Agadez-Bilma run.

Taoudenni-Timbuktu

Practically the only commodity carried is salt from the mines at Taoudenni in northern Mali. These salt mines have been in operation for over a thousand years and this caravan route likewise. Further north, the salt mines at Taghaza (Terhazza) have been abandoned for some decades now. This whole area is totally 'interdit' or forbidden to all because the salt mines are in fact a prison for political detainees and hardened criminals. Taoudenni is a most unpleasant place.

For the best recent description of this route, see Richard Trench's book

287

Forbidden Sands. He travelled from Tindouf in Algeria to Taoudenni and thence to Timbuktu by camel in 1977.

Teguidam Tessoumi-Agadez and Southwards

During September to March each year dozens of large caravans converge on the salt evaporation works at Teguidam Tessoumi to the north-west of Agadez. They take cakes of salt south to Tahoua, Sokoto, Maradi, Agadez, Zinder, Kano and other market towns along the way. Teguidam Tessoumi is along one of the two main pistes from Ain Guezzam to Agadez and motorists can watch the caravans loading up and departing south early every morning. On approaching the 'salines' or salt works, your car will be surrounded by dozens of urchins all offering their services as guides. Select one as a guide and another as a 'gardien' for your vehicle. The salines are inside a clay hill to the north-west of the village where there is a good view.

Agadez-South

Throughout the year caravans ply back and forth between Agadez and the towns and cities of northern Nigeria (Sokoto, Katsina, Daura, Kano, Maiduguri) as well as to Tahoua, Maradi, Zinder, Nguigmi, Dogondoutchi and even Niamey. They carry salt, dates and a few other commodities like camel cheese, goat skins and leatherwork. Northbound, most of the products carried are manufactured goods such as enamel bowls, perfumes, transistor radios, milk powder, sugar cones, and cotton goods. To join any of these caravans it would be necessary to meet with a major owner (usually an 'Alhaji') at a camel park near the market ('Kazua') at most towns in the region.

Nguigmi-Bilma-Ghat

A very rarely used route nowadays, but an extremely demanding one. Sometimes they continue to Djanet. (In 1977 it took 2½ months to do this journey.) However, because of marauding bandits from neighbouring war-torn Chad, no salt caravans have plied the N'guigmi-Bilma route recently.

Ma'atin-Kharga

This route is used about two or three times a year. The commodity taken north from Ma'atin near El Fasher in northern Sudan where it is mined as 'natron', an evaporite salt (mostly trona or sodium sesquicarbonate) which is used to tenderize chewing tobacco packed at Esna on the Nile. Usually it is taken north from El Kharga oasis by truck.

North of Agadez

Caravans frequently travel from Agadez into the Air Mountains to Iferouane, Timia and Arlit. Some infrequently travel further north to Tamanrasset via In Azaoua.

The camel caravan busines is definitely on the wane in the 1980s. It cannot compete with the truck. However, in an effort to protect the livelihoods of many desert dwellers, the Niger Government has legislated to make it illegal for truck operators to carry salt and dates between Bilma and Agadez. But it has been very difficult to enforce this law and for how long can such laws retard the inevitable march of progress?

Tourist Treks

There are several places where tourists can hire camels to go out into the desert such as at Tozeur in southern Tunisia and at Beni Abbes and Timmimoun on the edge of the Grand Erg Occidental. At Djanet camels are sometimes used (usually donkeys, though) to take tourists to the pre-historic

Would you buy a used camel from this man? A Hausa camel trader at Agadez in Niger. He might be an honest and reliable dealer but he might not be, and there are tremendous pitfalls waiting for the uninitiated westerner

rock art sites in the Tassili National Park.

It is also possible to hire camels and guides at Illizi to travel up the Oued Djerad to visit pre-historic sites there (impossible for any vehicle). It would be necessary to get to Illizi first to arrange this. Police at both In Amenas

SH 19

and Illizi have been most helpful.

Be warned! Life can be tough and ruthless in the Sahara. Some of last century's independent European explorers, like Gordon Laing and Alexandrine Tinne, paid for their experience in hiring camel caravans with their lives. Anyone contemplating independent travel by camel absolutely must read Geoffrey Moorhouse's **The Fearful Void.** He came very close to death in 1973 when he trusted people in the Sahara. Alternatively, contact an Altour office in Europe, Algiers, Djanet or Tamanrasset. Their price will be high but your life will not be in any real danger.

Perhaps the ultimate book on camel caravans currently available is Ritter, H. **Caravannes du Sel** (1981) Arthaud, Paris. Hans Ritter, a specialist in tropical medicine at the University of Munich, has travelled extensively by camel caravan in many parts of the Sahara and writes with first hand experience. He is also an excellent photographer.

26
Personal Health and Hygiene

The importance of maintaining good health during a journey such as this cannot be over-emphasized, and this chapter suggests a number of things you can do before setting out and while travelling to reduce the chances of infection, and lists some useful items for the medicine chest. More detailed advice can be found in K.E.M. Melville's invaluable book **Stay Alive in the Desert** and A.C. Turner's **The Traveller's Health Guide,** both published by Roger Lascelles, London. Another useful title which covers medical aspects of travel in Third World countries is Krook H. and Vanderspek J. **Survival Boek,** 1981, Uitgeverij Luitiugh, Utrecht, Netherlands. Werner, D. **Where there is no Doctor.** 1985, Hesperian Foundation, Palo Alto, California, is an excellent book full of practical advice. In Britain it is available from the Institute of Child Health, 30 Guildford Street, London WC1N 1EH. There is a companion book on dentistry. Walker, E. and Williams, G. **ABC of Healthy Travel.** 1989, British Medical Journal, London. Excellent very well-informed and technical. Written for doctors.

Personal Care

Set out with as clean a bill of health as possible. Make sure all tooth cavities are filled and all necessary vaccinations and all inoculations are done well before departure. In the same way that one must ensure the smooth running of the vehicle, an efficient body and clear thinking mind are equally essential. Preventive care and attention will minimise risks.

Animals: Avoid contact with dogs, cats, fennecs, and jackals. They can very easily give you rabies even though they may not be raving mad and foaming at the mouth. They can also give you fleas, lice, ticks and ringworm.

Anti-malaria tablets: Malaria is the biggest single cause of death in the world today, and WHO has declared that it is losing the battle against it. There are several suppressive malaria prevention drugs on the market (e.g. Paludrin, Nivaquin, Daraprim, Chloraquin, Camoquin). Some require one tablet daily, some weekly, and some two weekly. In the Saharan areas and West Africa the most frequently used are Daraprim and Nivaquin. Select your variety and stick to it.

Bilharzia: This is a parasite caught by direct contact with slow or stationary water, in which live the snails which carry it. The parasites leave the water and enter through your skin, and there is very little you can do to prevent it, except to keep out of such stretches of water. The disease is endemic throughout Africa from the Sahara to the Limpopo (except at high altitudes). Initial symptoms include blood in urine and stool, painful urination. The disease is debilitating. Tests at a tropical diseases clinic, on return to Europe, will confirm the case and drugs may be given to try to cure it.

Bites: Shake your shoes before putting them on; a hunting spider or scorpion, even a snake, may have found a nice place to sleep for the day. Be careful when dislodging rocks and fallen branches. Don't tease snakes.

Clothing: To avoid prickly heat wear light cotton clothing that allows plenty of air flow. Avoid synthetics.

Constipation: To avoid it, drink plenty of water and maintain a good quantity of roughage in the diet. If necessary eat dried fruits e.g. figs, dates and apricots.

Contraceptives: These are unavailable, generally, except in Nigeria and some of the more sophisticated modern cities. It is best to take everything you require with you. Keep them wrapped in plastic to protect them from the dust and, in the case of the Pill it is best to keep them in the coolest place in the vehicle, as some types are affected by extreme heat and light.

Cuts and Sores: Keep them clean and, if necessary, covered up. In Saharan temperatures and with the bacteria around, they can become infected and pustulous very quickly. The same applies to mosquito bites; resist the temptation to scratch them. (Bicarbonate of soda mixed to a paste with water and applied to the bite relieves the itch, though it is unscientific.)

Diarrhoea: It is almost inevitable that anyone travelling in the Sahara and Sahel will get some degree of lose bowels. To avoid diarrhoea, avoid situations most likely to cause it, e.g. unfiltered and untreated water, unwashed vegetables, fresh milk, cooked food sold by street vendors; and, sad to say, even local restaurants involve risk.

Drinking water: As a routine safety rule, all water for drinking, washing cutlery and crockery, and cleaning teeth should be filtered or treated. (See Chapter 23: Water.)

Monillia, Thrush and Allied Diseases: These bacterial growths in the vaginal region are encouraged by the climate in the Sahara and West Africa. To avoid them, wash and dry thoroughly and often, and wear fresh underwear each day. To try to cure them use pessaries and/or cream, available only on a prescription.

Salt intake: It is necessary to make up for increased perspiration and increased water intake. A teaspoon of salt in a glass of water tastes really good in the heat of the desert and is not usually nauseous. Salt tablets could be taken. Add plenty of salt to cooked foods. Also a salty thin 'bouillon' (soup) or Marmite mixed in hot water with extra salt can be a pleasant before dinner way of increasing salt intake. Lack of salt can lead to bad cramps and extreme weariness.

Sunburn: Don't allow yourslef to become sunburnt. Very gradually increase your exposure to the sun.

Treatment of Locals. Be extremely careful when treating local people's ailments. Eye diseases in particular are easily transmitted and difficult to cure. Wash very thoroughly immediately afterwards.

Venereal Diseases: Prostitutes in the Sahel region will not only give you the 'crabs', but the gonorrhoea they can give you will usually be of such a

Being a 'desert doctor' makes friends but requires caution as it is easy for the 'doctor' to contract illnesses

virulent type that it may not be curable with modern antibiotics; a ruptured bladder and sterility could result. Of course, it is a fact of life that AIDS is endemic in many parts of Africa and in most cases prostitutes are quite likely to be HIV antibody positive and therefore lethal. Do not risk your life!

Vitamin Pills: These are useful to supplement your normal daily food intake; you may be lacking some nutrients at times.

Water intake: In May-August water intake should be around 6 litres per person per day. (See Chapter 27: Survival.)

Washing: Wash completely as often as possible. To remain dirty is uncomfortable and also provides an ideal breeding ground for fungi and bacteria.

Some Major Desert Ailments

1. Heat Exhaustion   Resulting from lack of acclimatization, insufficient salt, water or the correct balance between the two, over exertion in the hot sun. Symptoms, cramp, weariness, lassitude, and apathy. Rest and increase salt or water intake, or both.

2. Malaria   Suppressive drugs do not guarantee that you will not contract malaria. Moreover, the only way malaria can be diagnosed is by laboratory analysis of a blood sample. However, if stuck out in the bush or desert, it is reasonable to treat a person for it as a precaution if some of the more usual malaria symptoms are present. These are: high temperature, fever, shivering and feeling cold, especially in the evening. It should be noted that symptoms vary considerably. Ideally, two types of suppressives should be

293

included in the medical kit, e.g. Daraprim could be taken once a week, but if malaria is reasonably suspected, then Nivaquin or Chloroquin could be taken in their heavy treatment doses strictly according to directions given by the manufacturer. Consultation should be sought as soon as possible. Note: All the Sahel and West Africa is a malaria endemic zone. So is the entire falaise from Bilma north to Djado.

3. Diarrhoea Occurs in mild and acute forms with shades in between. In its mild form it will probably go away in a day or two if left alone. If bad, then laboratory examination and skilled medical treatment are necessary, but in the Sahara this is rarely possible. So, if diarrhoea is accompanied by severe gripping abdominal pains, and perhaps by fever and vomiting then plenty of fluids should be given, with salt added (especially if muscular cramps are also evident) and a course of Sulphaguanadine tablets should be followed (e.g. 4 for an adult to start with and 2 every 4 hours for 18 to 20 hours). If this doesn't work and a doctor is unavailable then start a course of Entero-sediv or Guanamycin tablets. These will probably do the job but they will knock you back and make you too groggy to drive. (Do not bother with Enterovioform as they go brown and deteriorate in Saharan heat).

4. Scorpion Stings These result in intense localised pain and swelling. Some relief can be provided by immersion in cold water, or a scorpion anti-venom could be given. Relief is fairly quick after such an injection. Scorpion anti-venom is available from John Bell and Croydon Ltd., 50 Wigmore Street, London W1. Although painful for many hours, most scorpion stings are not usually dangerous to adults. However, the stings of three (*Androctonus australis, Buthus occitanus* and *Buthus quinquestriatus*) are neurotoxic and can easily be fatal (see Chapter 2).

5. Rabies If bitten by a dog which is suspected of being rabid or soon after mysteriously dies following peculiar behaviour, remove its head and take it to a hospital for saliva analysis. If positive a vaccination course must be begun immediately. However, do not expect that hospitals in the Sahara region will have the necessary vaccine (even in relatively affluent Algeria and Nigeria). It may be imperative for you to take quick action to obtain vaccine independently. Death is the usual outcome of contracting rabies and not being treated.
There are two types of vaccine available:
— duck egg vaccine which is injected daily for 14 days. This treatment does not have the best success rate and may have some unpleasant side effects such as nausea and loss of skin on hands and feet.
— inactivated rabies vaccine which is injected in a series of doses. It is expensive and effective. Available from Institute Merieux, Lyon, France.
The duck egg based vaccine may be available in some major centres like Algiers, Niamey or Kano and it may be necessary to travel there as quickly as possible. Invariably, the more effective inactivated vaccine would have to be especially flown out from Britain, France or Holland and especially cleared through customs. The French for rabies is 'la rage'.
Note: If bitten by a dog, one should have a tetanus injection regardless of whether it is rabid or not.

6. Snake Bites Usually there are two puncture marks about a centimetre apart and there could also be scratch marks from other fangs. Occasionally

A butcher at the Sokoto Market in northern Nigeria. The meat is freshly killed but being an open air stall without refrigeration one should select one's cut early in the morning. Before cooking or putting it in the 'fridge one should wash off the flies' eggs. In spite of this, the meat should be safe to eat if it is cooked properly

there is a swelling, reddening or bruising but the puncture marks may be difficult to discern

The first symptoms usually appear 15 minutes to two hours after the bite: double vision, drowsiness, nausea, sweating, faintness, diarrhoea, headache, pain in chest or abdomen.

Treatment:
— keep casualty at rest and allay fear
— apply a broad firm bandage around the limb, beginning at the bitten area. (As much of the limb should be bandaged as possible.)
— keep the limb as still as possible; using any rigid material as a splint (e.g. sand shovel or piece of timber)
— leave bandages and splint on until medical care is reached.
— do not cut or excise the bitten area
— do not apply an arterial tourniquet
— do not wash the bitten area as the snake involved may be identified by detection of venom on the skin
— watch for and treat any signs of respiratory arrest or circulatory collapse. (This information derived from The St. Johns Ambulance Association of Australia.)

If no snake bite kit is available, or a doctor, give the bitten person 4 Penicillin tablets (provided they are not allergic to them) and four capsules of Benadryl. Repeat 2 Penicillin tablets every 4 hours (see: Melville, K.E.M. **Stay Alive in the Desert).** Do not cut over the bite or use potassium permanganate. More harm than good usually results. Anti-snake bite kits

A bar at In Gall in Niger. This is a good place to meet local people as well as truck drivers and others able to give valuable advice about pistes. However, avoid using cups, glasses and other utensils provided. Instead, drink directly from the bottle. Generally, diseases caught in the countries of the Saharan region are far more virulent than the equivalent illnesses in western countries

and serum are available from Hoechst Pharmaceuticals, Salisbury Rd., Hounslow, to the west of London. Also Institut Pasteur, 25 Rue du Dr. Roux 72015 Paris. These kits are available for different parts of the world (except Australia). The relevant one for the Sahara is 'North Africa'.

A Typical Medical Kit

Unfortunately, many items included in this list are available only on prescription, even though essential for a long Saharan journey. Doctors in most countries are not allowed to prescribe these types of drugs for the purposes of a trip like this. So, unless you have a helpful doctor or chemist friend, problems may arise. However, in some countries like Niger and Nigeria most of the medicines quoted are available without prescription. It is possible just to walk into a chemist's shop and select them from the shelves.

Diarrhoea:	Entercine capsules
	Sulphaguanadine tablets.
	Lomotil tablets.
	Guanamycin tablets
	Entero-sediv tablets.
Laxatives:	Many brands available.
Allergy:	Phenergen tablets.
	Pyribenzamine tablets.
Tick bites:	Mecurachrome.
Wasp stings:	Wasp eze ointment. (A spray is available in U.K.)

Scorpion stings:	Anti-venom injection phial.
Snake bites:	Snake bite kit (see text above). Benadryl capsules.
Vomiting:	Primperan phials (syringe is necessary).
	Stemetil tablets.
Pain Relief:	Dymadon tablets.
	Aspirin tablets.
	A.P. Codeine tablets.
Anti-malarial:	Daraprim tablets.
	Nivaquin tablets. (Injection phial available).
	Chloroquin tablets.
	Camoquin tablets.
Eye ointment:	Golden eye ointment.
	Optrex eye wash and eye bath.
Sea sickness:	Sea legs tablets.
Cold remedies:	Febs Cold tablets.
	Contac 12 capsules.
	Dequadin throat lozenges.
	Cough linctus.
	Robitussin P.E. cough mixture.
Ointments:	Xylocaine ointment (antiseptic) for mucous membranes.
	Gentian violet jelly antiseptic cream.
	Desenex ointment for fungal infections.
	Bonjela antiseptic analgesic gel (for mouth infections)
	Movelat gel (for sprains and bruises and cold sores).
Nose drops:	Anustinprivien especially anti-allergy.
	Tyzine especially decongestant for children.
Ear drops:	Vosol (Good pre-swimming, anti fungal).
Powders:	Cicatrin antibiotic amino-acid powder.
	Desenex anti fungal powder.
Sleeping pills:	Mogozone mild sleeping tablets.
Salt:	Mopton salt tablets.
Water purifying:	(see Water chapter)
	Hallazone tablets.
	Puritabs.
	Sterotabs.
	Katadyne Micropur tablets, and powder.
General:	Penicillin tablets.
Vaginal:	Pessaries and applicator.
Burns:	Badional Gel.
Vitamins:	Various brands.
Dressings:	Sterilized gauze pads. Cotton wool.
	Band aid strips, circles, rectangles, etc.
	Surgical lint.
	2 triangular bandages.
	Surgical methylated spirits.
	Assorted plasters. Safety pins.
	Sprain bandages and clips.
	Scissors.
	Dettol or Savlon cream.
Insect repellents:	Aeroguard.
	Johnson's Protector. (These aerosols are sold only in Australia).
Disinfectant:	Bottle of Dettol.
Clinical Thermometer:	(in Centigrade).

27
Survival and Navigation

As can be seen from these preventative rules, your vehicle is vital; it must take top priority.

1. Know your vehicle's capabilities. Do not venture into the Ténéré, for example, with a beaten up old vehicle. Similarly don't take an outlandish vehicle like a London taxi or Fiat 126. In other words don't court disaster. Don't make yourself a liability on others; you may put their lives in danger too.

2. Know how to maintain and repair your vehicle. You should know how to do simple maintenance like oil changes, air cleaner changes, tappet, timing and point adjustment, fan belt replacement, battery checking, etc.

3. Daily vehicle inspection. This could let you know when to turn back before it is too late. (See Chapter 20: Vehicle Maintenance.)

4. Spares and tools. Carry an adequate supply of tools and relevant spare parts. This will vary for the make and type of vehicle. (See Chapter 20: Vehicle Maintenance.)

5. Take adequate fuel and water supplies. Allow for increased fuel consumption in difficult terrain. Allow extra water in case of delays. (See Chapter 23: Water.)

6. Set out with emergency survival equipment.
a. Emergency aluminium blanket.
b. Large sheet of strong plastic e.g. 2m x 2m.
c. At least one packet of 100g emergency rations.
d. Small compass (orienteering type).
e. Perhaps a pair of small marine rescue flares.

7. Note and record your speedometer reading and position regularly. In an emergency this can be vital in letting you know where you are.

8. Don't continue when lost. Stop, think, and if necessary retrace your tracks.

9. Do not set out with anti-freeze in the radiator. You may need to drink the water. (Anti-freeze is poisonous.)

10. Don't waste water. Always use a minimal amount of water for cleaning and washing up. You may need the water desperately later on.

11. Check out, if possible. On some routes, like the Tanezrouft and even between Sebha and Seguedine, you need not die if you break down, because there is sufficient traffic all year round for some vehicle to help you out within a week. On other routes a radio check on vehicle movements is made by authorities, as between Bilma and Agadez; and between Bilma and Nguigmi. If you have major breakdown problems and you checked out with the Police on departure then you could expect a search party to set out within a week of your being overdue. Do not try to cross these sections of desert without a guide and do not try to by-pass Police check out formalities. However, the risk of dying is still high; in July 1977 seven local people, with years of desert experience, died when their truck broke down near the Arbre du Ténéré.

12. Check in, on arrival. As a matter of courtesy and to prevent unnecessary and wasteful searches that could endanger others' lives.

13. Do not drive at night. This is a sure receipe for getting unnecessarily bogged and for getting lost. Many local drivers do travel at night because it is cooler, but they have lived all their lives in the desert and know the route extremely well. (Also, though this is not a matter of life or death, they do not cross dangerous stretches of desert to see the scenery, whereas the tourist presumably does.) However they too get bogged and lost at night.

14. Do not leave the piste. Unless you know exactly where you are going, have a compass, adequate equipment, and make notes about landmarks and directions, as you travel. You may find it necessary to retrace your tracks.

15. Observe convoy procedure. This is described in Chapter 22: Driving in the Sahara.

16. Personal Fitness. Make sure that everybody is capable of making the trip. Also, ensure that there is more than one driver in case of illness, or accident.

Emergency Survival

There is no step by step procedure, as circumstances vary, but of top priority is the need to keep a clear mind and to think logically. Panic, stupid decisions and delirium are disastrous.

Concentrate on getting your vehicle going again. It is your best hope for survival. To do so, you must use your wits to improvise and make use of the equipment and expertise available.

Keep well covered with clothes to minimize body water loss.

Don't do manual work during the day. Work at night or early morning to minimize body water loss.

Do not severely ration water supplies. You have to get yourselves out of this predicament, and clear and logical thought is essential. You may actually live longer by a day or two with severe water rationing but there is a very real danger of a gradual kidney breakdown and malfunction. This will manifest itself first in headaches and irritability, then in migraine, nausea, and finally delirium. Water use should be restricted to drinking only. With careful monitoring of urine colouring intensity, combined with points above (re: keeping covered, staying in the shade, and not doing any manual work in the heat of the day), these will minimize water loss. Water could be restricted to an intake of about 2 to 3 litres per person per day. This intake should be evenly spread between 08.00 and 20.00 hours (Water loss is lower during the cool night hours and body functions usually slow down after this time.)

Stay in the shade to keep cool and minimize body water loss.

Conserve all urine. This sounds unpleasant but it can be used as outlined in the following paragraph. Store it in an empty water jerrycan. Do not drink it as it is, as the concentrated waste products and toxins may actually speed up kidney decline, doing you more harm than good. Safari and Katadyn filters are incapable of rendering urine drinkable.

In the evening, dig a hole about a metre in circumference. In the bottom of the hole place an empty open tin, surrounded by wet, urine soaked sand. Spread a plastic sheet over the hole, anchoring it securely in the middle to weigh it down. Overnight, as heat radiates from the desert surface, water vapour from the wet sand will condense on the under surface of the plastic sheet and run down, dripping into the tin can. Alternatively, instead of wet sand, urine can be placed in containers at the bottom of the hole around the empty can (which should be in the centre).

As many stills like this, as possible, should be set up. In this way it is possible to make up for some of the water supplies used. It is also important that any water gained in this way should be thoroughly boiled (with a lid to catch the steam) or sterilized by adding tablets. One doesn't want to worsen the situation by encouraging diarrhoea and consequent dehydration.

Aircraft. Do not expect to attract the attention of aircraft overhead. They are usually large jet airliners (e.g. DC-10s and Boeing 747s) flying at about 10,000m (30,000 ft), and the chances of them seeing smoke from a burning tyre are extremely remote, and even then they could not be expected to take any action.

If you officially checked out and are awaiting rescue, for example in Niger, it will not come by air. If at all, it will come by Land Rover and more than likely along the piste or along the balises.

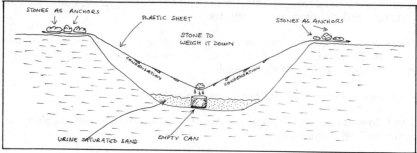

Flares. If you have flares, use them only when you actually see the dust of a passing vehicle on the horizon. This, or a previously prepared black smokey fire, could attract attention and induce vehicles' occupants to deviate and investigate. (Similarly if you should ever see a flare, or black smoke billowing in the distance, do go and check to be sure that it is not someone in dire need of your assistance.)

Do not leave the vehicle unless you know you can walk out. To do this you must know where you are, exactly, and you must know that at least one person can walk to safety, and help.

How to walk out. The route must be clear e.g. balises in good condition and at regular, visible intervals.

The person chosen to walk to help must be reasonably fit, known not to panic, and not prone to depression. A grim, determined 'battler' should be chosen.

The person should have a plastic jerry can with up to 15 litres of water in it, strapped to his back. This is heavy. He should also carry an emergency aluminium foil blanket and a bare minimum of food (preferably a 100g pack of survival rations). He should be clothed and carry a compass, an alarm clock, a cup and torch. He should walk only in the evenings. He should sleep a little during the night to gain maximum relaxation. During the early part of the morning while the sand is still relatively cool, he should dig a shallow depression to lie in (about 20 cm or 20 ins. deep), and, using the jerry can as a support, erect a 'tent' around himself, with the aluminium foil. There should be small holes at either end to allow passage of fresh air but at the same time prevent excessive entry of hot dry air. He should cover his face with clothing to ensure that he breathes in air that is as moist as possible. He should stay inside all day until about sunset, controlling, but not severely rationing his water intake all the time and trying to get as much rest as possible. Under no circumstances should he bury himself in the sand, for the hot, dry desert sand being hydroscopic, would virtually suck the moisture out of him during the day. He should keep going as far as he can like this to reach help.

How far he gets is an open question depending upon fitness and perseverance, temperatures, wind, softness of the sand and his luck. If, for example, he is contemplating walking in the Ténéré between Djanet and Chirfa, or between Fashi and the Arbre du Ténéré, 50 to 60 km would be about the maximum he could hope to travel during May to September.

If you left the piste or balises and struck out on your own before breaking down, then don't count on being able to walk out, following your own tracks. This is impossible in the Bilma Erg, for example, as the wind could obliterate your tracks within hours. In the northern Ténéré between Djanet and Chirfa it may well be possible within 50 or 60 km of these two places. Therefore, as much as possible, stick to the piste or balises.

Keep your cool. One of the most dangerous itineraries discussed in this guide is the Djanet to Chirfa route. It is dangerous not so much because of what it will do to you or your vehicle but because it is so lonely, especially in summer. In fact it is almost impossible to get lost because the balises are only 500m apart all the way. However, if your vehicle breaks down half way along the route, it could be three months before another vehicle passes, and it is impossible to walk out. Therefore, you must get that vehicle going again or perish. Hence the need to keep your wits about you, and not do stupid things, panic or give up.

301

Finally, for survival in the desert it is advantageous to have at least read a little more about the subject than is written here. For this, perhaps the best desert survival manual is K.E.M. Melville, **Stay Alive in the Desert,** (first published 1970, and now published by Roger Lascelles, London, 1981.) Dr Melville has many years of practical experience in the Sahara with oil companies. The book is short, concise, well laid out, informatively illustrated and inexpensive. It could save your life.

C.B. Radios

A Citizen's Band radio could be used to save your life, in dire emergency. (They are, however, illegal in Algeria.) U.S. 27mHz sets would be most useful, as not only do they have a high output (12 watts), but they are also available with single side band (SSB) facilities. This gives them a tremendous range over thousands of kilometres, especially at 'skip' times. In an emergency a continual 'Mayday' call would almost certainly be picked up by an amateur or 'Ham' radio operator, somewhere in Europe at least.

The advantages of CB sets over other VHF sets are primarily their relative cheapness, and their compact and robust structure. Unfortunately, German and Dutch CB radios are limited to AM and a very low output. British sets are limited to UHF and a similarly low power. Moreover it must be stressed that in Europe and Saharan Africa, U.S. sets are highly illegal but if used with discretion they could save your life. Because they are compact they should not attract too much attention at frontier posts, especially the combined CB-broadcast models, with the microphone removed.

Water Survival in the Desert

A man can last for a considerable period of time without food and indeed dehydration will suppress hunger. However, water is absolutely vital for survival in the desert and the hotter it gets the more water is needed. In fact, the amount of water required by the body to maintain a water balance necessary for survival increases exponentially as the ambient temperature increases.

The following figures are only approximate and assume rest in the shade at all times. In the desert, usually the average temperature can be taken as about 8°C below the daily maximum.

Daily Water Requirements to Maintain Water Balance		
Max. Temp.	**Average Temp.**	**Litres per 24 hr.**
43°C	35°C	5.1 litres
38°C	30°C	2.6 litres
33°C	25°C	1.2 litres
27°C	18°C	1.0 litres

Survival in the desert will also depend on one maintaining normal mental and physical efficiency. Dehydration will progressively lead to delirium, weakness and lack of muscular co-ordination. Maintaining a satisfactory water balance is vital. Any activity such as walking or digging will require considerably more water.

Desert Water Table — Days of Expected Survival							
Condition	Max daily shade temp	Total Available Water Per Person (litres)					
		0	1	2	3	4	10
Resting in the shade at all times	50°C	2½	2½	2½	3½	3	5
	45°C	3½	3½	3½	4	5	7
	40°C	5½	5½	6	7	10	13½
	35°C	8	8	9	10½	15	23
	30°C	10	10	11	13	19	29

		0	1	2	4	10
Walking only at night and resting in shade by day (Approx. distance walked in brackets).	50°C	1(40km)	2(40km)	2(42km)	2½(50km)	3(55km)
	45°C	2(40km)	2½(40km)	2½(42km)	3(50km)	3½(55km)
	40°C	3(40km)	3½(40km)	3½(42km)	5(50km)	5½(70km)
	35°C	4½(42km)	5(42km)	5(50km)	7(60km)	8(80km)
	30°C	7½(65km)	8(65km)	8½(70km)	10(90km)	12(105km)

It should be noted that walking across soft sand or parallel sand ridges can slow one up considerably (effectively reducing the distance covered by up to half).

* *   These tables have been adapted from tables in the British Ministry of Defence booklet: **Desert Survival-PAM(AIR)225,** published in 1975.

Some Basic Navigation

For most people travelling in the Sahara there will be no need for any special navigation techniques. Even though many pistes or tracks may be up to 20 kilometres across, there is generally a clear direction of travel as indicated by the tyre marks of previous vehicles. Most drivers are usually preoccupied with the need to find a way across the soft sand. On many occasions the authors have been concentrating on the sand in front while travelling along one of the main north-south pistes, looked out of a side window and on the distant horizon seen a moving black speck trailing a plume of dust yet travelling in the same direction and on the same piste.

In the flat Ténéré between Djanet and Chirfa, where only half a dozen vehicles may pass along the piste each year, one cannot really get lost as there are balises or beacons every 500 metres virtually all the way. However, if one is to strike out for any substantial distance from a known piste, then there are definite hazards and it is worthwhile knowing some rudimentary navigation techniques.

Landmarks

If you have good large scale maps or satellite photographs, then follow mountains, ridges or dune corridors if possible. However, you must be certain that the mountain or ridge you pick on at each stage of your journey is the correct one. Making a mistake of this sort in sand ridge country could be disastrous as you could be following up a dead-end or blind corridor between sand ridges and only have to turn back (if you can: soft sand may make turning very difficult).

Also bear in mind that desert terrain changes with time, especially in sand seas which can make even satellite photographs obsolete within days.

Direction Finding

In sand seas or vast flat expanses of featureless desert like the Tanezrouft or the northern Ténéré where there are no landmarks for hundreds of kilometres, there is a need to check constantly that one is still travelling in the intended direction. One of the consequences of not doing so is to find oneself travelling in large circles.

Provided that one does not need pin-point accuracy and only needs to keep going until one reaches a piste or mountain range, there are three simple ways of ensuring that one is travelling in the correct direction:

1. Watch the Sun

Point the hour hand of the watch towards the sun. Then bisect the angle between the hour hand and the 12 o'clock position on the watch face. This bisection will point directly south.

2. Shadow

At mid-day one's shadow will point towards the north, at sunrise to the west and at sunset to the east.

Note: In that part of the Sahara which lies to the south of the Tropic of Cancer

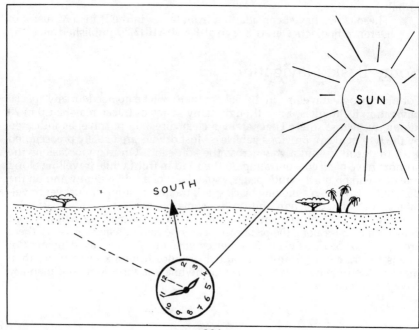

(23½°N), one's shadow and the direction of the sun at mid-day will be reversed for part of the period between April and September (the hot season or summer). For this reason it would be preferable to depend on a compass for direction finding. (The Tropic of Cancer lies just about 100 km south of Aswan, Kufra and Djanet and about 100 km north of Tamanrasset.)

3. Compass

All that is needed is a simple but robust and reliable orienteering hand compass (for example, those made by the Swedish 'Silva' company). Be careful to stand well clear of any vehicles or metal (ferrous) equipment (20 metres away, at least) to avoid interference with the magnetism of the compass. The compass needle will point to magnetic north which is not identical to true north. If you know, from maps you have with you, the difference between magnetic and true north, then make allowances for this. Otherwise, magnetic north will suffice because you will still strike that piste or range of mountains you were heading for.

If, however, you intend heading out across the desert without landmarks and wish to strike a well or an old camp with pin-point accuracy, you will need something more sophisticated than an orienteering compass if you are not to miss it by 20 to 50 kilometres.

For accurate dead reckoning, probably the simplest method for the layman is to obtain a Cole Sun Compass and have it mounted on the outside of the vehicle so that it may be watched as you drive. A sun compass does not depend upon magnetic fields to indicate a small shadow on the compass's calibrated flat surface. Again, account must be taken of the sun's position

A very simple, cheap and easy to make and use sun compass fitted into the bonnet mounted spare wheel of a Land Rover. A constant check on one's bearing can be maintained as one drives. However, this is not a Cole Sun Compass and does not make any pretence at accuracy and one has to take into account the seasonal variation in the sun's position when travelling in the tropics

SH 20

during the hot summer season if you are travelling south of the tropic of Cancer. If considering fitting a Sun Compass, it would be well worth consulting an excellent short article by D.N. Hall 'A simple method of navigating in Deserts' in the **Geographical Journal** Vol. 133, 1967, Part II, Pages 192 - 204. Most large public libraries will have a copy. It is indispensable.

Further up the scale in navigation complexity is position fixing at night by using selected stars. This requires an accurate and discerning knowledge of the stars and is fraught with hazards for those who are not absolutely certain of their own understanding of the night sky.

For even more sophisticated, accurate and certain navigation it would usually be necessary to undergo a formal training course in navigation and, in particular, the use of a sextant. A good text on navigation is: E.W. Anderson, **The Principles of Navigation** 1966, Hollis and Carter, London.

28
Trans Mediterranean

The ferry that one selects for crossing the Mediterranean should depend largely on which parts of north Africa and Europe one wishes to travel through before entering the Sahara, or after leaving it. For economy and time saving it is hard to match the Genoa-Tunis services. To get to or from the Sahara via Morocco and Spain will cost more in petrol and time than going directly via Tunis and Genoa, especially with a big fuel-hungry vehicle like a Range Rover or Mercedes Unimog.

From Spain to Tangier, Melilla, or Ceuta is only a short distance and facilities and accommodation on board are of little consequence in these few hours. However, the longer trips from Marseilles or Genoa to north Africa usually involve either two days and one night or two nights and one day. Therefore, on these long sea voyages facilities and accommodation should be considered. After an enjoyable, but very hot, tiring and dirty Saharan trip, it is sheer bliss to find beautifully clean cabins and showers, magnificent food, courteous and efficient service on the DFDS-Danish Seaways ferry service between Genoa and Tunis.

On ships like the 'Dana Corona', 'Dana Sirena', and 'Liberté' it is only possible to be booked into a cabin, and this is usually an indication of the style of vessel. These ships are one-class tourist cruise boats as well as car ferries. Thus the 'Liberté' caters for package round-trip cruises from Marseilles and back to Marseilles. Similarly, many passengers embarking on the 'Dana Corona' at Genoa have a ship cruise as part of a package holiday to some resort in Tunisia. These ships are therefore much more comfortable and luxurious than the average ferry, and offer organised entertainment, dances and cabarets as well as superb 'table d'hôte' dining. They are in marked contrast to the drab and dull ships of the Algerian line CNAM, where one has to sleep in aircraft type seats and where cabins are an expensive extra and the inferior meals available are not included in the fare.

The French SNCM (Société National Maritime Corse Mediterranée) service on the lovely modern 'Liberté' is superb but expensive. The authors have twice travelled on this vessel and relished the luxury of it. If one is to travel between Marseilles and Tunis or Algiers it is worth ensuring that one's sailing date coincides with the 'Liberté' rather than one of the other vessels.

It is very difficult to pay for the joint SNCM/CNAM service in Algeria with travellers cheques or foreign cash. Find out the cost first and then change

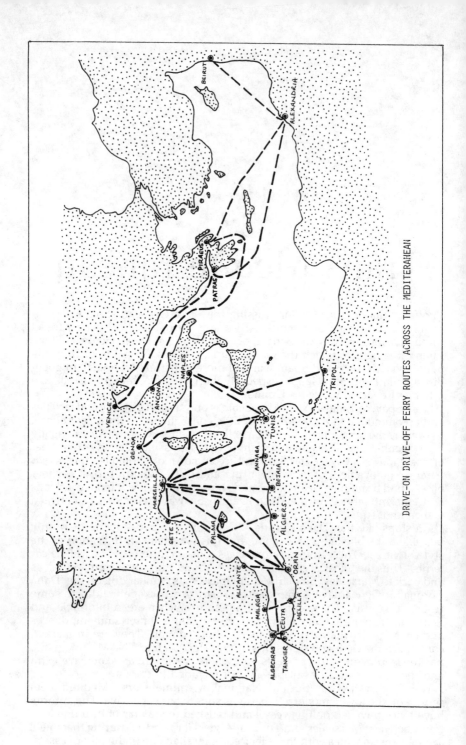

DRIVE-ON DRIVE-OFF FERRY ROUTES ACROSS THE MEDITERRANEAN

Trans Mediterranean Ferry Routes and Companies

Routes	Companies	Agents
Algeciras — Tangier Algeciras — Ceuta	: ISNASA Islena de Navegacion S.A., Estacion Naritima del Puerto del Algeciras, Algeciras, Spain. Tel: 652 850. Estacion Maritima del Puerto de Ceuta, Ceuta. Tel: 515 939	
Algeciras — Tangier Malaga — Melilla Algeciras — Ceuta	: Compania Transmediterrania Limadet, Estacion Maritima del Puerto del Algeciras, Algeciras, Spain. 3 Rue Henri Regnault, Boite Postale 244, Tangier, Tel: 33633 Estacion Maritima del Puerto de Ceuta, Ceuta.	Melia Travel, Ronkin 32, Amsterdam. Tel: 25 25 52 Voyages Melia, 31 Av de l'Opera, 75001 Paris Travel Melia, 12 Dover Street, London W1X 4NE. Tel: (01) 499 6731
Sète — Tangier	:Compagnie Marocaine de Navigation, 43 Avenue Abou Allal el Maari, Tangier.	G.I.B. Agency, Box 1311, 1410 BH Bussum, Netherlands. Tel: (02159) 15990 Gonrand Voyages, Talstrasse 66, 001 Zurich.
Marseille — Oran Alicante — Oran Marseille — Algiers Marseille — Bejaia Marseille — Annaba Sète — Oran	: CNAN Compagnie Nationale Algerienne de Navigation, 6 Boulevard Moh, Khemisti, Algiers. Tel: 64 04 20 9 Boulevard de la Soumman, Oran. Tel: 33 21 99 Offices in Annaba, Bejaia, Biskra, Skikda, Sidi-bel-Abbes, Tlemcen, Tizi-Ouzou and Setif.	SNCM, 61 Boulevard des Dames, Marseilles. Agencio Romeu, Plaza 18 Julio 2, Alicante, Spain. All SNCM offices in France
Marseille — Algiers Marseille — Annaba Marseille — Tunis	: SNCM — Societe Nationale Maritime Corse Mediteranée. 62 Boulevard des Dames, Marseille 13222. 12 Rue Godot de Mauroy, Paris 75009. All CNAN offices in Algeria.	CNAN 6 Boulevard Moh. Khemisti, Algiers. P & O Ferries, Arundel Towers, Portland Terrace, Southampton, SO9 4AE. Navitour, 8 Rue d'Alger, Tunis
Marseille — Tunis Genoa — Tunis	: CTN — Compagnie Tunisienne de Navigation, 5 Avenue Dag Hammarkjoeld, Tunis. All SNCM offices in France.	Tirrenia, Ponte Colombo (Gare Maritime), Genoa. Hoyman and Schuurman, De Ruytekade 124, Amsterdam. Tel: (020) 241 677
Genoa — Tunis Ancona — Patras — Alexandria	: DFDS — Danish Seaways, Ponte Calvi 1, 16126 Genoa. Tel: 20 58 06 20 Via 29 Settembre, 60100 Ancona, Italy. Tel: 20 04 46 Latham House, 16 Minories, London EC3N 1AD. Tel: (01) 481 3211. Sankt Annae Plads 30, DE-1295 Copenhagen K.	Anglo Algerian Coaling Co., 5 Rue Champlain, Tunis. Menatours, 28 Chamber of Commerce Street, Box 260, Alexandria. Zeetours, Postbus 996, Wilhelminakade, Rotterdam. Tel: 858 630 A/S Danske-Batene, Karl Johansgate 1, Oslo. Tel: 330 700.
Marseille — Naples — Tripoli	: General National Maritime Transport Co., 10 Garnata Street, Tripoli. Tel: 46 848 Omsr Street, Box 2451, Benghazi.	Aquitane Maritime Agencies, International House, 26 Creechurch Lane, London EC3A. Societa Navigazione Transceanica, Via Flaviogioia 15, Naples. Tel: 320 419
Naples — Palermo — Tunis Cagliari — Trapani — Tunis	: Tirrenia Line, Rione Sirignano 2, 80121 Naples. Tel: 660 333 Offices in Genoa, Palermo, Rome, Milan, Turin and Leghorn. All SNCM Offices in France.	Serena Holidays, 40 Kenway Road, London SW5 ORA. Tel: (01) 3736548 Suisse Italie S.A., Talaker 50, Postfach 8001, Zurich.
Venice — Piraeus — Alexandria	: Adriatica di Navigazione S.p.A., Zattere 1411, Palazzo Sociale, Venice 30123. Tel: 704 322	De Castro Shipping, 33 Sharia Calah Salem, Box 297, Alexandria. Tel: 35770 Gilnavi Ltd., 97 Akti Miaouli & Favierou, Piraeus. Tel: 4524 580 Sealink UK Ltd., Victoria Station, London SW1V 1JX. Tel: (01) 828 1940 Hoyman & Schuurman, De Ruytekade 124, 1011 AB Amsterdam. Tel: (020) 241 677
Alexandria — Beirut	: Alexandria Shipping & Navigation Co., 557 E1 Horreya Avenue, Box 812, Alexandria.	

money at the bank. This is a big problem on Fridays, Thursday afternoons and public holidays, and can be overcome by paying on arrival at Marseilles for the car, and to the purser, on board ship, for passengers.

Access to cars on ferries, while at sea, may be restricted. Enquire, as this varies.

It is preferable to buy tickets and make reservations at the actual terminal. Bookings through a travel agent should only be made several weeks in advance. Otherwise, you may find on arrival at the terminal that they have no knowledge of your booking.

Trans-Mediterranean shipping timetables and tariffs vary considerably from season to season. Summer tariffs can be 20% more than winter ones and it would be worth timing one's Sahara journey to take this into account. Similarly, some services like those operated by DFDS-Danish Seaways and the French SNCM are less frequent in the non-tourist or winter season. For details of fares, tariffs for vehicles and sailing dates it would be essential to study the most recent edition of the **ABC Shipping Guide** which is published monthly and available in most public libraries. All decent travel agents receive it on subscription. (Available from ABC Travel Guides, World Travel Centre, Dunstable, LU5 4HB, UK. Tel: 0582 600111.)

Some companies, such as the DFDS-Danish Seaways, offer a reduction in the tariff for vehicles carrying more than one person. Indeed, during the 'off-season' the vehicle may travel free if four or more fare paying passengers are carried.

Some companies, such as CNAM and SNCM, and Tirrenia Line, have a punitive rate for any vehicle regarded as a 'camping car' regardless of how small and compact it is. Such vehicles are charged at a flat rate per metre of length.

Some vessels have only limited space for high vehicles and have a surcharge for them. Thus DFDS-Danish Seaways have a penalty supplement for all vehicles over 2.15m in height. Therefore, if you must have a roof rack, be careful how high you load it. With regard to vehicle length, 4.25m and 4.5m seem to be the most commonly used dividing lines between short vehicles (and therefore cheaper tariffs) and long vehicles (more expensive rates). A selection of common vehicle lengths and heights is given below as a guide (excluding roof racks, bull-bars, extra spare wheels, etc.):

	Height mm	Length mm
Citroen 2CV	1600	3830
Datsun Patrol Stn Wagon	1850	4690
Fiat Campagnola long	1950	4025
Lada Niva	1640	3720
Land Rover 88	1970	3620
Land Rover 109 and 110	2070	4445
Mercedes Gelandewagen short	1985	3945
Mercedes Gelandewagen long	1975	4395
Mercedes Unimog U1300 short	2630	4750
Peugeot 504 car	1460	4490
Peugeot 504 Station Wagon	1550	4800
Peugeot-Dangel 504 Stn Wagon	1740	4800
Range Rover	1770	4470
Steyr Pinzgauer 710	2045	4175
Toyota Hilux	1790	4725
Toyota Land Cruiser BJ/FJ40	1970	3915
Toyota Land Cruiser FJ/HJ45	1960	4955

Toyota Land Cruiser FJ/HJ60	1820	4750
Volkswagen Bus 1968-1979	1960	4505
Volkswagen Bus 1980 onwards	1960	4570
Volkswagen Iltis	1830	3887
Volkswagen 181	1620	3780
Volvo C303	2145	4015

Between Algeciras and Tangier or Ceuta ferry services operate several times daily but during summer (especially July or August) it may be necessary to queue for many hours. The Malaga—Melilla service is once daily. Between Marseilles and Algiers the service is 5-6 times a week depending on the season. The Marseilles—Tunis service operates 10 to 14 trips a month. Most other services operate on a weekly or every 10 days basis.

At most ports the owner/driver is expected to drive his own vehicle on to

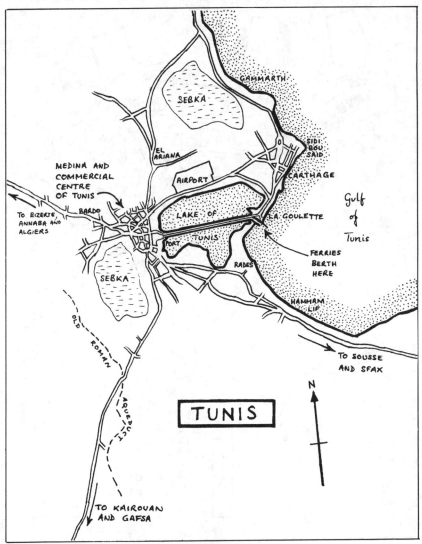

and off the vessel. In Algerian ports dock workers do this and one has to leave one's vehicle parked unlocked with the keys in the ignition. Do not leave valuables lying around inside the car. However, it might pay to leave a packet of cigarettes on the dashboard just to ensure that one's car is treated with special care.

The ferry terminal building at Algiers has a duty-free shop in the departure lounge area at which it is possible to buy good white and red Algerian wines at reasonable prices. These can be paid for in Dinars even though one has already surrendered one's currency declaration to customs officials.

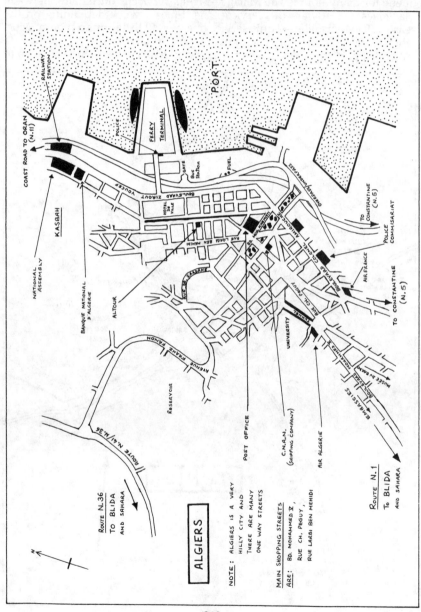

ALGIERS

NOTE: ALGIERS IS A VERY HILLY CITY AND THERE ARE MANY ONE WAY STREETS

MAIN SHOPPING STREETS
ARE: BD. MOHAMMED V,
RUE CH. PEGUY,
RUE LARBI BEN MEHIDI

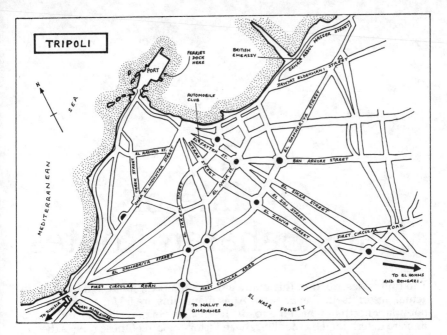

Note: During 1984 the British Embassy was closed. For consular matters involving British citizens, contact the Italian Embassy

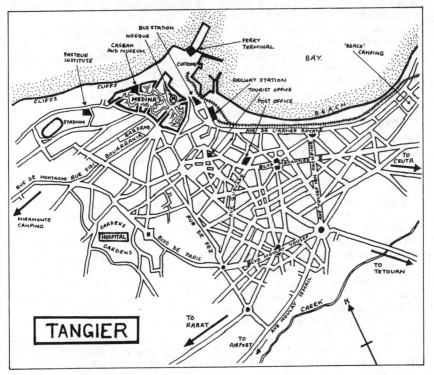

29
Outline of
Trans-Saharan Routes

The routes described in this guide are, in the north, limited to those in the actual desert itself. The Saharan Atlas mountains are taken as a convenient boundary north of which the roads, towns, way of life, climate, and vegetation are determined by Mediterranean factors. South of these ranges the real, vast, arid, harsh, and sometimes dangerous desert begins. Even though asphalt extends as far as Reggane, Tamanrasset and Sebha this does not detract from the essential character of this giant of a desert. It is still fraught with hazards for the unwary tourist.

For the southern limit of the area covered by route itineraries, the natural boundary is much more vague and transitional. The Sahel is a vast intermediate zone between desert and tropical tree savanna. It is an area that for three months of each year is essentially tropical, with apparently lush vegetation and lots of heavy rain. Yet, for the other nine months of the year it is largely desert and subject to the same dangers and pitfalls for the motorist as the Sahara itself. A piste that may require many hours of digging and laying sand ladders repeatedly to extract a vehicle from great seas of fine, soft sand, can six months later require the same tools, hard work and perseverance repeatedly to extract a vehicle from great seas of clinging mud. For these reasons it has been necessary to extend itinerary coverage into areas of the Sahel as far south as Kano: a city that for centuries has been the end of one of the trans-Saharan camel caravan routes.

Today there are two main trans-Saharan motor routes: the Tanezrouft and the Hoggar (the latter easily being the more popular). There are three other routes; the Tindouf-Mauritania, the Djanet - Ténéré, and Fezzan - Ténéré routes. The first has been impossible for the last few years, for political reasons, which make it very dangerous. (There is armed conflict between the Algerian backed Polisario movement, and the Moroccan backed Mauritanian government.) It is in fact illegal for tourists to travel this route, and it looks as if it will remain so for the next few years. For this reason itineraries of this route have not been included.

The two Ténéré routes traverse real sand desert, not actually experienced on the Tanezrouft or the Hoggar routes. Consequently they are little used by comparison, as they require vehicles more suited to desert conditions but they are included for the more intrepid traveller or the one who has more time, or has a suitable vehicle.

314

From the Ténéré and Fezzan there are pistes into the Tibesti region of Tchad (Chad): a desert region characterized by mountains, rising over 3200m (10,000 ft.), and active volcanoes. But the Toubou people of this area have been in revolt against the central government in the capital N'Djamena to the south. It is very dangerous (kidnapping and death by firing squad are facts of life here) and also illegal to enter the north of Tchad.

There is perhaps a sixth trans-Saharan route: from Tripoli to Sebha, then SE to Wau el Kebir, across the Rebiana Sand Sea to Kufra Oasis, and thence to El Uweinat, around the Egyptian border and into the Sudan to Wadi Halfa on the Nile. This route is over some of the remotest regions in the Sahara without tracks, with large ergs to cross and necessitating carriage of fuel for over 2000 km. It is clearly a route fraught with logistical problems of such magnitude that it is normally confined to major expeditions such as the Saviem one in 1977. Therefore, it has not been included in this guide. However, if you are contemplating travel in this region it would be worth contacting Klaus Daerr (Theresienstrasse 66, D-8000 Munchen 2, Germany) who has personal experience of crossing it privately in Mercedes 4x4 trucks. However, at the time of writing, travel on this route could be hazardous, even impossible, because relations between Egypt and the Sudan on the one hand and Libya on the other are very bad and there is considerable tension in the border area.

Routes from the Mediterranean to the Sahara

1. Through Morocco
Arrive at Tangier or Ceuta (Sebta) and head south via Tetouan to the Rif Mountains. These rise up to over 2,400m (7,500 ft) and can be seen snow-covered in winter, especially near the ski resort of Ketama. Unfortunately, tourists are often pestered by 'hashish' sellers, who may even force you off the road to sell you some. (Do not risk taking any into Spain or Algeria as penalties will always involve imprisonment.)

The Rif Mountains are very beautiful but travelling through them can be tortuously slow. The road returns to the coast at Al Hoceima, a pleasant seaside resort, with a good camping ground, which will be opened for you, in winter, if you ask at the nearby petrol station. Returning inland again, the road travels across plains to the city of Oujda. There is an Algerian consulate there.

Directly south of Oujda is a good road that runs within Morocco to the Algerian frontier at Figuig. This is a good shortcut to Bechar, the Saoura, and the Tanezrouft.

Alternatively east of Oujda after crossing the frontier, is a large historical town, Tlemcen. From here, there are good bitumen roads leading south across the big semi-desert high plateaus and Chotts to the Saharan Atlas range, where they cross into the desert via Ain Sefra, Laghouat and Ghardaia.

2. From Melilla
Directly inland to Oujda (see above).

3. From Oran
SW through vineyards, olive groves and wheatfields to Tlemcen, then across the high plateaus and Chotts to the Saharan Atlas ranges at Ain Sefra. Or, SE through Relizane or Mascara and over the Massif de l'Ouasenis to Tiaret, across the Chott plateau and the Saharan Atlas to Laghouat and Ghardaia.

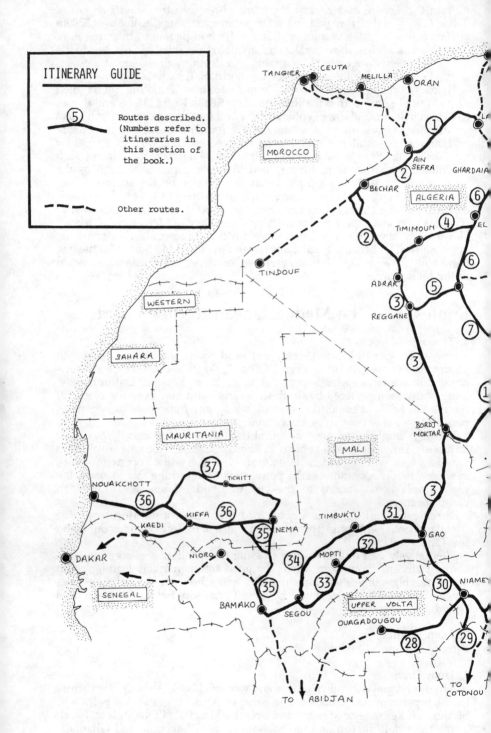

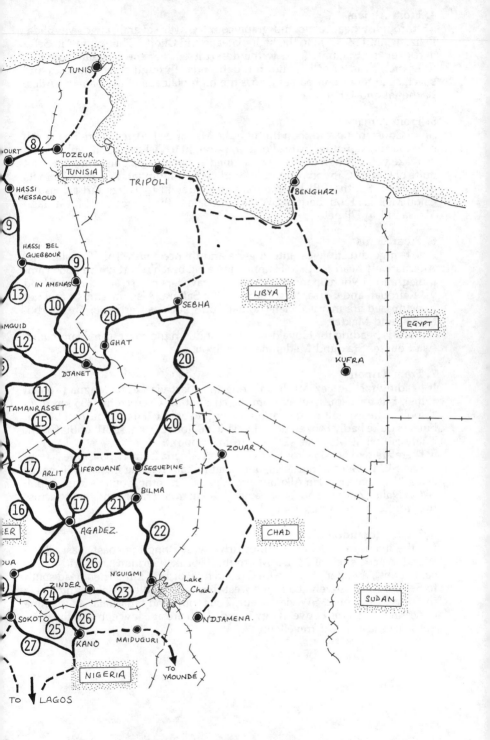

4. From Algiers

SE through wheat, olive and grape country over several ranges via Blida, Relizane, and Mascara to the high plateaus and Chotts. Thence, to Ain Sefra and over the Saharan Atlas to the desert itself. For the Hoggar route and to Djanet, head directly south through Blida, through some beautiful and spectacular mountain passes across the high plateaus to the Saharan Atlas, Laghouat and Ghardaia.

5. From Annaba

SE to Constantine and then through the Massif de l'Aures. Here it is worth side-tracking at Batna. Instead of going straight to Biskra a good asphalt road can take you through the Canyon d'Oued el Aboid: a magnificent gorge, not quite of Grand Canyon proportions but very beautiful and spectacular in its own right. South of Biskra the road goes straight to Touggourt across the Chott Melrhir. From here go SW via Ghardaia to the Hoggar, or SE via Hassi Messaoud to Djanet.

6. From Tunis

One can go directly west into Algeria and thence south from Constantine. Alternatively head south to Hammamet, a big beach resort with a good camping ground (where many trans Saharan travellers meet), and thence inland via Kairouan and Gafsa, to Tozeur and the Sahara. Also, in Tunisia and not to be missed are many ancient Roman ruins such as Carthage, Thurburbo-Majus, and Maktar.

If one is heading for Libya drive straight down the coast from Hammamet (via Sousse, Sfax and Medenine) to Tripoli.

7. From Tripoli

If heading for the Fezzan, head along the coast via Leptis-Magna (Roman ruins), but turn south away from the coast at Bu Gren (some 335 km from Tripoli). The asphalt road continues south to about 180 km south of Sebha, but it is quite badly broken up either side of Hon (278 km south of Bu Gren). There is fuel at Misurata (217 km from Tripoli).

There are two possible routes to Djanet in Algeria from Tripoli. One is from Sebha SW to Germa, Serdeles, and Rhat (Ghat on some maps) and thence across the frontier at Tin Alkoum into Algeria. The other route is from Tripoli SW to Nalut (266 km) and Ghaddames (584 km from Tripoli) and thence across the frontier to In Amenas in Algeria.

8. From Alexandria

For the main trans-Saharan routes drive west along the coast, past all the World War II sites of Mersa Matrouh, Tobruk (German and British war cemeteries), and Benghazi, to Bu Gren (a total of 1815 km). Then head south to Sebha. Alternatively, continue west through Tripoli to Gabes and Gafsa in Tunisia, and head SW via Tozeur, Touggourt and Ghardaia. At the time of writing, relations between Egypt and Libya are at a low ebb and the frontier is closed to most travellers.

30
Detailed Itineraries

Some of the words used in the Itineraries are drawn from other languages — Arabic, French, for instance. Readers are referred to the Glossary in Appendix B for explanations of these.

No.	Route	Page

KEY TO SYMBOLS USED IN MAPS.

● <u>ADRAR</u> — Larger or more important town or oasis.

○ MADAMA — Smaller settlement or locality.

(B F C W P) — Facilities available at a settlement.

C — Customs.

B — Bank.

F — Fuel.

P — Police.

W — Water.

River.

Intermittent water course.

Sand dunes or very sandy area.

Flat hammada (small stones and sand).

Mountains.

Scattered tussock grass.

Scattered low Acacia trees.

Trees in urban areas.

Palmeraie.

Swamp.

Asphalt road.

Unsealed or gravel road.

Piste or general direction of travel.

Bad corrugations.

Sandy section of piste.

Bridge or pass.

Escarpment or 'Falaise'.

HIGH GROUND / LOW GROUND

Important buildings.

International border.

Satellite television receiver.

Railway line.

321

Itinerary No. 1 : Laghouat — Ain Sefra

Distance   484 km.

Water   At all petrol stations and wells in other smaller oases.

Fuel   Petrol and diesel at stations at Laghouat, Aflou, El Bayadh, Ain Sefra.

This road is asphalt all the way with a good full width surface from Laghouat to Aflou and from El Bayadh to Ain Sefra. Between Aflou and El Bayadh the asphalt is narrow and it is often necessary, when passing oncoming traffic and overtaking other vehicles, partially to leave the sealed surface. All this route follows the relatively unspectacular Saharan Atlas ranges which are often lightly covered in snow during winter. Although definitely desert, there is always some vegetation consisting of low saltbush and tussock grasses with Oleanders and Tamarix bushes along oueds. In spring (May-June), the desert of these ranges bursts into magnificent displays of beautiful but short-lived flowers.

There are important pre-historic rock art examples along the way at El Bayadh and Tfout and to the south at Brezina and El Aboid Sidi Cheikh.

0	484	**Laghouat** A large oasis town with a modern light industrial area developing in the southern outskirts. Police, post office and Daira are to be found in the centre of town around the main square. Not a tourist oriented town, there are some modest hotels and it is served by SNTV buses and by Air Algérie. The petrol stations are to be found just off the western by-pass road.
		Leave town via the north along the main road to Algiers. Cross a large bridge over the Oued Djedi.
4	480	Turn off to west from the main north — south road. It is well sign-posted.
123	361	**Aflou** Bank, post office, police and fuel.
266	218	**El Bayadh** Bank, police, post office, fuel and a good bakery. No European-style hotels. Carpet weaving is one of the traditional crafts of the region. For rock engraving sites, ask at the petrol station. They will also give advice on how to find the Brezina engravings some 70 km to the south.
271	213	Road junction. Follow road to SW to Ain Sefra.
331	153	Road junction. For Ain Sefra keep going west. Asphalt road to south goes to El Aboid Sidi Cheikh about 60 km away where there are rock engravings and warm mineral springs.
391	93	**Ain Tazina** Spectacular large white spire which is a monument to those who died in the Algerian Revolution. No settlement.
404	80	**Chellala** Oasis overlooking a spectacular view of a massive arid valley and bare rocky mountains. Shop, police and Mosque but no other facilities.
468	16	**Tfout** Oasis village. Rock engravings are only 50 metres from the road about 300 metres east of the bridge across the palm lined oued and on the northern side of the road. Ask in the village for a guide to take you to further engravings 11 km to

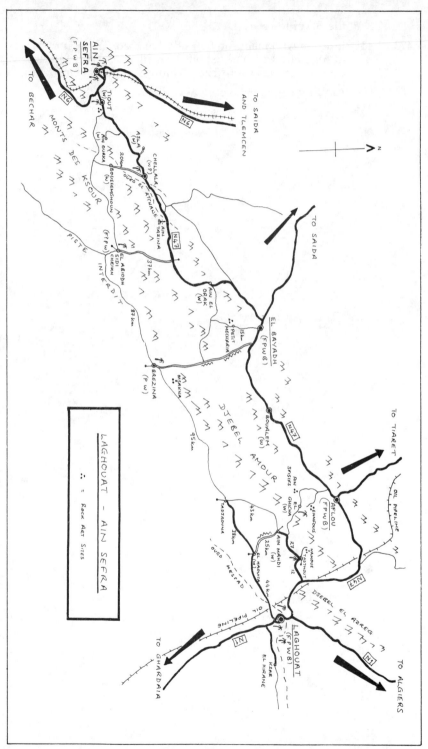

the SE of town.

473   11   Junction with main Ain Sefra-Bechar road. Travel northwards to Ain Sefra which is just off the main road. (Watch for speed traps or specially constructed humps as you enter town.)

484   0   **Ain Sefra** For details, see next itinerary.

Itinerary No. 2 : Ain Sefra — Adrar

Distance   847 km

Water   At all petrol stations and many small wells in major oases.

Fuel   Petrol stations at Ain Sefra, Beni Ounif, Bechar, Beni Abbes, Kerzaz and Adrar. They are all usually well stocked with petrol and diesolene.

The entire route is full width asphalt. Until Bechar the road travels through and just to the south of the Saharan Atlas ranges. South of Bechar it travels through the vast flat Hammada du Guir but soon enters the Saoura, a very large oued between two immense ergs, the Grand Erg Occidental and the Erg Er Raoui. This is one of the most beautiful routes in the Sahara and also one of the easiest to travel along.

0   847   **Ain Sefra** The town is just off the main road and lies at the northern foot of the Saharan Atlas Mountains just before the road passes through them to the real desert to the south. It can therefore be regarded as a gateway to the Sahara. Police, post office, petrol station, and bank. SNTV operates a bus service to Bechar and Adrar in the south and Oran in the north. There is a large military base nearby as this is a sensitive frontier zone. A railway station with passenger services to Bechar and to the north exists. There is good camping to the south of the town as the road enters the mountains.

49   798   **Moghrar** Formerly a French military outpost and now just a small village. Along most of the road from Ain Sefra to Bechar can be seen evidence of attempts by the French to stop raids by FLN guerrillas into Algeria from Morocco during the struggle for independence during the 1950s. The whole frontier zone is lined with over 1,000 km of dense barbed wire,

The legacy of France's resistance to the Algerian struggle for independence in the 1950s. In a futile attempt to prevent Algerian guerrillas crossing the Moroccan frontier, the French authorities erected a massive thousand kilometre barrier of entangled barbed wire, land mines and broken glass linked by a series of concrete forts built within sight of each other. Today, over thirty years later, it is all still there as mute testimony to man's folly

minefields and even broken bottles buried with the shards just protruding from the sand. There are small forts within sight of each other at strategic hilltops for the entire distance. As a result, with this legacy of lethal garbage, it can be dangerous to leave the road.

81 766 **Djenien Bou-Reg** Small village.

143 704 **Oued Zousfana bridge** Sometimes there is a military checkpoint here.

153 694 **Beni Ounif** Small frontier town. Police, petrol station, railway station but no bank (change money with Customs). Bakery, restaurant and shops. Nine kilometres to the north is the Moroccan frontier town of Figuig. Moroccan border post is open from 08.30 to 18.00 but the Algerian post is open 24 hours. Note: Fuel is much cheaper in Algeria than in Morocco but avoid the temptation to fill up your jerrycans as the Moroccans will charge you import duty on the fuel. Also, Algerian officials may confiscate certain issues of the Michelin 153 map.

267 580 **Bechar** A large modern town that is the administrative centre for the whole Saoura region. Many large apartment blocks. Police, Daira, post office, bank, petrol stations, supermarket, butchers, bakeries, market, two moderate to expensive hotels (Hotel Transat and Hotel de la Saoura), airport (with scheduled services to Tindouf, Adrar, Algiers) and an SNTV bus station. There is also a French Consulate and a public swimming pool.

Driving across the Oued Zousfana near Beni Ounif. It is only very rarely that water flows on the surface. The date palms in this palmeraie usually obtain their water from deep under the sand

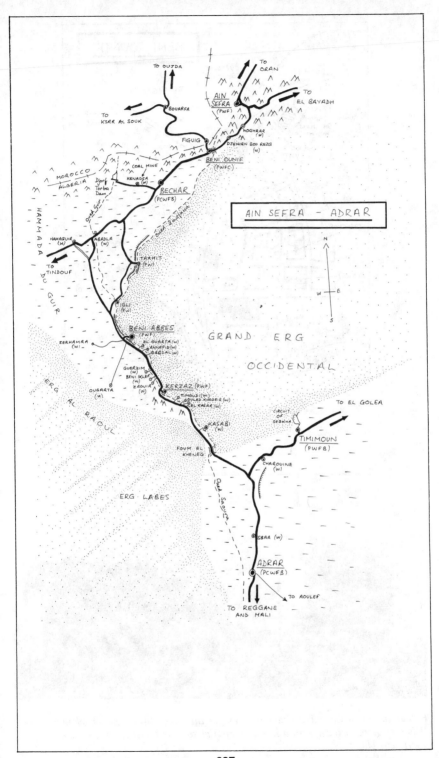

AIN SEFRA - ADRAR

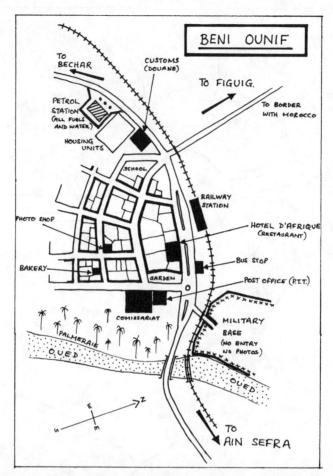

Bechar (formerly Colomb-Bechar) is no longer the sleepy little oasis of colonial times. It is a large busy town with a heavy industrial zone and suburbs of concrete apartment blocks

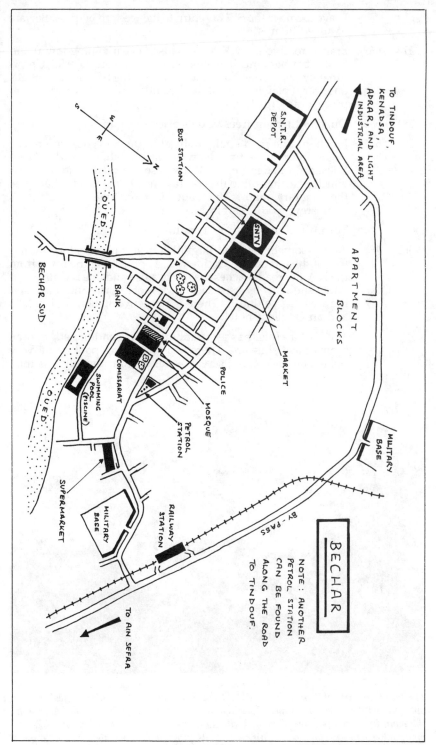

BECHAR

NOTE: ANOTHER PETROL STATION CAN BE FOUND ALONG THE ROAD TO TINDOUF.

TO TINDOUF, KENADSA, ADRAR, AND LIGHT INDUSTRIAL AREA

S.N.T.R. DEPOT

BUS STATION

APARTMENT BLOCKS

SNTV

OUED

BECHAR SUD

OUED

BANK

MARKET

COMISSARIAT

SWIMMING POOL (PISCINE)

POLICE

MOSQUE

PETROL STATION

MILITARY BASE

SUPERMARKET

MILITARY BASE

RAILWAY STATION

BY-PASS

TO AIN SEFRA

Leave town via the SW or return to the western by-pass. Beware of speed bumps.

278	569	Branch road to the NW to Kenadsa (a coal mining town) and to the barrage and irrigation scheme at Torb Djorfa. Unfortunately, when one has almost reached the barrage a sign tells one very plainly that it is forbidden for all foreigners to proceed any further.
281	566	Oued with palm trees. Good place to camp.
290	557	Junction. The road straight ahead to the SW goes to Tindouf (route interdite — forbidden to tourists while the Moroccan-Polisario problem persists). It is also the main road to Adrar which branches off to the south some 91 km from Bechar. (See the itinerary map.) This route is monotonous and not as interesting as the Tarhit deviation.

Turn off to the south to Tarhit.

362   485   **Tarhit** (sometimes spelt Targhit) A beautiful oasis town at the foot of the Grand Erg Occidental. Approaching the town from the NW the road reaches the top of a rise and one is confronted rather suddenly by a spectacular view of this romantic oasis and the vast erg behind it. There is no petrol station, but police, and an excellent hotel.

The Tarhit Hotel has a restaurant, is air-conditioned, and all rooms have showers. There is a swimming pool and a very polite and welcoming service — all for considerably less than

The beautiful oasis of Tarhit (Targhit). At the foot of some spectacular dunes, the village is built between the Oued Zousfana and the Grand Erg Occidental. Although the main livelihood is date growing, virtually every house has television and, like so many other oases in Algeria, Tarhit receives its programmes via satellite from Algiers

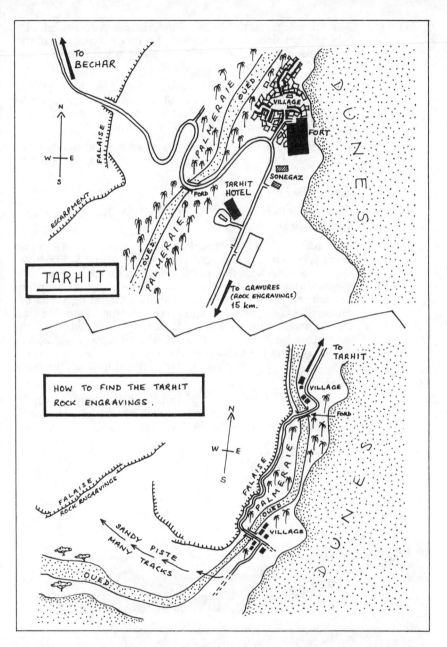

TO
BECHAR

N

W — E

S

FALAISE

ESCARPMENT

PALMERAIE

OUED

OUED

PALMERAIE

VILLAGE

FORT

SONEGAZ

FORD

TARHIT
HOTEL

TO GRAVURES
(ROCK ENGRAVINGS)
15 km.

D U N E S

TARHIT

HOW TO FIND THE TARHIT
ROCK ENGRAVINGS.

N

W — E

S

TO
TARHIT

VILLAGE

FORD

FALAISE

PALMERAIE

OUED

VILLAGE

FALAISE
ROCK ENGRAVINGS

SANDY PISTE
MANY TRACKS

OUED

D U N E S

the equivalent government run luxury hotels in other towns.
This one is very proudly run by the municipality. From Tarhit
it is well worth walking up into the enormous sand dunes,
especially in the late afternoon — it is very beautiful. Some
12 km to the south of the town via the palmeraie, there is an
asphalt road which degenerates into a piste and leads to the
rock engravings and paintings. They are in excellent condition
but at present unprotected from tourist vandals and graffiti.

331

365	482	For Adrar leave Tarhit by the same hill that you entered it by. About 5 km along this asphalt road is a new asphalt road that branches off to the SW — a 96 km short cut to the main road south. There is some lovely scenery.
394	453	Sign written on the ground with stones: 'El Aouedj 4 km Puits.' It points to some wells to the SE in the Oued Saoura after descending a steep sandy track down the escarpment. Beware. It may be impossible to drive back up this track.
426	421	**Igli** Oasis village with palmeraie and an agricultural development programme. Post office, police station and a municipal garage.
442	405	Junction with main road south.
484	363	Turn-off to Beni Abbes 15 km to the east. This is a good full width asphalt road.

Beni Abbes Police, supermarket, Daira, petrol station and post office (open in morning until 11.00 and re-opens at 13.00). An expensive hotel with air-conditioning, bar, sauna, tennis courts, swimming pool, etc. (Hotel Rym). There is also a cheap one without most of these facilities (Hotel du Grand Erg). There is an excellent little museum and zoo run by the Centre National de Recherche sur les Zones Arides. It has displays of the prehistory and the wildlife of the Saoura region. The swimming pool (piscine), at the Ksar is broken down and derelict. Camel excursions can be arranged through the Hotel Rym.

To the south of the town is a humble little hermitage run by the Petites Soeurs de Jesus and founded by Charles de Foucauld before he went to live in the Hoggar.

The chapel built by Father Charles de Foucauld in 1902 at Beni Abbes

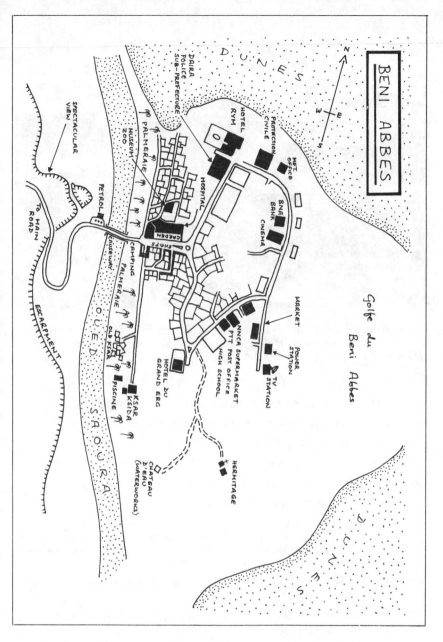

To leave Beni Abbes return to the main road. At the junction with the main road there is also an almost indiscernible piste heading west to Zerhamra some 30 km away and to Oued Merlook where there are rock engravings and Neolithic remains. It is piste for the experienced only.

488   359   Piste to Ougarta 40 km to SW. No balises.

538   309   Side road east to village of El Ouata in the Oued Saoura only

Looking across the dry Oued Saoura that marks the western limit of the massive Grand Erg Occidental. This sea of sand extends for 450 kilometres without a break and without any sign of plant or animal life. Yet it is one of the Sahara's smaller ergs

2 km away. Post Office.

543	304	Side road east to the village of Annefid only 5 km away.
545	302	Side road east to the village of Agdal only 7 km away.
549	298	**Foum El Erg** Beautiful erg.
559	288	Side road to oasis of Guerzim a few km to west.
568	279	Side road to oasis of Beni Iklef to west.
585	262	Village of Zaouia on the west side of the road.
592	255	**Kerzaz** Oasis in between two ergs with a palmeraie and picturesque well pumps. Police, clinic, restaurant, and petrol station. The old town is 5 km to the south along a good asphalt road. Turn off at the petrol station.
622	225	Side road to oasis of Timoudi some 18 km to the east along a piste.
635	212	Good asphalt side road to oasis of Ouled Khodeir about 11 km to the east.
638	209	Side road to El Kasar 7 km away to the east along a piste.
648	199	Side road to Ksabit some 12 km away to the east along a piste. Café at turn-off.
657	190	Foum El Kheneg — large oued and concrete causeway.
720	125	Junction with asphalt road to Timimoun and El Golea. For Adrar continue south.

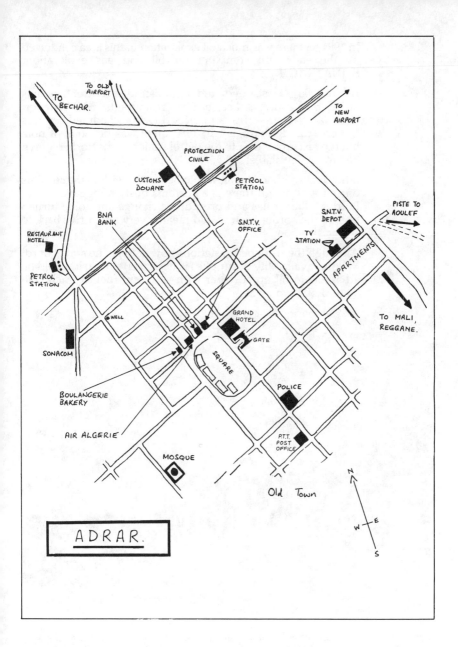

767	80	Café.
788	59	Café.
799	48	Recently a military road block has been set up here.
807	40	**Sbaa** Actually three villages (Sbaa, Tsabit and El Gueirara) each with its own palmeraie and system of underground water channels or 'foggaras'.

In 1981-83 there was much oil exploration in this area conducted by the state run company for oil and gas exploration: SONATRACH.

847   0   **Adrar** A large oasis town and administrative centre. Customs office, post office, police, bakery, restaurants, SNTV depot, bank, Air Algérie office and airport (with scheduled services to Bechar and Ghardaia). In 1983 there was no hotel of note but the restaurant next to the petrol station to the north of town has rooms available.

If heading south to Mali, it would be worth a visit to the customs office for although there is a customs post at Reggane and at Bordj Moktar, rules and procedures change and to be turned back at the border itself would mean a very long drive back to Adrar

Although there are petrol stations now at Reggane and at Bordj Moktar, availability of supplies is never certain. So it would be advisable to fill up at Adrar with sufficient fuel to reach Gao some 1,503 km away.

Part of the central square at Adrar with most of the buildings constructed in the so-called 'Sudanese' red mud style not unlike buildings in Timbuktu, Mopti and Djenne in Mali

Itinerary No. 3 : Adrar — Gao

Distance   Approx. 1,503 km (Four wheel drive is not necessary.)

Water   Adrar and Reggane at the petrol stations. Take sufficient to last you all the way to Gao, though it is occasionally possible to obtain some at Bordj Moktar.

Fuel   Petrol and diesel fuel is available at Adrar and Reggane. There are new pumps at Bordj Moktar (sometimes they have fuel). It is worth filling up at Reggane with sufficient fuel to get you all the way to Gao.

The 'Tanezrouft' route can be boring or fascinating depending on how one regards almost 1,500 km of flat nothing. It is not as rough on vehicles as the Tamanrasset — Arlit piste. There are big stretches of 'feche feche' but, if you keep your speed up, there should be no problems. Fuel is a headache, as so much must be carried. This is where large thirsty engines like those of the Range Rover and Chevrolet Blazer are at a disadvantage: so much space inside the vehicle has to be devoted to carrying jerrycans. Diminutive motors with a frugal consumption like those of the Citroen 2CV have a distinct advantage.

Police in Adrar may insist that you travel in a convoy of at least two vehicles, and might wish to check on fuel supplies and whether or not you have two spare wheels. Note: report to the police in Gao before heading north across the Tanezrouft.

There are banks and therefore money change facilities at Adrar and Gao but nothing in between. Therefore, it would be wise to carry sufficient cash in CFA or Mali francs (buy these in Europe before you leave for the Sahara) to pay for the 1,000 CFA francs per car 'Laissez-passer' at Tessalit.

0 1503   **Adrar** The route is quite clear from the television station onwards to the east of town. The asphalt road has been completed all the way to Reggane. On the way some impressive foggaras can be seen. North bound travellers would be advised to call in to customs office in Adrar on arrival.

            Note: if going on to Reggane and then to Aoulef and Ain Salah or coming from these places, there is no need to report to customs or police. If arriving in Adrar from Mali, it is necessary to change foreign currency into 1,000 Algerian Dinar per person at the bank before reporting to the customs.

            Between Adrar and Reggane there are numerous ancient little oases to the west of the road each with its palmeraie irrigated by subterranean water brought there by an elaborate network of foggaras. Note how each village is engaged in an endless battle against encroaching sand by continually building walls of palm fronds.

31 1472   **Zaouiet-Sidi-Abdelkader** A modern village constructed in 1979-80 by the Algerian government as a model people's commune. School, police, shops and garage. Palmeraie.

135 1368   **Reggane** The settlement appears sooner than expected. Very clearly seen are the ominous remains of a former French prison for political prisoners. The area to the south of the town was

337

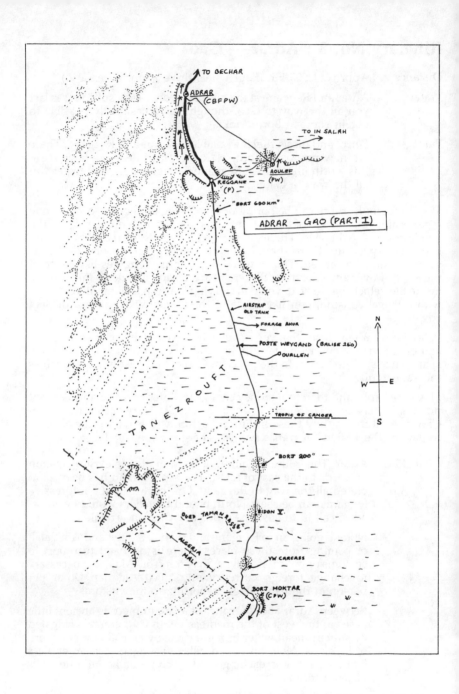

TO BECHAR

ADRAR
(CBFPW)

TO IN SALAH

AOULEF
(PW)

REGGANE
(P)

"BORJ 600 KM"

ADRAR — GAO (PART I)

AIRSTRIP
OLD TANK

FORAGE AHUR

POSTE WEYGAND (BALISE 260)

OUALLEN

N

W — E

S

T A N E Z R O U F T

TROPIC OF CANCER

"BORJ 200"

OUED TAMANRASSET

BIDON V.

ALGERIA

MALI

VW CARCASS

BORJ MOKTAR
(CPW)

338

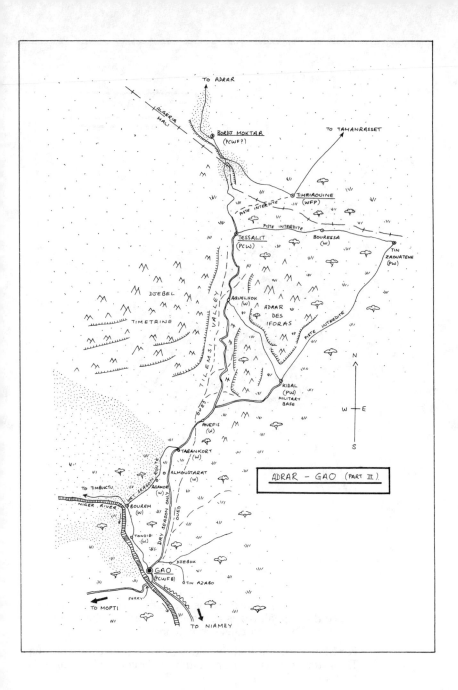

ADRAR – GAO (PART II)

339

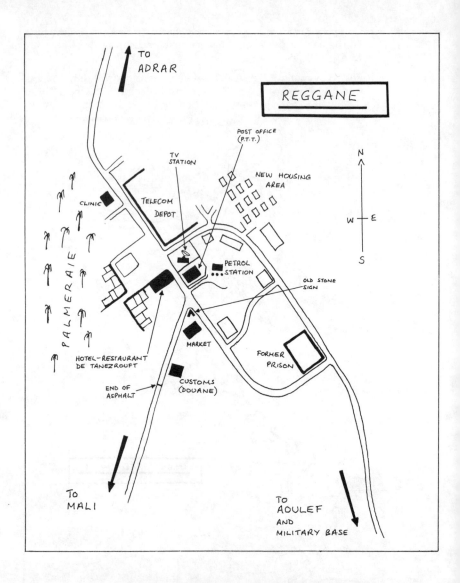

the site of some French atmospheric nuclear test in the 1950s, hence the asphalt roads that seem to lead nowhere to the SE of town. These can cause some confusion.

For Mali, turn south at the old signpost in the centre of town. Then stop at the customs post. (If travelling from Mali, also visit customs in Adrar.)

145	1358	500m of soft sand.
175	1328	Sign 'Bordj 600' (i.e. km to Bordj Moktar).
280	1223	Sign 'Bordj 500'.
335	1168	Airstrip with marker. Storage tank and pump. No longer in operation.

350	1153	To the east of the piste are sign posts indicating 'Forage Ahur 17 km'.
385	1118	**Post Weygand** (or Balise 250). Merely a collection of derelict steel huts. A sign says 'Gao 1112 km' and 'Bechar 968 km'. A little used piste heads to the east of here to Ouallen, an uninhabited old military post 70 km away. Keep on southwards.
425	1078	Sign 'Bordj 350'.
475	1028	Sign 'Bordj 300'.
493	1010	Tropic of Cancer. Around here the piste passes between some dunes, and there is some soft sand.
575	928	Sign 'Bordj 200'. Soft sand.
625	878	Sign 'Bordj 150'.
645	858	**Bidon V** A tower and some derelict huts. Some sandy sections north and south of here.
		Airstrip. The Oued Tamanrasset dissipates into the desert here.
695	808	Sign 'Bordj 80'.
725	778	Sign 'Bordj 50'.
756	747	Feche feche on a slight rise.
775	728	**Bordj Moktar** Wide shallow oued on the northern approach. Military outpost. Repeat Customs and Police formalities. Water supplies — tap. New petrol station. For 32 km south of the frontier post to the Mali border the piste is not very clear.
807	696	Mali frontier.
935	568	**Tessalit** Mali frontier post. If you don't have a visa for Mali you may be sent all the way back. No fuel, no money changing facilities; there is a very small store and a rudimentary Campement. You may need 2,000 Mali francs or 1,000 CFA in cash per vehicle to pay for the 'Laissez-passer'.
1033	470	**Aguelhok** A small Touareg village with a well. There is an open prison and also a small bar run by 'Suleiman'. Police control post.
1060	443	A piste branches off to the SE to the village of Kidal some 123 km away. Do not go there as it is also a military base and tourists are most unwelcome.
1205	298	Branch piste to Kidal in the NE, 95 km away.
1218	285	**Anefis in Daran** Small Touareg village. Police control post. It is here that the sparse grassland of the northern fringes of the Sahel begins.
		South of Anefis the piste follows the Oued Tin Daren to Tabankort.
1258	245	**Tabankort** Small Touareg village. Well (dirty). Police control post. The piste from here southwards divides into two. One is direct to Gao but only to be used in the dry season (Tabankort — Gao is 194 km). The other is longer via Bourem to the SSW.

Using the all weather vehicle piste, there are patches of sand and many different vehicle traces. About 2-3 km north of Bourem is the piste to Timbuktu heading west.

| 1408 | 95 | **Bourem** A village on the Niger River. Police. German aid project. A corrugated piste south to Gao. |

| 1493 | 10 | Police check point. |

| 1503 | 0 | **Gao** On arrival or shortly before departure for the north, one should first check in with the police and customs (wear long trousers). Obtain photographic permits and, if necessary, extend your visa. From customs one should obtain an import permit for the vehicle. For this, one needs to have obtained the necessary stamps from the post office. |

There is a bank. In most cases CFA francs are also acceptable in Gao. (1 CFA franc = 2 Mali francs.) Petrol stations, hotel, pharmacy, hospital and airport with services to Mopti and Bamako as well as to Niamey. There are several garages, the best being the Dutch organised co-operative one. A site not to be missed is the tomb of Askia Mohammed (see Chapter 6: History).

For the ferry or 'bac' across the Niger to the road to Mopti head south for 7 km.

For the steamer service up the Niger River to Timbuktu and Mopti and for further details and a map of Gao see Itinerary No. 30.

Itinerary No. 4 : El Golea — Adrar

Distance   569 km (For maps see Itinerary No. 6).

Water   At petrol stations at El Golea, Timimoun and Adrar.

Fuel   Petrol stations at El Golea, Timimoun, Adrar and M'Guiden.

There is a good full width asphalt road all the way. Towards Timimoun the road passes the southern edge of the Grand Erg Occidental where there are big sand dunes.

0	569	**El Golea** Heading south the road climbs up onto the plateau which overlooks the town.
63	506	Take the turn-off to the west. Straight ahead goes south to In Salah and Tamanrasset. It is well signposted.
213	356	**M'Guiden** Tiny settlement with petrol station. Also, turn-off to larger oasis of El Homr some 15 km to the north.
353	216	**Timimoun** A large oasis town. Main centre for a prosperous agricultural region known as the Gourara. There are other villages in the 'sebka' or fertile depression to the north, the whole sebka being surrounded by dunes of the Grand Erg

The lovely Hotel Rouge de l'Oasis at Timimoun. Sadly, this famous hotel had to be abandoned in 1981 because large parts of it collapsed

343

Occidental. Police, clinic, post office, bank, airport, Air Algérie office, SNTV depot, petrol stations (2). The Timimoun local government or Wilaya makes great efforts to attract tourists to the area. There is a cultural festival during the first two days of April: well worth seeing. It is also worthwhile travelling around the sebka for a few days; the circuit of the villages being 52 km. Apart from the scenery, fossilized wood and roses of sand can be seen.

Hotels: Hotel Gourara, a modern air-conditioned government run hotel that is expensive but has tremendous views of the sebka.

The Hotel Rouge de l'Oasis had its roof collapse in 1981 and has been closed since. It is a beautiful Sudanese-style red mud building. It would be well worth trying to have a look inside before it becomes too derelict.

398	171	**Asfaou** A small oasis.
418	151	**Chaiouire and Tinkran** Two villages with palmeraie. Police station.
444	125	Junction with the main north-south route from Bechar. Head south for Adrar.
498	80	Café.
508	61	Café.
521	48	Military road-block sometimes (e.g. in 1981 and 1983).

Inside the Hotel Rouge de l'Oasis. Every interior wall of this red mud building is covered with delicate patterns which were traditional for this part of the Sahara. One door has a plaque fixed to it which states that the Grand Duchess of Luxembourg stayed here for a time in 1926

344

529	40	**Sbaa** Actually three villages, Sbaa, Tsabit and El Gueirara, each with its own palmeraie and system of foggaras.
569	0	**Adrar** For detailed description, see Itinerary No. 2.

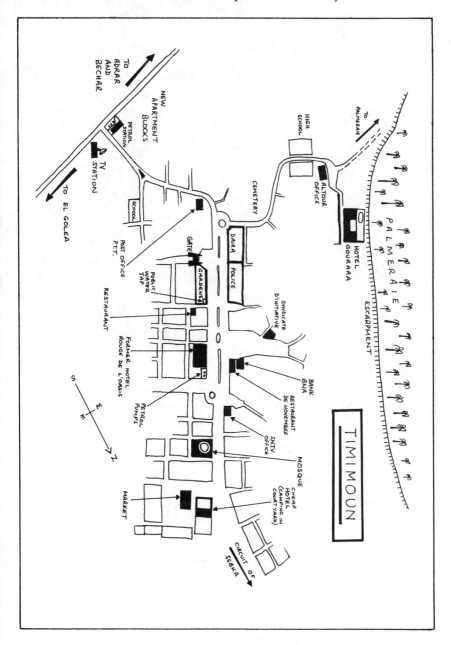

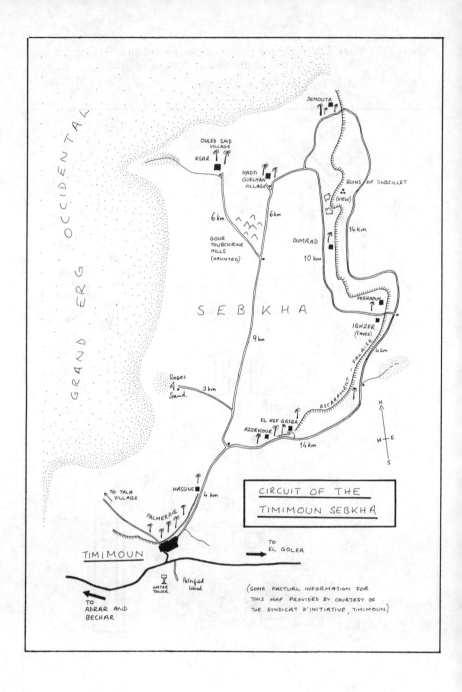

CIRCUIT OF THE
TIMIMOUN SEBKHA

(SOME FACTUAL INFORMATION FOR
THIS MAP PROVIDED BY COURTESY OF
THE SYNDICAT D'INITIATIVE, TIMIMOUN.)

Itinerary No. 5 : Reggane — Ain Salah

Distance   273 km. (For route map see Itinerary No. 6. For map of Reggane see Itinerary No. 3. For map of Ain Salah see Itinerary No. 6.)

Water   At Reggane, Aoulef and Ain Salah, at the petrol stations. At other oases, the local well.

Fuel   Petrol stations at Reggane, Aoulef and Ain Salah.

This is an open desert piste without any balises. Follow the most recent tyre marks in the sand. Four wheel drive is not necessary but two wheel drive vehicles should travel with reduced tyre pressures for much of the way; otherwise expect to become bogged a few times.

0	273	**Reggane** For Aoulef follow the asphalt road south for about 5 km beyond the settlement. Just opposite a small village and palmeraie, a signpost indicates the route to Aoulef which starts as a made-up gravel road rising up and over an escarpment to the east. The asphalt road actually continues south for another 5 km towards a fort and a warning notice: 'Zone Militaire — Access Interdite'. Do not proceed and take no photos. (You can be seen from the fort.)
40	233	At about 40 km out of Reggane, it would be wise to stop and reduce tyre pressures to about 60% of normal to avoid getting bogged.
97	176	Keep to the northerly tracks as there is much feche feche to the south. Keep speed up.
102	171	**Timokten** A village with a palmeraie. Junction with piste direct to Adrar.

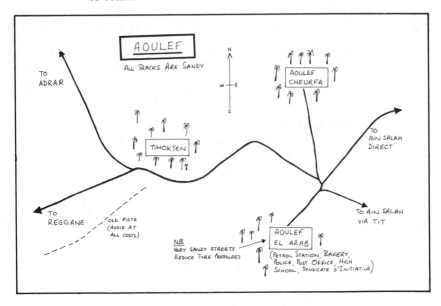

| 109 | 164 | **Aoulef el Arab** Large village with palmeraie and foggaras. Also, petrol station (at entry to town), high school, bakery, police, post office, hotel (hotel Charef), 'syndicate d'initiative'. All are located close to or in the central square. For water, ask at the petrol station and they will probably give you a bucket and rope in order to pull water up from the nearby foggara. It is good water — though should still be treated. |

Note: the streets are very sandy. Do not enter town without tyres deflated at least 50%.

Fresh vegetables are usually in abundance, especially tomatoes.

For Ain Salah, leave via the NE piste.

114	159	Airstrip. Drive across part of it.
119	154	Well. Dried up and full of sand. There is a lone acacia tree to the north in the distance.
204	69	Small sandy and rocky pass. Lots of blue-grey rocks. After this pass, increase tyre pressures to normal as the piste steadily becomes more rocky. (Reduce pressures here if travelling west.)
218	55	Signpost to In Ghar or In Rhat some 15 km to the south. This piste is only just discernible. In Rhat is a small oasis with a palmeraie.
225	48	Petrified trees. The remains of temperate rain forest 'Araucaria' trees now found only in the SE of Australia, New Zealand and southern Chile. Please don't take souvenirs.

From here on the piste becomes more sandy. Lower tyre pressures again.

248	25	Signpost to Sebhket el Melch to the south. No recognisable piste.
270	3	Join the asphalt road that travels between Ain Salah and the Palmeraie d'El Barka. Turn left and east for Ain Salah. Turn right and SW for 'Camping Chez Alhaji Abdul Rahman'. If travelling from Ain Salah to Aoulef, turn right and west of the asphalt about one kilometre after emerging from the Ain Salah palmeraie. (There is no signpost. Just follow all the tyre tracks but lower tyre pressures about 50% first.)
273	0	**Ain Salah** Enter town from the west via the palmeraie. All facilities. (For details, see Itinerary No.6.)

Itinerary No. 6 : Ghardaia — Ain Salah

Distance	669 km.
Water	At petrol stations at Ghardaia, El Golea and Ain Salah. Along the 400 km between El Golea and Ain Salah there are no facilities for obtaining water. The Tademait Plateau is a terrible place to run out of water.
Fuel	Several petrol stations at Ghardaia, two in El Golea, one at Hassi Fahl and one at Ain Salah.

The road is full width asphalt all the way with some lengths of reconstruction to the south of El Golea. South of Ghardaia it passes through caramel coloured dunes which can extend across the road. Do not hit this sand at speed. This would severely damage your vehicle.

0   669   **Ghardaia** Really five towns, (Ghardaia, Melika, Beni Isguen, Ben Noura, and El Atteuf) in a fertile shallow gorge, known collectively as the 'M'zab'. There is a sixth town, Berriane, about 45 km to the north, and a seventh, Guerrara about 120 km to the north east.

The Mozabites are an Islamic sect that broke away from the mainstream of Islam a schism about 900 years ago. Essentially Berbers who fled into the desert, they possess a puritanical zeal, not unlike that of Calvinists, that sees merit in success in the world of commerce. Thus, these five towns have a commercial atmosphere about them, unknown to the rest of Algeria. The man sitting outside his shop may well have a BMW parked around the back and shares in a supermarket in France. It is a friendly town(s) with an architecture both beautiful and unique.

The area is also famous for its woven rugs (beautiful, but expensive). It is a good place to have servicing done to any make of vehicle. The service will be prompt, and efficient. (If stranded in Tamanrasset or Adrar, come to Ghardaia rather than Algiers, for spare parts for your vehicle.)

Police station, post office, two banks, motor insurance, cinema, hospital, airport (jets to Algiers, Tamanrasset, Djanet, Bechar, etc). There is an air-conditioned bus service to Algiers, and good, ordinary bus services to El Golea, Tamanrasset, Timimoun, and Ouargla (all run by SNTV). Tours of the M'zab are operated by Altour (the government tourism organization) with an office at the Hotel Rostimedes.

An expensive hotel (Hotel Rostimedes), a more moderate one (Hotel Transatlantique), and a cheap one (Hotel Napht). Camping ground surrounded by a high wall and guarded by a fierce dog.

Leave the M'zab via the south. As the road climbs out of the valley there is a spectacular view of Beni Isguen. For the next 5 to 10 kilometres the road passes through the Ghardaia industrial complex and the airport.

18   651   Turn off to west. Asphalt road to Metlili some 20 km away. This

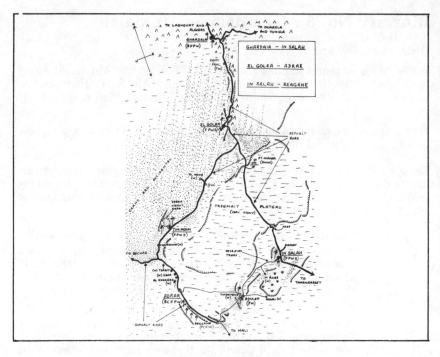

is a Chaamba village and palmeraie.

24	645	Branch road (well signposted) to the east to Ouargla and the oil and natural gas installations of this area. The flares of burning waste gas can be seen from dozens of kilometres away during the night. This branch road continues to Djanet and to Tunisia.
111	558	**Hassi Fahl** Drinkable water, small village and new petrol station.
225	444	Piste to Ouargla branches off to the east. Not only is this a Piste Interdite but it is also rarely used.
263	406	Television satellite receiving station and quite spectacular view overlooking El Golea and the distant dunes.
269	400	**El Golea** Large oasis town. Petrol stations, police, post office, bank, several bakeries, market, cafés, airport and an Air Algérie office. Two hotels (an expensive one, the Hotel el Boustan, and a more moderate one, the Hotel du Tademait). There is also an Altour office which can arrange camel tours. The old Chaamba fort or Ksar to the east of the town is well worth a visit.

To the north of the town 4 km away in the suburb of Bel Bachir is the tomb of Father Charles de Foucauld who established the hermitage at Assekrem (see Chapter 8: Explorers, Conquerors and a Saint). His heart is, however, interred in Tamanrasset. There is a community of the Little Sisters of Jesus nearby.

El Golea is a main centre of the Chaamba people, a warlike nomadic group. They were used by the French to crush the

350

A glimpse of the old city of Ghardaia as seen from the Hotel Rostimedes. Ghardaia is just one of several ancient Mozabite cities close together at this point along the edge of the M'Zab Valley in the middle of arid stony desert

Touaregs at the Battle of Tit in 1902, near Tamanrasset. South of El Golea the road passes between two ergs. Sometimes there is sand across the road. It may seriously damage your suspension if you take it at speed.

334	335	Branch road to the west to Timimoun and Adrar (asphalt). Continue south.
375	294	The road rises straight up onto the vast flat expanse of the Tademait Plateau. A desolate area, totally devoid of vegetation and covered only with stones. At this point there is a gravel road to the east of the ruins of Fort Mirabel, a former French Foreign Legion outpost, some 15 km away.
486	183	Small café all by itself in the middle of a vast flat area of nothing.
576	93	**Ain El Hadjadj** No buildings or anything, just a beautiful pass as the road winds its way down to the big plain on which Ain Salah is situated.
663	6	Turn off to the Ain Salah airport in the east and to the oasis of Foggaret-es-Zoua which has a palmeraie and an elaborate system of foggaras. To the east of Foggaret-es-Zoua there is a little used piste to Bordj Omar Idriss some 580 km away. It is a 'Piste Interdite' and would need approval from the Diara in Ain Salah and an experienced guide before being attempted. It is difficult. This piste also has a branch which goes to Amguid and ultimately to Djanet and is equally difficult. Both pistes are for the experienced only.
669	0	**Ain Salah** A large oasis — mainly Arab but a few Touaregs.

Built largely of red-brown mud, there are increasingly a lot of modern concrete buildings, such as apartment blocks, being erected. Police, airport, Air Algérie office, SNTV office, petrol station, bank, bakery, restaurants and hospital. A moderately priced hotel (Hotel Badjouda) and an expensive one (Hotel Tidikelt). There are several mechanics in the town. The authors can thoroughly recommend the one next to the Restaurant du Carrefour which is operated by Bousidi Abderrahmane and

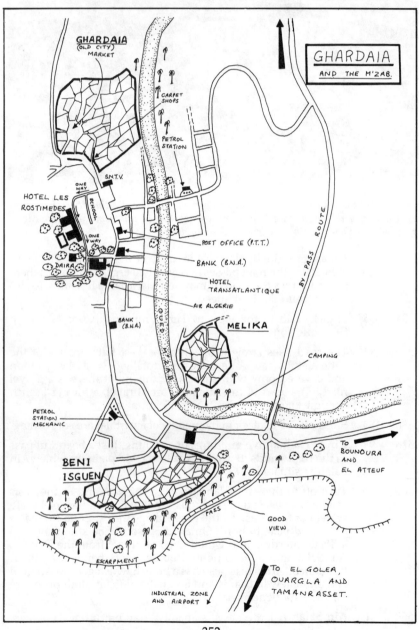

GHARDAIA
(OLD CITY)
MARKET

GHARDAIA
AND THE M'ZAB.

CARPET SHOPS

PETROL STATION

S.N.T.V.
ONE WAY
SCHOOL
HOTEL LES ROSTIMEDES
ONE WAY
DAIRA

POST OFFICE (P.T.T.)

BANK (B.N.A.)

HOTEL TRANSATLANTIQUE

AIR ALGERIE

BANK (B.N.A.)

OUED M'ZAB

BY-PASS ROUTE

MELIKA

CAMPING

PETROL STATION MECHANIC

BENI ISGUEN

TO BOUNOURA AND EL ATTEUF

PASS

GOOD VIEW

ESCARPMENT

INDUSTRIAL ZONE AND AIRPORT

TO EL GOLEA, OUARGLA AND TAMANRASSET.

called Mechanique Trans Saharien.

It is always worth a visit to the Restaurant du Carrefour. Its proprietor, Alhadji Abdul Rahman, is a Touareg from the village of Adriane near Tamanrasset and is genuinely very sympathetic to overland travellers. A man who bridges two cultures, he is a mine of information about the region and has friends all over the world. He can give valuable advice on pistes and

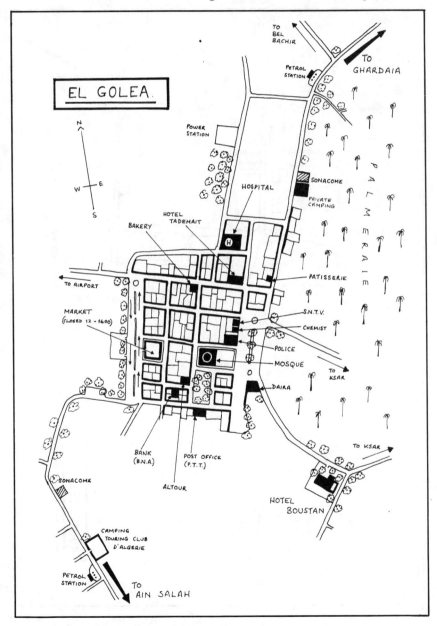

conditions as well as on how to obtain items such as jerrycans and sand ladders (p.s.p.) or where to sell them. He is very friendly but this is genuine and he is not a con-man. In 1982 he opened a protected camping area just south of the town. Having done some skiing himself in Switzerland, he is now famous for his ability to ski down the slopes of sand dunes near Ain Salah.

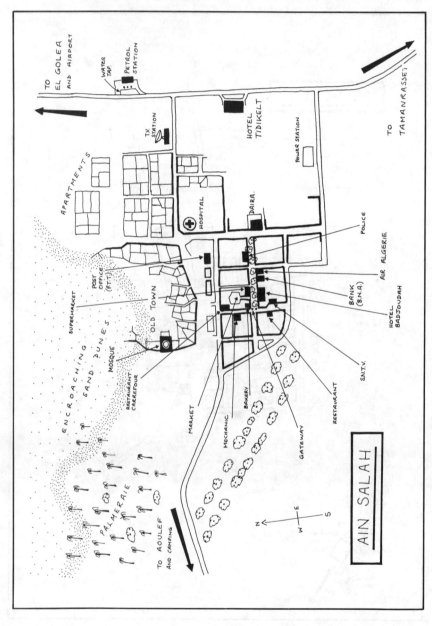

There is a palmeraie to the west of the town with many small irrigation canals. (Do not wash in these as they are believed to carry Bilharzia or Schistosomiasis). Unfortunately, this palmeraie has in the past been overused by tourists and there is a lot of rubbish lying around. It is preferable to camp in the open desert or at Alhadji Abdul Rahman's camping area where there are showers and a piscine.

There are scheduled flights to Ghardaia and to Tamanrasset by Air Algérie. There are also daily SNTV bus service to Ghardaia and Tamanrasset.

Alhaji Abdul Rahman (or Abderrhamane), proprietor of Ain Salah's Restaurant du Carrefour and one of the notable characters of the Sahara. He is renowned for his hospitality and helpfulness

The red mud 'Sudanese' style gateway in the commercial centre of Ain Salah

Itinerary No. 7 : Ain Salah — Tamanrasset

Distance   658 km.

Water   At petrol station and at Camping at Ain Salah; at petrol station at Árak and at Ain Ecker; at well in village at Ain Amguel and at Tit; at hotels at Tamanrasset if you are a guest. If not it is best to drive out to the Tahabort spring at 'Chez Jojo' north of town along the piste to Assekrem.

Fuel   Petrol stations at Ain Salah, Arak, Ain Ecker and two in Tamanrasset. However, stations along the way between Ain Salah and Tamanrasset may run out of supplies. Therefore, carry sufficient for the whole distance.

In theory the road is now full width asphalt all the way between Ain Salah and Tamanrasset. However, south of Ain Salah it has become very broken up in places. South of Arak it is so badly broken up and for such long distances that it is impossible to drive on and pistes have been established to the side of the road for many kilometres at a time. Progress can be very slow and frustrating.

Along the way it is worthwhile making a conscious effort to leave the main road and explore especially in the Erg Mehedjibat to the east of the road about 15 km north of Arak and in the mountains to the south of Arak. Therefore it is still useful to take spare jerrycans and a set of sand ladders or p.s.p.

0	658	**Ain Salah**
88	570	Turn-off to Amguid 406 km away to SE. A very lonely and difficult piste, for experienced travellers only. Seek advice in Ain Salah before attempting this route.
254	404	Small group of dunes to the east of the road make a spectacular place to camp. Just leave the asphalt and head east across the gravel desert.
273	385	Entrance to Arak Gorge, a passage through an otherwise impenetrable block of mountains. Roadworkers camp, a zeriba café and an old disused petrol pump.
282	376	**Arak** A few humble stone and zeriba houses, a petrol station and a café (coffee and tea only — no soft drinks or alcohol).
332	326	The road travels through the Monts du Mouydir. Not always visible here is Meniet well. Sometimes there is a Touareg encampment. Nearby is a Neolithic site (3460 BC) of major archeological importance.
390	268	Signpost indicating 268 km to Tamanrasset. Leave the road here and head west following other vehicle tracks to the tomb of the Marabout Moulay Hassan. This is a humble white-painted building with little pinnacles and usually flags on the roof. It is the custom for all vehicles heading in either direction to drive around this building three times as a mark of respect for this Moslem holy man who died here while on a pilgrimage to Mecca. About a kilometre to the south of this tomb is the carcass of a burned out Volkswagen Kombi. Apparently its American owners did not know about this custom, did not

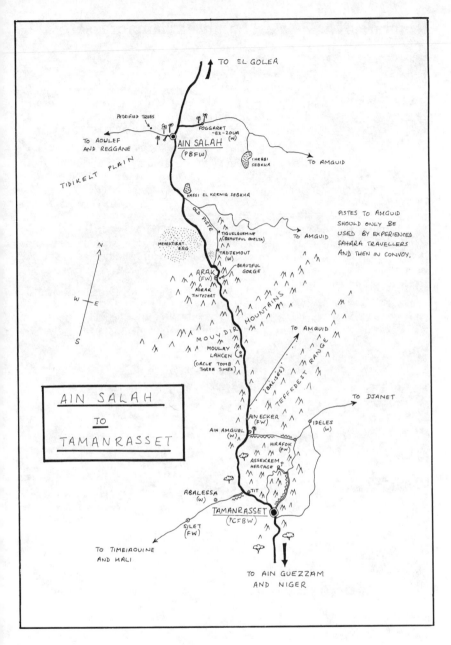

encircle the tomb three times and the vehicle was engulfed in
flames as plastic jerrycans of petrol carried on the roof exploded.

There is a small café near the tomb

478 180 Turn off to NE to Amguid. A piste for the experienced.

492 166 **Ain Ecker** Police station, café and petrol station. This was also
the site of some French nuclear tests during the 1950s. Beware

The mausoleum of Moulay Hassan (Moulay Lacene). All vehicles should drive around this building three times as a mark of respect for this Marabout or Moslem holy man who died on his way to Mecca

ot lots of barbed wire lying around on either side of the road. Like some of the bleak windswept buildings scattered around, this was left by the French when they abandoned the site upon

Algerian independence in 1962 and moved their nuclear testing programme to the south Pacific.

502	156	Turn off to SONAREM mine to the east. (In dire emergency, they will help with vehicle repairs.)
520	138	Several turn-offs to the east to military camps.
533	125	**Ain Amguel** Village with well and a small palmeraie.
540	118	Branch road to Djanet 612 km to the east and to Hirafok some 93 km away along a piste.
574	84	Café.
616	42	Turn-off to Abalessa some 60 km away in the west. This piste also takes one to Silet, Tim Missao, Timeiaouine and Bordj Moktar on the Mali frontier.
618	40	**Tit** Touareg village. Site of a battle in 1902 at which the French crushed the power of the Kel Ahaggar Touaregs.
639	19	**Outoul** Village with well and café.
648	10	Turn-off to airport 2 km to west.
649	9	Piste for western approach to Assekrem (120 km away) branches off to NE. Can be difficult to find.
658	0	**Tamanrasset**

Tamanrasset

With the expansion of the tourist industry and, in 1978, the completion of the asphalt road, Tamanrasset has grown incredibly in size and in population, but in the process it has lost much of its 'back of beyond' appeal. There are now apartment buildings, a television station which receives its programmes by satellite, a multi-storey air-conditioned hotel, light industries and a supermarket. Yet the Kel Ahaggar Touareg men of the region can still be seen in great numbers in the town with their traditional robes and veils walking the streets maintaining their dignity in spite of this alien culture and technology which has taken over the region and which now dominates their society. Nevertheless, it is rather despressing to see the shantytown slums or 'bidonvilles' that these dispossessed now inhabit, in and around Tamanrasset.

Water Water can be a major problem for tourists spending a day or two in town unless one stays at a hotel or at the official new Camping area. Alternatively, it would be worth driving out to the Source Tahabort about 15 kilometres along the way to Assekrem. Here there is a spring at the side of a mountain and a restaurant, 'Chez Jojo', which has unfortunately become a little run down since the proprietor, Jojo, went to jail. There is now a lot of rubbish lying around as it is common for overland travellers to camp in the area.

Accommodation Hotel Tahat — a modern air-conditioned hotel. Expensive but it has all modern amentities. It is a wonderful place to clean up and relax in after a lot of hard work travelling in the desert. Hotel Tin Hinane — a quaint place that is a remnant from the more relaxed colonial past. It has become run down. Camping — there is a new camping ground to the east of town

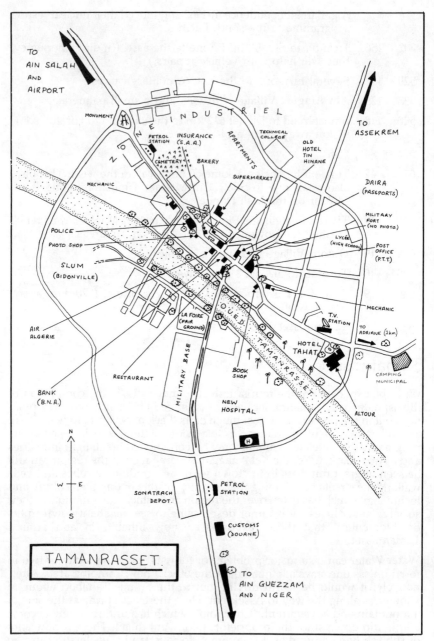

near the village of Adriane (Hadriane) run by the Tamanrasset Municipality. It has water taps, showers, a bar and a restaurant.

There are several restaurants. Bank hours are 8.30 to 13.00 and 16.00 to 17.00 daily except for Fridays. There is an Altour office in the Hotel Tahat. The authors have found it to be helpful and efficient. A lot of package tours are flown directly from Europe (via Algiers) and tourism has become big business. See Chapter 11 for details of tours in the Hoggar offered by Altour.

One of many southern European style restaurants in the more picturesque old colonial parts of Tamanrasset. South of Tamanrasset, the Sahara becomes increasingly African in culture rather than Mediterranean

Mechanic There are several garages and prices are regularised by the government. Thus, there is little opportunity for bargaining. However, spare parts are in short supply and, if available, expensive. The exchange of spares that one has brought with one for the services of a mechanic is always appreciated and an acceptable way of paying for repairs, even if they are simple things like tyre tubes, distributor points or gaskets. A good mechanic who can be recommended by the authors is Rikab Mohammed Rabah in the Ksar el Fougani area of town on the way to the Hotel Tahat opposite the bookshop.

Formalities On arrival from the south (i.e. Niger),
1. Report to customs at the southern extremity of town. Obtain permit for vehicle and declare currency and other valuables like cameras. Don't use your Carnet here if you have one. It will be necessary to change foreign currency into 1,000 Algerian Dinars per person visiting Algeria,
2. Report to Daira in centre of town next to the old fort (no photos!). Your visa and passport will be checked and stamped. In some cases you may be asked to go to the hospital for a malaria test or for other inoculations if your international health certificate is out of date.
   Note: you must go through these formalities in Tamanrasset even though you may have seen customs and immigration authorities at Ain Guezzam or Bordj Moktar.
3. Buy vehicle insurance from the S.A.A. office in town. This should cover the period of your stay in Algeria. Allow for delays or an extension of the time originally planned to spend in Algeria. To buy an extension to the vehicle insurance is very expensive and cumbersome. (See Chapter 14 on Vehicle Documents.)
Of course steps one and two above should be undertaken in the reverse order if travelling south. If you intend heading for Mali via Timeiaouine, it would

361

be worth visiting the Daira and customs in Tamanrasset first. There is now a Mali Consulate in Tamanrasset which can issue visas.

Places in the Hoggar

Tazrouk A Touareg village with many irrigated vegetable gardens. Water available from irrigation channels, or preferably from the spring along the oued, about 3 km from Tazrouk, by a small village with a well. Plenty of fresh vegetables to buy.

Along the Oued Teberber, about 7 km from Tazrouk are four big fig trees. In the rocks all around can be found ancient engravings of giraffes, cows, camels, etc. and the ancient now forgotten Libyan script (see Frobenius, O. **Ekade Ektab,** Graz, 1937).

23 km SW of Tazrouk the track along the oued reaches the main Ideles — Tahifet piste.

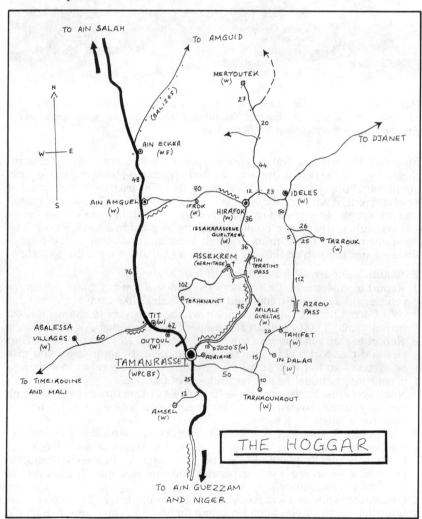

Assekrem Spectacular view! One of the highlights of any Saharan excursion. A series of trachyte volcanic plugs juts out from a generally granite massif, to form magnificent sheer faced mountains. A view matched only by such places as the Victoria Falls, the Grand Canyon, and New Zealand's Fjords.

It is best to arrive in the late afternoon, camp in the car park, (which is always dirty), and climb up to the Hermitage to watch the view as the sun sets. However, the sight not to be missed is the sun rise. You must be at the top before the sun rises. It takes between 10 and 30 minutes to reach the Hermitage, depending on fitness. But, the sight is ample reward for the steep climb.

In the hermitage is a small library of books on the Hoggar, Foucauld, and other subjects pertaining to the region. Also there is a small, very beautiful and serene chapel where 'Les petits frères de Foucauld' (two Catholic monks) celebrate mass every morning. Entry is by invitation only.

Mertoutek A group of isolated Touareg villages about 80 - 90 km north of Hirafok. There is a palmeraie and vegetable gardens. Infrequently visited by tourists. Many prehistoric rock engravings in the nearby hills. It is worthwhile arranging for a local guide to take you, by donkey or camel, for two days into these hills, called the Taffedest. About 15 km south of Mertoutek, it is possible to leave the piste on the right and head directly north to Amguid. There are no tracks, balises, or traces of other vehicles, but for those really wishing to do their own thing, or save time, it can be very interesting, if you are well prepared and travel in convoy.

Sunrise from the hermitage built by Father Charles de Foucauld in 1906 at Assekrem high up in the Hoggar Mountains. A sight not to be missed

Itinerary No. 8 : Tozeur — Ghardaia

Distance   592 km

Water   From petrol stations, palmeraies, public taps etc. in Tozeur, Nefta, El Oued, Touggourt, Ouargla and Ghardaia.

Fuel   Petrol stations at Tozeur, El Oued, Nefta, Touggourt, Ouargla and Ghardaia. Invariably adequate supplies available.

The route passes the beautiful Chott el Djerid, a large salt lake bordered with palmeraies and oases. In Algeria it passes through the Souf region, an area famous for its large succulent 'deglet nour' dates. This is also an area of continually moving sand dunes, so that almost daily the date farmer has to remove sand from his palmeraie. Further into Algeria the route goes through part of the main oil and gas producing regions of the country: flares from the burning waste gas can be seen for miles around, especially at night. Ghardaia is one of a group of five Mozabite towns in a lovely deep oued.

The whole distance is on good full width asphalt road, with no problems.

0   592   **Tozeur** Large town on the edge of the Chott el Djerid, with a big, beautiful palmeraie.

             Five big hotels (Continental, de L'Oasis, Splendid, Djerid, and des Palmiers). Bank, petrol stations, post office, railway station, many shops. Known for its fine brilliantly coloured and patterned rugs. A town which is very much geared to the tourist industry. A new airport capable of receiving jumbo jets, is under construction.

23   569   **Nefta** A smaller version of Tozeur. Petrol Station, bank, Police,

The business centre of Tozeur. Note the Australian Eucalyptus tree - very common around the northern limits of the Sahara

Tourist Information Office, keen to take you on any number of guided tours through the Souf region and the beautiful Chott. These tours, though some are expensive, seem quite worthwhile, and the pride and enthusiasm of the tour operators is most encouraging. Market, two big hotels (Sahara Palace, and Hotel Mirage), and a special hotel run by the Touring Club of Tunisia (the Marthala), which is more modest than the other two. A palmeraie which is very pleasant for camping, though another palmeraie further out of town, towards El Oued, is more private. Note: fuel and oil are cheaper in Algeria than in Tunisia.

66	526	Tunisian frontier post. Between the two border posts is about 5 km of no man's land, littered with the skeletons of cars, stripped for spare parts, rather than have import duty paid on the complete vehicle.
71	521	Algerian frontier post. Declare currency. Buy insurance with foreign cash (e.g. French or Swiss Francs, DM or US$) as there are no facilities for changing travellers cheques. Change foreign money into 1,000 DA per person on entry to Algeria.
83	509	Junction with bitumen road from Tebessa in the north.
147	445	**El Oued** Large oasis town. Police, bank (hours 08.30 to 13.00 and 14.00 to 16.00). There is an expensive hotel (Hotel du Souf), and three medium priced hotels (Trans-atlantique, Hotel d'Or Noir, and Hotel En-Nakhil), and a cheap but adequate one (Hotel de l'Oasis). Camping En Nakhil a few kilometres along the route to Tunisia. Also a hospital, petrol station, Daira, post office, airport (scheduled flights, by jet to Algiers); bus services by SNTV to Ghardaia, Touggourt, Biskra, and Tebessa

Rug shops at Tozeur, which is renowned for its distinctive rug and mat weaving

(departures near Hotel des Dunes). The 'Syndicat d'Initiative' can organize tours by camel in the Souf region.

Leave town via NW but then turn off to Touggourt on the left. (Straight ahead goes to Biskra and Algiers.)

A small mausoleum on the edge of the palmeraie just west of Nefta. In the background is part of the massive Chott el Djerid saltpan or 'sebka'

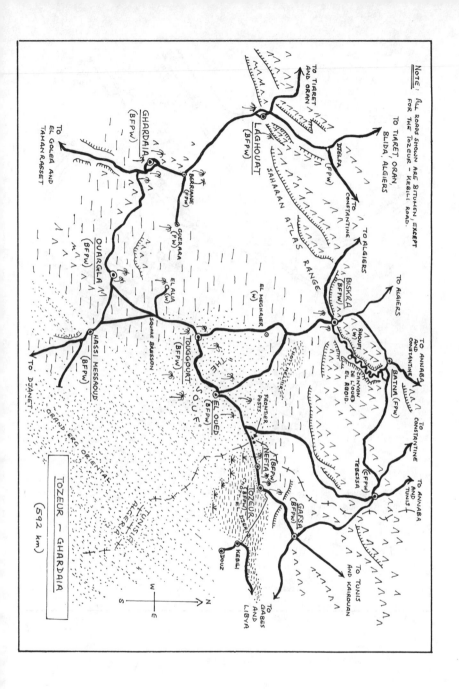

TOZEUR ~ GHARDAIA

(592 km)

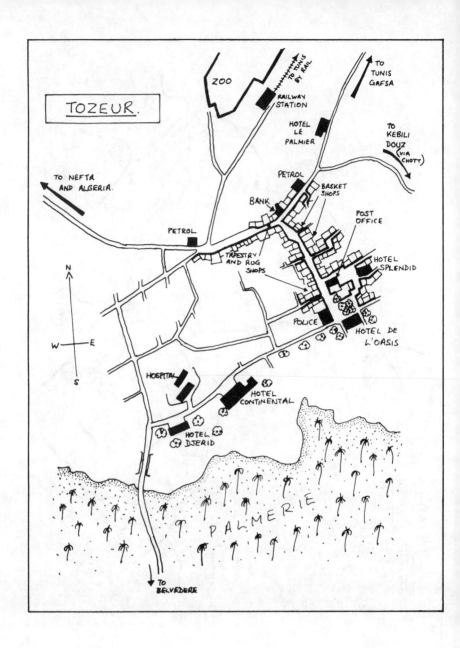

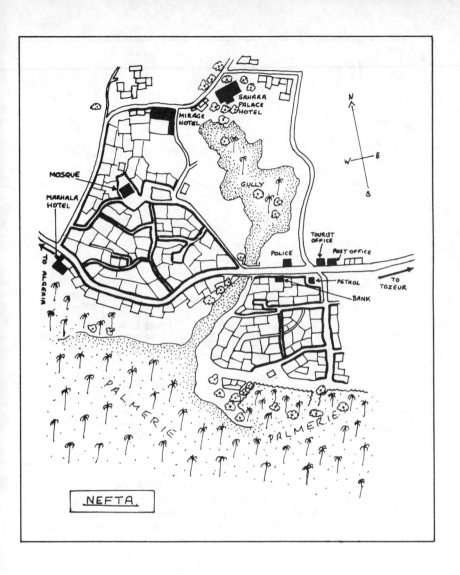

NEFTA.

SH 24

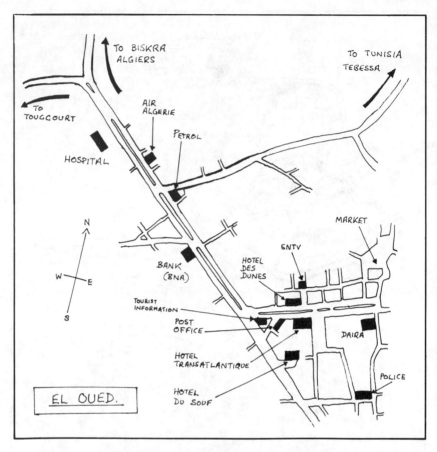

EL OUED.

242 350 **Touggourt** Large oasis town. Police, bank, post office, hospital, airport, hotels, (An expensive one, Hotel de l'Oasis; a moderate one, Hotel du Hoggar), railway station, Tourist Office (Syndicat d'Initiative), bakery (usually bakes in morning only), petrol station.

Bitumen road to the south is excellent. Main road to the north goes to Biskra, Algiers, and Constantine. Good camping in the open desert after 20 km south of the town.

306 286 Branch road (asphalt) to the west goes to El Alia only (51 km away).

322 270 **Square Bresson** Nothing here except a major fork in the road. Route to SSE goes to Hassi Messaoud and Djanet. Continue to SSW to Ouagla. Between Touggourt and Ouagla are several roadside stalls where jerrycans are sold (or can be sold), and where one can buy really beautiful roses of sand.

403 189 **Ouargla** Enter the town a few kilometres after joining the Ghardaia — Hassi Messaoud road. There is an old town, to the north, but Ouargla is very much a modern oil boom town, geared to the oil industry rather than local agriculture or tourism. Two quite expensive hotels (Transatlantique, and Hotel

370

el Mehri), petrol station, Police, post office, airport (services to Algiers), hospital, Daira. Road to west is fast wide bitumen.

| 568 | 24 | Junction with main Algiers — Ghardaia — In Salah — Tamanrasset road. Many oil flares in the vicinity. |
| 592 | 0 | **Ghardaia** Enter the M'zab valley from the south after passing through the light industrial area and the turn-off to the airport. For details of Ghardaia, see Itinerary No. 6. |

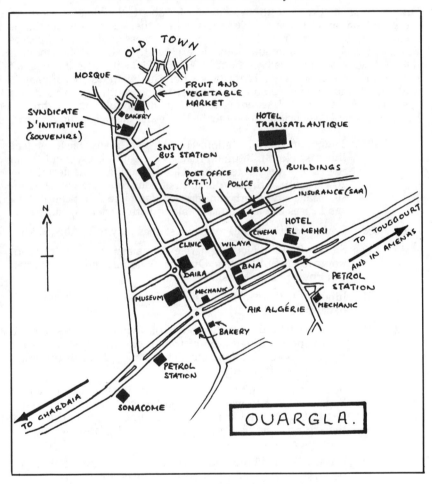

OUARGLA.

Itinerary No. 9 : Touggourt — In Amenas

Distance   903 km

Water   At petrol stations en route.

Fuel   Petrol stations at Touggourt, Hassi Messaoud, Hassi Bel Guebbour (Closed 12.00-1600), In Amenas.

Full width asphalt road all the way except for about 10 kilometres north of the petrol station at Hassi Bel Guebbour where there is narrow tar that is breaking up in places. From Touggourt to Hassi Messaoud the road passes through largely flat hammada stony desert. South of Hassi Messaoud, it follows a wide flat stony valley (about 20-30 km wide) with magnificent giant sand dunes on either side. From Hassi Bel Guebbour to In Amenas is undulating and broken hammada, but just to the south of the road is a spectacular escarpment descending to an equally undulating and broken hammada some 200 m below. Report to the Police and the Daira at In Amenas.

0	903	**Touggourt** Petrol station. Town with many facilities (see Itinerary No. 8). Bitumen road to the south is excellent. Main road to the north is to Biskra. Good camping in the desert after 20 km south of the town. South of Touggourt are several roadside stalls where jerrycans are sold (and bought). Beautiful big sand roses are also on sale, along with ancient spearheads.
64	839	Branch road (asphalt) to the west goes only to El Alia (51 km).
80	823	**Square Bresson** Nothing here except a major fork in the road. Route to the SSW goes to Ouargla, Ghardaia and Tamanrasset. Continue SSE to Hassi Messaoud.
152	751	Junction with road from Ouargla in the west. Oil flares will usually be visible.
172	731	**Hassi Messaoud** A totally modern oil town with blocks of apartments, prefabricated administration blocks, a gas processing plant, truck repair depot, etc. Petrol station, Police, post office, Air Algérie office, airport.
		South of the town the road soon enters the Gassi Touil, a very large oued or hammada between two sections of the massive Grand Erg Oriental. It is worth spending a night at the foot of the erg and climbing up to the top in the late afternoon or early morning.
529	374	**Hassi Bel Guebbour** Small transport depot only, but with a petrol station. A café is just opposite the petrol pumps. (Beware of the deep sand at the pumps!)
590	313	**Hassi Tabankort** 61 km exactly, after Hassi Bel Guebbour is a signpost to Hassi Tabankort on the northern side of the road. Nobody lives there but there is warm artesian water gushing from the big bore just 3 or 4 km from the main road. Ideal for a wash.
674	229	Branch road to the south to Hassi Mazoula 55 km away on tar seal. If camping in this area keep an eye open for fossils, especially in dried up water courses.

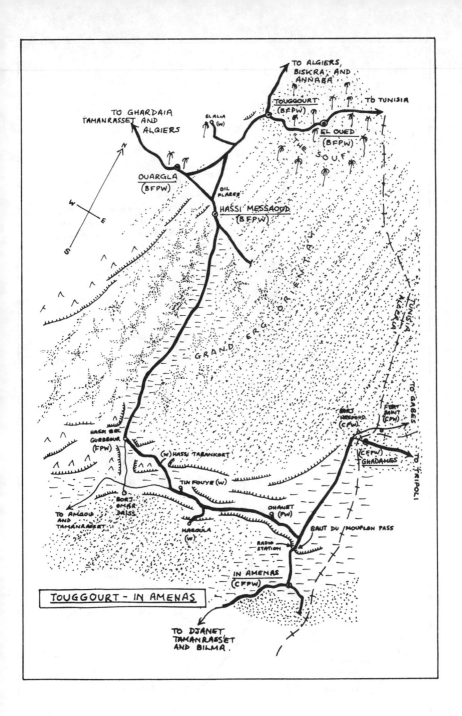

TOUGGOURT - IN AMENAS

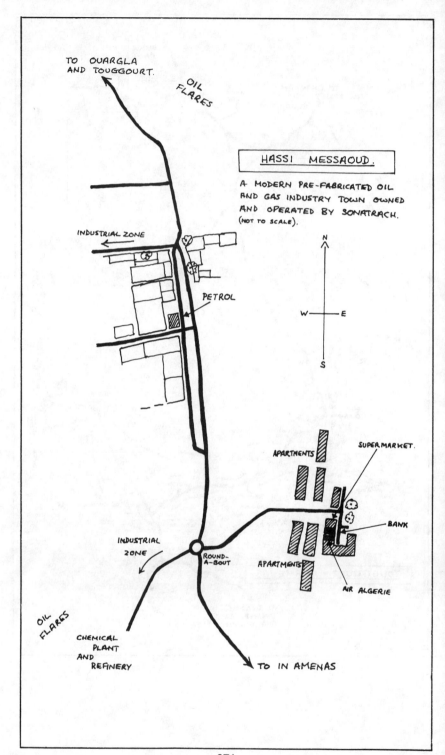

TO OUARGLA
AND TOUGGOURT.

OIL FLARES

HASSI MESSAOUD.

A MODERN PRE-FABRICATED OIL
AND GAS INDUSTRY TOWN OWNED
AND OPERATED BY SONATRACH.
(NOT TO SCALE).

N
W — E
S

INDUSTRIAL ZONE

PETROL

APARTMENTS

SUPERMARKET.

BANK

INDUSTRIAL ZONE

ROUND-A-BOUT

APARTMENTS

AIR ALGERIE

OIL FLARES

CHEMICAL PLANT AND REFINERY

TO IN AMENAS

721	182	About this point it is worth leaving the road for 100 - 200 metres to the south. There is a spectacular view over a vast arid plain below — a veritable moonscape. Several spots like this, all to the south of the road.
786	117	**Ohanet** Small settlement connected with the oil industry, about 2 km to the north of the main road.
796	107	Asphalt road to the north to an oil exploration depot.
808	95	A small dirty road branches off to the east where there is a guelta, usually with water.
836	67	Junction with asphalt road from the north from Bordj Messouda, Ghadames in Libya, and the Tunisian Sahara. At Bordj Messouda you will probably be turned back, unless you have a visa for Libya or a visa and permission to enter the south of Tunisia (see Chapter 12: Visas).
		Turn southwards for In Amenas. The road follows an oil or gas pipeline.
844	59	**Saut du Mouflon** Small radio station and a magnificent pass descending about 200 m to the arid eroded plain below.
903	0	**In Amenas** Another oil town. Entirely modern but largely prefabricated. Police, Daira, post office, cinema, bar, shops, petrol station, airport (actually partly in Libya), with scheduled services to Algiers, hospital (in 1978 had a very helpful, English-speaking, Egyptian doctor).

It is essential to report to the Daira. Fill out a form indicating details of journey to Djanet. This is sent by telex to the Daira in Djanet. Then report to the Police. It is possible to camp just outside the Police station, in fact they ask you to do so. (It is not compulsory to accept the invitation.)

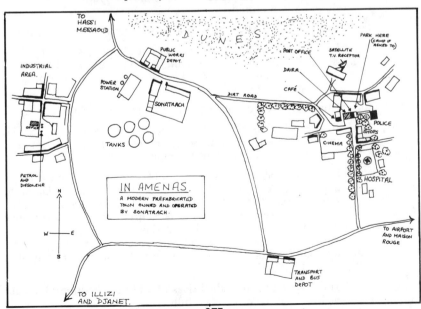

Itinerary No. 10 : In Amenas — Djanet

Distance   677 km

Water   In Amenas, at petrol station; El Adeb Larache, 1 km to west of the road; Hassi Issendjel, well in the old fort, polluted; Illizi, at petrol station, at Police and at gardens; Iherir, 25 km off the main road, at spring near village; Guelta, 140 km south of Illizi; Fort Gardel, near the 'hotel'; Djanet, many public taps throughout the town.

Fuel   Petrol station at In Amenas, Illizi, Djanet.

South from In Amenas the route is rough and passes through very irregular terrain. South of Illizi, it rises up onto the Fadnoun Plateau, of bare rocky hills, but descends by two spectacular passes to the plains that form the Erg D'Admer at the foot of the Tassili N'Ajjer. 4x4 vehicle is not necessary.

0	677	**In Amenas** Report to Daira and Police. Fill up with fuel; sufficient for Djanet. (Although usually well stocked, there is no guarantee of supplies at Illizi.) Leave town via the SW along a good bitumen road.
48	629	Asphalt road comes to an end. Good corrugated gravel road continues.
117	560	**El Adeb Larache** Tiny oil encampment with a few trees and a well just off the road.
123	554	Be careful to take branch to the right (SW) at a fork in the road marked only by Arabic signs. (Road to the left disappears after 20 km).
206	471	**Hassi Issendjel** Ruined fort about 3 km to the east of the road. It is possible to drive to it. The walls are graffiti covered and the well is polluted.
209	468	Series of small dunes, right across the road. Can be difficult.
257	420	For about 20 km there is a danger of becoming lost as the piste descends onto a large flat plain. Keep to the SW all the time. Some tracks head SE. Avoid these as they disappear or go to Tarat at the Libyan fontier.
275	402	**Illizi Airport** No buildings, just a stony runway.
280	397	**Illizi** Small oasis. Police, Customs (report to both), shop, SNTR workshop, petrol station, (not guaranteed to have any supplies), hotel under construction, hospital.

From Illizi just about the best tour of rock paintings and engravings exists. A six day tour can be taken up the Oued Djerid to see the prehistoric art discovered in 1931 by a French soldier. The ultimate expert on this art is Henri Lhote, **A la découverte des fresques du Tassili.** This oued is really a big long twisting gorge with a sometimes flowing stream with an occasional inhabited palmeraie. There is a very humble hotel to stay at in Illizi, the Aba Kada.

The road south from Illizi rises up onto the Fadnoun Plateau; really a vast area of rocky hills.

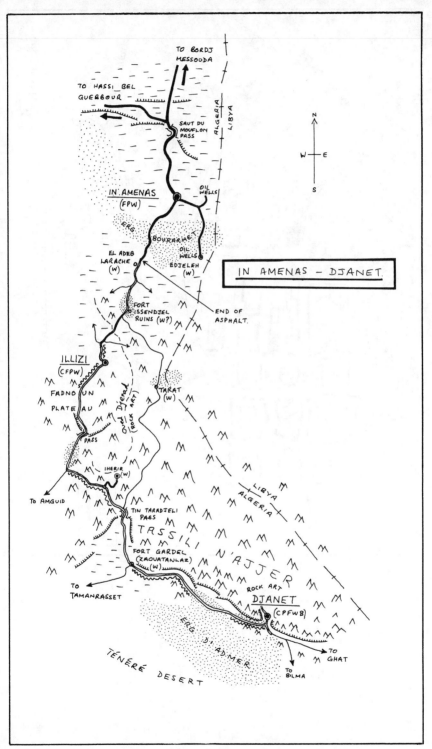

IN AMENAS – DJANET.

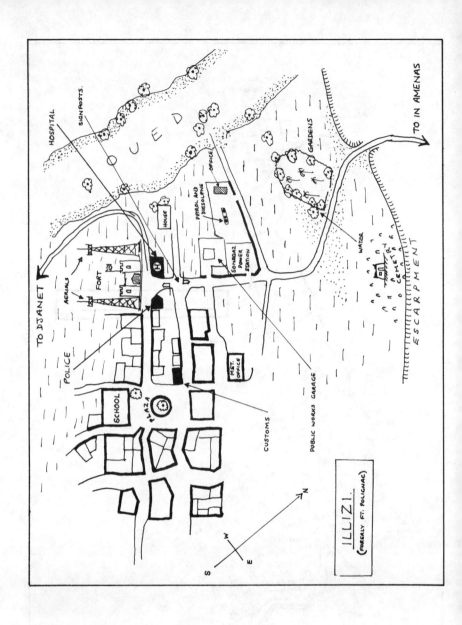

ILLIZI.
(FORMERLY FT. POLIGNAC.)

TO DJANET

TO IN AMENAS

OUED

ESCARPMENT

HOSPITAL
SIGN POSTS.
OFFICE
GARDENS
WATER
HOUSE
PETROL AND DIESOLENE
FORT
AERIALS
POLICE
SONELGAZ POWER STATION
CEMETRY
SCHOOL
PLAZA
MET. OFFICE
CUSTOMS
PUBLIC WORKS GARAGE

N
W
E
S

378

392	285	About 285 km north of Djanet by a stripped 2CV panel van carcass there is, 100 metres to the west, an incredibly high cliff which drops about 3-400 metres to an eroded bare plain below. The view is fantastic. Shortly afterwards, about 10 km later, there is a steep pass as the road winds its way down to the rolling plain below. It is sights like this that show one how big and timeless the Sahara is and how really insignificant mankind is by comparison.
490	187	**Iherir** 25 km (and two hours) off the main road to the NE, along a tortuously slow and rough, hand made road. It is not suitable for normal two wheel drive cars. The big problem is leaving Iherir up the steep rocky mountain pass where low range is a big asset. A normal VW bus will only just make it, but one with a big engine and limited slip differential should have no trouble (one did it in 1978). However, this diversion from the main road is well worth the effort. Iherir is a tiny Touareg village in a lost world all of its own, inside a canyon. The floor of the canyon supports a tiny population which depends on irrigation from a spring, and a palmeraie, for its existence. They are friendly and hospitable. On arrival it is best, as a matter of courtesy to present yourself to the 'chef du village'. You may then wish to spend the afternoon walking up the lovely guelta, with a guide, to see some prehistoric rock paintings.

No shops or any other facilities. This is an unspoilt 'Shangri-la'. Please be very respectful of the inhabitants and the environment.

View from the top of the pass at Tin-Taradjeli in the Tassili N'Ajjer about 150 km north of Djanet

510   167   **Col Tin Taradjeli** Beautiful pass which descends to the foot of the Tassili N'Ajjer.

547   130   **Fort Gardel** (or Zaouatenlaz). Remains of an old French fort. Also, a cluster of Touareg zeribas and a 'Hotel and Café' (charming zeriba only, but the local people are very proud of it). Here a reputable Touareg guide, Ibrahim Ben Balous, offers his services for a tour of the local guelta, to rock paintings and engravings, with unlimited photography. A round trip of 40 km.

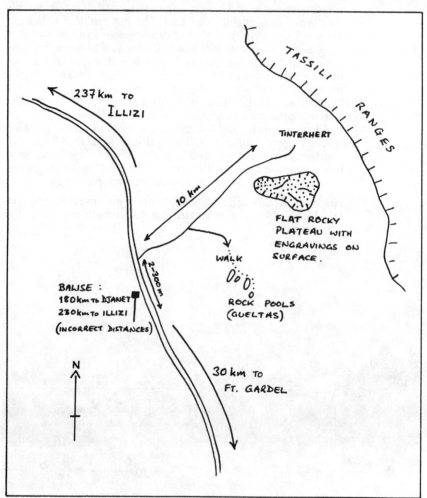

Tinterhert Rock Engravings

The rock engravings (or petroglyphs) at Tinterhert lie on the hard flat bare rocky surface of a rocky plateau about 7km south of Col Tin Taradjeli. There are engravings of ostriches, a rabbit, antelopes and a large bull covered in spiral decorations. Most of them are on flat rock facing the sky. Contact registered guide Ibrahim Ben Balous at the Zaouatenlaz village near the old Fort Gardel

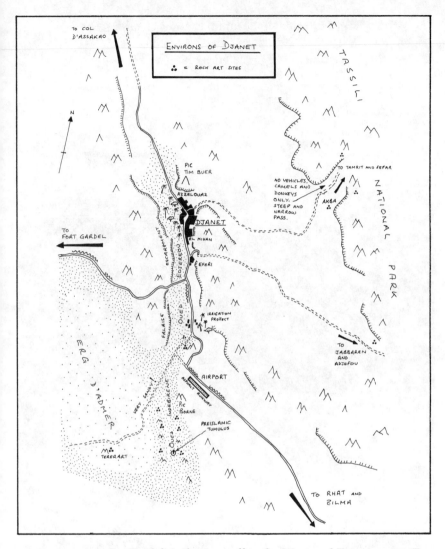

At Ft. Gardel, is the turn off to the West and Tamanrasset. For Djanet, head SE along the foot of the mountains.

632   45   Signpost (illegible) points to piste that heads west out into the erg. As the main piste approaches Djanet it runs between the Erg d'Admer and the Tassili N'Ajjer mountains. Often there is very soft sand on either side of the piste preventing one from leaving it. One just has to endure the corrugations at times. However, with a 4x4 vehicle with very low tyre pressures one can leave the piste more often.

677   0   **Djanet** The piste emerges from some hills into the Djanet Oued. It joins the road between Djanet and the airport, and heads north for 5 km into the town.

Report to the Daira on arrival. Post office, bank, airport

381

Djanet, overlooking the main square and hotel with Pic Tim Beur in the background

(scheduled services to Tamanrasset and Algiers), Customs, museum (good), shops, bakery, cinema, military base, television, meteorological station, two mechanics (see map: the

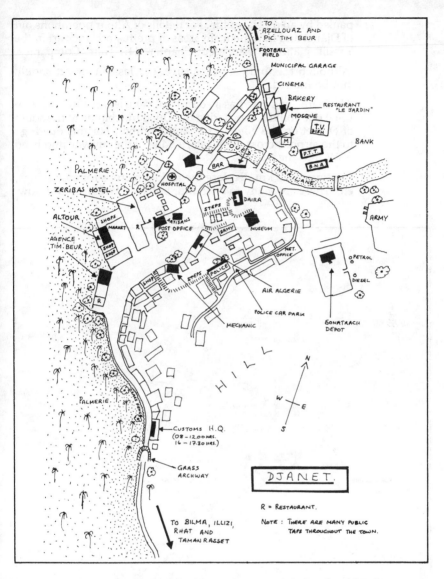

one in the middle of town is Ben-Dahan Ahmed Baba — very helpful), butcher, café. Petrol station. There are also many taps, all over town, for good water. Hotel des Zeribas: simple accommodation in furnished zeribas, with restaurant attached. It is illegal to camp in the palmeraie, but about 2-3 km south of the turn-off to Illizi and Tamanrasset, on the airport road, there is an oued where you can camp peacefully. The Algerian government tourist office (Altour) runs several tours by camel or donkey, up into the Tassili to see the prehistoric paintings and view the mountains.

Note: You must have a guide for day tour into the Tassili National Park. Individual groups are not allowed to go unaccompanied by an official guide. For details of Altour operations out of Djanet and into the main areas of pre-historic rock art in the Tassili National Park see Chapter 11: Tour Companies.

Although the tours are expensive, the Tassili rock art should not be missed.

Alternatively if one has a sound 4x4 vehicle, (or VW-Bus with LSD) one could try exploring the Oued Indebirene to the south of Djanet on the edge of the Erg d'Admer. For this oued, go to the airport, cross the western edge of the runway and head SSW into the oued.

Continue 5-10 km. Explore the rocky outcrops for engravings, etc. There are many to be found, but keep tyre pressures low.

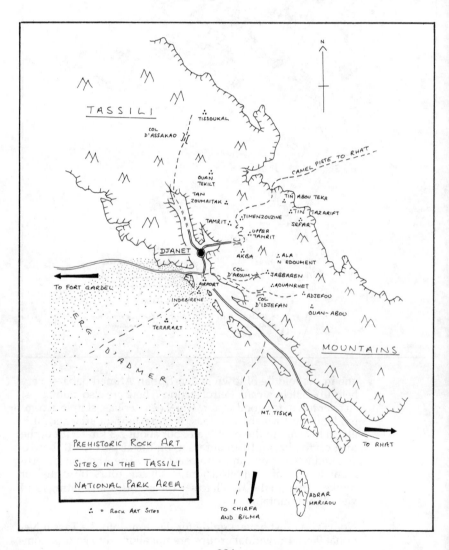

Note: If leaving Djanet across the Ténéré to Bilma, you must check out with Customs and the Police. Also, you will need at least 50,000 CFA or 1,000 French francs in cash to buy petrol at Bilma or Dirkou (not travellers cheques).

Itinerary No. 11 : Djanet — Tamanrasset

Distances   Via Ain Amguel: 730 km. Via Tazrouk and Tahifet: 818 km. Via Assekrem: 659 km.

Water   Fill up in Djanet, many public taps. Ft. Gardel,plenty of water from well. Serouenout, water, undrinkable. Ideles, good water. Hirafok, good water. Ain Amguel, water from irrigation canals. Tahifet, well. Tamanrasset, from hotel or camping municipal. Otherwise, there is a spring and a restaurant at Tahabort, 15 km along the road from Tamanrasset to Assekrem (see Itinerary No. 7).

Fuel   Djanet, usually adequate supplies of normal, super and diesolene. If not, wait a few days, as there are no other petrol stations en route. Tamanrasset, usually good supplies at petrol station to the south of town.

The route is reasonably clear the whole way with only one or two difficult sandy patches. 4x4 vehicle and convoy not necessary. However, during the summer months it is very lonely and during the whole trip you may not see another vehicle until Tamanrasset.

0   730   **Djanet** Before leaving you should notify the Daira of your intentions. Leave town via the south.

3   727   Turn off to NW for road to Fort Gardel. Straight on goes to the airport, Rhat in Libya, and Bilma in Niger. Corrugated road all the way to Ft. Gardel. Sometimes not really possible to leave it because of soft sand. Beautiful scenery.

131   599   **Fort Gardel** (Officially Ft. Gardel is called Zaouatanlaz.) Old fort, a zeriba 'hotel and café' and an excellent guide (see Itinerary No. 10).

At Ft. Gardel turn west, cross the oued and turn south just after the big tree.

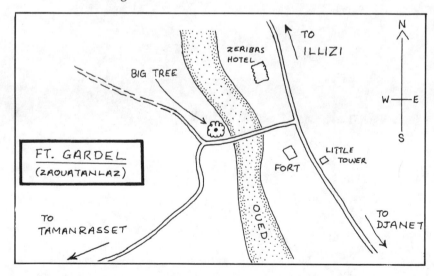

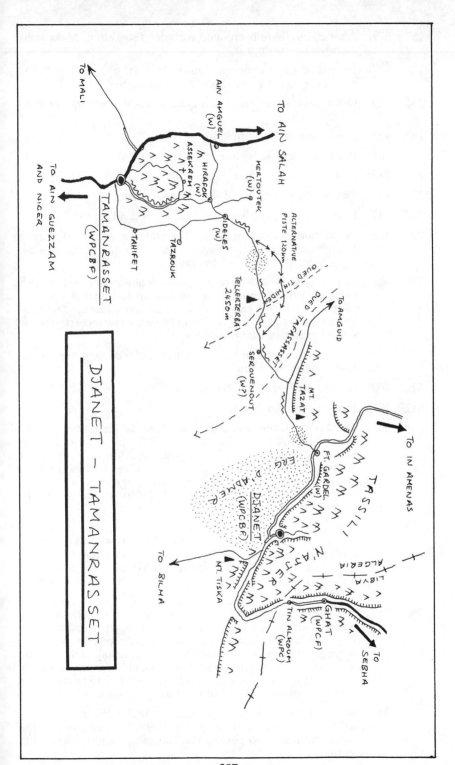

DJANET — TAMANRASSET

151	579	After 20 km there is an oued with deep sand in it. Make your own tracks through it.
243	487	Triangular stone structure. This indicates the junction with the road to Amguid to the NW. Keep going SW.
251	479	**Oued Tafassasset** This oued is very sandy. Keep up speed to get through.
257	473	Some dark brown dunes.
269	461	Patches of low sand dunes.
270	460	Deep ruts in the sand. Sharp curves.
272	458	Old Simca wreck. Sand. But route is clear.
288	442	Stony corrugated piste, with flat topped hill to the south.
292	438	**Serouenout** Abandoned fort. The water is undrinkable even though only one metre down. No inhabitants. Lots of rubbish lying around; beware of punctures.
298	432	About 6 km west of Serouenout is an alternative piste which takes a northerly route for about 120 km and rejoins the main piste about 70 km east of Ideles. This route has no balises at all but it is easier on the vehicle as there are fewer corrugations. Follow tracks of other vehicles.

The following description is for the regular piste, not the alternative northerly route.

322	408	Narrow valley. A few thorn trees.
342	388	Stony desert for 4 km.
348	382	**Oued Tin Hiden** and **Amadrar Hamada** Hard surface and generally good going. To the south of the piste is the volcanic massif of Tellerteba which rises up to 2,450 m. To climb it approach from the SW up a narrow valley. Proper climbing equipment is needed as this is a challenge even for experienced mountaineers (see R. Frison-Roche and P. Tairraz, **50 Ans de Sahara**).
417	313	If travelling from the west, there is an alternative piste with fewer corrugations but no balises which runs to the north of the regular piste. About 70 km east of Ideles and 4 km after a balise labelled 'FG 250', follow vehicle tracks to the north. This piste rejoins the regular piste about 6 km west of Serouenout.
381	349	Very sandy area. On the surface the sand looks dark but is white underneath; it is softer than you think. This is where a wandering dune has blocked out the old piste. Make your own way. It is very bumpy, deep, soft sand. It will usually take you by surprise, but keep up speed if you possibly can. If necessary wait until your engine has cooled a little bit before crossing this patch. From here the piste is generally good to Ideles.
487	243	**Ideles** Touareg village. Water obtainable from the oasis irrigations channels. If lucky, vegetables can be bought at the oasis. No hotel, no petrol. You can camp at fort. Very good signposting.

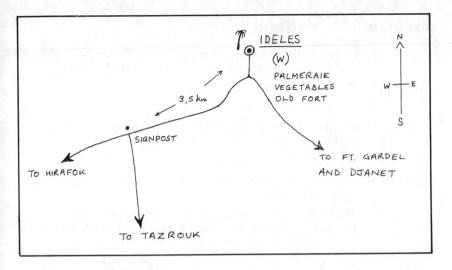

510   220   Piste to Mertoutek branches off to the north. A pleasant oasis some 91 km away. Rock engravings can be visited with a guide and donkeys. See the brief route description at the end of this itinerary.

522   208   **Hirafok** Touareg village. Irrigated vegetable gardens. Branch road to the south goes to Assekrem along a tortuous and at times very washed out and rocky road. A VW Bus is quite capable of doing it safely. West of Hirafok there is a good slightly corrugated road to Ain Amguel. About 20 km before Ain Amguel there are two routes to take. One goes directly to the village by following the sandy bed of the oued, while the other follows a more southerly route and joins the main asphalt Ain Salah — Tamanrasset road about 7 km south of the village. If you are desperate for fuel head north to Ain Ecker where there is a petrol station (no guarantee of supplies — you may have to wait a day).

612   118   Junction with main north-south trans-Sahara road. Ain Amguel is about 7 km to the north. It has a well, irrigation canals and a palmeraie.

646   84   Café.

688   42   Turn-off to Abalessa some 60 km away in the west. This piste also takes one to Silet, Tim Missao, Timeiaouine and Bordj Moktar on the Mali frontier.

690   40   **Tit** Touareg village. Site of a battle in 1902 at which the French crushed the power of the Kel Ahaggar Touaregs.

711   19   **Outoul** Village with well and café.

720   10   Turn-off to Tamanrasset airport 2 km to the west.

721   9   Piste for the western approach to Assekrem (120 km away) branches off to the NE. Can be difficult to find.

730   0   **Tamanrasset** For details of Tamanrasset and of excursions in the Hoggar area, see Itinerary No. 7.

Excursion to Mertoutek

91	0	Depart north from main Tamanrasset — Djanet piste. (This is 12.3 km east of Hirafok and 22.7 km west of Ideles.)
76	15	Oued. Lavafields.
61	30	Deep sand and stones.
47	44	Junction of pistes. East to Mertoutek (indicated by sign written on the ground in stones). West to Ain Ecker.
26	65	Tracks to NE to Amguid.
12	79	Twisting piste with many curves, the last curve goes over a mountain saddle.
0	91	**Mertoutek** Village (Kel Ahaggar Touaregs) with well and small palmeraie. Ancient rock engravings in the area are well worth visiting. Ask at the village for a guide with donkeys.

Mertoutek is a small Kel Ahaggar Touareg village in the Teffedest Ranges. Nearby rock engravings are well worth a visit (Photo by courtesy of Keith Smith)

Itinerary No. 12 : Fort Gardel — Amguid

Distance	480 km
Water	Fill up at Djanet. There is a well at Fort Gardel but there may not be any water in the guelta at Amguid. It is essential to take good supplies of water.
Fuel	Fill up at Djanet as there are no other petrol stations until one arrives at Ain Salah, Hassi Bel Guebbour or Ain Ecker. Carry fuel supplies for at least 1,050 km from Djanet plus reserves.

This piste should present no serious problems except for a few sandy sections along the Oued Tafassasset. However, it is only for the experienced and well equipped with at least two robust vehicles. There is very little traffic and with a major breakdown in a lone vehicle one could easily die of thirst while waiting for other traffic. The other problem is that very large volumes of fuel and water have to be carried but beware of the consequences of overloading the vehicle.

0	480	**Fort Gardel** Officially known as Zaouatanlaz. Old fort, a zeriba 'hotel and cafe'. Depart as if for Tamanrasset by heading west across the oued and turn south just after the big tree.
20	460	After 20 km there is an oued with deep sand in it.
50	430	Mt. Tazat is the peak some 8 km to the north of the piste.
112	368	Turn-off to SW to Tamanrasset. For Amguid, follow the Oued Tafassasset in a NW direction. Balises usually every 10 km but bad corrugations.
185	295	Mt. Toukmatine can be seen some 5 km to north.
210	270	Cross the Oued in Touf.
240	240	Pass the Erg Tihodaine which lies to the NE.
307	173	Follow the Oued Tedjert in a NE direction.
415	65	Pass between the Erg Guidi to the south and the Adrar Ahellakane to the north. Turn SW until ...
462	18	Join the Ain Ecker — Amguid piste at Oued Taghmert n' Akli. Head north.
480	0	**Amguid** A military post with corrugated iron sheds but no supplies at all. There is a ruined village and a guelta which sometimes has water.

Itinerary No. 13 : Ain Ecker — Hassi Bel Guebbour

Distance	672 km.
Water	Ain Ecker, on tap at the petrol station. Amguid, a guelta but no guarantee of water. Bordj Omar Driss, in the palmeraie. Hassi Bel Guebbour, at café.
Fuel	There are petrol stations which sell petrol and diesel fuel at Ain Ecker and Hassi Bel Guebbour. If they have temporarily run out, wait a day or two for supplies to arrive as one must carry sufficient for at least 700 km of piste and allow for reserves.

This piste is not frequently used. A major breakdown could result in death as one waited for other traffic to give assistance. A convoy of at least two robust vehicles driven by experienced people is necessary. If heading south, it might be diplomatic at least to advise the police at Hassi Bel Guebbour of one's intended route.

For the first 200 km or so from Ain Ecker north there are balises about 10 kilometres apart. Some have disappeared, though. Either side of Amguid, as one follows the Oued Irharrhar, there are some very sandy sections.

0	672	**Ain Ecker** Petrol station, water and a former French nuclear bomb testing site (during the early 50s). Beware of lots of barbed wire in the sand if one leaves the asphalt.
14	658	Leave the asphalt at the old triangular masonry cairn and turn-off to the NE for Amguid. Once on the piste it is clear and mildly corrugated.
114	558	Garet el Djenoun (Mountain of Ghosts) at 2330 m to the east

The 2330m high Garet el Djenoum or Mountain of Ghosts is an important landmark along the piste south of Amguid (Photo by courtesy of T. McCleay)

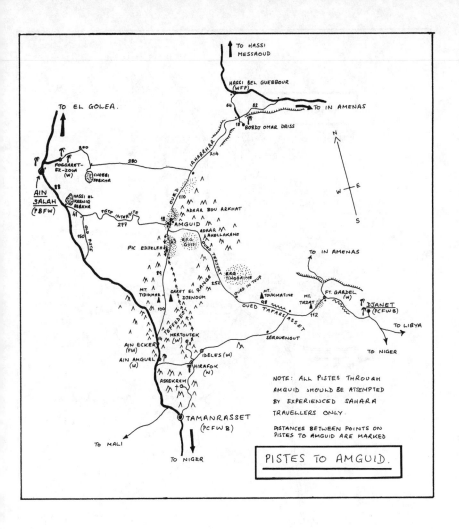

PISTES TO AMGUID.

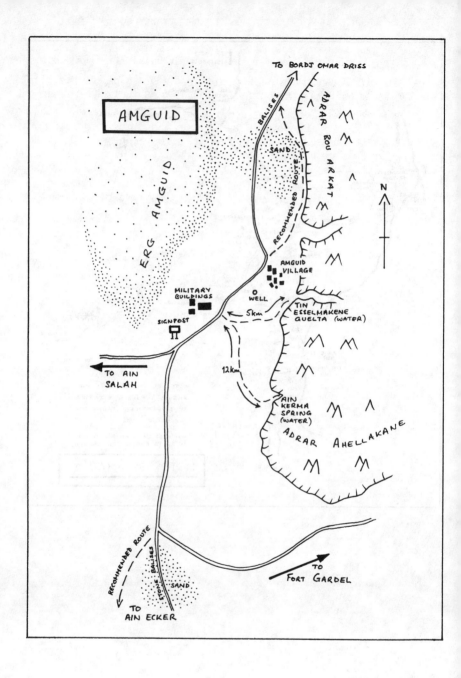

AMGUID

and Mount Tidikmar at 1462 m to the west. There are Neolithic remains and rock engravings at the base of Mt. Tidikmar.

154	518	The piste starts to follow the Oued Tagmert n' Akli in a NNE direction becoming northerly as it joins the Oued Irharrhar.
203	469	The regular piste passes to the east of Pic Edjeleh (a small peak of 702 m). However, it has become sandy. Instead, depart from the balises and follow vehicle tyre tracks to the west of the peak. Also at this point, an extremely rarely used route heads SE up the Oued Irharrhar eventually to emerge near Mertoutek and Ideles.
266	406	Join the Amguid — Ft. Gardel piste which comes from the SE.

If going south to Ain Ecker, one should at this point follow the vehicle tyre tracks to the SSW rather than the old piste.

284 388 **Amguid** A military post with corrugated iron sheds and no supplies available. There is a ruined village and a guelta which sometimes has water in it.

For Hassi al Krenig on the main Ain Salah — Tamanrasset asphalt road: head SW and follow the tracks to the old Ain Salah — Tamanrasset piste, head north along it and rejoin the new road at Hassi al Krenig. Note: this is a 'Piste Interdite'. Do not get caught using it.

For Bordj Omar Driss, leave Amguid via the NNE.

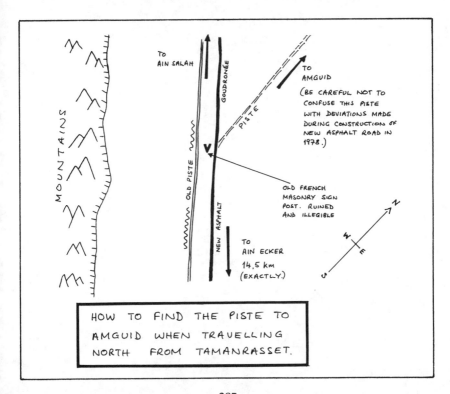

HOW TO FIND THE PISTE TO AMGUID WHEN TRAVELLING NORTH FROM TAMANRASSET.

301	371	Cross a dune. Then, with the Erg Amguid in the west and following vehicle tyre tracks close to the Adrar Bou Arkhat mountains in the east, one should join up with the balises once more.
326	346	The piste turns NE along the valley of the Oued Irharrhar.
394	278	The piste to Foggaret ez Zoua and Ain Salah (some 580 km away) branches off to the east and is marked by a triangular masonry cairn. It is a good piste that shouldn't pose any serious problems. About 200 km before Ain Salah is another masonry cairn. Turn NE for Foggaret and Ain Salah.

For Bordj Omar Driss, instead of heading east for Ain Salah, continue NNE along the Oued Irharrhar by following the balises.

608	64	**Les Quatre Chemins** A crossroads. Go south for 14 km to Bordj Omar Driss (formerly Fort Flatters) where there is an old fort, a village and a palmeraie.

For Hassi Bel Guebbour, turn north. One soon joins a section of old asphalt road for about 18 km. The remaining distance is badly corrugated piste.

672	0	**Hassi Bel Guebbour** Police, petrol station and a café.

Itinerary No. 14 : Tamanrasset — Bordj Moktar

Distance   709 km.

Water   Tamanrasset, at hotel, camping ground or try petrol stations. Wells at Abalessa, Silet, Tim Missaou (to the south of piste), Timeiaouine. Bordj Moktar could be a problem: there is a tap.

Fuel   Fill up at Tamanrasset as there is no guarantee of supplies at the petrol stations at Silet, Timeiaouine and Bordj Moktar. This may mean carrying sufficient fuel to get to Reggane or Gao, i.e. more than 1,500 km. The same applies if travelling from Gao or Reggane.

From Tamanrasset to the Abalessa turn-off is the new (1978!) now broken up asphalt road. An easy to follow, sometimes corrugated, piste takes one to Abalessa and Silet. Further on to Timeiaouine can present difficulties especially for the inexperienced. (Mark Thatcher got lost and ran out of fuel along this section during the 1982 Paris-Dakar rally.) A robust vehicle capable of carrying sufficient fuel, water and victuals is necessary. Even with four-wheel drive one might expect to get bogged in sand once or twice but much more in a lower slung vehicle like a Citroen 2CV. This is a desolate rather plain part of the Sahara but towards Timeiaouine the cram cram (vegetation of very scattered grasses and small Acacia trees) begins to appear. Late in 1984 it became possible to drive directly from Timeiaouine to Tessalit in Mali. However you should discuss this with police at Tamanrasset, Timeiaouine and Tessalit. Of course, if you travel from Tamanrasset to Adrar via Timeiaouine, there is no need to see either customs or the Daira before leaving Tamanrasset, although it would pay to show your evidence of this to the police at Bordj Moktar. There is now a Mali consulate in Tamanrasset which can issue visas.

0	709	**Tamanrasset** Leave town by the main north road to Ain Salah.
42	667	Turn off to Abalessa in the west. At first, there is a mildly corrugated piste which is sometimes graded. This eventually degenerates into a series of tracks.
102	607	**Abalessa** Actually several villages: Iglene, Tafirt and Abalessa, all to the north of the piste. To the SE of Abalessa is the Tombeau d'Aramouk — where the legendary Tin Hinane is buried. Abalessa is the centre or capital of the Ahaggar Touaregs. Their traditional leader, the Amenokol, lives here.
		For Silet, head SW across the Tahalgha massif along a rough corrugated piste.
144	565	**Silet** Touareg village. Petrol station but no guarantee of supplies. There is a large volcanic crater some 45 km to the north.
187	522	Pass through the Adrar Isket pass (901 m) about 2 km south of the peak.
239	470	Join the Oued Tamanrasset and head along it to the west.
281	428	Leave the Oued Tamanrasset and head SW with the low Adrar Timekerkaz hills to the south.
309	400	**Tim Missaou** Wells to the south of the piste. Sometimes a small

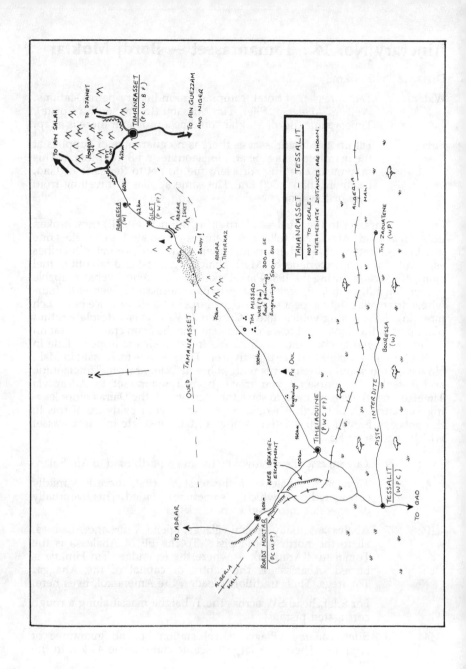

TAMANRASSET - TESSALIT

NOT TO SCALE.
INTERMEDIATE DISTANCES ARE SHOWN.

TO AIN SALAR

TAMANRASSET (P C W B F)

Hoggar

TO DJANET

62km

TO AIN GUEZZAM AND NIGER

60km

ABALESSA (W)

42km

SILET (P W F?)

ADRAR ISKET

95km

ADRAR TIMERKAZ

SANDY

OUED TAMANRASSET

70km

TIM MISSAO
WELL (7m)
Rock paintings 300m SE
Engravings 500m SW

100km

PC OIL

ENGRAVINGS

160km

TIMEIAQUINE (P W C F ?)

100km

KREB BEKATIEL ESCARPMENT

TO ADRAR

100km

BORDJ MOKTAR (P C W F?)

ALGERIA
MALI

ALGERIA
MALI

TIN ZAOUATENE (W P)

BOURESSA (W)

PISTE INTERDITE

TESSALIT (W P C)

TO GAO

N

Touareg encampment. Six kilometres to the east, Henri Lhote discovered five rock paintings of horse-drawn chariots.

409 300 Pic Oul, a small peak which stand out in the monotonous reg.

569 140 **Timeiaouine** A village with police, petrol station (no guarantee of supplies), a school and small shops. Customs post (report if arriving from the south). Leave the settlement to the NW and follow the Oued Djoudene.

669 40 Join the main Tanezrouft piste at Kreb Bekatiel escarpment. Ascend this falaise and head NW.

709 0 **Bordj Moktar** Police, customs and petrol station with no guarantee of supplies.

Itinerary No. 15 : Tamanrasset — Iferouane

Distance   Approximately 719 km

Fuel   Fill up at Tamanrasset before Customs formalities because Customs officers count your money. No more fuel available until Arlit or Agadez.

Water   Fill up at Tamanrasset (your hotel or at Jojo's) for although there are wells at In Azaoua, In Ebeggi and Tadera they may be dry, very deep, polluted or sulphurous. It would be best to take enough to get to Iferouane.

This piste leaves the hills of the Hoggar Massif some 50 km south of Tamanrasset and one enters open vegetationless desert. Near Tadera one encounters the first real signs of vegetation: very scattered thorn trees and grasses (cram-cram).

Permission from the Daira at Tamanrasset should be obtained before travelling this route from the north. (You may meet military personnel en route.) Between the turn-off 107 km south of Tamanrasset and Tadera the piste is extremely desolate and is rarely used. From Tadera south or east it is equally rarely used but much more beautiful. If travelling from the south make sure that you check out with Police and Customs at Arlit but it might not be wise to let them know that you intend travelling via In Azaoua.

Note: the inability to improvise and overcome a mechanical breakdown is likely to result in death from thirst because with so little traffic the chances of rescue are very remote. Preferably travel in convoy.

0   719   **Tamanrasset** Visit Police de Frontiere for passports at the Daira and then go to Customs at the southern exit of town. If arriving from Niger, the Daira may send you to the hospital for a malaria test before even looking at your passports. Declare currency at Customs. Carnets should not be used in Algeria (see Chapter 14: Vehicle Documents).

Head south through rocky hills for about 60 km along the new asphalt road. The route then opens out into the Oued Tin Amzi.

10   709   Turn-off to Amsel 2 km to the west.

100   619   End of new asphalt road (late 1983). Some construction work further south. Do not drive on newly completed road if rows of stones have been placed across it. This means that it has not yet cured and officials have been known to impound the passports of offenders.

107   612   For Ain Guezzam continue south (see Itinerary No. 16) but for In Azaoua and Iferouane turn ESE along a little used piste.

215   504   **Oued Tagrina** Sandy area. This is the path of an ancient north-south camel caravan route. There are many quite spectacular large wind eroded rock spires.

In Ebeggi Well site several kilometres to the north of the piste.

377   342   **In Azaoua** Uninhabited. Well with water (deep). A notice board announces arrival at the Niger—Algeria frontier. The almost indiscernible ruins of Fort Flatters lie to the east of the piste.

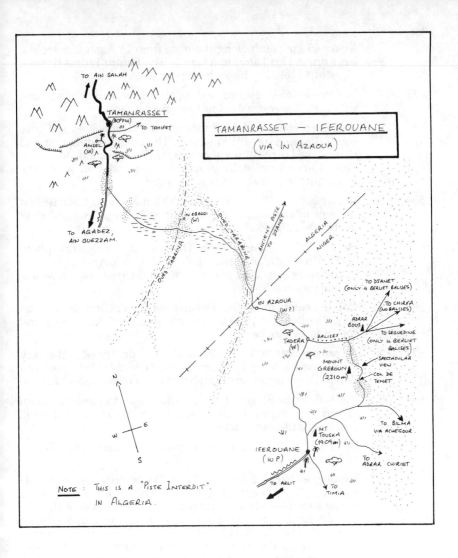

TAMANRASSET — IFEROUANE
(VIA IN AZAOUA)

TO AIN SALAH

TAMANRASSET
(BCPFW)

TO TAHIFET

AMSEL
(W)

TO AGADEZ,
AIN GUEZZAM.

IN EBEGGI
(W)

OUED TAHRAINE

ANCIENT PISTE
TO DJANET

OUED TAHRINA

ALGERIA

NIGER

IN AZAOUA
(W?)

TO DJANET.
(ONLY 4 BERLIET BALISES)

TO CHIRFA
(NO BALISES)

ADRAR
BOUS

TADERA
(W)

BALISES

TO SEGUEDINE
(ONLY 4 BERLIET
BALISES)

SPECTACULAR
VIEW

MOUNT
GREBOUN
(2310m)

COL DE
TEMET

TO BILMA
VIA ACHEGOUR.

MT
TOUSKA
(1909m)

IFEROUANE
(W P)

TO ADRAR
CHIRIET

TO ARLIT

TO
TIMIA

N
W   E
S

NOTE : THIS IS A "PISTE INTERDIT".
IN ALGERIA.

401

SH 26

About 45 km south along the piste from In Azaoua there is a large dune. Head around it via the SW. Before Tadera the first signs of vegetation begin to appear (cram-cram).

472   247   **Tadera-er-Roui** Deserted well containing very mineralised and sulphurous water only 2 m from the surface.

The direct route to Iferouane is marked with balises and goes south. Iferouane is 191 km away. The piste heading east and also marked with balises goes to Adrar Bous and Col de Temet. This is an exceptionally beautiful route and well worth the extra distance, time and cost involved.

534   185   Berliet Balise No. 17. A further 30 km away to the east and without intermediate balises is Adrar Bous, an isolated peak in the Ténéré noted as a site for neolithic remains.

For Col de Temet head south. This is a very sandy area. About 35-40 km south of Berliet Balise 17 is a magnificent view overlooking a gigantic sea of dunes in the east. To the west is Mt. Greboun (2310 m).

589   130   **Col de Temet** Uninhabited steep pass. Ascent and descent can be difficult as the piste is not only steep but very sandy and full of large stones.

629   90   Approximately 40 km south of the Col de Temet is the very rarely used Saviem Piste across the Ténéré to Achegour and Bilma. Only very experienced travellers in convoy should use it.

664   55   Turn-off to the SE goes to Adrar Chiriet, an isolated mountain among the dunes of the western Ténéré. There is a small Touareg settlement there.

694   25   Mt. Touska (1909 m) and the junction with the piste from Tedera in the north.

719   0   **Iferouane.** Large Touareg village. Wells. Irrigated vegetable gardens. Campement set up in 1973 to observe the total eclipse of the sun. There is also another camp operated by a Niamey based tour company but it is not open to private tourists. Police post with radio contact to Arlit. School. No fuel. British missionary Frank Baggot has been very helpful. If arriving from the north, particularly from Algeria, one should then go to Arlit and report to Customs and Police.

Itinerary No. 16 : Tamanrasset — Agadez

Distance		897 km
Water		Fill up at Tamanrasset. There is water at In Guezzam, (unpredictable cleanliness). There is an artesian bore at Assamaka with sulphurous water. There are wells at In Abangarit, Tegguidam Tessoumi and south of there.
Fuel		Fill up at Tamanrasset, before Customs formalities, because Customs count your money on departure at Tam, and at In Guezzam. Very rarely is there fuel at In Guezzam; no more fuel until Agadez. 4x4 vehicles are not necessary.

0   897   **Tamanrasset** 'Police de Frontiere' for passports at the Daira, and then Customs, just south of town. If arriving from Niger, the Daira may send you to the hospital for a malaria test, before looking at your passports. Declare currency at Customs. Carnets should not be used in Algeria (see Chapter 14: Vehicle Documents).

Just south of the petrol station there is a turn-off to Tahifet in the east. Continue south along a road which curves its way through rocky hills for 60 km south of Tamanrasset. A new asphalt road is now under construction.

10   887   There is a branch road to Amsel 2 km to the west (market gardening centre).

100   797   End of new asphalt road (late in 1983). Some construction work further south. Do not drive on newly completed road if rows of stones have been placed upon it. This means that it has not yet cured and officials have been known to impound passports of offenders.

107   790   Do not take the turn-off to In Azaoua in the east. Permission from Tamanrasset Daira is necessary to travel this piste. Tourists have died on this route; it is easy to get lost without a guide.

280   617   Signpost 'Dunes de Laouni'. Some deep sand.

285   612   **Ruined Laouni Fort** Just south of here leave the piste and head SW towards the distant hills. This is a regularly used deviation around a very badly corrugated piste. Follow the most numerous and recent tracks, and keep up speed as there is much feche feche. The alternative is painfully slow corrugated piste.

357   540   **Gara Eckar** Both the piste and the deviation converge at these magnificent outcrops of wind eroded sandstone rocks. Worth spending the night here. Ideal for photography in the late afternoon or early morning. If heading north instead of following the corrugated piste, follow the tracks to the north west of Gara Eckar along the foot of the escarpment. This will lead to the ruins of Fort Laouni.

South of Gara Eckar, avoid the piste and travel alongside it, often through 'feche feche'.

416   481   **In Guezzam** Algerian frontier post. See the Police first for

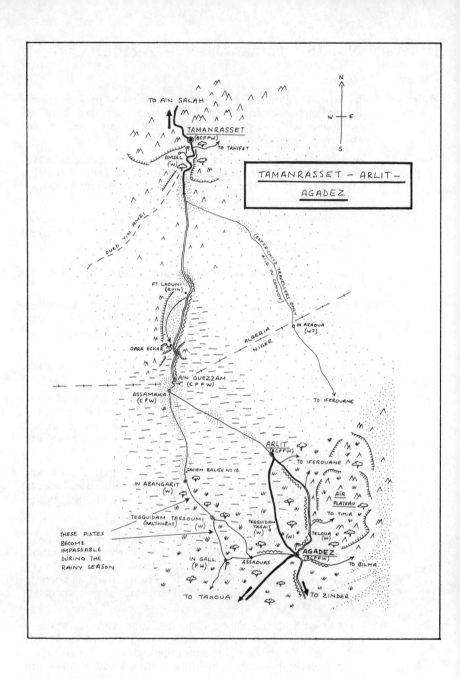

Right: Part of the beautiful wind eroded sandstone rock formations at Gara Eckar about 60 km north of Ain Guezzam. An ideal spot to camp overnight.

404

passport control (open 08.30 till lunchtime, and thence to sunset). Then see customs. This is a repeat of formalities at Tamanrasset.

On leaving for the south follow the corrugated piste past the gardens, for 3 km. About 200m after the old Kombi shell on the left, leave the piste and follow the vehicle tracks on the left. Build up speed and follow these tracks (but not in them) all the 25 km (16 miles) to Assamaka, which consists of a few buildings, on top of a hill, surrounded by very deep soft sand.

441 456 **Assamaka** Niger military frontier post. Have your Carnet stamped here (first see Chapter 14: Vehicle Documents). On approaching Assamaka from the north or south, keep up your speed. Do not slow down until you have climbed the sand hill, and have to stop, right at the frontier post itself. No photography is allowed. Plenty of sulphurous bore water. The post is open from 08.00 to 12.00 and 16.00 to 18.00. Note: in summer only, Algeria is one hour ahead of Niger.

For Tegguidam Tessoumi, head south on a bearing of 170°. Kep speed up. (Use Arlit route in the rainy season, July - August.) Several big sandy patches, and seas of bull-dust especially 85 km south of Assamaka. There are balises every 5 km, but the piste deviates from them sometimes. Niger frontier officials have been known to force travellers heading southwards to go to Arlit and then to Agadez instead of going via Tegguidam Tessoumi.

For the route via Arlit, see Itinerary No. 17.

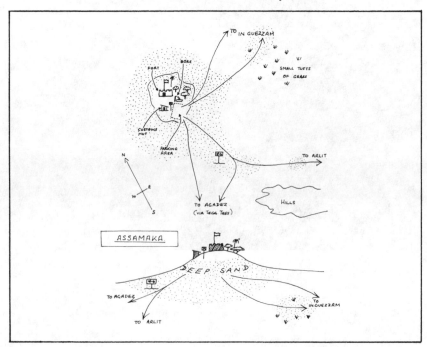

595	302	**Saviem Balise** A large white and blue triangular column erected by a West-East Saharan expedition in 1977.
602	295	**In Abangarit** A small Touareg village with a well (15m). First sight of low Sahel thorn trees.
704	193	**Tegguidam Tessoumi** A large permanent village with a thriving salt extraction industry. Ask a boy to guide you over the salt workings. Many boys will offer. Select one and pay only one. In the mornings camels are loaded with salt to be taken for sale in Tahoua, Sokoto, Kano, etc. A Japanese salt research project is visible nearby. For Assaouas, head east and then SE. Many wells on the way. Touareg camel cheese can be bought at the roadside.
829	68	**Assaouas** Well. Junction with piste between Agadez and In Gall.
897	0	**Agadez** Visit Police first; they usually require 2 passport photos (there are several photographers in town). No need to see Customs if all was okay at Assamaka. If heading north to Algeria, see Customs about your Carnet if you used it to enter Niger (see Chapter 14: Vehicle Documents). Bank hours: 08.00 to 11.30 and 15.30 to 16.30. Monday to Friday.

Agadez

Banks: B.D.R.N. Monday to Friday. 08.00 to 11.00 and 15.30 to 16.30.

Police: Present passports, fill out forms (fiches), give details of your journey. They may keep passports overnight or for afternoon.

The salt evaporation ponds at Tegguidam Tessoumi, one of the attractions of taking the route direct from Assamaka to Agadez rather than going via Arlit

Customs: Necessary only if heading north and if you need exit page of Carnet stamped and removed.

Hospital: Good under the circumstances.

Garages and Spares: Several 'bush' mechanics, but capable and ingenious. Some spare parts available.

Post Office: (P.T.T.) Monday to Friday. 08.00 to 12.00 and 15.00 to 17.00. Poste Restante service. Money Order service, called 'Mandat Postale'.

Buses: SNTN Bus service to Zinder, then Niamey. Leaves from the bus station (Gare Routière). (See map.)

Trucks. Cheaper than buses and go all directions, leaving from the lorry park (see map). Allow 10,000 CFA minimum to Niamey from Agadez.

Airline: Air Niger flies: Niamey — Agadez, Monday & Friday; Agadez — Niamey, Tuesday & Saturday. Military flights: Agadez — Bilma, first and third Tuesday each month, returning Wednesday. Tourists can use this service.

Camping: Oasis Camping' along the old piste to Arlit to the NE of town. Swimming pool, bucket type cold showers, lots of shade, restaurant. There is a new camping ground 5 km outside Agadez along the new asphalt road to Arlit but with no shade.

Hotels: Hotel de l'Air, formerly the Sultan's Palace, but very simple, with showers, fans and air conditioning available; restaurant; bar.

Religion: Mosques: The famous one in the centre of town and another one near the airport. Usually tourists are unwelcome inside. Church: There is a catholic church at the back of the town, next door to the mission. A

The famous mosque at Agadez in northern Niger, Agadez has for centuries been a major crossroads of camel caravan routes in the Southern Sahara.

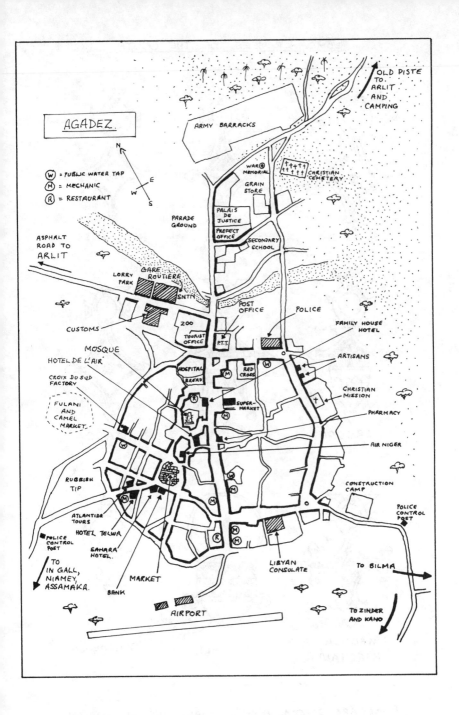

Some Crosses of the South.

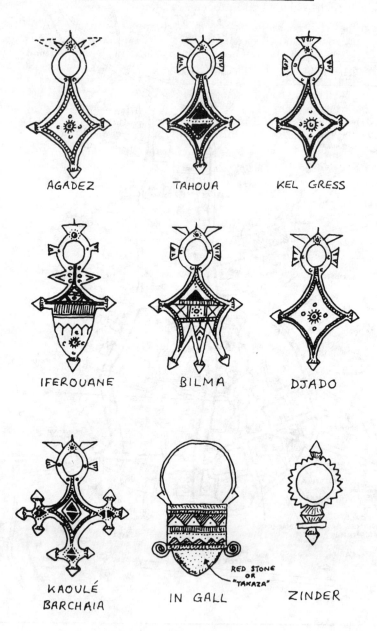

AGADEZ   TAHOUA   KEL GRESS

IFEROUANE   BILMA   DJADO

KAOULÉ BARCHAIA   IN GALL   ZINDER

RED STONE OR "TAKAZA"

There are several others. Many are on display in the Niamey Museum.

Christian cemetery near the road which goes to Oasis Camping holds the graves of French soldiers and European residents.

Silversmiths: The most famous artisan, Mohammat Kumama and his two partners have a workshop near the market. Another two artisans can be found in a back street near the mission. Better deals and superior quality are obtained by buying direct, rather than from street vendors. Inspect all three workshops before buying. They will all make jewellery and statuettes to order. The silver used in the region is not pure; it is nickel silver. If you desire, it is possible to have them use silver ingots you supply. These are relatively inexpensive in Europe, and they assist the artisans who have increasing difficulty buying local silver, which is now quite scarce.

Other Souvenirs: Leather work including pouffes, bags, Fulani and Touareg money purses, sandals, snakeskins, Touareg camel saddles; pottery, basket work and old swords. Many of these items are less expensive and of superior quality in the Chief Artisan's shop of the Niamey Museum.

Market: In the centre of the town, selling groceries; bread; grass mats; souvenirs as mentioned above; vegetables; meat; salt; dates; etc. Friday is a day for prayer, therefore shops and markets are closed for the early part of the afternoon.

Festivals: Two Salah festivals (The Birth of the Prophet, Mohammed; and the Moslem New Year) are very spectacular occasions, in Agadez, and should not to be missed if you are in the area at the time. (See page 82 for date information.)

Diplomatic: Libyan Consulate. Check visas and translations here if you are travelling to Libya. There is also a new Algerian consulate.

For broken down vehicles beyond repair, or for fuel to Bilma, see Alhaji Atta, near the Libyan Consulate.

One of several skilled silversmiths in Agadez, Ahnou Amini uses the 'lost wax' method to cast his silver jewellery. A wax model of the cross required is encased in clay. Molten silver is then poured into a hole in the clay casing. The wax melts and is displaced by the molten silver and runs out of another hole. When the silver has cooled, the clay is then broken away and all that is left to do is to clean up the new silver cross with a metal file and polish it

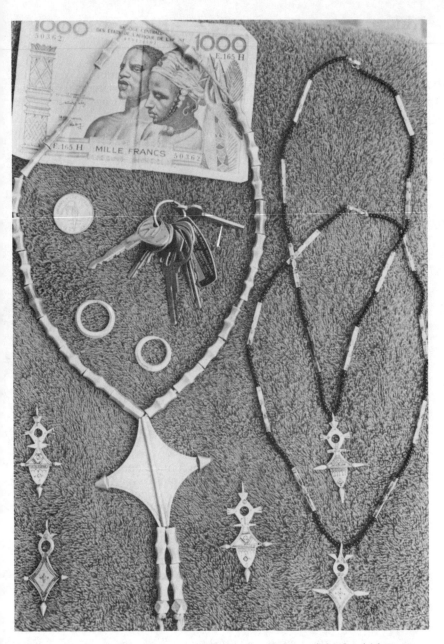

Typical jewellery of the Agadez region. The smaller 'Crosses of the South' have been made for the tourist trade. The two rings and the large cross are old traditional family heirlooms bought from a destitute Touareg which were about to be melted down to make smaller tourist crosses (The keys, coin and note are in this photograph for scale purposes.

Itinerary No. 17 : Agadez — Arlit — Assamaka

Distance   469 km.

Water   Fill up at Agadez at public taps or at the Camping. Well at tiny
village of Anou Araghenne, but next convenient water is at the
petrol station in Arlit where one should fill up again as the water
at Assamaka is abundant but sulphurous.

Fuel   Fill up in Agadez with enough to reach Tamanrasset (about
650 km) as there is no guarantee of supplies being available at
Arlit and it is rare to find fuel available at Ain Guezzam.

From Agadez to Arlit there is a new (1981) asphalt road which was specially
constructed to transport uranium 'yellow cake' from the mine at Arlit to
Niamey. This new road circuits much of the more attractive part of the Air
uplands and takes a direct route to Arlit, passing only one tiny oasis along
the way, Anou Araghenne. Beware, the heavy trucks are often reluctant to
move over for smaller vehicles to pass or to overtake. •

North of Arlit there are balises every kilometre to Assamaka but many have
fallen over and are covered by sand and in many cases the preferred piste
deviates from the line of balises.

   0   469   **Agadez** Before leaving town for the north or immediately upon
arrival from Algeria and Arlit, check out with customs and
police. (Have Carnet discharged if you used it to enter Niger
from the south.) Leave town via the NW, past the Gare
Routière.

  61   408   **Anou Araghenne** Tiny settlement to the east of the road with
a well.

 233   236   Uranium mine and police post. There is a turn-off to Iferouane
in the east.

 243   226   **Arlit** Approach town from the south. Report to Customs, then
Police (if coming from the north your passport may be held until
you buy insurance that is valid for Niger); and then the Gen-
darmerie (the latter only just before you leave). Post office, bank,
airport (with scheduled services to Niamey and Agadez). There
is a big largely French expatriate compound area with bars,
pools, etc. but it is usually closed to tourists. There is a very
small oasis with vegetable gardens and a well, about 5 km across
the desert directly north of the town. There is an airport with
scheduled flights to Niamey. There is a camping ground with
showers just outside Arlit along the new asphalt road to
Agadez. There are plenty of signs in town promoting it and
giving directions.

Leaving Arlit, head NWW past the uranium processing plant
and airport on the left. Balises start at the factory with the
distance marked on them. They are spaced every kilometre all
the way to Assamaka. (Beware: there is a maze of tracks on
leaving Arlit near the factory.) The piste to Assamaka has no
really big sandy patches and can be crossed at speed.

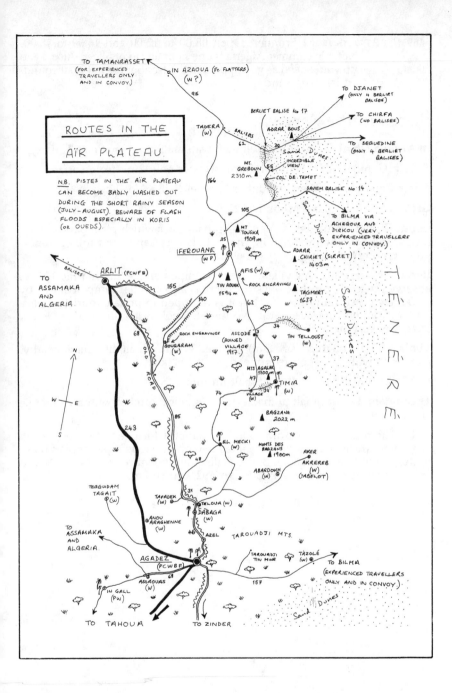

ROUTES IN THE
AïR PLATEAU

N.B. PISTES IN THE AïR PLATEAU
CAN BECOME BADLY WASHED OUT
DURING THE SHORT RAINY SEASON
(JULY - AUGUST). BEWARE OF FLASH
FLOODS ESPECIALLY IN KORIS
(OR OUEDS).

TO TAMANRASSET
(FOR EXPERIENCED
TRAVELLERS ONLY
AND IN CONVOY.)

IN AZAOUA (Ft. FLATTERS)
(W?)
95

TADERA
(W)

BALISES
62

BERLIET BALISE No 17

ADRAR BOUS
39

MT.
GREBOUN
2310 m.

COL DE TEMET

Sand Dunes
INCREDIBLE
VIEW.
55

TO DJANET
(ONLY 4 BERLIET
BALISES)

TO CHIRFA
(NO BALISES)

TO SEGUEDINE
(ONLY 4 BERLIET
BALISES)

SAVIEM BALISE No 14

TO BILMA VIA
ACHEGOUR AND
DIRKOU (VERY
EXPERIENCED TRAVELLERS
ONLY IN CONVOY.)

166

105

MT
TOUSKÁ
1909 m
25

IFEROUANE
(W P)

AFIS (W)

ROCK ENGRAVINGS

ADRAR
CHIRIET (SIRRET)
1403m

T E N E R E

ARLIT (PCWFB)

TO
ASSAMAKA
AND
ALGERIA

BALISES

155

TIN AOUAK
1594 m

62

TAGMERT
1637

140

ROCK ENGRAVINGS
BOUGARAM
(W)

ASSODÉ
(RUINED
VILLAGE
1917.)

34

TIN TELLOUST
(W)

68

OLD
ROAD

N

W   E

S

243

85

74

MTS AGALAK
1700 m
47

TIMIA
(W)
VILLAGE
(W)
34

37

BAGZANE
2022 m

EL MECKI
(W)

MONTS DES
BAGZANS
1900m

AKER
AKREREB
(W)
(GABELOT)

48

ABARDOUGH
(W)

TEGGIDAM
TAGAIT
(W)

TAFADEK
(W)
31

TELOUA (W)

DABAGA
(W)

ANOU
ARAGHENNE
(W)

46

AZEL

TAROUADJI MTS.

TO
ASSAMAKA
AND
ALGERIA.

AGADEZ
(PCWBF)

TAROUADJI
TIN MINE

TAZOLÉ
(W.)

TO BILMA
(EXPERIENCED TRAVELLERS
ONLY AND IN CONVOY.)

ASSAOUAS
(W)

68

157

IN GALL
(PW)

Sand Dunes

TO TAHOUA

TO ZINDER

Sand Dunes

469   0   **Assamaka** Frontier. Open 08.00 to 12.00 and 16.00 to 18.00. Note: in summer Algeria is one hour ahead of Niger. Also, keep up your speed as you approach the frontier post; it is surrounded by deep sand.

Places in the Air

In Azaoua Uninhabited ruin. Well with water at 5 m. Sometimes Touaregs.

Tadera Uninhabited. Well: sulphurous water only 2 m. from surface.

Adrar Bous Uninhabited. Mountain. Berliet Balise No. 17.

Greboun Uninhabited. Mountain 2310 m.

Col de Temet Uninhabited. Very steep pass over which piste passes. Both ascent and descent are difficult. The piste is very sandy and full of stones. Low tyre pressures necessary. Spectacular.

Iferouane Large Touareg village. Wells. Campement, set up in June 1973 to observe the total eclipse of the sun. There is also another camp operated by a Niamey based tour operator, but it is not open to private tourists. Police post with radio contact to Arlit. No fuel. School. British missionary Frank Baggot is very helpful.

Timia Large Touareg (Kel Oui) village. Wells. Small tin mine nearby. Palmeraie with irrigation from nearby kori. School.

El Mecki Small village. Well. Small tin mine.

Tegguidam Tagait Small nomadic Touareg encampment with a palmeraie and school.

Note: The routes east of Adrar Bous to Djanet, Chirfa, and Seguedine can be without trace, and a guide or someone with previous experience of these routes, would be invaluable. Berliet Balises are not at regular intervals and are very far apart, e.g. 102 km, 82 km, 92 km, 90 km.

Itinerary No. 18 : Agadez — Tahoua — Sokoto

Distance	615 km.
Water	Agadez, at the many public taps. Abalak, well with pump to NE of village. Tahoua, Birni N'Konni, and Sokoto, at petrol stations.
Fuel	Fill up at Agadez with sufficient for at least 400 km to Tahoua. Petrol stations also at Tahoua, Birni N'Konni and Sokoto. (Nigerian fuel is almost as cheap as in Algeria.)

From Agadez south to Tahoua and all the way to Sokoto there is a beautiful full width asphalt road. Unfortunately, this new road by-passes many interesting little towns and villages. The old piste with its horrendous 'ornières' still exists between the villages of In Gall and In Waggeur but these places are now connected to the new asphalt road by quite good, though corrugated, gravel roads (see route map).

About 150 km south of Agadez the new road rises up over the Falaise de Tiguidit. From here southwards the vegetation changes from that of the cram cram desert type to the grass and thorn trees of the Sahel. By Tahoua this in turn begins to give way to more dense growth with tall grass and larger trees and even some of the grotesquely big and fat Baobab trees. As well as the nomadic Fulani or Puel people with their cattle, there are more settled villages and large fields of millet have been planted by Hausa farmers.

0	615	**Agadez** Take the westerly route out of town past the camel market and rubbish tip. If asked to, stop at the police checkpoint on the way out. Theoretically, one is supposed to check in with the police at every town between Agadez and Niamey.
150	465	**Falaise de Tiguidit** and branch road (gravel) to In Gall some 48 km away to the NW. At In Gall there is a fort, village and market. There is much petrified wood about 2 km east of town along the old piste. North of In Gall is the salt producing oasis of Tegguidam Tessoumi.
240	375	Junction with gravel road to Tofamanir and In Waggeur.
260	355	**Abalak** Large mud village with many shops and a most welcome bar. Major cattle watering point to the east of the village — many Fulani can be seen.
360	255	About 40 km north of Tahoua at Tounfafi, there is a large man-made lake which attracts many beautiful water birds.
400	215	**Tahoua** Large town laid out by French, with streets in a grid pattern. If asked to by Police at entry to town, check in at Police station. Campement/hotel, banks, boulangerie, 3 petrol stations, post office, airport, CFAO supermarket, hospital and quite large market (see Tahoua map). Alternative route to Niamey via Filingué leaves town via the west.
		For Birni N'Konni return to main Agadez — Niamey road and head south along excellent bitumen road.
507	108	Road joins main Zinder—Niamey road and heads west. Police check point.

SH 27

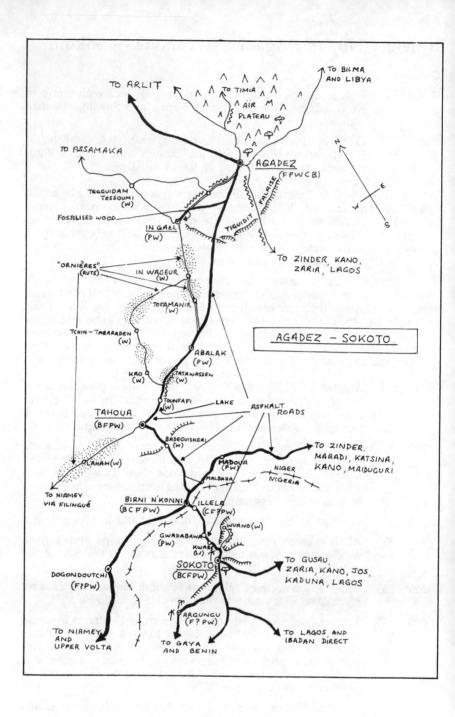

Street scene at the border town of Birni N'Konni

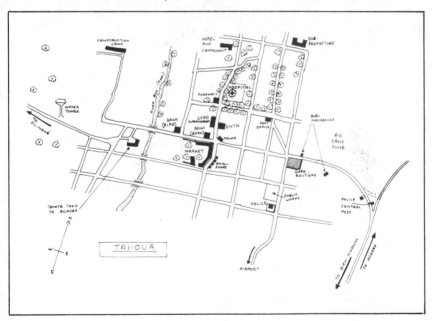

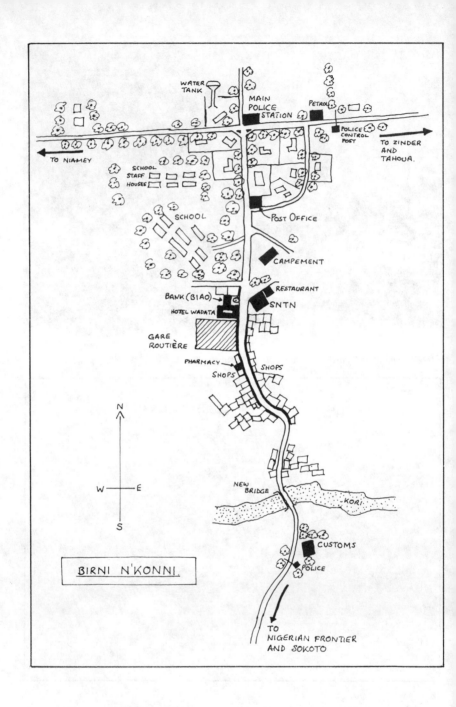

BIRNI N'KONNI.

522	93	**Birni N'Konni** Report to Police if asked to at barrier on entry to town. There is petrol station, bar and a bank; also an SNTN agency. For Illela and Sokoto head directly south. For Niamey go west from the Police station. Niger frontier post is to the south of the town (see map of Birni N'Konni). When entering Niger, obtain a 'laissez-passer' for your vehicle.
532	83	**Nigerian frontier post** Don't forget to ask for currency declaration. Nigerains usually require a Carnet for the vehicle.
534	81	**Illela** Market town. Petrol station but rarely has supplies. Market day is Sunday.
564	51	**Gwadabawa** Large market town. Mosque. Small shops, Police station and two secondary schools.
582	33	**Kware** Large village near Lake Kware which supplies water to the city of Sokoto. Beware of Bilharzia in the lake.
602	13	Bridge across the Rima river (usually dry).
608	7	Road from Wurno joins from NE.
615	0	**Sokoto** Enter town from NE across Sokoto River (see Sokoto map). All facilities.

Sokoto

Banks Several: Union Bank of Nigeria (formerly Barclays), First Bank of Nigeria (formerly Standard), Bank of the North, United Bank for Africa, and

Trumpeters herald the arrival of the Sultan of Sokoto during the festivities at the end of Ramadan

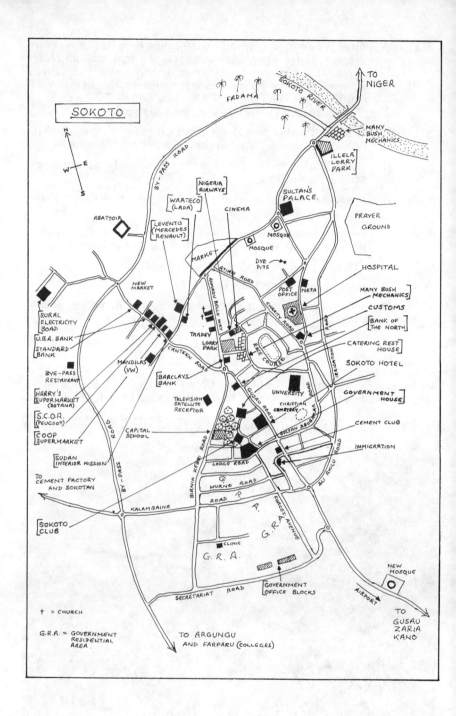

SOKOTO

even a branch of the Nigerian Central Bank. Hours 08.00 to 14.00 with early closing on Fridays. Monday to Friday, closed Saturday and Sunday.

Petrol Several: but supplies can be limited and long queues are possible. However, the price is cheap.

Garages and Spares: Volkswagen: Mandilas. Peugeot: SCOA. Mercedes & Renault: Leventis. Lada: WAATECO. However, good, new, and cheaper spare parts can be obtained from the Ibo shops in the Sabon Gari area, behind the lorry park.

Shopping: Sokoto has a very large market open daily except Sunday. Friday is the special big market day. There are also supermarkets e.g. TRADEV, Harry Brothers, Co-op, and Chellerams.

Accommodation: Sokoto Hotel is a big modern air-conditioned hotel, but is expensive. The government run Catering Guest House is run down and dirty. Alternatives are the privately run Cement Club Rest House and Howeidy's Rest House, each with air-conditioned rooms, showers and attached restaurant. There is also an S.I.M. rest house.

Bars and Restaurants: There are many, most with a distinctly modern African atmosphere e.g. Charity Hotel, Nasara Club, Rima Valley Hotel, Sahara Club, Bye-Pass Hotel.

Customs: Capable of handling the importation of a vehicle, but it is preferable to go to Kano for this.

Police: No need to report to Police.

Immigration: The Immigration Office will handle visa extensions. Hours 8.00 to 17.00 Monday to Friday.

Post Office: Hours 8.00 to 17.00 Monday to Friday.

Historical: The site of Sokoto was chosen as Shehu Usman Dan Fodio's capital in 1806 after a successful Jihad (Holy War). There are two large mosques (and a third one under construction near the airport). The present Sultan of Sokoto, Sultan Abubakar II, is the direct descendant of the Shehu. As a result, he is the spiritual leader of all Hausas and Moslems in northern Nigeria and Niger. The end of Ramadan fasting does not occur either in Niger or Nigeria until the Sultan has sighted the new moon. The 'Sallah' at the end of Ramadan (Id el Fitri) and at the Birthdate of the Prophet Mohammed are both very colourful and spectacular occasions, with processions of knights in chain-mail armour, and musicians, from the prayer ground to the Sultan's Palace. Shehu Usman Dan Fodio's tomb (or 'hubbare') is worth a visit. No women are admitted, visitors must take off their shoes and on leaving give money ('gaisuwa') to the guide. (It is at the Sultan's mosque.) On Thursday evenings between 09.00 and 11.00 musicians play outside the Sultan's Palace to welcome, and usher in, Friday (a Holy Day), which officially begins on Thursday, at sunset.

The Sokoto Sultanate was defeated in a battle against the British Frontier Force in 1903, at the site of the present race course. In the Christian cemetery, a grave, claimed to be that of the early explorer, Clapperton (died 1827), can be seen.

Traditional Artifacts: Red goat leather is tanned locally, and for centuries was sent across the Sahara, by camel, to Morocco. This is the famous 'Moroccon Leather'. Leather pouffes, bags, purses, etc. can be bought from the government run Sokotan factory, or from two specialized traders: Alhaji

Abdullahi Haido (front of Sokoto Hotel) and Alhaji Ladan (near Sultan's Palace). There are traditional indigo dye pits at Wurno (30 km to the NE) and behind the small market opposite the Post Office.

Traditional Hausa boxing, using one arm only, can be seen at the special boxing stadium next to the Giginya Memorial College most evenings (next to the race course).

Transport: The main lorry park for buses, 'mammy wagons', taxis and Transit vans to the east, south and west. The Illela Lorry Park should be used for public transport to Birni N'Konni. There are taxis all over town for local journeys.

Airport: Daily flights by Fokker F28, and Boeing 737 jets to Kano, Kaduna and Lagos. A new airport, capable of landing jumbo jets has been completed 25 km along the Argungu road.

Surame Ruins Built by the Kanta of Kebbi, a noble of the Songhai Empire, who rebelled in 1516, and set up his own kingdom. This is now a completely abandoned city, but there are many stone walls still intact. North of Kware turn off to the west to Binji or Bankari, where the services of a guide should be obtained. The old city is 5 km south of here along a very rough, little used track, but satisfactory for a Volkswagen.

Argungu: 99 km to the west of Sokoto, along a good asphalt road. Excellent museum with traditional artifacts and historical relics. (Ask for directions.) A guide will escort you around the museum, explaining the exhibits. It is customary to tip him with a naira at least. There is also an imposing Emir's Palace.

During three days at the end of February every year, there is the spectacular Argungu Fishing Festival. The Sokoto River is dammed for several months and fishing is restricted. On the day of the festival hundreds of local fishermen plunge into the river with their gourds and nets to see who can catch the biggest fish. The results are staggering, producing fish (Giwan rua) over 50 kg in weight and nearly 2 m long. There is a government Catering Rest House, a petrol station (unreliable supplies), several schools, small shops, and a police station.

Birnin Kebbi: Small town with bank (Union Bank), petrol station, small shops, market and a hospital.

Kamba: Nigerian Customs and Immigration post.

Sokoto - Kamba - Dosso Route: All roads are a good asphalt surface.

Itinerary No. 19 : Djanet — Bilma

Distance   865 km.
Note: Allow an extra 20-25 km for the return trip to Djado, and allow for the extra distance if travelling up on to the Djado Plateau.

Water   Djanet, from the many taps in town. Chirfa, well near school (1m). Djado, none to drink. Seguedine, well to SE of town (2m). Dirkou, well near barracks, and in palmeraie (2m). Bilma, at piscine, and well near fort, opposite the post office (1m). There is also a well at the tiny oasis of Aney. These are the only sources of water on the entire route.

Fuel   Djanet usually has good supplies of diesolene, normal, and even super, but if necessary wait for a few days. At Bilma and Dirkou it is usually necessary to locate the Libyan 'Jerome' (or his assistant Ibrahim Mohammed), for they sell Libyan diesolene and normal from both oases in lots of 200 litres for 50,000 CFA. Sometimes, if there is no fuel at either depot, it is necessary to wait a few days. If travelling across the Ténéré from Agadez it might pay to have supplies sent out in advance, in 200 litre drums, to Bilma by arrangement with a local cartage contractor in Agadez such as Alhaji Atta (see Agadez section). This could lessen the cost of fuel but needs advance organization.

To cover this distance through the Ténéré to Bilma a lot of fuel should be carried for safety. This route is infrequently used, especially in the hot season (May to August). To run out of fuel or have a major breakdown could be disastrous, as it could entail waiting for perhaps three months for another vehicle to pass and find yours with dehydrated corpses lying around. This is no exaggeration, as the seven marked graves near the Arbre du Ténéré show; even Hausas and Touaregs die when their vehicle breaks down. Here your life depends on your vehicle. It must be in good condition. You must know how to carry out simple and sometimes improvised repairs. You must carry sufficient fuel for each vehicle. As a guide, here are some examples of the number of jerry cans needed by different vehicles in addition to their normal full fuel tanks.

14 : 4 cylinder Land Rover   25 : 6 cylinder petrol Unimog
15 : Range Rover   10 : VW Bus.

It should be pointed out that only a big (Type 4) engined VW Bus with limited slip differential should be taken. Even then it should be lightly laden and driven by an experienced person. Alternatively, a four wheel drive "Syndiro" VW Bus is very capable of travelling this route.

For this journey, two vehicles is an absolute minimum, and it is preferable to have three. Travel in a pre-determined order, and if following, never lose sight of the vehicle ahead, or its tracks. If these rules are not followed there is a very real danger of vehicles losing each other, and not knowing whether one has broken down or has just gone on ahead. Much fuel can be wasted in useless searches. Similarly, the lead vehicle should always keep a following vehicle in sight, or stop and wait every few minutes.

On leaving Djanet for the south, no authorities are interested in how well your vehicle is equipped or even whether it is capable for the journey. The Police are interested only in commodities like whisky and cassette tapes.

425

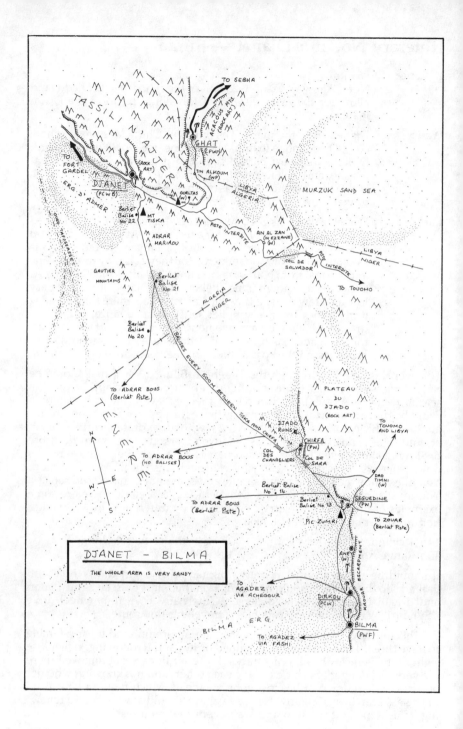

Consequently, nobody is interested in whether you make the journey, or not. **WARNING:** It should be noted that in Autumn 1979 four Land Rovers were lost and their occupants never seen again along this route. The Algerian authorities subsequently banned all travel between Djanet and Chirfa (except with special permission from the Interior Ministry in Algiers, which is rarely given). The penalties for breaching this ban are severe and always include confiscation of the vehicle and equipment.

There are no radio or telex messages as is the case with the Bilma to Agadez and In Amenas to Djanet routes. You're on your own totally.

Always stay with the known route. Follow balises unless the route is known. The Michelin map 153 is accurate and remarkably detailed. Apart from the area around Tiska, the route is simple to follow. Yet it is worth noting that even a large professional expedition financed by a large truck manufacturer got lost at Seguedine: a piste junction so clear that all four pistes to Bilma, Djanet, Libya and Tchad can be seen at one time from the foot of nearby Pic Zumri. In other words, keep cool and make logical decisions.

Note: There are two types of balises mentioned in this itinerary; those erected every 500 m by the French colonial government, and those erected by the Berliet expedition in 1960. All are numbered.

0	865	**Djanet** Before departure visit Police (closed 12.00 - 14.00 hours) and the Customs on the way out of town (see Djanet map). Head south past the piste that goes to Tamanrasset and Illizi and go to the airport.
7	858	**Airport** Turn east at the airport and drive along the northern edge of the runway. Then head SE along the mildly corrugated piste to Rhat (Ghat) with mountains on both sides. But do not take any tracks to the south through the mountains until after you've passed a yellow signpost indicating the route to Rhat (Ghat) to the east.
40	825	This signpost is about 40 km from Djanet. Continue SE. Take the first opportunity to follow a well formed piste southwards through a wide gap in the mountain range. This piste soon disappears, and it is necessary for you to find your own way southwards over several ranges of low hills until you see the
70	795	big conical shape of **Mt. Tiska.** Head around Tiska in a wide arc on the western side until you are due west of the mountain. Then head SE past a final low range of hills (about 3 km south of Tiska) until you hit the balises which are 500 metres apart all the way SSE to Niger across the flat featureless Ténéré to Chirfa.
130	735	**Adrar Mariaou** Small range of hills to be seen some distance to the east.
190	675	**Berliet Balise No. 21** From here the Berliet piste branches off in a SSW direction to Adrar Bous. For this route a guide is essential as the balises are at irregular intervals of between 58 and 101 km apart and vehicle tracks disappear quickly. Just south of this balise, for 30 km you must often go uphill in sometimes deep sand which could be quite difficult. Keep up speed, and do not slow down for about 40 km.

Mount Tiska, a vital landmark that one must find and keep to the west of when travelling between the Ténéré desert and the oasis of Djanet

There are balises (marker posts) every 500 metres for 570 kilometres across the northern Ténéré from Mount Tiska to Chirfa. They are a great help in this massive totally bare and flat desert but this piste is so lonely that if a lone vehicle should break down it could be months before other vehicles pass by and discover the broken down vehicle and some dehydrated corpses. Travelling in convoy is essential in the Ténéré

231	634	At Balise 231 there is soft sand. Keep up speed and do not use brakes.
510	355	At Balise 510 there is a piste departing towards Adrar Bous. This has no balises and is rarely used except by an Italian tour operator from Agadez. A guide is essential, unless this route is known from experience.
540	325	**Chirfa** Small Toubou village of about 30 families. Possesses a two teacher primary school, small store, well, and an old ruined ex-French army fort. There is a Guarde Nomadique. He and the Directeur of the school are most helpful and informative. They both speak French and Hausa, and will provide a schoolboy (eager to improve his French) as a guide for the Djado ruins. A tip of 1,000 CFA after the trip to Djado is sufficient.

Djado Ruined city about 10 km to the north of Chirfa. Abandoned for at least 200 years, probably for a variety of reasons; among them are: malaria, Touareg raids, Arab slave raids, and an increasing salinity of the oasis water. Probably inhabited by the ancestors of the Toubous at Chirfa, who also speak of a great monster with a snake's head that used to fly over from the Djado Plateau and eat the people whole!

The route to Djado is sandy. Be careful of thorns. Do not try to drive over the last sand dune just before the ruins, without

The ruined town of Djado. Some 250 years ago the inhabitants were forced to give up their town for several reasons: increasing salinity of the nearby water supply made irrigation impossible, total lack of rain, a malaria epidemic, and raids by Touaregs

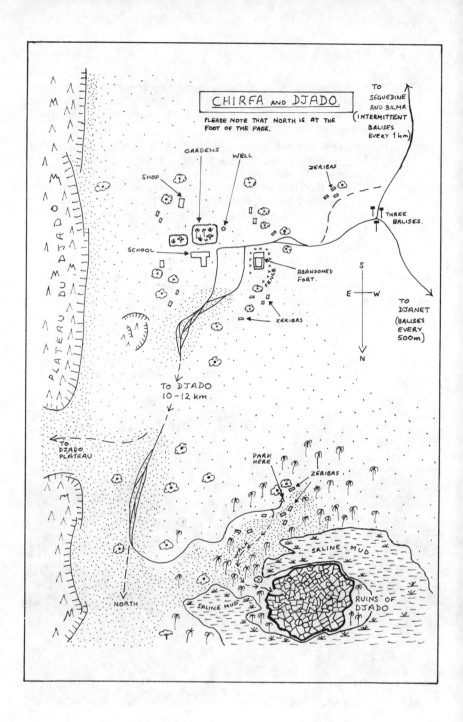

CHIRFA and DJADO.

PLEASE NOTE THAT NORTH IS AT THE FOOT OF THE PAGE.

430

first inspecting it on foot. Preferably park among the empty zeribas to the south of the city. Nobody lives at Djado, but zeribas are used as shelters by people from Chirfa who come to collect dates. In the ruins, beware of snakes, and crumbling walls and roofs. Also, avoid camping near Djado because at night it swarms with malaria-carrying mosquitoes.

Djado Plateau If time and fuel permit, it is worthwhile driving up on to the Djado Plateau to the NE. There are many beautiful neolithic stone arrowheads, etc. at these sites. However, please respect the historical and cultural importance of each site. It would be advisable to take a guide from Chirfa, after consulting the Directeur or Guarde Nomadique, as this really is a very rarely visited part of the Sahara.

Southwards For Dirkou and Bilma leave Chirfa by the direction you entered it until you reach three balises within 5 metres of each other. They are about 2 km west of Chirfa. Then head directly south, trying to stay close to the balises which are now 1 kilometre apart. However many have fallen over and are buried now.

588 277 **Col de Sara** A hardly noticeable ridge of rocks in the flat sandy landscape.

591 274 **Piste to Madama** Branches off to the east. This point is marked by a stone balise and writing in stones in the sand. Directions are very clear from this point.

630 235 **Berliet Balise No. 13** Piste to Adrar Bous branches off to west. Balises are irregular (between 82 and 102 km apart). Not often used, though very flat, easy terrain.

670 195 **Seguedine** is reached from both north and south by sighting the conical peak of Pic Zumri, which will make itself abundantly clear if you are on the right course. Head to the east

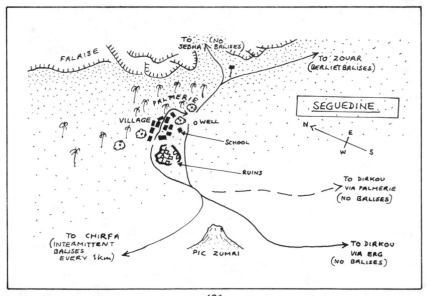

431

of Zumri until directly east of it. Go down the hill towards the palmeraie in the distance, in the east at the foot of a falaise or escarpment. This is Seguedine, a small Toubou village of about 30 families with a one teacher primary school, several wells, a store, a Guarde Nomadique and a palmeraie. There is a store of petrol belonging to the Italian tour operator: Vittorio Goni. There is also a very small cluster of ruined mud houses.

The pistes to Libya and Tchad branch off in their different directions halfway up the falaise to the east of Seguedine.

On leaving Seguedine for Dirkou, go to Pic Zumri again and head south following other vehicle tracks. There are no balises and the tracks may be up to 20 km apart, but still heading in the same direction and parallel with one another. Keep just out of sight of falaise about 20 km to the east. If conditions are hazy follow other tracks, stopping to check your bearing with a compass every 10 to 20 km. Sometimes the sand is deep and soft. Tyre pressures must be low.

815   50   About 150 km south of Pic Zumri the tracks will converge in a SSE direction as you arrive at Dirkou.

There is an alternative route that travels directly south of Seguedine via the palmeraie at the foot of the falaise all the way to Dirkou. This route is very sandy and often it is not possible to keep up the necessary speed to get through. However, it does go past the rarely visited village of Aney: Toubou oasis with a well and old fort. Probably the best way to visit it is to take the Ténéré route (20 km away from the falaise) for about 70 km south of Pic Zumri. Then head directly east to the falaise, whereupon you should head south till you hit the village.

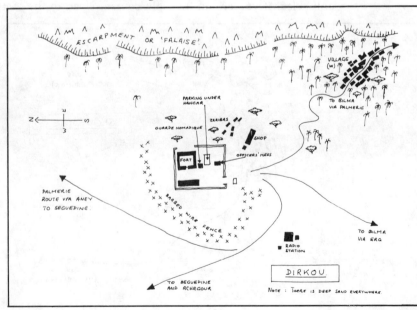

820   45   **Dirkou** Military base and frontier post. Check in with military on arrival, no matter where you have come from: Djanet, Libya, Tchad, Bilma or Agadez. Coming from Djanet this is your first passport control. You might be told to wait under a large hangar for several hours while your passport is processed. If heading for Agadez direct from there via Acheggour or via Bilma and Fashi, the Guarde Nomadique may retain your passports until you find a guide for the Ténéré crossing to Agadez. There are two or three professional guides who live in the small (Bli bli) village in the palmeraie about 3 km SE of the military fort. (One satisfactory guide is Abari Derri who owns a store near the military encampment.) There is a fixed rate for a guide from Bilma or Dirkou to Agadez (or vice versa) per vehicle. It is expensive and often one feels the guide is not worth it. But his knowledge of the route may prevent you making navigational errors, which would cost you your life.

Apart from the palmeraie and the local people, there are no other attractions at Dirkou. Nevertheless, it is mandatory to visit this oasis not only for passport and Customs formalities, but also so that the Police can monitor vehicle movements in the Ténéré. A daily exchange of vehicle movement information is made by radio with the Police in Agadez. If you are overdue, the Police will look for you. (Though this does not mean that they will find you!)

Also, while in Dirkou, try to locate the Libyan 'Jerome'. If he is in Dirkou try to arrange to buy fuel locally (if crossing the Ténéré via Acheggour), or at Bilma (if crossing via Fashi). If he

The centre of Bilma looking down the main street from the fort. Tyre pressures need to be low while driving around the few streets of Bilma

433

is at Dirkou, he can if necessary arrange for you to buy fuel from his assistant in Bilma. Otherwise look for him in Bilma.

To Bilma There are two routes. One is via the palmeraie and the several villages along it. For this route you leave Dirkou via the SE and wind your way through palm groves, and over sand dunes, joining up with the other alternative route about 10 km north of Bilma. This latter route is via the open desert and is probably quicker. For this, you leave Dirkou via the SSW and follow tracks across flat sand for 45 km to Bilma. No balises. The route you choose will be dependent upon which route your guide wishes you to take, and if looking for 'Jerome' it is best to take the palmeraie route, as this is the one he generally uses.

865   0   **Bilma** Post Office, military fort, Police, several stores, wells, fuel depot, airport, bakery shop, grain store, salt extraction industry. You must report to the Police (at the fort) soon after arrival.

It is best to visit the 'salines' in the early morning before 9.00 a.m., for as the day gets hotter work ceases. Generally the best time to visit Bilma is during September to December. During this time, the 'Azelai' takes place, when thousands of camels, in gigantic caravans converge on Bilma to load salt for the markets at Agadez and places as far away as Sokoto and Kano and Maiduguri.

There are flights out of Bilma to Agadez by military aircraft every first and third Wednesday of the month. The people of Bilma and Dirkou insist that they are neither Touareg, nor Toubou, nor Kanure, but rather, 'Bli bli'.

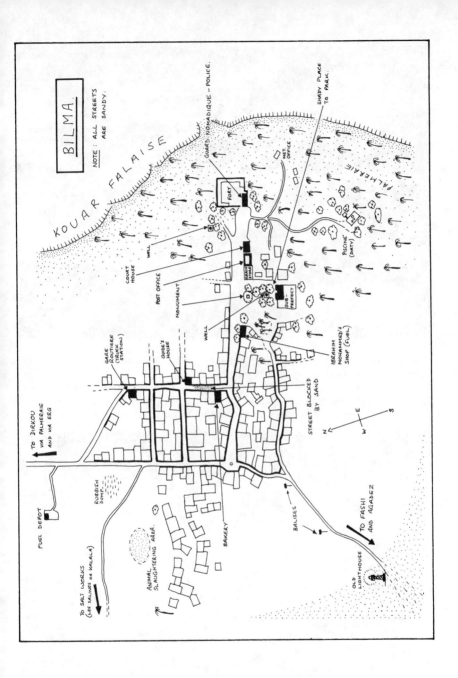

435

The evaporation ponds at the saltworks at Bilma. Earth with salt in it is collected from nearby salt pans or 'sebka' and mixed with water in these ponds. As the water evaporates, a thin crust of concentrated salt crystals floats on the top, as can be seen on the ponds in the foreground and to the right of this photo. Each day a man wades in these ponds and scrapes up the floating salt crystals

While still slightly damp the salt scraped from the top of the evaporation ponds is then moulded into different shapes. In the background are the classic biblical pillars of salt, which are usually slightly better quality

436

Itinerary No. 20 : Seguedine — Sebha

Distance   1028 km.

Water   Fill up at Seguedine (see map of Seguedine). Some available from military posts at Madama and Gatrun. Also at Zouilia, Traghem, Ghoddua and Sebha.

Fuel   Fill up with sufficient fuel at Dirkou, 150 km south of Seguedine, as none is available till Sebha. A four cylinder petrol Land Rover will need at least 15 jerrycans of fuel, in addition to the normal tankful.

Documents Libya requires the first few pages of the passports and health certificate translated into Arabic, and this must be an 'official' translation. Visa must be obtained in advance (see Chapter 12: Visas). A Carnet for the vehicle is not usually required. If entering Libya from the south it would be wise to visit the Libyan Consulate in Agadez to check over your personal documents. The ability to speak some Arabic would be a distinct advantage in Libya. Do not import alcohol, and be very discreet with photography.

The route has some difficult sandy sections, and it is easy to lose one's way. Two vehicles are essential and it would be best to over estimate fuel needs for the journey. There is an irregular Libyan run truck service from Sebha to Agadez, via Dirkou.

At the time of writing northern Chad has recently been the scene of some very bloody fighting and seems likely to remain a troublespot for some time to come. As such travel by tourists in the north-east of Niger and the south of Libya currently has the potential to be exceptionally dangerous. A violent death could not be ruled out. The authors, having narrowly escaped political violence recently in Iran, would not knowingly take a similar risk in the southern Sahara.

0	1028	**Seguedine** (see map) Drive east out of the palmeraie and up the sandy slope towards the falaise. Pass to the left of the Berliet balise, leaving the piste to Chad which goes eastwards. Head north climbing a small sandy pass, after which the piste is easier.
60	968	**Dao-Timni** Police control post. Go behind the fort to go to Madama. Towards Madama no piste is usually evident.
265	763	**Madama** Military fort. Check in with military. To leave Madama retrace your own tracks till you find recognizable piste again. Head north.
375	653	**Mt. Toummo** (1022m) Libya — Niger Frontier.
493	535	**Bir Musciuru** This is the main difficulty after Toummo; a horrible pass. The piste is not well defined. Look for stone balises and vehicle tracks (traces).
523	505	Approximately 30 km north of Bir Musciuru the piste joins the one coming from Chad. This junction may not be noticed, though there is a signpost.
573	455	**Ouirh El Sehir** There are two deep wells, one 500m to the SF and the other just a few paces NE. About 5-10 km to the north there is feche feche. 15 km to the north is a signpost to Tedjere

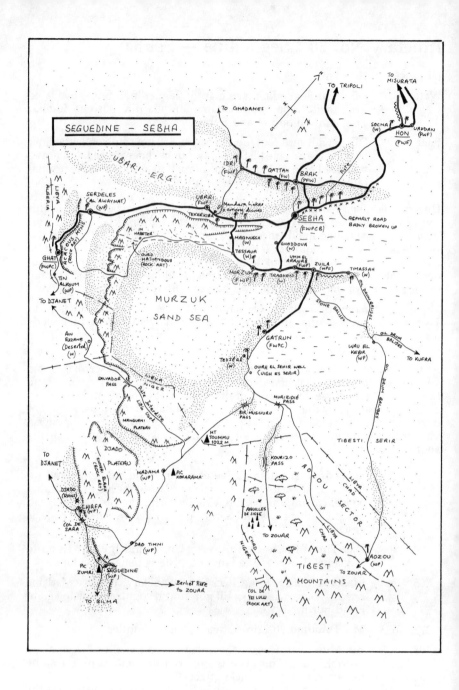

SEGUEDINE - SEBHA.

438

Seguedine as seen from the Pic Zumri. The oasis is among the palm trees at the foot of the distant escarpment. The piste to Libya passes up through the hills directly behind the settlement. The piste to Chad goes east (to the right) behind the settlement along the foot of the hills

about 20 km to the west. Continue north to El Gatrun.

678	350	**El Gatrun** Libyan military fort. Customs and Immigration formalities. Petrol is sometimes available and there are money changing facilities. You will be well received if you can speak at least some Arabic. A new asphalt road now extends northwards (under construction for the 100 km north of El Gatrun during 1982).
807	221	**Magadul** Oasis with palmeraie and well.
828	200	**Zouila** Oasis with palmeraie and petrol station. A gravel road goes east to the small oasis of Tmessa.
863	165	**Ummel Araneb** Small oasis with palmeraie.
906	122	**Traghen** Small oasis with palmeraie. An asphalt road west goes 52 km to the large oasis and oil town of Murzuk where petrol is available. Head north from Traghen to Sebha.
956	72	**Ghoddua** Palmeraie. Water.
1028	0	**Sebha** Large town. Police, hotel, petrol, airport, (scheduled flights to Tripoli). Centre for agricultural transformation of this part of the Sahara. Col. Gaddafi was born in Sebha. The town is also a major military base. Please exercise discretion with your camera. North of Sebha there is a good full width tar sealed road, to Tripoli, some 1004 km away. But in long sections either side of Hon (362 km north of Sebha) it is badly broken up and potentially very damaging to your vehicle.

439

SE of Sebha a good full width asphalt road is being extended SE to Ghat some 588 km away. During 1983 the last 100 km were under construction. A piste then continues on to Djanet in Algeria. There are important examples of pre-historic rock art north of **Ghat** in the Acacous ranges. Ghat is the frontier clearance point, but it is necessary to repeat formalities at the tiny post of Tin Alkhoum at the border. Ghat (sometimes spelled Rhat) is also the main centre for the Kel Ajjer Touaregs.

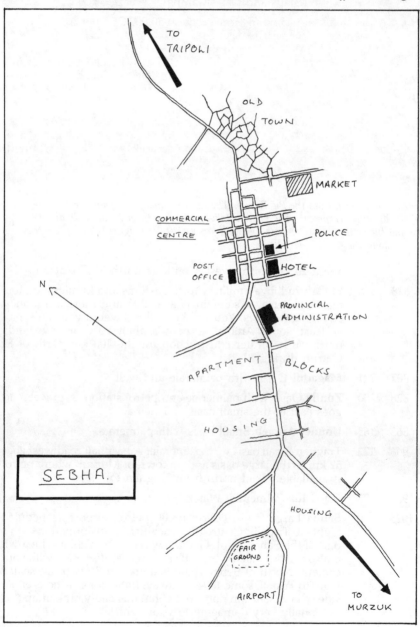

Itinerary No. 21 : Bilma — Agadez

Distance   610 km

Water   Bilma: plenty of good water outside Prefecture, opposite fort, and at piscine. Fashi: several small very shallow holes in the palmeraie, usually quite dirty. Arbre du Ténéré: saline and rather dirty water, from the well (40 m deep). Agadez: plenty, at public taps and Oasis Camping.

Fuel   Bilma and Dirkou: from Jerome at 50,000 CFA per 200 litres (see Djanet-Bilma Itinerary).

Before departure report to Police at Bilma Fort. They will radio details of your journey to Agadez. If you are overdue, Agadez Police will look for you. So, report your arrival in Agadez. There is a Police radio post at Fashi, but you do not have to report to them.

Tyres should be extremely low for the entire length of the journey to the Arbre du Ténéré (e.g. Range Rover with 1.0kg in front and 1.2kg at rear). There are balises every kilometre but in many places they have been buried by shifting parallel sand dunes. At times, the route deviates from the balises. Usually there are no tracks to follow as the wind obliterates them within 24 hours. Traffic is feeble on this route, and it is possible to die waiting for help. For these reasons, notifying the Police, taking a good guide, and having at least two sound vehicles are essential prerequisites for a successful crossing. 4x4 vehicle is advisable.

0	610	**Bilma** Leave Bilma via SW. Within two kilometres pass an old lighthouse (it used to be a real working lighthouse, to guide people across the Sea of Sand, in French colonial times). Then the route climbs up on to the Bilma Erg. This can be difficult as it is uphill in soft sand with a vehicle laden up with fuel and water.
160	450	**Falaise,** or escarpment. About 10 km before Fashi, the route descends through a very sandy pass to the Fashi palmeraie. This pass is dangerous because although it is very sandy it is also riddled with loose sharp rocks and stones. These could play havoc with the tyres as they have to remain at low pressure.
170	440	**Fashi** Large village of over 200 families. Has a school, shop, and Police station, with radio. Large pleasant palmeraie for good camping without getting too close to the town. Beware of thorns under the Acacia trees. To the east of town human skulls can be seen lying around on the ground. Bird life is quite phenomenal.

Leave Fashi by SW and climb up on to the erg again. For the first 40 km the dunes are not of the parallel type but high rolling type, and the sand is still soft. Further on, the dunes strike up the normal NE to SW parallel pattern, but get shallower to the west. By the Arbre du Ténéré they have disappeared completely, leaving just the vast, flat, empty Ténéré.

311	299	**Grave of Abubakar Kantana** This grave (about 30 km from the Arbre du Ténéré) is the first of seven, scattered over the next 30 km. The last is tragically only 3 km from the well at the

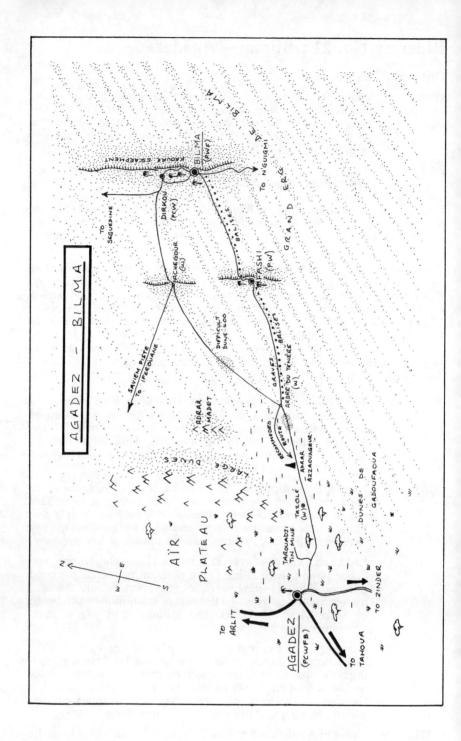

AGADEZ - BILMA

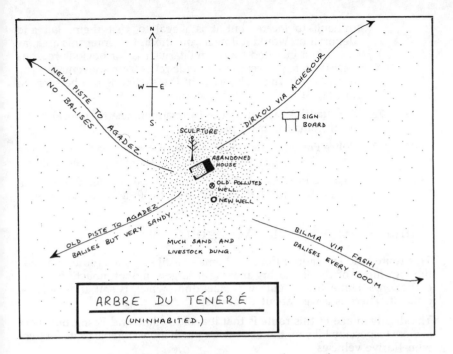

ARBRE DU TÉNÉRÉ

(UNINHABITED.)

Arbre. It is very sobering to see these sad graves.

341 269 **Arbre du Ténéré** Here one joins the piste from Dirkou via
Acheggour. There used to be a solitary tree alone in this vast
plain, but it was knocked down by a truck in 1973. The bits and
pieces have been salvaged, bolted together with steel supports
and this famous tree is now on display in the Niamey Museum.
In its place is a steel sculpture. There are two wells, one polluted
by a dead animal, but the other holds dirty saline water at a
depth of 40m.

On leaving the Arbre for Agadez do not follow the balises. This
route has become very sandy. Instead, follow the tracks to the
NW which deviate from the balises, but rejoin them about 80
km further on at Adrar Azzaouageur. The site is surrounded
by goat, sheep and camel dung and corpses. It can be crowded
with camel caravans between September and January.

421 189 **Adrar Azzaouageur** This small conical hill effectively marks the
end of the flat sandy Ténéré and the stony undulating Air
Plateau. Tyre pressures must be increased to the normal amount
for corrugated piste.

From here to Agadez the piste is more defined as it travels over
ridges, down rocky gullies, and through patches of thorn trees.
At times there are deep ruts, or 'ornières'.

453 157 **Tazolé** Here there is an airstrip occasionally used by the army.

South of here among the crescent dunes of the Ténéré (the
Dunes of Gadoufaoua), there are the complete intact skeletons
of Dinosaurs (*Ouranosaurus nigeriensis*) and a giant prehistoric
crocodile (*Sarcosuchus imperator*). Not only is the exact spot

443

difficult to locate, but it is illegal to visit them. Jail and deportation would follow if you attempt to enter this area, as it is often guarded by the military. It is for obvious reasons necessary to protect these unique relics from souvenir hungry tourists. Alternatively, casts of the skeletons can be seen on display at the Niamey Museum.

538	72	**Tarouadji** A piste from the Tarouadji mines (tin mines) to the north joins the main piste.
607	3	**Police Post** Piste joins main Agadez to Zinder road, near a Police post. Give personal and vehicle details to the policeman there.
610	0	**Agadez** Report to Police on arrival (see Agadez map). Bank hours 08.00 to 11.30 and 15.30 to 16.30. Monday to Friday.

Bilma — Agadez via Achegour

This route is 40 km shorter than the Bilma - Fashi - Agadez route. It avoids the big dunes of the Bilma Erg making it largely monotonously flat. The exception is Dune 400: a solitary parallel dune which is soft and could be difficult. There is a well about 10 m deep at Achegour.

The disadvantage of this route is that it avoids Bilma and Fashi. But there is more (especially Libyan) traffic, as it is a much more suitable route for two-wheel drive vehicles.

Itinerary No. 22 : Nguigmi — Bilma

Distance   840 km

Water   Nguigmi: at petrol supply point. Koufey: small well at village (artesian supply). Ngourti: several wells at village (11m). Bedouaram: in ruined fort there is a very deep well (30m); the water would need to be filtered. Bilma: at piscine, opposite fort, opposite prefecture.

Fuel   Nguigmi: petrol station (but supply is not guaranteed). Bilma: see Jerome or his assistant Ibrahim Mohammed. (Supplies not guaranteed, and sold for 50,000 CFA per 200 litres.) If no fuel at Bilma try Jerome's depot in Dirkou.

To travel the full length of this route a good guide is essential. Ask around in Nguigmi, or Bilma or Dirkou. As far as Bedouaran there are recognizable traces of previous vehicles. But north of there vehicle traces are obliterated quickly by shifting sand. Especially between Dibella and Bilma, where there are hundreds of parallel sand ridges to cross, a guide is absolutely essential as their pattern varies from month to month and only an experienced eye can pick up the subtle similarities with the landscape encountered on previous trips. Also, traffic is extremely rare and virtually non-existent between March and December, so three 4x4 vehicles with good equipment are essential. Similarly, because of the soft sand and because of the zig-zag path necessary to find passages through and over the dunes, fuel consumption for this route is phenomenal, e.g. a 4 cylinder petrol Land Rover should carry 550 to 600 litres of petrol. As a result it is preferable to travel this route south to north, as in the more difficult northern section you will have less fuel and water to carry having already used much of it.

Allow between 5 and 10 days to do the trip and carry water on the basis of at least 10 days travelling.

The route starts in low thorn bush country or Sahel, but by Bedouaran this has thinned out into desert with scattered grass and thorn tree patches, and the beginning of low parallel sand dunes. Between Agadem and Bilma there are hundreds of big dunes to traverse. This is real desert.

Be very careful, especially when the sun is high, not to lose track of the relief in front of you. There is a very real danger of accidentally going over the steep leeward side of a dune. If this does happen don't try to steer out of it, you will roll sideways down to the bottom. Similarly don't brake, as this will cause your front to dig in and you may cartwheel down the slope. If anything, it is best to just ride it out straight to the bottom, and hope everybody has their seat belts on.

Be careful where you point your camera in the area as there is a prison for political detainees at Nguigmi and the authorities are quite sensitive.

While the civil war continues in neighbouring Chad, this route is potentially hazardous because it is so close to the frontier. Camel caravans no longer operate this route because there have been attacks by bandit groups from Chad. The Niger military are also particularly sensitive and there is always the danger that trigger happy soldiers in a highly charged situation could open fire on innocent tourists.

0   840   **Nguigmi** Head north along laterite road (after checking out at Police post). This road soon develops 'ornières'.

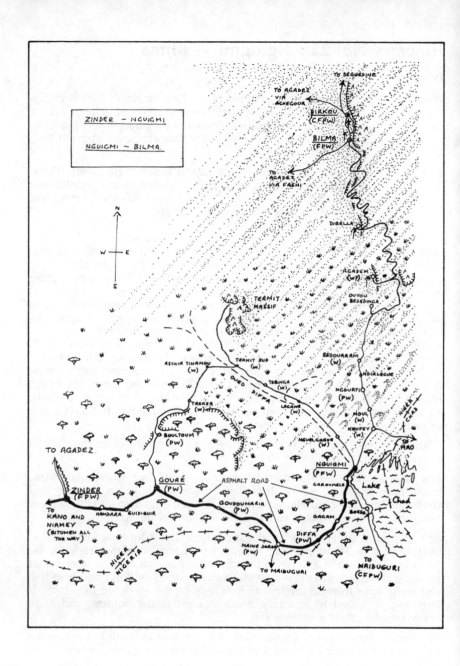

70	770	**Koufey** A small Kanuri village with artesian water supply. To the east, the piste to Chad travels across the frontier to Mao. This is guerrilla war territory. Not only does the Chad government forbid tourism here but also it is extremely dangerous. Head NNE from Koufey.
136	704	**Ngourti** A small village with good water (11m).
183	657	**Bedouaran** A nomad village, water at 6 m. From here a guide is essential.
313	527	**Agadem** Abandoned fort by a falaise and palmeraie. Uninhabited, Doubtful water in well at fort (5m).
415	425	**Dibella** Abandoned village at palmeraie near very small falaise. Usually no water. From this point the dunes northward are very big and steep.
840	0	**Bilma** Although Bilma is only 130 km from Dibella as the crow flies it takes over 400 km of tortuous travel to cross the many sand ridges. N.B. Report to Police at fort on arrival.

Massif de Termit There is a little used piste NW from Nguigmi to N'guelgague (water can be found 20 m down), Lagane (water is 15 m down), Malam Tebinga (water 20 m down) and to Termit Sud (water 24 m down); a total distance of 260 km. At Termit Sud a piste extends SW via Aschia Tinamou (water at 70 m), Tasker (water at 16 m down) and Boultoum (water at 41 m) and to Gouré on the main Zinder - Nguigmi road.

However, some deep Saharan tour operators e.g. Jerrycan, have taken groups north from Termit Sud to the Termit Plateau, and thence across the low Ténéré Erg to Agadez. A guide would be essential, but it would be a most interesting journey, requiring less fuel than the trip to Bilma from Nguigmi. The Termit Plateau is littered with seabed fossils and Neolithic hand tools, and is very rarely visited.
N.B. 50 km South of Tazolé on the Agadez-Bilma piste are the Dunes of Guadafawa, where Dinosaur skeleton remains are protected by law, and access is strictly forbidden.

Itinerary No. 23: Zinder — Nguigmi

Distance   602 km. Asphalt road all the way.

Water   Zinder: at petrol stations. Gouré: at encampment. Nguigmi: at petrol point.

Fuel   Petrol stations at Zinder, Diffa (not guaranteed), Nguigmi (not guaranteed).

0   602   **Zinder** Leave town by SE past the fort and prison.

177   425   **Gouré** Small town with post office, market, shops, petrol station (rarely functions), Campement, airstrip.

399   203   **Maine-Soroa** Campement, market. Border post if travelling to Nigeria. Police station.

506   96   **Diffa** Police post, market, petrol station (not guaranteed).

602   0   **Nguigmi** Market town close to Lake Chad. Petrol station (not guaranteed), shops, post office, airport, pharmacy. Report to Police on heading north to Bilma. Ask them for advice on recruiting a guide, which is essential. No bank. (Note: also no bank at Bilma, Dirkou, etc.)

Itinerary No. 24 : Niamey — Zinder

Distance   909 km

Water   No problem, available at all petrol stations.

Fuel   Petrol stations at Niamey, Dosso (usually but no guarantee), Dogondoutchi (sometimes), Birni N'Konni (usually but no guarantee), Maradi and Zinder.

The route is full width asphalt except for 52 km of narrow tar just west of Zinder. The countryside is low tree savanna all the way. Consequently there is good private camping and usually plenty of firewood.

0	909	**Niamey** All facilities. See map and special section on Niamey.

Leave city via the SE past airport. Check out at Police post just after airport.

107	802	**Birni Nguare** Petrol station rarely functions. Market. Junction with laterite road north to Fillingué
140	769	**Dosso** No bank, but usually fuel. Stores. Post Office. Report to Police at station near lorry park, only if asked to, at station on entry to town.

If heading south to Benin or Nigeria, turn off to the south at the petrol station on the Niamey side of the town. If heading west go straight through the town.

277	632	**Dogondoutchi** Main road by-passes town. Report to Police in town only if asked to at barrier. Post Office. Chemist shop. Petrol stations (sometimes fuel).
422	487	**Birni N'Konni** Usually fuel available. Post Office. Bank. Campement (hotel), bars, restaurant, Police station, secondary school (see map). Report to Police only if asked to at barrier on entry to the town.
437	472	Road to Tahoua branches off to the north. Stop at Police post only if asked to at barrier on entry to the town.
457	452	**Galmi** Cement factory.
476	433	**Madaoua** Sudan Interior Mission (U.S.A.) and hospital.
672	237	**Maradi** Town is 2 km south of main road. Banks. Post Office. VW and Peugeot agency (Sonida). Market. Lorry park. (See map).
764	145	**Gazaoua** Large village with market and shops.
795	114	**Tessaoua** Large village with roadside stalls.
857	52	**Takieta** Village at junction with main Zinder — Kano road. Narrow tar to Zinder.
909	0	**Zinder** All facilities: Petrol stations. Lorry park. Banks. Two hotels. Supermarkets. VW and Peugeot agency (Sonida). Airport. Police. Post Office. Report to Police only if asked to do so. Renault agency, Sonimeg.

SH 29

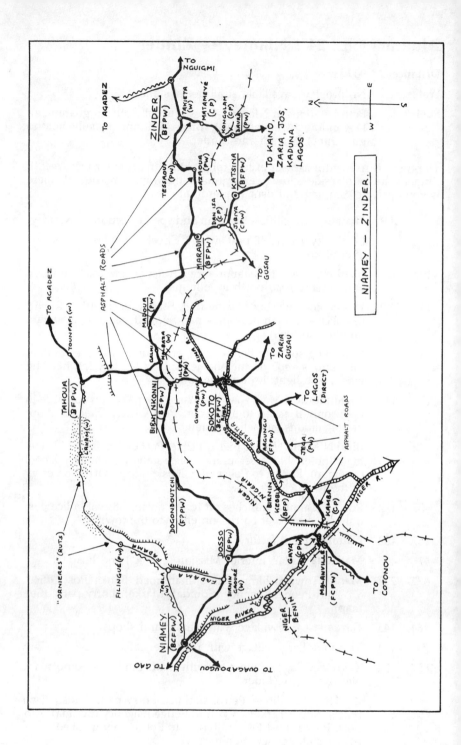

Itinerary No. 25 : Kano — Maradi

Distance   314 km (For map see Itinerary No. 27)

Water   Petrol stations at Kano (on tap), Bichi, Yashi, Katsina, Maradi; and near market at Jibya.

Fuel   Kano: many petrol stations, but supplies are dependent upon transport from the south and electricity for pumps (frequent black-outs). If necessary wait several hours in the queues, as there is no assurance of fuel at Katsina and rarely any elsewhere, until Maradi. Katsina: several petrol stations, but supplies may run out. Maradi: regular supplies at several garages (but considerably more expensive than in Nigeria).

Many small villages enroute, have pumps, but very rarely have petrol. Some of these are Bichi, Tashi, and Jibya. The road is bitumen all the way and should cause no problems.

0	314	**Kano** Leave the city via the NW, past the central market, lorry park, and military barracks.
40	274	**Bichi** Town with market, non functioning petrol station, and two large secondary schools. Many shops and small mechanics' workshops.
92	222	**Yashi** Market village at junction with main road south to Talata Mafara and Lagos. Beware, many big trucks.
174	140	**Katsina** Traditional Hausa trading city. Many shops, petrol stations. Impressive city wall and Emir's palace. Famous for the celebrations and ceremonies at the Salah at the end of Ramadan. During these festivities there is a spectacular charge of knights in traditional armour and regalia. Not to be missed if you are in the area at the time. These horsemen abruptly end their charge right in front of their Emir's grandstand with much colour, noise and dust.
		Leave Katsina by the NE. There is by-pass road around the city.
219	95	**Jibya** Market town on border. Stop at the Police barrier. There is a branch road to the SW to Gusau and Sokoto. On leaving the town go through Customs and Immigration formalities, not forgetting Carnet and currency declaration. (On entering Nigeria from the north ask for this currency form).
229	85	**Dan Isa** This is a market town. Go through frontier formalities.
314	0	**Maradi** Large town. Several petrol stations. Police (report only if asked to). Large Hausa market. Mosque. VW and Peugeot agency (Scoa-Sonida).
		For Zinder or Birni N'Konni leave Maradi by the north and 2 km out of town join the main Zinder-Niamey road.

Kano

The largest city in Northern Nigeria, with a population of about a million. It is essentially an African city with a history going back over a thousand

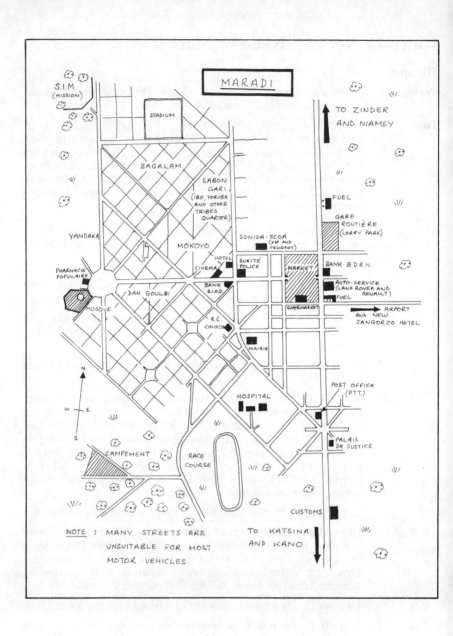

years, as a trading centre and a crossroads of the trans Saharan camel caravan routes and the bush routes to Yorubaland and the West African coast.

It still has impressive remnants of a city wall. There is a very important mosque in the centre of the old city, near the Emir's Palace. The traditional indigo dyeing industry is still in operation and the dye pits can be seen near the gates to the old city called 'Kofar Mata'. Kano is the centre of a very important agricultural region which produces large quantities of cotton and groundnuts (peanuts). Unfortunately, with the oil boom currently experienced by Nigeria, both these commodities have fallen behind in production. In 1978 there weren't even enough groundnuts to operate the big Kano mills for one day.

There is no need to report to the Police.

Hotels: Central Hotel is the main expensive international standard hotel with restaurants, swimming pool, bars, tennis courts, and air-conditioning in all rooms. A new expensive hotel is the Daula. A good but cheaper and less elaborate hotel is the Kandara Palace Hotel in the Syrian quarter but all rooms have air-conditioning and showers.

There are other smaller and cheaper, more modest hotels, of varying repute. Another large international standard hotel can be found 80 km south of Kano: the Bagauda Lakes Hotel, with parklike grounds and air-conditioned rondavels.

The Sudan Interior Mission operates a Guest House (no smoking or drinking) with very clean but simple chalets with fans and showers. Family style meals are served (do not start eating before grace has been said). Their iced tea is delicious.

Camping: The Kano Club used to allow overlanders to camp at the back of the premises. Camping is now a problem as the population around Kano is quite dense for miles around. The club does allow overlanders to have Monday to Friday membership. Facilities include bars, lounge, pool room, tennis, badminton and squash courts, swimming pool and a good restaurant.

Restaurants: Eating out French style is not a feature of ex-British Nigeria. The few top class restaurants are confined to the Central Hotel, Magwan Water Restaurant, Kano Club, Pink Peacock and Lebanese Club. There are hundreds of small street-side restaurants which sell Hausa, Yoruba and Ibo food.

Post Office: 08.00 to 17.00. Poste Restante service.

Banks: Hours—08.00 to 14.00 with early closing on Fridays. There are many banks, the biggest being Union Bank of Nigeria (formerly Barclays), First Bank of Nigeria (formerly Standard) and Bank of the North. Also, African Continental Bank, Arab Bank, International Bank for Africa, and Savanna Bank.

Hospitals: There is a big Kano State Hospital where queues are likely to be long. There is also a specialist eye hospital run by the Sudan Interior Mission which draws patients from all over West Africa and is capable of major eye surgery.

Tourist Office: There are no tourist information facilities. However, road maps of Nigeria and street maps of Kano are sold at the Central Hotel bookstall.

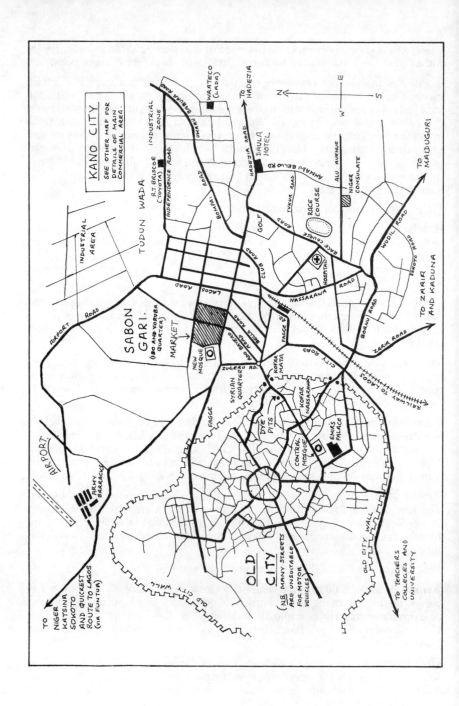

Garages: Mercedes, Renault: Leventis Motors. Volkswagen: Mandilas, Allens. Peugeot: SCOA. Bedford, Opel: Niger Motors and U.T.C. Fiat: Allens Motors. Lada, Polski-Fiat: WAATECO. Land Rover, Morris: BEWAC. Toyota: R.T. Briscoe.

Airlines: KLM, UTA, Sabena, British Caledonian, Nigeria Airways, and Egyptian Airlines, all operates services out of Kano to Europe and the Middle East. They have booking offices in the centre of Kano. There are also daily flights by Boeing 737 or Fokker F28 to Sokoto, Kaduna, Jos, Maiduguri and Lagos.

Buses: Hundreds of small private operators run services by coach, mini-bus, VW bus, and Peugeot taxis, all over Nigeria, from the lorry park. The Mid-West line operates a fast coach service all the way south to Lagos, from its depot near the railway station.

Railway: Daily train service south to Kaduna, Ilorin, Ibadan and Lagos.

Diplomatic: Lebanese Consulate in Sokoto Rd., off Wudil Road. Niger Consulate, Alu Ave; near the racecourse.

Shopping: There are several large department stores and supermarkets e.g. Levantis, Chellerams, Kingsway. The central Market is one of the biggest in West Africa. The Sabon Gari area to the north of the town is full of very useful small shops, like chemists, motor car parts, electrical goods, motor repairs, bookshops, etc.

Souvenirs at very inflated prices can be found at the stalls opposite the Central Hotel.

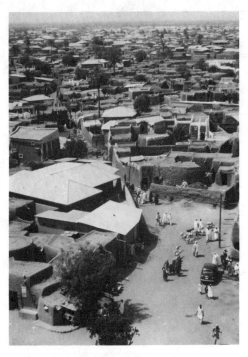

Inside the old city of Kano. For centuries this Hausa city has been a major trading centre and today it has a population approaching a million

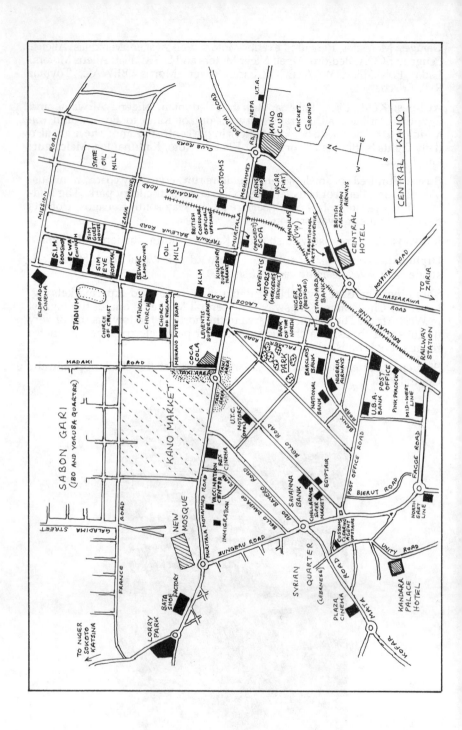

CENTRAL KANO

Itinerary No. 26 : Kano — Agadez

Distance   736 km.

Water   On tap at petrol stations at Kano and Zinder. Wells at Tanout (near Fort) and Aderbissinat (at village, 15m). Public taps at various places in Agadez. There are also several wells on the way, but the water can be a hundred metres down.

Fuel   Kano: many petrol stations throughout city, but availability depends on the arrival of fuel from the south, and on whether there is electricity to operate the pumps. You may have to wait many hours in queues. However, fuel is cheap in Nigeria and enroute to Zinder you are unlikely to find supplies, even though there are several towns with pumps e.g. Daura. Zinder: several petrol stations, usually no problems. Tanout: sometimes available from a trader, in 200 litre lots. You will find this man, beside the main road, under some trees, near the market. Agadez: several petrol stations, but if not available wait several days for supplies to arrive.

The road to Zinder is asphalt all the way, although there is a section of narrow tar mainly in Niger. Between Zinder and Agadez there is a made up laterite (gravel) road, but it is usually badly corrugated and for this reason it may be preferable to take the Tahoua route. During 1985, work started on building a new asphalt road from Zinder to Agadez. Most of the route northwards is through increasingly sparse Sahel, thorn tree semi desert. Therefore, there is usually plenty of firewood for camp fires, and usually there is a sparser population after Daura so that your privacy should not be disturbed. North of Zinder ostriches are frequently seen.

Kano, Daura and Zinder are essentially Hausa towns, but many Fulanis will be seen with their livestock, especially at wells, and further north the Kel Gress Touaregs will predominate.

0	736	**Kano** Leave the city via the NW past the central market, the lorry park, and the military barracks, along the road to Katsina. See Kano street map.
20	716	Leave the main Katsina road and head north.
137	599	**Daura** Traditional Hausa town, with an Emir's palace, and remnants of a city wall.
150	586	**Kongolam** Frontier barrier. Have Carnet processed. Don't forget currency declaration.
185	551	**Matameye** Frontier barrier.
213	523	**Takieta** Join main Zinder - Niamey road and head east.
237	499	**Zinder** Large town with all facilities. Two hotels, two banks, VW and Peugeot agencies (SCOA), two supermarkets, a market, lorry station, etc.

Report to Police if asked to. It is possible to sell surplus Naira at an inferior rate (ask at petrol stations, or at Central Hotel), and conversely one can buy Naira, at a very favourable rate (but be careful if taking them into Nigeria). There is no satisfactory camping in town. Several petrol stations.

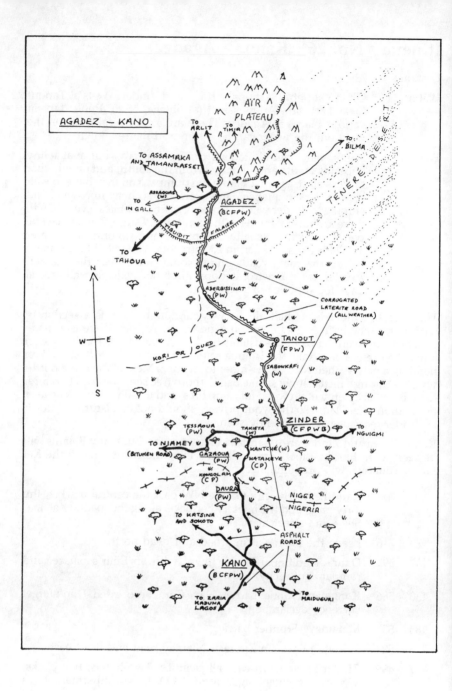

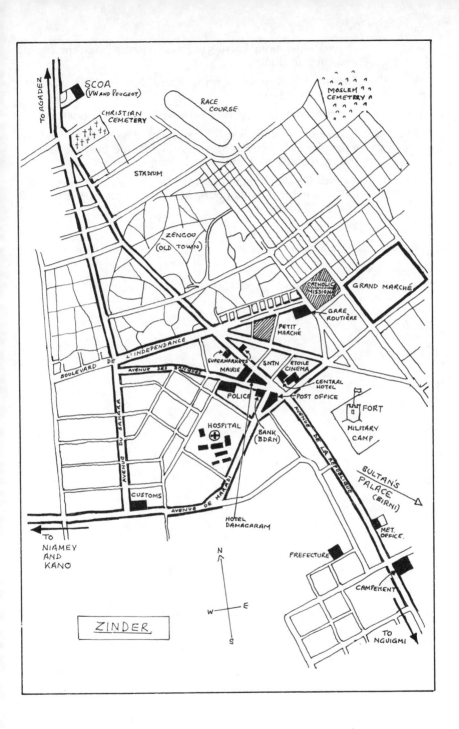

Leave Zinder along corrugated road (laterite), past the airport and rubbish dump.

397 339 **Tanout** Small town with military fort. Petrol available, sometimes. Market.

575 161 **Aderbissinat** Small village with well and police post.

654 82 **Falaise de Tiguidit** Small escarpment. The road descends to a flat plain which leads to Agadez. Often it is possible to leave the corrugated road and travel alongside it.

736 0 **Agadez** On outskirts of town stop at Police post. Then report to Police in town. Bank hours: Monday to Friday 08.00 to 11.30 and 15.30 to 16.30.

Itinerary No. 27 : Sokoto — Kano

Distances   Sokoto - Gusau - Jibya - Katsina - Kano   695 km.
                  Sokoto - Gusau - Funtua - Yashi - Kano   647 km.
                  Sokoto - Gusau - Zaria - Kano   607 km.

Water   Widely available in all towns and villages en route.

Fuel   Petrol available from petrol stations at Katsina, Malamfashi, Gusau, Funtua, Samaru, Zaria, Sokoto and Kano. However, supplies can run out and it may be necessary to wait several hours and even days for deliveries. Some smaller localities have local traders who sell petrol infrequently from small tanks, with hand pumps e.g. Denge, Maru, Talata Mafara, Mainchi, and Yashi. Here the price may be more than the legal 18 kobo per litre.

All roads are full width tar seal except for Gusau - Jibya section which is narrow tar (single vehicle width only) and broken up in places.

Denge Small village. Birthplace of Sultan of Sokoto. Roadside stalls. Sometimes petrol.

Talata Mafara Boom town due to construction of mammoth irrigation scheme at nearby Bakalori, by large Italian company. Hospital shops, bank, Italian town, schools, and sometimes petrol.

Mainchi Cotton mill, roadside stalls, sometimes petrol.

Maru Large secondary school, roadside stalls, sometimes petrol.

Gusau Large town served by railway. Many petrol stations, schools, three banks, government catering rest house (for accommodation and meals),

The massive granite rock at Kotorkoshi. Well worth a climb

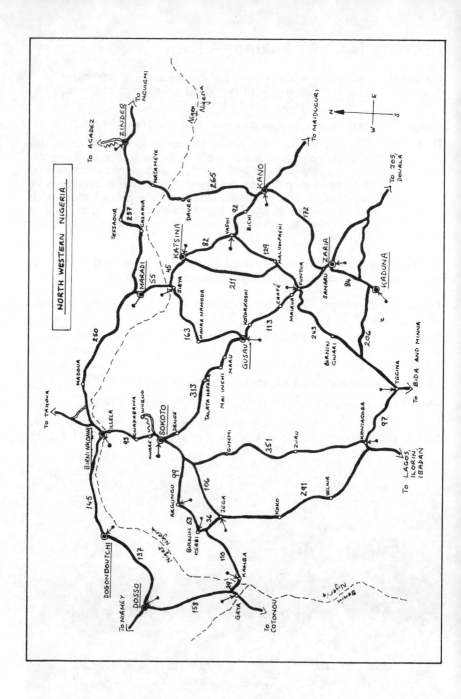

mechanics, shops, groundnut mill.

Kotorkoshi Small village at foot of gigantic granite rock. Well worth spending a day climbing. Rock is about 20 km in circumference and just on 330m (1,000 ft.) above the surrounding countryside (about the size of Ayers Rock in Central Australia). There is no need for climbing gear.

Chafe Small but bustling village. Sudan Interior Mission and many roadside stalls.

Mairua Small village but with very good government run catering rest house overlooking a lake. Good food, accommodation and cold drinks.

Funtua Town with many shops, bank, petrol stations and schools. Road junction with main roads to Sokoto, Kano, Zaria and Lagos.

Samaru Junction of roads to Sokoto, Kano and Zaria. Big Amadhu Bello University complex. Airport, shops, restaurants, petrol stations, mechanics.

Zaria Old Hausa trading city with wall and impressive Emir's Palace. Railway station, supermarkets (Leventis, Chellerams), petrol stations, teaching hospital, VW agency (Mandilas), Peugeot agency (SCOA), Leyland agency (BEWAC), Mercedes and Renault agency (Leventis), Ford agency (Allens), racecourse, Club etc. Government catering rest house and government conference centre, each provide reasonable accommodation and meals. Many local hotels.

Kaduna Former British capital of Northern Nigeria. Large colonial style town with gracious avenues in the 'best' suburbs, but more African style houses everywhere else. Centre for many international organisations. Former Northern National Asssembly building, large racecourse, Club (members only), airport, many banks, VW and Peugeot agency (Mandilas and SCOA respectively), Leyland general agency (Leventis), Ford agency (Allens), General Motors, Bedford, Chevrolet and Opel agency (U.T.C.), Lada agency (WAATECO), Toyota agency (R.T. Briscoe). British High Commission and Consulate, British Council, many petrol stations, and supermarkets (Leventis, Kingsway and Chellerams). For cheap, new and very good motor vehicle spare parts, visit the Ibo traders shops in the Sabon Gari area. Accommodation is a problem, apart from the very expensive luxury Hamdallah International Hotel and the Durbah Hotel. Offices of K.L.M., British Caledonian, Niger Airways and Sabena.

All routes in and out of the city are via the north.

Kaura Namoda Railhead. Small tobacco growing area. Bank. Occasionally petrol.

Malamfashi Large market village. Shops, schools and sometimes petrol.

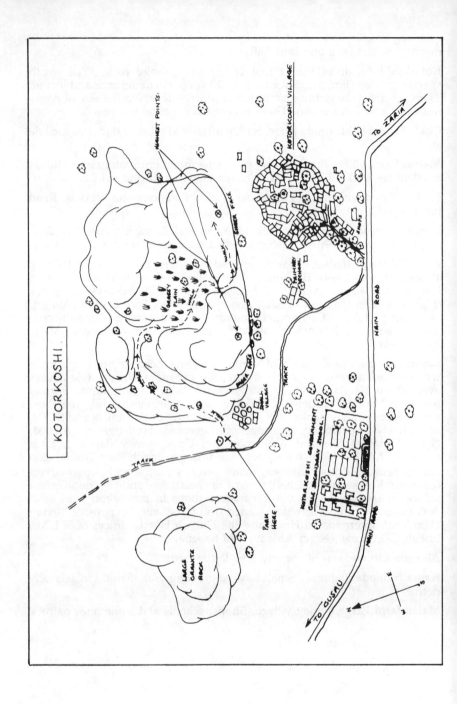

KOTORKOSHI

HIGHEST POINTS.

TO ZARIA

KOTORKOSHI VILLAGE

SHOPS

TIMBER FACE

WALK

PRIMARY SCHOOL

GAME PLAIN

WALK

MAIN ROAD

WATER FACE

WALK

SMALL VILLAGE

TRACK

TRACK

KOTRAKOSHI GOVERNMENT GIRLS SECONDARY SCHOOL

PARK HERE

LARGE GRANITE ROCK

MAIN ROAD

TO GUSAU

N
E
S
W

464

Itinerary No. 28 : Niamey — Ouagadougou

Distance   520 km.

Water   Niamey and Ouagadougou at petrol stations, and from wells at most villages enroute.

Fuel   Petrol stations at Niamey (no problems), Fada N'Gourma (no regular supply), Ouagadougou and Koupela.

From Niamey to Kantchari there is a good but corrugated laterite road. Between Kantchari and Ouagadougou a new asphalt road will be completed during 1985. Most of the country is low savanna vegetation, affording privacy when camping and plenty of firewood.

0	520	**Niamey** Head west from the centre of Niamey, across the Niger River by Pont du Kennedy.
3	517	Junction: turn right for Ouagadougou and left (south) for Say and Parc du W.
70	450	**Lamorde Torodi** Niger frontier post. End of asphalt.
147	373	**Kantchari** Burkina Faso (Upper Volta) frontier. Sometimes (rarely) petrol is sold. Market village.
297	223	**Fada N'Gourma** Market town. Sometimes petrol is sold. Air strip. Police station. A road heads directly south from here to Benin. For Ouagadougou head west along asphalt road.
385	135	**Koupela** Police station. Village with a market and roadside stalls. Sometimes petrol is sold. Junction with main road from Togo to the south.
520	0	**Ouagadougou** Banks, international airport, petrol stations. Report to the Police on arrival. Several hotels, including luxury class (expensive) one. U.S. Embassy, but no British Representative. Toyota, Land Rover, VW Peugeot, and Renault agencies. Camping can be a problem as one has to travel a long way out of town (city) to find an open area of countryside and privacy.

South from Ouagadougou there is a good full width bitumen road to the coast at Accra. To the NW is a laterite road to Mopti. To the west is a well used laterite road to Bobo - Dioulasso and thence either to the south to Abidjan or north (bitumen) to Bamako.

An interesting return route to Niamey is via Kaya and Dori. There is no guarantee of fuel at either place and the road is sometimes officially closed in the rainy season (July—August). Border formalities are at Dori and Tera (in Niger).

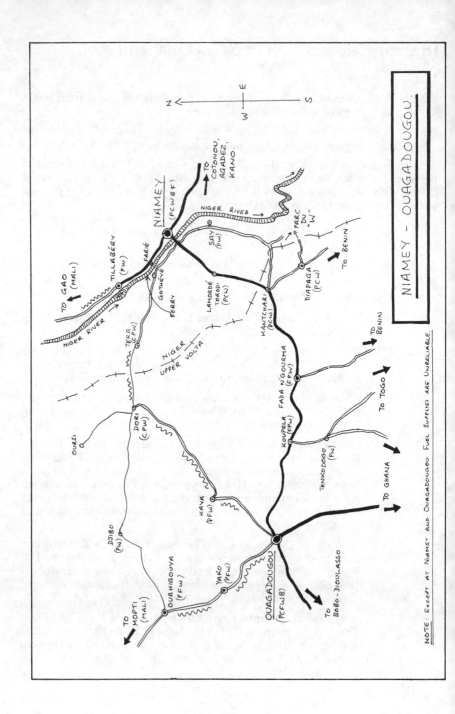

NIAMEY – OUAGADOUGOU

NOTE: Except at Niamey and Ouagadougou Fuel Supplies are Unreliable.

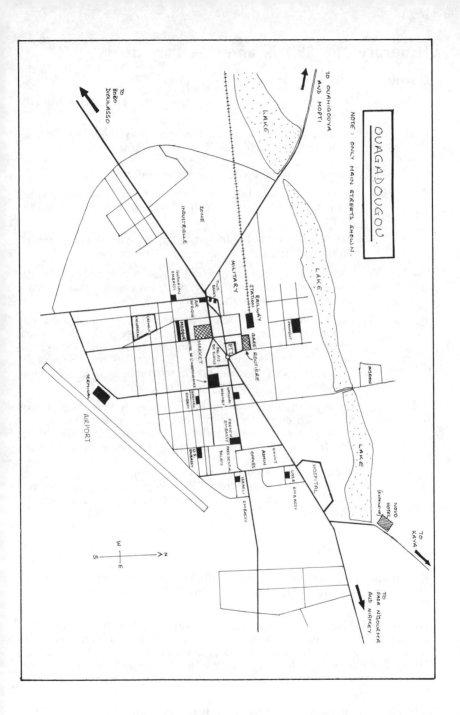

Itinerary No. 29 : Niamey — Parc du W.

Distance: 150 km.

Water   Niamey at petrol station. Say, from river. La Tapoua, from the Campement.

Fuel   Niamey at petrol stations. Say, rarely available. La Tapoua, sometimes available from Park administration.

0	150	**Niamey** Leave the city via Pont du Kennedy.
3	147	Junction at end of bitumen. Turn right for Ouagadougou but left (south) for Say and Parc du W. A mildly corrugated laterite road.
50	100	**Say** At entrance to the town is a Police post. Without entering the town, turn right along a good laterite road.
100	50	**Tamou** Turn left (south). Straight ahead goes to Upper Volta, only a few kilometres away. Narrow smooth laterite road, through savanna, bush country.
150	0	**La Tapoua (Parc du W)** See administration to check in and pay park entrance fee. There are actually three parks next to each other, but in three different countries, Niger, Burkina Faso and Benin. The Park administration sells excellent road maps of the park and it is worthwhile asking where the best game viewing places are. It is obligatory to have a guide.

For accommodation at the hotel, it may be necessary to book at the Office of Tourism in Niamey. Best game viewing time is late in the afternoon and early morning, especially during the dry season. Game to be seen include: lions, elephants, warthog, crocodiles, waterbuck, buffalo, roan antelope, reed-buck, harte-beest, duikers, oribi, hippos, porcupine, rock daissies, aardvarks, cheetahs, jackals, spotted and striped hyenas, leopards, baboons, vervet monkeys and big ground hornbills.

Niamey

On arrival in Niamey see the Sûreté with two passport photos; the Police at the barriers on the edge of town will not let you leave unless you have done so.

Hotels: There are four big international standard hotels, with restaurants, swimming pools, beer gardens, bars, and all rooms air-conditioned and with showers. They are expensive. They are, in order of price range: the Grand Hotel, Hotel Sahel, Les Roniers, and the Hotel Terminus. Slightly cheaper but still with air-conditioning, though without a swimming pool, is the Hotel Rivoli.

Camping: Camping Rio Bravo has a lovely setting on the banks of the Niger, about 20 km north of Niamey (see Niamey — Gao itinerary). It has become run down recently. There is now a new camping ground near the US embassy with good facilities.

Boubon: Campement on an island in the Niger River about 25 km north of

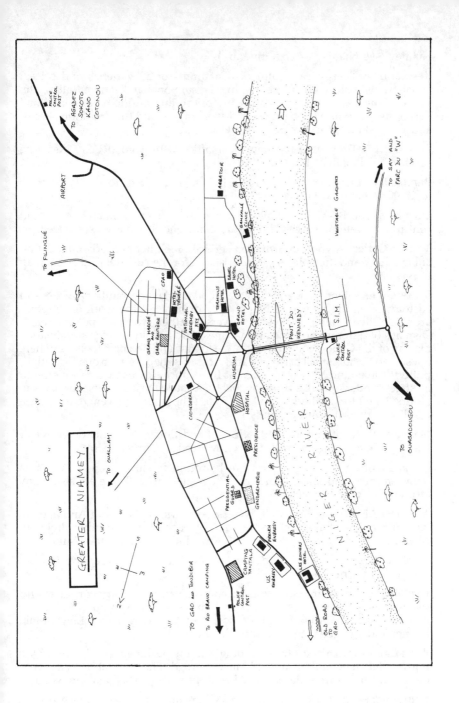

GREATER NIAMEY

469

Niamey (see Niamey — Gao itinerary).

Restaurants: There is a wealth of restaurants of all varieties and prices: Lebanese, French, Vietnamese, Benin, Hausa, Songhai, Djerma, Italian, etc. Three of the best and more reasonably priced are: Le Vietnam (near Hotel Terminus), Le Safari Club (opposite Rivoli and behind the Zed Club Disco), and the restaurant in the Sahel Hotel.

Post Office: There is a big new post office with a good Poste Restante service and Philatelic Bureau

Banks: Two main banks: BDRN and BIAO. Hours 08.00 to 12.00 and 16.00 to 17.00 Monday to Friday.

Hospitals: Tourists will normally be turned away from the main hospital and sent to a private one e.g. Clinique de Gamkalle. It is very expensive.

Tourist Office: A good information service. Book here for accommodation at Parc du W and the hotel Ayorou. Also ask for the very detailed street map of Niamey.

Museum: Excellent. Free entry. Really good displays of traditional dress and customs of all the people of Niger. Live displays of the work of different artisans (silversmiths, weavers, carvers, leather workers, potters, etc.). Displays of different housing and villages, and a really excellent prehistoric display of the Gadoufaoua dinosaur, paleolithic and neolithic tools etc. There is also a zoo, and a small bar. The Chief Artisan's shop sells top quality leather, pottery, silver and brassware, etc., at fixed prices lower than those offered by street vendors and of a superior quality. A catalogue is available for perusal. Hours: 08.00 to 12.00 and 15.30 to 17.00. (The Arbre du Ténéré is also on display in the Museum grounds.)

Garages: Peugeot and VW: SONIDA. Land Rover, Renault, Opel: Niger Afrique. Toyota, Simca Ford: CFAO. Mercedes, Citroen: SEAN.

Cheaper, but good, spare parts can be found in small shops in the area between the grand Marché and the Nouveau Marché. There are also many efficient back street mechanics' shops.

Airlines: Air Afrique, Air Mali, Nigeria Airways, U.T.A., and Air Niger all have offices. Several direct flights to Paris each week and other flights to Abidjan, Algiers and Lagos as well as to Zinder, Agadez and Kano.

Gare Routière: near the Grand Marché. SNTN operate bus services to Gao, Agadez and Zinder.

Diplomatic: There are embassies or consulates or honorary consulates for the following nations: (see the street map for some locations) Algeria, Belgium, Britain, China, Egypt, France, West Germany, Israel, Libya, Mali, Netherlands, Nigeria, Sweden and USSR.

Bush Camping: The best free camping is in the bush between 10 and 15 km north of Niamey on the Gao and Tillabery road. The population is not very dense and there are quite a few trees to provide privacy and firewood.

Shopping: Several large supermarkets where many European type groceries can be purchased are to be found, near the Grande Marché and opposite the Petit Marché. (Items for sale include mushrooms and lettuce, regularly flown in from Paris.) There are also the Petit Marché, the Grand Marché and the Nouveau Marché. The Petit Marché is handy for fresh vegetables (e.g. lettuce, cucumbers, carrots, onions, tomatoes, cabbage, potatoes, cassava,

Niamey from the Pont du Kennedy which takes traffic for Burkina Faso (Upper Volta) across the Niger River

The pottery market in the centre of Niamey. These are all products of a thriving industry at the village of Tondibia on the banks of the Niger River some 40 km north of Niamey

471

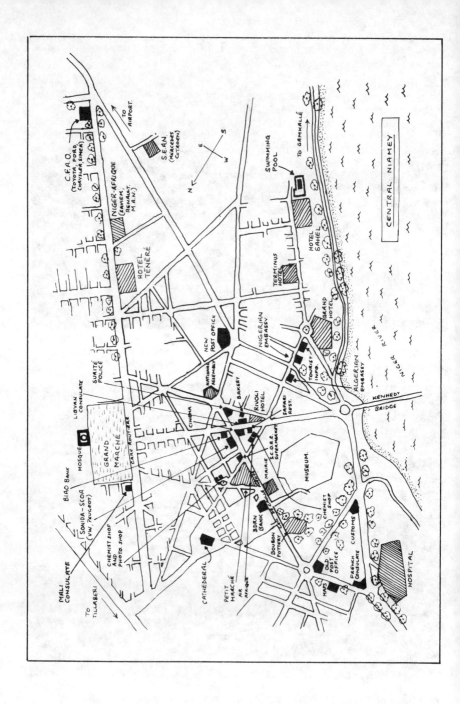

CENTRAL NIAMEY

472

yams, garlic), fruits (mangoes, bananas, pineapples, pawpaws, oranges, melons, etc.), eggs, meat, herbs and spices, etc.

Bakeries: one next to Rivoli Hotel and one behind SCOA - SONIDA. Souvenirs are probably best purchased from the Chief Artisan's shop at the Museum, though for Malien artifacts street vendors are quite reasonable. There is a Boubon pottery market opposite the BDRN bank. There are several big chemists shops (e.g. Pharmacie Nouvelle next to Air Afrique, Pharmacie Centrale behind the Petit Marché). Films and camera equipment are available from the photography shop next door to the Pharmacie Centrale. French newspapers, and magazines (including Time and Newsweek) are available at the bookshop between the Rivoli Hotel and the Libyan Information Centre, and nightly in the restaurants, in particular the Sahel Hotel's restaurant.

Itinerary No. 30 : Niamey — Gao

Distance 443 km. It is planned to complete a new asphalt road between Niamey and Gao late in 1985.

Water Niamey, at petrol stations, camping ground or hotel. Tillabery, at petrol station. Ayorou, at campement. Gao, at petrol stations. The whole route is never more than 5 km east of the Niger River and there is always water in it.

Fuel Niamey: At petrol stations, no problems. Fill up here. Tillabery: At petrol station, but no guarantee of supply. Ayorou: There is a petrol station, but it rarely has fuel at the pumps. Gao: At least three petrol stations, but they can at times run out. Wait till supplies arrive or, if desperate, visit the gouvernorat. N.B. If heading north up the Tanezrouft route there is no fuel available until Reggane, a distance of 1,368 km. If heading west, there is usually fuel at Mopti, a distance of 617 km, but to the NW at Timbuktu there is usually no fuel. (A distance of 424 km from Gao.)

Between Niamey and Tillabery there is a good, full width bitumen road which passes through low semi-arid savanna or 'sahel' country. This gets more sparse in Mali towards Gao. Between Tillabery and the frontier there is a good, but corrugated laterite road. Between the frontier and Gao it is similar, but not as well maintained. All the way there is good private camping in the bush with plenty of firewood. North and south of Ayorou there are at least two groups of giraffes (the only giraffes to be found in the whole of West Africa). They, like the lions, which are also sometimes seen in this area, are protected by law, and should not be molested.

0 443 **Niamey** There are two routes out of town for the north. One is an extension of the road past the market, around the back of the town. The other is on the river side, through the exclusive northern suburbs, past the Presidency, but not going past Les Roniers and the U.S. Embassy; instead, turning right at a well signposted junction and joining the back route at the Police checkpoint. Before the Police allow you to leave Niamey, they may require to see evidence in your passport that you have been registered with the Surété in town.

20 423 **Camping Rio Bravo Turn-off** This track descends down an escarpment to the pleasant surroundings of the camp ground on the banks of the Niger about 3 km from the main road.

25 418 **Boubon** This is a Djerma village, about 6 km off the main road on the banks of the Niger. It specializes in clay pottery (on sale in the centre of Niamey). On an island opposite, is a Campement in idyllic surrounding, with rondavels to stay in, a restaurant and swimming pool. It is necessary to leave your vehicle at Boubon village (you must hire a guard and lock it) and travel 50 metres of river across to the island, on a 'pirogue'. A favourite spot for Niamey expatriates, at the weekends.

62 381 **Farie** A small village where there is a ferry service to the laterite road that runs up the west bank of the Niger to Dori in Birkina Faso.

120	323	**Tillabery** A Djerma town with an important market (special market day is Sunday). Petrol sometimes available at pump in town. Police station. Northwards from Tillabery there is a made-up road (laterite).
208	235	**Ayorou** A major Songhai centre with an important market. Police station. Petrol is rarely available. Very good Campement, Hotel Amenokol, which is privately run with restaurant, bar, swimming pool, etc. A very worthwhile trip by pirogue to an island in the middle of the river where there is spectacular birdlife, or, a longer canoe trip north, upstream, can take one to see plenty of hippos. (See hotel office.) It is also possible to go downstream to Niamey, by canoe, which would also be an exciting trip.
255	188	**Labazanga** The frontier post. There is a police check point a short distance before the Niger border post. On the Mali side there is only one check point.
348	95	**Ansongo** A Songhai town with an important market. Many roadside stalls. Report to the Police.
443	0	**Gao** Police on entry to Gao. Then you must report to the Police in town to register, and to extend your visa, (two photos are necessary). Obtain a permit to take photographs. The Police have to see and record camera numbers, etc. The permit is supposed to be valid for the whole country.

The tomb at Gao of the great Songhai emperor Askia Mohammed Turé. Gao was once the capital of the large Songhai empire as well as a dynamic trading centre during the fifteenth and sixteenth centuries (Photo by courtesy of Ida and Pieter Kersten)

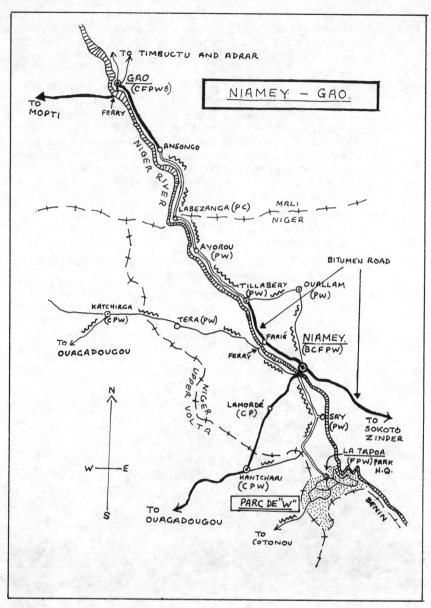

Correction: Ansougo to Gao is not sealed.

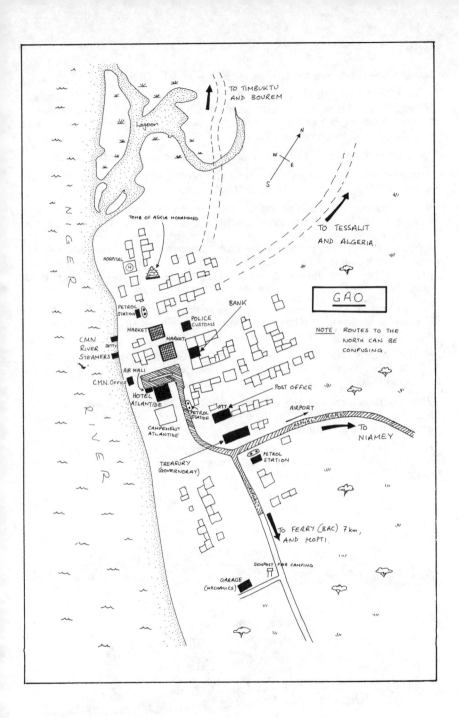

Gao

Banks: See map of Gao. It is possible to use CFA francs in Mali.

Hotel: The Hotel Atlantide is government run, simple but very friendly and helpful. The building has a typical 1930 French colonial atmosphere. Showers, air conditioning, bar and restaurant. There is also a Campement of a lower standard, near the banks of the river.

Note: 'free camping' near Gao is actively discouraged by the police.

Airlines: Air Mali has an office near the ferry company offices. There are scheduled flights to Bamako and Niamey.

River Steamers: Three vessels are used on the service between Gao and Koulikoro (57 km east of Bamako) which is run by the government owned Compagnie Malien de Navigation: the *Mali*, the *Generale Soumaré* and the *Kanga Moussa* (the latter being the more modern). It would be advisable to travel only by de luxe (air conditioned), first and second classes which have private cabins, for third and fourth class are dormitories and deck space only. All except fourth class are served meals as part of the fare.

Depending on the seasonal flow of the river it takes between 5 and 8 days to travel from Koulikoro to Gao (possibly even slower upstream). The boats operate at the following times of the year:

Koulikoro - Mopti	= July-August
Koulikoro - Mopti - Gao	= September-February
Mopti - Gao	= December-February

Bus: There is a regular, weekly bus service run by SNTN to Niamey. But, it is also possible to go to Niamey by small Toyota Hi-Ace bus. These operate an irregular but frequent service.

Ferry: For the ferry or 'bac' across the Niger and piste to Mopti travel 7 km south of the town. It is a scheduled service and has a fixed scale of charges. Don't be persuaded otherwise.

Public transport on the Niger River

Itinerary No. 31 : Gao — Timbuktu

Distance	424 km. (For map see Itinerary No. 32.)
Water	At Timbuktu and Gao.
Fuel	Only at Gao.

Usually necessary to have a 4x4 vehicle, because sand dunes have to be crossed. These sand dunes extend right down to the Niger River.

0	424	**Gao** Check out with the Police and make sure visa has been extended. Fill up with fuel. North of Gao the piste follows the east bank of the Niger River to Bourem. Very difficult in the rainy season (July-August).
95	329	**Bourem** Small Songhai fishing and market village. From Bourem the piste to Timbuktu heads west, while that for the Tanezrouft route to Algeria branches off to the NNE.
232	192	**Bamba** A very small oasis between the piste and the Niger River to the south. Just west of Bamba for about 30 km there is very deep sand. It is here that all traces of previous vehicles can be lost in the shifting sands.
277	147	On the south bank of the Niger is a small Songhai village Gourma Rharous. A 15 tonne capacity ferry service used to take vehicles across to a piste south, to the main Gao - Mopti road, 149 km away.
424	0	**Timbuktu** Police station. Report and get photography permit. Campement on banks of river. No bank. There is an air service to Gao and the paddle steamer 'Générale Soumaré', calls in to the nearby port of Kabara, when the river is navigable. Sometimes there is petrol at Timbuktu, but there is no guarantee. Directly north of Timbuktu a piste extends for 765 km to the saltworks at Taoudenni. This is a prison and tourists are forbidden access. It is one of the loneliest habitations in the Sahara.

For more details on Timbuktu, see Itinerary No. 34 Timbuktu-Segou.

Itinerary No. 32 : Gao - Mopti

Distance   600 km.

Water   Gao: at petrol stations and river. Wells at Hombori, Bini, Douentza, Bore, Kona. Sevare: petrol station. Mopti: petrol station and campement.

Fuel   Petrol stations at Gao (not guaranteed), Sevare and Mopti.

This has been a difficult piste, following oueds, crossing dried up river beds, up and down rocky river banks, and negotiating very deep ornières, with grass on the hard centre lump. However, at the time of writing there was asphalt from Gao to Doro with further sections under construction.

   0   600   **Gao** Leave Gao via south and cross Niger River by ferry or 'bac' (service three times daily). After the river there is 90 km of new asphalt road.

  90   510   **Doro** There are reputedly several prides of lions about 30 - 40 km south of the piste. Recruit a guide in Doro.

 162   438   **Gossi** Just east of Gossi a very rough and sandy piste from Gourma-Rhazarous 149 km to the north joins the main Gao - Mopti road. West of Gossi the piste improves steadily.

 250   350   **Hombori** Songhai village with small market and impressive flat topped mountains, the highest being Mt. Hombori Tondo (1155m). Wells. Police post.

                  A section of new asphalt road to the east of the village. Between Hombori and Douentza, the road passes an area of beautiful cliffs.

 398   202   **Douentza** Impressive mosque. No Police post. Gandamia falaise to the north, and the beginnings of the Bandiagara falaise to the south. Asphalt road the rest of the way to Mopti.

 458   142   **Bore** Village with pretty mosque. Wells.

 514   86   **Kona** Market village at junction of Gao - Mopti road with Mopti - Timbuktu road.

 588   12   **Sevaré** Police station. Good clean Campement with air-

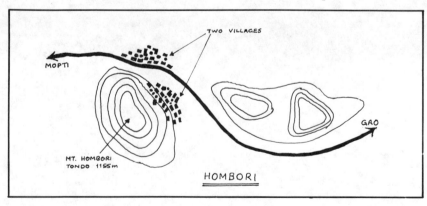

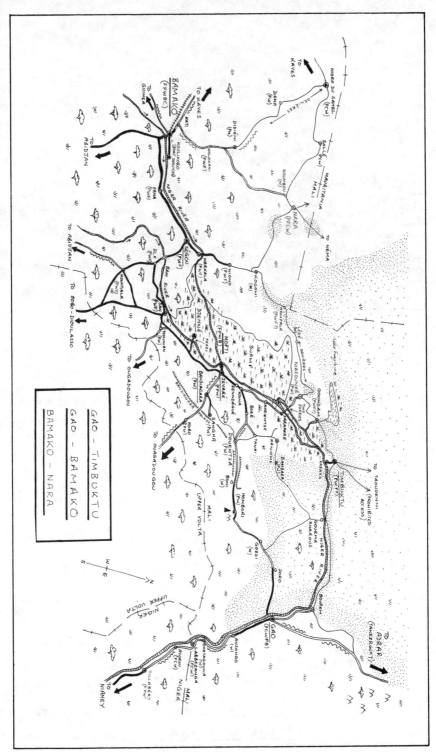

481

Hombori Tondo half way along the main piste from Gao to Mopti (Photo by courtesy of Pieter and Ida Kersten)

conditioning, showers, and a bar selling cold drinks. Report to the Police, and get photography permit. Airport with flights to Bamako. Mopti is twelve kilometres to the west of Sevaré.

600   0   **Mopti** Police, bank, big impressive mosque, a port with a fish market, and a paddle steamer service. Water is not drinkable, usually.

Dogon People

Sixty three kilometres east of Sevaré, along a corrugated laterite road, is a small town, Bandiagara, situated at the top of the Bandiagara Escarpment. Here the Dogon people live in villages at the foot of the cliffs, in a peaceful existence almost untouched by the 20th century. They are naturally friendly, and remarkably unaffected by tourists (there are in fact very few tourists, compared to Tamanrasset and Agadez).

At Bandiagara the Police will want to see your photography permit, or issue one.

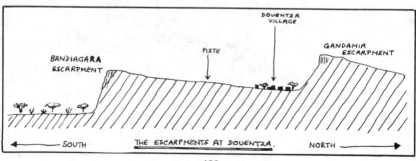

482

Forty four kilometres further on is Sangha. Park your vehicle at the Campement and hire a guide to conduct you on one of three tours (2 hours, 3½ hours or a full day), all on foot. On each tour you visit a Dogon village and inspect the ancient cliff burial grounds.

Part of a Dogon village at the foot of the Bandiagara Escarpment (Photo by courtesy of Freddie and Marie Hicks)

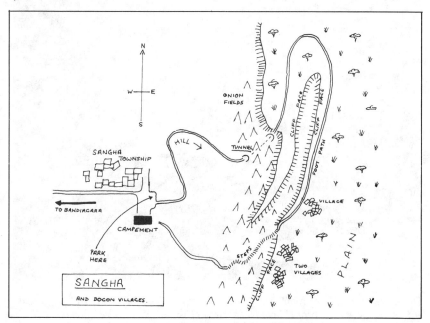

Itinerary No. 33 : Mopti — Bamako

Distance   646 km

Water   Most towns and villages along the way have public taps or wells. The route is also never very far from the Bani River.

Fuel   Petrol stations at Mopti, Sévaré, San and Segou usually have supplies. There are pumps at Sofara, Bla and Fana.

Theoretically, the entire route is sealed with asphalt. However, between Sévaré and San reconstruction is under way (1983). Between Segou and Bamako the narrow width tar road is in a bad state and there are many badly corrugated and rutted detours. Between San and Segou the road is good full width asphalt.

This route passes through Sahel country consisting of Acacia thorn trees and scattered tussock grass. Towards Bamako the vegetation becomes more woodland savanna with increasing numbers of other deciduous trees including the large bulbous Baobabs. There are good possibilities for open free camping.

   0   646   **Mopti** Commercial centre and major river port based on the confluence of the Niger and Bani rivers and built on three islands linked by dykes. Founded during the 19th century as a Moslem Fulani theocracy, it quickly became the commercial centre of what is now Mali (until the railway reached Bamako). It is noted for its red mud architecture, spectacular mosque and bustling markets. (Market day in the Grand Marché is on

The red mud mosque at Mopti on the banks of the Niger River. This style is typical of this part of West Africa (Photo by courtesy of Freddie and Marie Hicks)

484

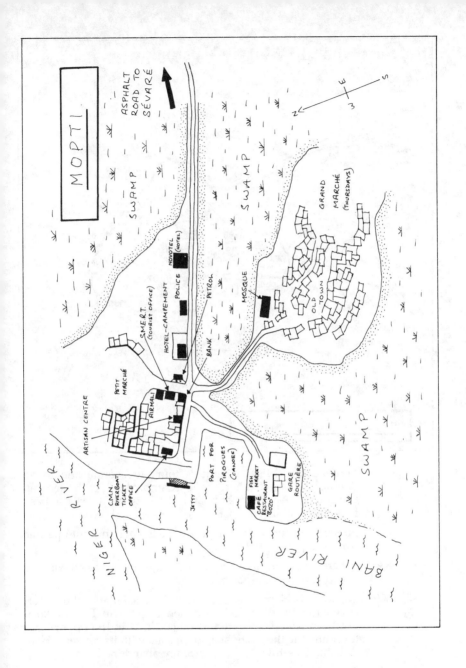

MOPTI

ASPHALT ROAD TO SÉVARÉ

SWAMP

SWAMP

SWAMP

NIGER RIVER

BANI RIVER

NOVOTEL (HOTEL)
POLICE
SMERT (TOURIST OFFICE)
HOTEL–CAMPEMENT
PETROL
BANK
MOSQUE
GRAND MARCHÉ (THURSDAYS)
OLD TOWN
PETIT MARCHÉ
AIR MALI
ARTISAN CENTRE
CMN RIVERBOAT TICKET OFFICE
JETTY
PORT FOR PIROGUES (CANOES)
FISH MARKET
CAFÉ RESTAURANT "BOZO"
GARE ROUTIÈRE

N E S W

485

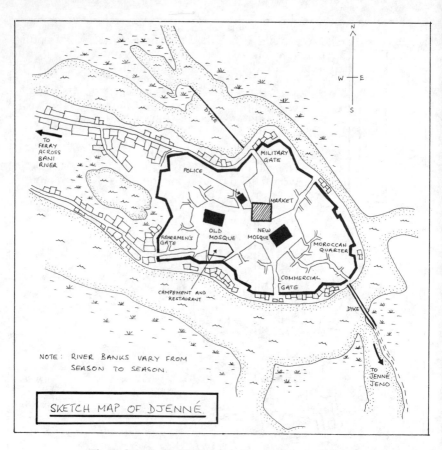

SKETCH MAP OF DJENNÉ

Thursdays.) SMERT organises tours to Djenné and to the Bandiagara area. There is a Campement with separate bungalows. An old river boat at the jetty has been used as a floating hotel in the past.

Fill up with fuel before departing. Also obtain photo permits from the police.

12   634   **Sévaré** Commercial centre at crossroads. Fill up again with fuel if you can. Motel at airport.

37   609   Turn-off to Hamdullahi. Hamad Bari, a Fulani who experienced the Jihad or Holy War led by Usman Dan Fodio in northern Nigeria, also led a similar Jihad in the upper Niger founding the theocratic state of Macina with its capital at Hamdullahi. This town is now virtually abandoned.

101   545   Turn-off to the west to Djenné. Not to be missed. A bad gravel road for about 30 km takes one to the Bani River where it is possible to leave one's vehicle with a paid guardian and cross by pirogue (or canoe) to Djenné. Alternatively, have the vehicle ferried across the river and then drive on to Segou directly across the floodplain (dry season only).

About 2 to 3 km south of Djenné along a dyke or causeway archeologists have unearthed the ruins of the ancient trading city of Jenne-Jeno. Its economy prospered by trading the agricultural surplus from the surrounding fertile floodplain with gold from the south and salt from Taoudenni and Taghaza in the central Sahara. It has been described as 'the oldest known city, and perhaps the most important Iron Age site, in Africa south of the Sahara' (S. and R. McIntosh **National Geographic,** September 1982).

From about 1200 AD there was a gradual population shift to the present site fo Djenné which coincided with the rise of Islam in this part of the Sahel and saw the rapid rise of Djenné as a major trading city and Islamic cultural centre. The people of this city today are largely the Sarakolés (traders and cultivators), the Fulani (pastoralists) and the Bozos (fishermen and boat people or 'piroguiers').

The mosque at Djenné was built in 1906 as a spectacularly beautiful replica of the original 14th century one destroyed during a Jihad led by Hamad Bari then ruler of the Fulani run Macina theocracy. It is, nevertheless, a classic example of the red mud architecture of this part of the Sahel and southern Sahara. (Don't forget to leave your shoes outside before entering. Note also, that women are not allowed inside.)

Note: report to police on arrival in Djenné. Today life still goes on in Djenné much as it did in ancient Jenne-Jeno. Like Timbuktu, Agadez, Katsina and the old parts of Kano, it is a

The mosque at Djenné which was built in 1906 as a replica of the original fourteenth century building destroyed during a holy war in the nineteenth century (Photo by courtesy of Pieter and Ida Kersten)

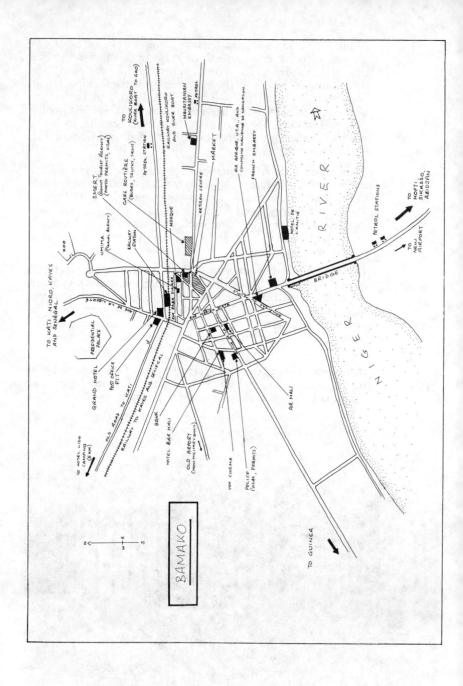

BAMAKO

N
W E
S

200

TO KATI NIORO, KAYES
AND SENEGAL

TO KOULIKORO
(RIVER BOAT — TO GAO)

RAILWAY KOULIKORO
AND RIVER BOAT

MAURITANIAN
EMBASSY

PETROL

MARKET

PETROL STATION

ARTISAN CENTRE

MOSQUE

RAILWAY
STATION

UMPA
(TRAVEL AGENCY)

SMERT
(GOVT TOURIST AGENCY)
(PHOTO PERMITS, VISAS)

GARE ROUTIÈRE
(BUSES, TRUCKS, TAXIS)

AIR AFRIQUE, U.T.A. AND
COMPAGNIE MALIENNE DE NAVIGATION

FRENCH EMBASSY

HOTEL DE
L'AMITIÉ

R I V E R

N I G E R

BRIDGE

PETROL STATIONS

TO
MOPTI,
SIKASSO,
ABIDJAN

TO
NEW
AIRPORT

PRESIDENTIAL
PALACE

GRAND HOTEL

POST OFFICE
P.T.T.

OLD ROAD TO KATI

RAILWAY TO KAYES AND SENEGAL

BANK

HOTEL BAR MALI

OLD AIRPORT
(NON-MILITARY ONLY)

VOX CINEMA

POLICE
(VISAS, PERMITS)

AIR MALI

TO HOTEL LIDO
CAMPING (5 KM)

TO GUINEA

good example of a traditional African town with its fine geometric red mud brick building architecture that is sensibly adapted for coolness in this hot climate. Monday is market day in front of the mosque. (Don't forget photo permit.) The artisans of Djenné are noted for their jewellery. There is a Campement with rooms and meals available.

171 475 Turn-off to the SE to Tominian and to Burkina Faso.

212 434 **San** Commercial centre. Fuel supplies. A good asphalt road heads south to Bobo Dioulasso in Burkina Faso. For Bamako, head west towards Segou. There is a small Campement. Also, a picturesque red mud mosque built in typical Sahel style.

323 323 **Bla** Road south to Sikasso and Ivory Coast. Possibility of fuel supplies.

368 278 Bridge across Bani River.

411 235 **Segou** Commercial and administrative centre for major irrigation schemes on the Niger River floodplain. There is a barrage and bridge across the river at Sansanding some 40 km away along the road north to Timbuktu. This barrage controls supplies of water to a large FAO and government funded rice, sugar and cotton growing project. There is a Campement belonging to the Office du Niger, the irrigation authority. Fuel supplies are usually available. Monday is market day. Founded originally by Bozo fishermen, Segou became a major centre of the ancient Bambara-Toucoulour empire. In 1890 the French captured the town from Ahmad the Fulani ruler of the Bambara-Toucoulour Empire. Ahmad's palace and the even grander one

Entrance to the main market at Bamako (Photo by courtesy of Ida and Pieter Kersten)

of his father (Alhadji Umar) can be seen in the middle of the old walled part of town.

For Bamako, head west.

643 3 Junction with main north-south road between Bamako and Ivory Coast.

646 0 **Bamako** Founded in 1650, it is the capital and commercial centre of modern Mali. All facilities. Obtain photo permit, 'carte touristique' and report one's presence at SMERT, the state tourist agency in the Boulevard du People. There are two relatively expensive hotels: the Grand near the railway station and the Amitié on the banks of the Niger. To the NW of town along the old road to Kati is the Hotel Lido with restaurant, swimming pool and a camping area.

The Niger River boat or steamer service leaves from Koulikoro on the north bank of the river some 57 km to the east of Bamako along an asphalt road (see section on Gao for details).

Because the piste to Kayes in the NW and on to Senegal is so bad and totally impassable in the wet season it is usual for travellers to put their vehicles on the train and travel with them into Senegal or vice versa. The alternative is travel the pistes north into Mauritania and thence by asphalt road to Nouakchott or on to Dakar.

The train service between Dakar and Bamako is twice weekly and takes about three days. Unless one is prepared to be jam packed into a carriage one should travel first class in a couchette wagon or sleeping car. However, one is also able to travel on the platform wagon with one's vehicle. In this case take sufficient food and water for at least three days and rig up a tent or tarpaulin for protection from the sun. In 1983 it cost about US$110 per tonne between

The modern Grand Mosque in central Bamako (Photo by courtesy of Pieter and Ida Kersten)

490

Tambacounda and Bamako for the vehicle.

Vehicles should be lashed to the platform truck at each corner with at least 5mm gauge wire rope. A single length of about 30 metres should do. Thicker gauge would be too difficult to tie. Carnets de passage should be stamped at Kadira (Senegal) and at Kayes (Mali). Note that only platform trucks marked as belonging to 'Regie des Chemins de Fer du Mali' are generally permitted to leave Senegal.

Itinerary No. 34 : Timbuktu — Segou

Distance   715 km.

Water   Between Timbuktu and Léré water is obtainable from the river in flood season especially (September - February). Otherwise most villages have public wells.

Fuel   Timbuktu, Goundam and Niafounké have pumps but supplies of fuel are not always available. Fill up whenever you can.

This piste is difficult. It is always sandy especially between Timbuktu and Goundam where dunes have to be crossed. There are Acacia thorn trees everywhere which are a puncture menace. There are often deep 'ornières' especially either side of Niafounké, a ' the piste is often obliterated by the constant trampling of livestock. This may require the occasional use of a compass to check one's general bearing.

Because of the distance and perhaps quite a lot of low gear work, it is necessary to carry a lot of fuel for at least 720 km. This adds to the weight of the vehicle making progress just that much more difficult and in fact increasing one's fuel consumption.

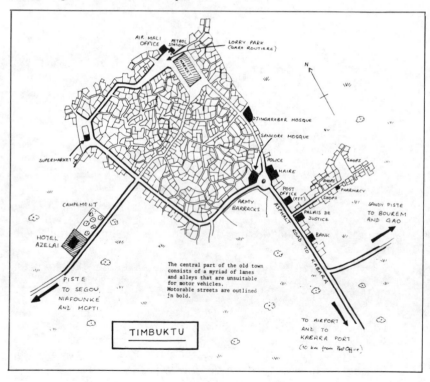

Timbuktu

Since the publicity of Rene Caillié's and Gordon Laing's visits in the early nineteenth century (see Chapter 8), Timbuktu has been regarded by westerners as the mysterious and fabulously rich city further away than the back of beyond. In fact it is a rather depressing lack lustre town in a state of decline and has been for at least three hundred years. It used to be one of the great trading centres at the end of the ancient trans-Saharan caravan routes trading in gold, slaves and grain from the south and salt, dates and processed goods from the north. On the banks of the Niger, it was also a major river port. Now Timbuktu is no longer on the river, which has shifted south, and the town's population has dropped from about 100,000 at the time of Askia Mohammed Turé of Gao (1493-1529) to about 7,000 today.

In 1324 the great Emperor of Mali, Mansa Musa, made his famous 'hadj' or pilgrimage to Mecca with a massive entourage and so much gold that his arrival in Cairo caused inflation that was almost disastrous for the Egyptian economy. On his return during the next year, he passed through Timbuktu and directed that a great new mosque be built under the supervision of Ibrahim es Sahelia, a Moorish poet and architect from Granada in Spain. This is the Djingerebur or Great Mosque of Timbuktu which, although it has been modified and re-surfaced many times, still stands in all its red mud magnificence today.

During the fifteenth century Timbuktu became a major centre of Islamic learning with a university based around the other mosque, the Sankore. It was during this time that the great Songhai Empire under Sonni Ali Ber and then Mohammed Askia Turé was established and ruled from Gao but with Timbuktu being an integral part of it. This was when Timbuktu really was a fabulous city of learning and material wealth. But, with the collapse of Songhai, the city was sacked in 1591 by an army from Sultan Mansour of Marrakesh which had crossed the Sahara to defeat Songhai and capture the wealth in its cities. Great caravans of gold and other treasures were expropriated and taken north to Morocco. Yet Timbuktu's reputation lived on even during the dark century of rule by the animist Bambara Kingdom of Segou which followed the withdrawal of the Moroccans.

In the early nineteenth century Islam returned to Timbuktu with the Fulani jihads or holy wars started by Usman dan Fodio of Sokoto and Hamad Bari of Hamdullahi when, like Mopti and Djenné, it became part of the Macina theocracy.

In 1894 it was captured by the French under Major (later Marshall) Joffre and in 1960 it became just one of many rural towns within the present Republique du Mali.

The old part of the present-day Timbuktu would probably not have changed much since Caillié and Laing saw it in the early nineteenth century. Its red mud buildings, markets and polyglot mixture of peoples can also be seen in many West African Sahel towns from Maiduguri, Agadez, Kano and Sokoto through to Gao, Mopti, Djenné and Segou. However, the mystical attraction still lingers on in the minds of Westerners to such an extent that the French airline UTA and Air Afrique have now constructed a new luxury hotel, the Azelai, to international standards with 42 air-conditioned bedrooms and all modern facilities to attract airline based package tour operators. However, this should not dissuade other more intrepid travellers from going there. Only don't be disappointed when you get there. Timbuktu's

The once fabled but now almost forgotten Timbuktu. Tradition relates that before its first settlement in the eleventh century, there was only a well known as 'Tim' on the site. It was looked after by an elderly Touareg woman called 'Buktu'. Recently, it was hoped that the city's fortunes might be revived with the completion of the air-conditioned Azelai Hotel. However, in February 1985, the weekly flight from Bamako crashed at Timbuktu killing nearly fifty package tourists from Europe. Since then, the new hotel has remained virtually empty (Photo by courtesy of Keith Smith)

mystery and glory lies in the past.

Between December and April is the period when the 'Azelai' takes place: salt bearing camel caravans arrive from Taoudenni more than 750 km to the north. Do **not** attempt to go to these desert salt works as they are in fact a terrible prison and access is strictly forbidden by the authorities.

There are scheduled air services by Air Mali out of Timbuktu's airport (to the south of town) to Gao, Mopti and Bamako. The C.M.N. river steamers call in at Kabara some 7 km to the south of town along an asphalt road. For details see the Gao section, end of Itinerary No. 30.

In the new part of town are the post office, police station and a supermarket which sells imported canned and processed products. For accommodation there is the luxurious Azelai Hotel and an older colonial-type Campement where it is also possible to stay in Touareg style tents. Very reasonable meals and rooms are also available at Baba Cisse's Restaurant.

| 0 | 715 | Leave town via the west. Fill up with fuel. Note: the direct route to Mopti via Niafounké, Korientze and Kona is not normally motorable between September and February because that is when the Niger is in full flood (even though this is not the rainy season). Between Timbuktu and Goundam there is much sand and some low dunes have to be crossed. The piste may be obliterated by livestock footprints. |
| 97 | 618 | **Goundam** An agricultural village (irrigation of wheat, millet, rice and maize) situated on the shores of Lake Télé. Also noted for its fine weaving. There is a Campement. Sometimes there |

494

is fuel. 34 km to the SE on the Niger River is the village of Diré where river steamers stop. There is a rarely used piste north from Goundam to the very beautiful Lake Faguibine which has dunes on its northern shoreline.

Main piste westwards is very sandy.

147 568 **Tondidarou** Small village but nearby is the site of well over a hundred large pre-Islamic stone monuments or megaliths whose origins are still fairly obscure.

185 530 **Niafounké** Village with Campement and the rare possibility of fuel supplies. If heading for Mopti, this is where one makes the first of two river crossings by ferry (except during the flood season — September to February).

321 394 **Léré** Village on Lake Tanda.

Between Léré and Nampala the piste is much firmer but there are also deep ornières.

413 302 **Nampala** Village. Police post.

465 250 Beginning of irrigated fields. Water is brought from the barrage at Sansanding near Markala along the Canal du Sahel.

556 159 **Kogoni** Village. Police post. Piste to NW goes to Nara 158 km away and on into Mauritania.

606 109 **Niono** Police post. Fuel. Important centre for rice irrigation programme. Asphalt road from here south.

675 40 **Sansanding Barrage and Bridge** across the Niger River. This irrigation scheme was started in 1948 with French government and F.A.O. assistance. It has not been quite as successful as planned (the acreage under cultivation is 30% less than it should be). Crops grown are cotton, rice and sugar cane.

677 38 **Markala** Commercial centre and river port.

715 0 **Segou** Fuel supplies. Campement. For further details see Itinerary No. 33.

Itinerary No. 35 : Bamako — Néma

Distance   560 km

Water   From wells at villages en route, especially at Nara.

Fuel   Fill up at Bamako with as much as possible as there is not likely to be any available for the 577 km en route. In fact, there may not be supplies until Kiffa, a total of 1,072 km.

This route can be waterlogged during the rainy season especially north of Nara. Between Nara and Néma it will be sandy at the best of times and only very well equipped vehicles should be used to attempt this route. There is a new all-weather gravel road between Didieni and Nara.

The vegetation changes from savanna woodland near Bamako, through sahel to desert at Néma.

0   560   **Bamako** For details see Itinerary No. 33. Fill up with fuel. Leave town via the north through the Manding Escarpment. The road is sealed as far as Kati.

20   540   **Kati** Sometimes fuel available.

124   436   **Kolokani** Small town. Police post. Junction with roads leading to Banamba in the east and Koulikoro to the south-east.

163   397   **Didieni** Village. Road continues NW to Nioro du Sahel and thence to Kayes. For Nara head NNE. This section could be inundated with water in the rainy season (July-September).

348   212   **Goumbou** Village. Turn-off to west for Balle and Nioro du Sahel (270 km). A little used piste. Continue NE for Nara.

The partly excavated ruins of Koumbi Saleh, once the capital city of the ancient empire of Ghana and dated by archaeologists at around 1200 AD. The remains of the city's Mosque are shown here (Photo by courtesy of Ida and Pieter Kersten)

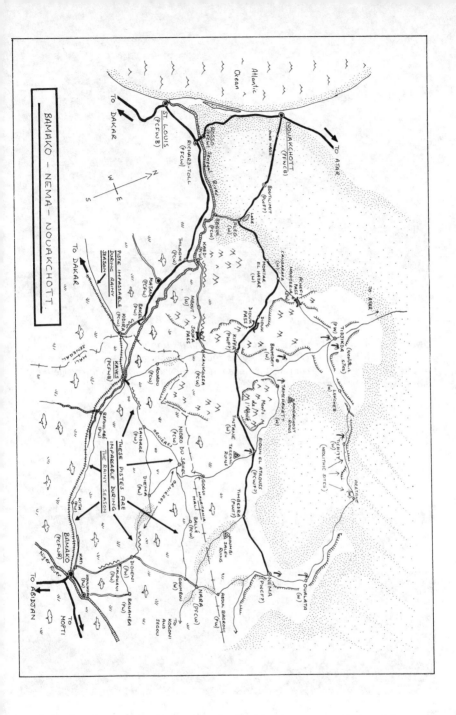

BAMAKO – NEMA – NOUAKCHOTT.

Ornières between Nara and Nioro du Sahel. They are typical of most pistes in northern Mali. A robust vehicle with good ground clearance and sand tyres is a big advantage. Nevertheless, both on the piste and in the surrounding countryside large thorns are a major hazard (Photo by courtesy of Ida and Pieter Kersten)

Part of the new asphalt road to Nouakchott in Mauritania. It is typical of some of the new roads that are increasingly found in the countries of the Sahel. They are boring, fast and deceptively easy to travel on. Some of the dangers are overheated engines, wandering livestock (as seen here), drifting sand and pot holes (Photo by courtesy of Ida and Pieter Kersten)

377   183   **Nara** Village. Police post. Mali customs. Discharge Carnet here. A possibility of fuel supplies. To the west of town is a sandy piste heading NW to Timbedra in Mauritania where there is a Customs post. However, along the way, about 45 km south of Timbedra, are the ruins of Koumbi Saleh, once the capital of the ancient empire of Ghana (carbon-14 dated around 1200 AD). Today, this once important city consists of about 2 km² of stone ruins and 4 km² of cemeteries but these, together with many other potential sites in the area suggest that early African urban society existed here at least before 1000 AD. A major excavation of the Koumbi-Saleh ruins took place in 1950. Note that there is still a village called Koumbi-Saleh. As the piste from Nara in the SE may vary considerably especially towards the well at Bousteila, it pays to ask the way whenever possible.

The piste for Néma passes the airstrip to the north of the village, is sandy and is likely to be flooded in the short rainy season.

425   135   **Abdel Bagrou** Village. Police post. Report to it as it is the first contact with Mauritanian officialdom.

560   0   **Néma** Frontier formalities for Mauritania. Have your Carnet stamped. Post office. Market with good supplies of vegetables. Beautiful mosque and decorated mud houses. Airstrip with weekly service to Nouakchott. Petrol station but supplies are not always available. Néma is at the SE end of the beautiful and archeologically important Tichitt-Oualata Escarpment. For details see Itinerary No. 37.

Note: At Nioro du Sahel there are Customs, Police, fuel, shops, a good hospital, an airport.

Itinerary No. 36 : Néma — Nouakchott

Distance   999 km

Water   At public wells in all major oases.

Fuel   Supplies are not guaranteed anywhere along this route until Nouakchott. There are possibilities of fuel being available especially at Néma, Timbedra and Kiffa but also at Ayoum al Atrous, Aleg and Boutilimit. Fill up whenever supplies are found to be available.

This route consists of a corrugated gravel road from Néma to Timbedra but from there all the way to Nouakchott is a recently completed asphalt road. The entire route should be asphalt late in 1985. As far as Aleg it passes along the northern fringe of the Sahel vegetation zone but from there to Nouakchott it crosses open often sandy desert.

0	999	**Néma** Police. Frontier formalities. Fill up with fuel if possible. For further details see Itinerary No. 35. For Nouakchott head west along a gravel but corrugated road which is sometimes in very bad condition.
110	889	**Timbedra** Post office. Police post. Customs post. Petrol. Simple lodgings available. Well. Junction with piste from Nara in Mali along which are also the ruins of Koumbi Saleh former capital of the ancient empire of Ghana (see Itinerary No. 35). Start of asphalt road to the west. Sand dunes.
280	719	**Ayoun al Atous** Customs and Police post. (Report here if heading south to Nioro du Sahel.) Post office. Government clinic. Lodgings available. Restaurant. Possibility of fuel. Good vegetables for sale.
495	504	**Kiffa** Post office. Police post. Government clinic. Market. Lodgings available. Possibility of fuel. Piste with corrugations and ornières goes south to Kankossa (customs post and palmeraie) and then on to Kaedi on the Senegal River (customs post, airstrip, government clinic and fuel supplies). To the NW of Kiffa the asphalt road crosses the Diouk pass after about 100 km.
597	402	**Cangarata** Village. Turn-off to Tidjikja and Tichitt Escarpment to the NE (see ItineraryNo. 37).
737	262	**Aleg** Police post. Post office. Possibility of fuel. Corrugated piste to SW goes to Bogue some 70 km away on the Senegal River. Asphalt road continues NW across open sandy desert.
845	154	**Boutilimit** Police post. Rare possibility of fuel supplies. Well.
999	0	**Nouakchott** Capital of Mauritania. All facilities. Port. International airport. There are at least seven fairly expensive hotels with air-conditioned rooms. The Marhaba Hotel is government owned and run by S.M.T.H. (Société Mauritanienne de Tourisme et d'Hostellerie). Most of the restaurants are in the beach area. Not to be missed is the Musée National because of its displays on the Tichitt Escarpment archeological sites. The

government supported artisans' shop is on the corner of Kennedy and Nasser Avenues.

Itinerary No. 37 : The Tichitt Escarpment

Néma lies at the SE extremity of the Tichitt-Oualata Dahr or Escarpment. This forms a semi-circle around a giant depression known as the Aouker which is today filled with sand dunes. However, 5,000 years ago this depression was a massive inland lake and the surrounding countryside was a tropical savanna. In 1954 at the foot of the escarpment near Tichitt, Teodore Monod discovered the remains of some fortified villages constructed of stone by neolithic fishermen and cultivators. These ruins predate by several thousands of years sites previously known to archeologists as the earliest examples of urbanisation in Africa.

Other ruins have now also been found along the escarpment. Monod's discovery thirty years ago is now seen as a major breakthrough in the rediscovery of African pre-history.

To travel the full length of the Tichitt-Oualata Dahr is well worth the trouble but requires extensive experience of remote Saharan travel as well as necessitating several well equipped Land Rover or Unimog type vehicles in convoy. The distance from Néma to Tidjikja is 640 km through almost vegetationless, very sandy open desert usually without discernible vehicle tracks and no human settlement (except for the very humble villages at Oualata and around Tichitt). A mechanical breakdown that could not be rectified for a lone vehicle would be absolutely disastrous. For a vehicle travelling in convoy it would mean abandoning it to the desert as the logistics and costs involved in return to recover the vehicle are not worthwhile even for an expensive one like a Unimog.

Air Mauritanie services Tidjikja, Tichitt and Néma once a week.

Route Description
No distances are given because these are so variable.
Total distance from Néma to Tidjikja would be in excess of 640 km.

From Néma to Oualata the piste winds in and out of the escarpment.

The ancient town of Oualata is partially abandoned now but there is a mosque and the occupied houses that remain are beautifully decorated. There is a police post, a well and a palmeraie.

Between Oualata and Tichitt the piste is only partially marked with balises and is exceptionally sandy. Some 50 km before Tichitt is the tiny settlement of Aghrijit. Nearby is the site discovered by Teodore Monod in 1954.

Tichitt has a police post, airstrip (weekly service), a mosque and a small market.

From Tichitt to Tidjikja the piste is difficult to follow but after the well at Zik it rises up through the escarpment on to a plateau.

Tidjikja is a large oasis with an old fort, police post, airport, palmeraie, market and sometimes fuel. There are other neolithic sites nearby. A piste to the north goes to Atar (rarely used). A piste heads south to Kiffa via the Oued Taskast. Some 150 km NE of Kiffa in the Aouker sand sea are the ruins of the ancient trading city of Aoudaghost which thrived between the ninth and fourteenth centuries AD. It is through Aoudaghost that the Berber Almoravids first conquered this part of West Africa during the late eleventh century. The site of the Aoudaghost ruins is protected by law and a permit to visit it is

Oualata, a partly abandoned town at the eastern end of the Tichitt Escarpment. The decorative style of buildings is unique and quite beautiful. To reach Oualata from Néma, there are two routes: the escarpment piste (well defined and relatively easier) and the valley piste (guide advisable). Both are very sandy and traffic is infrequent (Photo by courtesy of Alain and Yolande Cottereau)

obtainable from the prefecture at the nearby village of Tamchekket.

To the SW of Tidjikja a fairly well used piste goes to the main asphalt road that leads to Nouakchott. The junction with this asphalt road is at Cangarata some 208 km away after crossing the Acheft Pass and passing through the oasis of Moudjeria.

Appendix A

Conversion Tables

A pocket calculator is an invaluable asset in the Sahara.

Volume
1 pint = 600 ml
1 Imp Gallon = 4.54 litres
1 US Gallon = 3.78 litres
22 Imp Gallons = 100 litres
44 Imp Gallons = 200 litres
                 = Fuel drum size
1litre = 1.76 pints
1 litre of water weighs 1 kg
20 litres = 4.4 gallons = Jerrycan size
500 ml = .9 pint

Length
1 mile = 1.6 km
1,000 feet = 305 metres
100 metres = 328 feet
1 km = 0.63 miles

Mass
1 kg = 2.2 lbs
1 tonne = 1000 kg = 2,200 lbs

Temperature

°C	°F	
127	260	
105	220	
100	212	(Water boils at sea level)
82	180	
60	140	
55	131	
50	122	
45	113	
40	104	
37	98.4	(Blood heat)
35	95	
30	86	
25	77	
20	68	
15	59	
10	50	
5	41	
0	32	(Water freezes)
-10	14	

To convert Celsius to Fahrenheit
Double it, subtract 10% and add 32.
eg 20°C = 20x2 = 40 -10% = 36 + 32 = 68°F

Tyre Pressures

kg/cm² and p.s.i.		kg/cm² and p.s.i.	
0.5	= 7	2.0	= 29
0.7	= 10	2.1	= 30.6
0.8	= 11.4	2.2	= 32
0.9	= 13	2.3	= 35
1.0	= 14.5	2.5	= 36
1.1	= 16	2.6	= 38
1.2	= 17.5	2.7	= 39
1.3	= 19	2.8	= 41
1.4	= 20.3	2.9	= 42
1.5	= 22	3.0	= 43.5
1.6	= 23	3.1	= 45
1.7	= 24.8	3.2	= 47
1.8	= 26	3.3	= 48.5
1.9	= 27.5	3.4	= 50

Distance
Kilometres to Miles

km	miles	km	miles
5	3.1	60	37.5
10	6.3	70	43.8
15	9.4	80	50.0
20	12.5	90	56.3
25	15.3	100	62.5
30	18.8	110	68.8
35	21.9	120	75.0
40	25.0	130	81.3
45	28.2	140	87.5
50	31.3	150	93.8
		160	100.0

For fast conversion from km to miles, halve the
figure and add a quarter of the result.

e.g. 40 becomes 20 + 5 = 25
60 becomes 30 + 7.5 = 37.5

International Times

Africa

Algeria	GMT + 1
	GMT + 2 (Summer)
Burkina Faso	GMT
Chad	GMT + 1
Egypt	GMT + 2
Ghana	GMT
Ivory Coast	GMT
Libya	GMT + 2
Mali	GMT
Mauritania	GMT
Morocco	GMT
	GMT + 1 (Summer)
Niger	GMT + 1
Nigeria	GMT + 1
Sudan	GMT + 2

Europe

Belgium	GMT + 1
	GMT + 2 (Summer)
Britain	GMT
	GMT + 1 (Summer)
France	GMT + 1
	GMT + 2 (Summer)
Germany	GMT + 1
Greece	GMT + 2
	GMT + 3 (Summer)
Holland	GMT + 1
	GMT + 2 (Summer)
Italy	GMT + 1
	GMT + 2 (Summer)
Spain	GMT + 1
	GMT + 2 (Summer)
Switzerland	GMT + 1
Yugoslavia	GMT + 1

Fuel Consumption

M.p.g. to km per litre	Litres/100 km to m.p.g.
10 = 3.5	5 = 56.8
11 = 3.8	6 = 47.3
12 = 4.2	7 = 40.5
13 = 4.6	8 = 34.6
14 = 4.9	9 = 31.5
15 = 5.3	10 = 28.4
16 = 5.7	11 = 25.8
17 = 6.0	12 = 23.7
18 = 6.4	13 = 21.8
19 = 6.7	14 = 20.3

Fuel Consumption

M.p.g. to km per litre	Litres/100 km to m.p.g.
20 = 7.1	15 = 18.9
21 = 7.4	16 = 17.7
22 = 7.7	17 = 16.7
23 = 8.1	18 = 15.8
24 = 8.4	19 = 14.9
25 = 8.8	20 = 14.2
26 = 9.1	21 = 13.5
27 = 9.5	22 = 12.9
28 = 9.8	23 = 12.3
29 = 10.1	24 = 11.8
30 = 10.6	25 = 11.4
31 = 10.9	26 = 10.9
32 = 11.2	27 = 10.4
33 = 11.6	28 = 10.1
34 = 11.9	29 = 9.8
35 = 12.3	30 = 9.5
26 = 12.6	31 = 8.6
37 = 13.0	35 = 8.1
39 = 13.7	37 = 7.7
40 = 14.2	40 = 7.1
45 = 15.8	45 = 6.3
50 = 17.7	50 = 5.7

Appendix B

Glossary

Some words used in the text may be unfamiliar to readers from different parts of the world. There are Algerian, Australian, American, British, French, German and Nigerian words for many different things. It is therefore necessary to provide a list of some of the more common different usages.

Ad darak = Arabic for a road block or check point.

Ain = Arabic for a natural spring (e.g. artesian water).

Asphalt = Bitumen = Tar sealed = Tarmac = Macadamised = Paved road = Goudronné (French).

Autocar = Autobus = Car = All French for long distance bus.

Balises = Markers along a desert piste to indicate the direction of travel.

Berliet balise No. 21 in the vast expanse of nothingness of the Ténéré. Some balises are spaced apart at regular intervals such as every 500 metres, every kilometre or every 5 kilometres. They are usually just a steel pole, or they may have distances marked on them but in many cases they consist of just an old 200 litre drum or a crude cairn of stones. Provided they have not been removed or covered by drifting sand, they are relatively easy to follow. On the other hand, as with the Berliet and the Saviem balises, some are very far apart and spaced at irregular intervals. For example, the distance between Berliet balises No 21 and No 20 is 101 km but the distance between Berliet balises No 20 and No 19 is only 58 km and at no point can one Berliet balise be seen from the other. Good navigation skills are still needed when following this type of balise system. In other words, the balises are there not to follow but to provide accurately known points from which one can check one's navigation and progress

Barrière des pluies (French) = A barrier erected across unsealed roads in West Africa, during the rainy season, to prevent traffic using the road. The same system is used in the north of Australia. It prevents roads being 'chewed up' by heavy vehicles.

Bidon = Oil drum in French; often used for balises.

Bidonville (French) = Slum area with houses made out of flattened oil drums and other rubbish.

Bogged (Australian) = Stuck (English) = Ensablé (French). The car is in soft sand or mud unable to get sufficient traction to move forwards or backwards.

Billet = Bon = Ticket or coupon.

Bordj = Arabic for a fort.

Boulangerie (French) = Bakery (English)

Bull Dust (Australian) = Extremely fine, pulverised, powder dust that does not settle properly. It remains in semi-suspension, giving the impression of hard ground ahead.

Bull Bar (Australian) = Bush bar = Crash bar (English) = Roo bar (Australian) = A heavy steel structure erected on to the front of a vehicle to minimize accident damage, when in collision with livestock, wild animals and trees.

Bush (Australian and African) = Bundu (Southern Africa) = Generally refers to Savanna country; a mixture of trees and grass.

Camion (French) = Truck or lorry.

Campement (French) = A hotel in Africa with fairly basic facilities and an area to camp in.

Camping (French) = A privately operated camping ground with toilet and other facilities.

Campmobile = camping car = campervan = small panel van with bed and other furniture built into it and often a glass fibre elevating roof. This is distinct from a motor caravan which is normally a larger van or small truck.

Carte = French for a map.

Carte-postale = French for post card.

Carnet = Carnet de Passages en Douane = Internationally recognised customs passport for a vehicle.

Carte gris = French for vehicle registration document.

Casse = Cashier in French. Similar to Le Guichet.

Chalets = Term used in Nigeria to describe motel type rooms detached from the main hotel building complex. Characteristic of government run Catering Rest Houses in Nigeria.

Cheche (Arabic) = Turban. (Tagelmoust in Tamahaq, the language of the Touaregs.)

Col = French for a small pass across a range of hills.

Co-operant = French version of the US 'Peace Corps' or the British VSO or Canadian CUSO : people who are sent to poor countries as part of an aid programme and who generally get paid less than they would in their home country.

Corrugations (African and Australian) = Tole ondulée (French) = Welblech (German) = Washboard (English) = Thousands of small parallel ridges which lie across an unsealed road. They are caused by fast moving traffic.

Cous-cous = A North African Arab dish of granulated wheat flour steamed over broth, usually with meat and other vegetables added. Packets of 'instant' cous-cous are available in supermarkets in Algeria, Morocco and France.

Cram-cram = The low scattered tussock grass which generally marks the end of the real desert and the beginning of the southern Sahel. Usually grows in association with small scattered Acacia thorn trees (see Chapter 2 : Flora and Fauna).

Cric (French) = A car jack.

Daira = Roughly equivalent to a local government office in Algeria.

Douane (French) = Customs.

Ensablé (French) = Stuck in sand.

Erg (Arabic) = A vast sea of rolling sand dunes, devoid of vegetation and usually several hundred kilometres across.

Essence (French) = Petrol (English) = Gasoline (American).

Expatriate (English) = Term applied to foreigners living and working in African countries, usually on contract to a government, or working for a company. They may be of British, French, Indian, Egyptian, Canadian, etc. origin. It does not apply to settlers.

Faddama (Hausa) = Irrigated flat area on either side of a river.

Falaise (French) = Escarpment (English) = A range of hills rising steeply from a plain.

Feche feche = A type of sand which is very soft and seemingly bottomless and may even have a deceptively hard crust. It may extend for only a few metres or even for kilometres. It is to be avoided at all costs because it is nearly impossible to drive through long distances of it without getting bogged. It is very difficult to extract a bogged vehicle from feche feche.

Fiches (French) = Forms (English) = Given to you to fill in, by police and Customs.

Foggara (Arabic) = Underground water canals, used to bring water to an irrigated oasis (esp. near Adrar). They are very efficient as they minimize water loss through evaporation.

Forgeron (French) = Artisan usually skilled as a silversmith, who will also do other minor metal work like soldering cables, making funnels out of old cans, etc.

Fourgonette (French) = A small panel van, e.g. a VW Kombi.

Fulani = Fulbe = Puel = Puel Bororo = Nomadic cattle keepers of the southern Sahel region.

Gare Routière (French) = Lorry Park (Nigeria) = place where passenger carrying trucks arrive and depart.

Gasoil (French) = Diesolene (English) = Derv (in Britain) = Distillate (in Australia) = Diesel fuel.

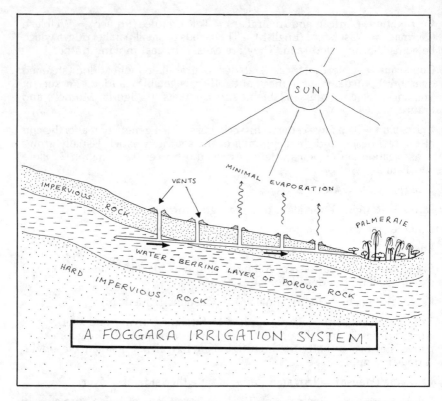

A FOGGARA IRRIGATION SYSTEM

Gravures (French) = Engraved rock art, usually pre-historic.

Guelta = A semi-permanent water hole usually in a sheltered spot among mountains or rocky hills.

Guerba (Arabic) = Water bag made of sheep or goatskin.

Guichet (French) = Cashier's window or counter.

Hammada (Arabic) = Stony desert plain.

Harmattan = An unpleasantly cold dry NE wind which brings very dusty conditions to the southern Sahara, the Sahel and sometimes even the coast of West Africa during October to February. A bad time of the year for cracked lips and feet and for contracting eye, ear and respiratory diseases.

Jack (English) = Cric (French) = Tool for lifting up a vehicle.

Kazua (Hausa) = Market (English) = Marché (French).

Kerosene (Australian, American, African) = Paraffin (English) = Petrole (French).

Kori (Hausa) = Oued (Arabic) = Waddi (Arabic) = dried up sandy river bed which rarely has water flowing in it.

Ksar (Arabic) = A fort or the old fortified centre of a town.

Laissez-passer = A special form which permits one to travel usually in one's vehicle. This form must be obtained in Niger and Mali and produced upon demand by the police.

Looking along a line of vent holes which mark the underground path of one of several 'foggaras' which take underground water to a palmeraie south of Adrar. This ancient and very ingenious system of irrigation is used extensively in the Saoura and Tidikelt regions of southern Algeria. It is also used a lot in southern Iran

Laterite road = West African term for a road made up of a type of leached stony material characteristic of many tropical lands. Usually a red-brown colour.

Lorry Park = A Nigerian and Ghanaian term for a place where passenger carrying trucks arrive and depart. The French is **Gare Routière.**

LSD = Limited Slip Differential = Autobloquage = Sperrendifferentiale = Special differential that limits the degree to which both wheels will spin uselessly in conditions of poor traction such as in mud or soft sand.

Mammy wagon = A passenger-carrying bus characteristic of Nigeria and Ghana, made up of a basic truck chassis, bonnet and windscreen, with a rickety, crooked wooden body built on to it.

Marché = French for market. Sometimes referred to as 'la foire' or the fair ground.

Marque = French for make of car.

Matelas = French for mattress. These can sometimes be rented at camping grounds.

Moto = French for motorcycle.

Narrow tar = Asphalt or bitumen road which is only wide enough for one vehicle. If vehicles have to pass, then each travels for a short but sufficient distance with only two wheels on the sealed road with the other two wheels on the gravel edge or berm.

513

A Nigerian 'Mammy Wagon' characteristically packed with people

Neame tree = An Indian species (*Azadirachta Indicata*) which was introduced to West Africa by colonial administrations Provides excellent shade and is found in many villages throughout the southern Sahel.

Normale (French) = Benzin (German) = Regular (English) = low octaine petrol.

Ornières (French) = (See ruts, below)

Oued (Arabic) = Waddi (Arabic) = Kori (Hausa) = dried up sandy river bed which rarely has running water in it.

P.S.P. = Perforated Steel Planking = Pierced Steel Planking = Marsden Plating = 10 foot (3.3m), long sheets of steel, which are interlocking, and perforated to reduce weight, and used in the Sahara and the Pacific during World War II for making temporary air strips. Just about the best tool available for debogging a truck. Lighter aluminium ones are available for Land Rovers, VW-Buses, etc.

Paillote (French) = Portable woven grass mat tents used by the Touaregs of the Southern Sahara.

Palmeraie (French) = A palm tree grove.

Paraffin (in Britain) = Kerosene (in Africa, Australasia and USA) = Petrole (French).

Petrol (English) = Essence (French) = Gasoline (USA).

Pijotte = Peugeot in Nigeria.

Pirogue (French) = Dug out canoe (English) = Canoe made from a single tree.

Piscine (French) = A swimming pool. In the Sahara, such places usually do not have proper filtration systems.

514

Piste (French) = A desert track which is essentially not a made up road but a commonly used 'direction' of travel. It may be several kilometres wide in some sections.

Piste Interdite = A piste or track that it is forbidden to travel along without prior approval from a governmental authority (e.g. from a Daira in Algeria).

Plateau (French) = Light pick-up truck such as a Peugeot 404.

Poste restante = Service operated by many post offices whereby mail addressed to an individual and labelled 'Poste Restante' is held for collection for that person at the post office.

Raid = Alternative French word for expedition or excursion into a rugged area.

Rondavel (Southern African) = A round thatched roofed house or motel room, usually found at game parks, and at some rest houses.

Ruts (English) = Ornières (French) = Parallel deep trenches filled with sand, along which vehicles have to travel. They are not made deliberately but result from many vehicles following the same path through a particularly sandy or muddy section of piste.

Sahel = Usually used to describe a dry vegetation area where the most prominent plants are scattered grasses and low thorn trees.

Salines (French) = Salt workings e.g. Bilma, Tegguidam Tessoumi, and Taoudenni, where salt is extracted by traditional evaporation methods.

Sand ladders (English) = Short steel ladders used in place of P.S.P.

'Taxis-brousse' or bush taxis at Tahoua in Niger. These four-wheel drive taxis are used to carry fifteen or more passengers along the sandiest pistes in the Sahel and across the Sahara

515

Sebka (Arabic) = A dry salt lake or salt pan.

Souder (French) = Weld or solder (English).

Sûreté (French) = Special security police who are a mixture of detective and secret police.

Tassili = Touareg language (Tamahaq) for rocky plateau.

Taxis-brouse (French) = Bush taxis = Term applied to VW-Buses, Peugeot station wagons and pick-ups, and Toyota Land Cruisers, that carry people inter-city or even from Agadez to Libya.

Thongs (Australian) = Jandals (New Zealand) = Flip flops (English) = Open plastic sandals.

Tole ondulée = French for corrugations (literally undulating iron) = Welblech (German).

Tracks = Used in this book in the plural form only to describe the marks left by a previous vehicle in the sand. (Also called Traces).

Truck = Lorry (English) = A large vehicle designed to carry goods and with a load capacity of over one tonne. It does not apply to Land Rovers, Land Cruisers, etc.

Ute (Australian) = Pick up (English) = Bakkie (Southern Africa) = Plateau (French) = Two door car type vehicle with the rear made into a large load carrying area like that of a truck e.g. Peugeot 404, Land Rover Pick up, Isuzu - Chev Luv, Holden Ute. Usually they have a load capacity of between ½ and 1½ tonnes.

Village = African settlement with almost no modern amenities. It can range from only 2-3 families to over 2,000 inhabitants. The English term Hamlet is not relevant to the African situation.

Volunteer = Expatriates working in less developed countries, very minimal pay conditions e.g. Peace Corps (U.S.A.), V.S.O. (British), Co-operants (French), C.U.S.O. (Canadian), V.S.A. (Australian and New Zealand).

Zeriba (Arabic) = House built of reeds or grasses, in Algeria.

Zit (Arabic) = Oil.

Zone interdite = An area such as a military range, sensitive border or even a dam construction site where entry by foreigners is forbidden without approval.

A typical zeriba, a hut made of millet stalks and common throughout the central Sahara. This zeriba at Arak in southern Algeria is used as a roadside café (Photo by courtesy of Lindsay White)

Appendix C

Abbreviations

A.B.U. = Ahmadhu Bello University, Zaria, Nigeria.
Altour = The current abbreviation for the Office Nationale Algérienne du Tourisme, sometimes previously known as A.T.A., SONATOUR or ONAT.
B.N.A. = Banque Nationale d'Algérie.
B.I.A.O. = Banque Internationale pour l'Afrique Occidentale.
B.D.R.N. = Banque de Developpement de la République du Niger.
C.F.A. = Communauté Financière d'Afrique.
C.M.N. = Compagnie Malienne de Navigation.
C.N.A.N. = Compagnie Nationale Algérienne de Navigation.
C.N.R.S. = Centre Nationale des Recherches Sahariennes, Paris.
C.T.N. = Compagnie Tunisienne de Navigation.
I.F.A.N. = Institut Francais d'Afrique Noire, Dakar.
I.G.N. = Institut Geographique National, Paris.
L.S.D. or LSD = Limited Slip Differential.
N.E.P.A. = Nigerian Electric Power Authority.
P.T.T. = Postes, Telegrammes, et Telephones.
P.S.P. Perforated Steel Planking.
S.I.M. = Sudan Interior Mission (American)
S.M.E.R.T. = Societé Malienne d'Exploitation des Resources Touristiques.
S.N.E.D. = Societé Nationale d'Edition et Diffusion, Algiers, the government publisher.
SONACOM = Societé Nationale des Constructions Mechaniques, Algiers, manufacturers of SONACOM trucks and distributors of all new vehicles imported into Algeria and their spare parts.
SONATRACH = Societé Nationale pour la Recherche, la Production, le Transport, la Transformation et la Commercialisation des Hydrocarbures, Algiers. (Oil and gas exploration and marketing company.)
S.N.T.N. = Societé Nationale des Transports Nigeriennes, Niamey, government truck and bus operating company.
S.N.T.V. = Societé Nationale des Transports de Voyageurs, Algiers, government long distance bus company.
S.N.T.R. = Societé Nationale des Transports Routières, Algiers, government long distance truck company.
S.N.M.C.M. = Societé Nationale Maritime Corse-Mediterranée, Paris, French ferry operator.
SWB and LWB = short wheel base and long wheel base.
4WD and 4x4 = four wheel drive.
2WD = two wheel drive.

Note: 'Pierre Noire' This mysterious little black stone developed by the Roman Catholic order, the White Fathers, is supposed to be able to draw venom out of a snake bite area. It must be strapped to the bite area, and soaked in milk for several hours afterwards to remove the poison it has withdrawn. It is supposed to work. For further information contact: Les Pères Blancs, 5 Rue Roger-Verlomme, 75003 Paris, France.

Insurance

Personal medical and accident insurance is essential. A stay in hospital in Niamey could cost around US$200 per day! Alternatively, an emergency air-fare could be prohibitively expensive if a stretcher case, drip feed and nurse have to be paid for.

Campbell, Irvine Ltd., (48 Earls Court Road, London W8 6EJ) offer a special overlander's policy at the following rates (1986):

1 month £35	4 months £110
2 months £60	5 months £135
3 months £85	6 months £160

Some other policies actually exclude overland travel, so read them carefully.

Index